John Donne

and the Theology of Language

John Donne
and the Theology of Language

Edited by
P. G. Stanwood
and Heather Ross Asals

University of Missouri Press
Columbia, 1986

University of Missouri Press, Columbia, Missouri 65211
Printed and bound in the United States of America

Library of Congress Cataloging in Publication Data

Donne, John, 1572–1631.
John Donne and the theology of language.

Bibliography: p.
Includes index.
1. Donne, John, 1572–1631—Quotations. 2. Language and languages—Religious aspects—Quotations, maxims, etc. 3. Theology, Anglican—Quotations, maxims, etc. 4. Devotional literature, English. 5. Sermons, English. I. Stanwood, P. G. II. Asals, Heather A. R. (Heather Anne Ross), 1940- III. Title.
PR2246.A83 1985 230'.33 85–1031
ISBN 0-8262-0477-5

∞™ This paper meets the minimum requirements of the American National Standard for Permanence of Paper for Printed Library Materials, Z39. 48, 1984.

Who does not triumph with joy,
when hee considers what God hath done?

Acknowledgments

This book is a collaborative effort: the initial idea, the selection and arrangement of the passages, and the composition of the headings belong to Heather Ross Asals; the annotations, glossary, citations, bibliography, and all of the formal presentation of the texts are the work of P. G. Stanwood; both editors have joined in the writing of the general and chapter introductions. Mr. Stanwood is responsible for the final editing and preparation for the press of the entire volume.

The frontispiece engraving appears by permission of the Houghton Library, Harvard University. It is from John Donne, *Letters* (1651), Wing D 1864 (Keynes, no. 55).

Both editors wish to acknowledge the support of the Social Sciences and Humanities Research Council of Canada in the form of a Research Grant during the early stages of this project.

P. G. S. H. R. A.
Vancouver and Toronto
Feast of the Transfiguration
6 August 1985

Contents

General Introduction

> *Invention*, and *Disposition*, and *Art*, and *Eloquence*, and *Expression*, and *Elocution*, and *reading*, and *writing*, and *printing*, are secondary things, accessory things, auxiliary, subsidiary things; men may account us, and make account of us, as of *Orators* in the pulpit, and of *Authors*, in the shop; but if they account of us as *of Ministers and Stewards*, they give us our due; that's our name to you.[1]

"Rest your selves upon the *Calling*," Donne says in continuing the passage above, referring to his own ministry and to the ministry of the whole Church. To understand this calling became Donne's life's work—the preacher who remained always a poet, determined to use all he knew and could learn about language in order to be a Christian orator who might with divine eloquence instruct, and please, and persuade the world around him.[2] "I ame / The Trumpet, at whose voice the people came," the prophetic last line of Donne's *Anniversaries* ("The Progres of the Soul" [1612], line 528), anticipates the exaltation of the Second Prebend Sermon (29 January 1625), where Donne looks forward with his congregation to the end of time in an "everlastingnesse" of joy "super-invested in glory." The means by which Donne reached this stage of calling, and the terms in which he understood and defined it, form the subject of this present volume. But while others have written about Donne, this book lets Donne write about himself.

When we study sixteenth-century poetry, we are helped in understanding its theoretical basis and the language itself by such critical works as Sidney's *Defense of Poesie* (1583) and Puttenham's *Arte of English Poesie* (1589). Sidney attempted to define what poetry is: he did not aim to give directions, or commentary, nor to describe versification; his primary purpose was to declare the nature of poetry, on the

1. John Donne, *The Sermons of John Donne*, ed. Evelyn M. Simpson and George R. Potter (Berkeley, 1953–1962), 6:103–4. References to Donne's sermons will be to volume and page number of this edition.

2. See St. Augustine, *De doctrina Christiana*, 4.13.29, whose admonitions, which Donne followed, are paraphrased above: "Oportet . . . eloquentem ecclesiasticum, quando suadet aliquid, quod agendum est, non solum docere, ut instruat, et delectare, ut teneat, verum etiam flectere, ut vincat" (It is necessary that the Christian orator, when he urges something that is intended for practice, should not only teach in order to instruct and please in order to hold attention, but should persuade in order that he be victorious). Cf. note 3, below.

one hand, and to celebrate the good effects of poetry, on the other. Poetry is imitation, Sidney writes, paraphrasing Aristotle; and with confidence typical of the Renaissance, he elevates this belief into terms of the "peerless poet," who, better than any other man, is able to teach virtue and the good life. The poet shows the way, but also gives "so sweet a prospect into the way, as will entice any man to enter into it." Although Sidney's *Defense* did not appear until 1595, almost ten years after his death, Puttenham independently reflected the same emphases of his younger contemporary. Puttenham's pedestrian work is valuable mainly for its effort to provide an English vocabulary for classical rhetoric, and so to give the kind of specialized detail that Sidney assumes or ignores.

In the seventeenth century, Ben Jonson's *Timber, or Discoveries* (written about 1630, but published posthumously, in 1641) is a digest of readings and judgments (such as a commonplace book offers) about poets and poetry, mainly secular and "classical." This is the kind of poetry generally written by Jonson himself and his followers, of "eloquence" and "wit," where natural facility is tamed by the discipline of art and of close consideration. But a treatise that outlines the fundamental assumptions of a devotional literary art of the earlier seventeenth century is lacking—a work comparable to Sidney's, Puttenham's, or Jonson's. Although the present volume cannot really make good this absence, the passages gathered here display Donne thinking self-consciously about the nature of his task as a theologian and writer. Since Donne speaks not only about theology but also about "character," "image," and so on—the special concerns of language—we may be able to see a "text" on the nature of the written word, sacred, but also at times secular. A "theology of language" necessarily underlies Donne's preaching, and, by implication, much else of his devotional writing as well as the religious and homiletic work of his contemporaries.

Nothing is more essential to a first step in understanding the literature of devotion than an appreciation of Donne's conviction that the proper design of language is a preparatory exercise for one's full and final participation in God's design, in His divine harmony: "And what I must doe then, thinke now before" ("Hymne to God my God, in my sicknesse"). This life is no parenthesis "that might be left out, as well as put in," Donne argues in one of his sermons (3:288). Every minute counts, especially the minutes spent at meditating and composing what to say, for "*Breath is speech*, but *Breath is life too*." Our speech is the manifestation of God's Spirit at work in us (4:252). Because of the critical situation of each "moment" of composition, even prepositions and conjunctions have great significance (9:70–72, 312). "Nothing is to be neglected as little, from which great things may arise," Donne comments (9:70), citing the Damascene (that is, St. John of Damascus, c.675-c.749). Nothing, indeed, can be too slight in the consideration or the analysis of a text.

Behind Donne's exhortation that every word of a text be scrutinized rests his training in the law and the scholastic logic which requires the examination of "terms." Knowledge of Donne's background is thus a prelude to our understanding of his basic assumptions about the nature and purpose of language. Logos is logic, and Christ is reason, as Donne frequently declares (e.g., 5:103–4; 4:119). Language is an "outward thing" which "apparells" God (5:158–60; 4:142)—indeed, the very material of language is sacred. And the act of writing results in a "chirograph," which is the liturgical representation of Christ's death on the cross (8:346–48; 10:196). Under such circumstances, every "particle" of the grammatical and argumentative structure of a sermon (or poem) bears closer examination than we have heretofore allowed. The soul of religion, or language, demands our meticulous and skilled attention, and our willingness to believe that it points in the direction of "last things."

This volume began as a text for undergraduates; we had hoped that we might provide a book that would corroborate university teaching of seventeenth-century poetry and aid students in entering a world different from the one in which we all live, where the special concerns of Donne and his contemporaries about the nature of speech and writing have been forgotten. The topics and their various headings developed out of several readings of the sermons and were not preconceived or imposed at the beginning. But the project grew much larger than we had at first planned, and its audience changed to include, finally, teachers and scholars of seventeenth-century literature, history, and theology as well as its general students. The project grew inevitably: the section on voice and character (or "persona"), for example, led naturally to a section on Donne's beliefs about human personality; the section on personality led, in turn, to Donne's theories about typology, and "names" working typologically. Links (and some overlapping) occur between these and all the chapters; but what has evolved is the necessary pattern dictated by the sermons themselves.

Donne's literary theory was influenced not only by his training in logic but also by his knowledge of Greek and Hebrew. His articulation of the necessary relationship between past and future, between "hath" and "will," reflects his knowledge that in Hebrew (which, he asserts, is the language that God spoke) the two tenses are interchangeable (e.g., 9:335). Donne was not alone in understanding this point, and we may ask if the same knowledge influenced George Herbert, or if

Herbert had heard Donne speak of it before he wrote "Praise II." In this poem, Herbert alternates stanzas that express man's expectation of God's love with declarations of salvation: "I will love thee . . . Thou hast heard me." Whether Donne and Herbert learned from each other or from common sources, the particular concept that mixes past and future provides one example of the interest of the material assembled here. We are led by it to consider seventeenth-century devotional literature at large, and to look for the temper of an age and the forces that lie behind it.

Typical of many of the preachers of his time, Donne appeals to numerous patristic sources: the Damascene, Basil, Jerome, Tertullian, Justin Martyr, Origen, Chrysostom, Ambrose, Cyprian, Gregory Nazianzen, and especially Augustine, whose writings affected Donne profoundly.[3] Of Augustine's many works, *De doctrina Christiana* (*On Christian Instruction*, begun about 396, completed 427) should be particularly mentioned. In four books, this study describes (in books 1 and 2) those subjects that are necessary for anyone to master who would read and interpret the Scriptures: science, history, logic, rhetoric (or "eloquence"), among a variety of topics. Book 3 deals with the interpretation of the Scriptures, or what we would now call "hermeneutics." In book 4, which St. Augustine wrote long after the first three books, we are shown how to present or expound the truths of religion that we have previously comprehended. This final book is thus a kind of manual of homiletics, drawing terms and concepts from the rhetorical writings of Cicero, Quintillian, and other pagan authorities as well as examples from St. Cyprian, St. Ambrose, and the Scriptures. Augustine is at some pains to describe the practical use of the three styles—high, middle, and low (or grand, moderate, and subdued)—and their ends, as if the man who would be eloquent must teach, please, and persuade according to the appropriate level or style, though Augustine is careful to avoid linking theme or subject matter to one level or another. These ideas are implicit in Donne's own theory and practice, and sometimes acknowledged, as in the passage from a late sermon that closes this book. In quoting and paraphrasing Augustine's *De doctrina Christiana*, Donne recognizes the basic assumption of his master, that in spite of the rules of classical rhetoric, with its gradations of style, the subject of a Christian orator is always Christian revelation. Donne understood this lesson well: "Let all things concur in the name of God, to the advancing of his pur-

3. See the discussion of Donne's sources by Simpson and Potter in *The Sermons of John Donne*, 10:345–64, "The Early Fathers, Especially St. Augustine": "Augustine is quoted or referred to about 700 times in the whole edition" of the sermons (p. 346).

pose, in his ordinance, which is, to make his will *acceptable* to you, by his word."[4]

The scriptural commentary of the Fathers influenced Donne's theology, his rules for textual interpretation, and his understanding of the process of the Logos that operates in language. Moreover, Donne himself writes in his early polemical work *Pseudo-Martyr* (1610) that he studied the apologists of both the Church of Rome and the Church of England before he determined his Anglican course, that he "survayed and digested the whole body of Divinity, controverted betweene ours and the Romane Church."[5] Donne's decision to follow the "Catholique [not Roman] Church" affects his sermons (and his literary theory), as Chapter 8 on Image particularly shows. He reveals, to some extent, a predictable overreaction to the "abuses" of "a *painted Church*, on one side . . . a *naked Church*, on another"; for "*the word of God is not beyond Sea*" (6 : 284–85). While his learning is broad, his sympathies are finally selective and specific; Donne's commitment to the English Church and its "*via media*" ("Neither too mean, nor yet too gay," in Herbert's words) is complete, and one shared also by others such as Herbert and Vaughan; and even Milton and Crashaw, who appear to be at opposite extremes of this *via media*, responded to assumptions like Donne's.

Simpson and Potter notice three phases in the development of Donne's sermons,[6] but his literary and theological ideas remain largely the same, from his first to his last sermon, for Donne wrote out of certain unchanging preoccupations. Nevertheless, there are changes or inconsistencies. One of these occurs in Chapter 6 when Donne dis-

4. See the crucial statement of St. Augustine in *De doctrina Christiana*, 4.27.34: "Is erit . . . eloquens, qui poterit parva submisse, modica temperate, magna granditer dicere" (He will be eloquent who can speak about slight subjects in a "subdued" style, ordinary subjects in a moderate style, great subjects in a grand style). Erich Auerbach analyzes the significance of this statement, borrowed in fact from Cicero, in *Literary Language and Its Public in Late Latin Antiquity and in the Middle Ages* (London, 1965), pp. 34–39; cf. Sister M. Geraldine Thompson, "'Writs Canonicall': The High Word and the Humble in the Sermons of John Donne," in *Familiar Colloquy: Essays Presented to Arthur Edward Barker*, ed. Patricia Bruckmann (Ottawa, 1978), pp. 55–67. In his comments on style (see below, pp. 253–54), Donne freely adapts *De doctrina Christiana*, 2.27.55; cf. Augustine's *De doctrina*, 1, in connection with Donne's understanding of "*Uti-Frui*" in the discussion of image (Introduction to Chap. 8).

5. Quoted from the preface in the text given in *John Donne: Selected Prose*, chosen by Evelyn Simpson and edited by Helen Gardner and Timothy Healy (Oxford, 1967), p. 50.

6. These phases correspond with the different periods of Donne's ministry, early, middle, and late: from his ordination in 1615 to his induction as dean of St. Paul's in 1622 (the Lincoln's Inn and Whitehall years); from 1622 to 1625, the death of James I; and from the accession of Charles I until Donne's own death in 1631. Over the years, Donne's style and confidence mature, he becomes more assured, and he feels his subjects more intensely.

cusses the "trinities." In a passage of about 1621, he aligns the Son with the faculty of Understanding (Wisdom), the Holy Ghost with the faculty of Will (Goodness), and (by implication) the Father with the faculty of Memory (Power) (p. 142). In a later—and on this point more elaborately developed—sermon (of 1629), Donne alters the arrangement. Here "in this first naturall faculty of the soule, the Understanding, stands the Image of the first Person, the Father, Power . . . in the second faculty which is the Will, is the Image, the Attribute of the second Person, the Sonne, which is Wisdome . . . in the third faculty of the soule, the Memory, is the Image of the third person, the holy Ghost, that is, Goodnesse" (pp. 146–47). To move from these to other perplexities proves the statement of a much later poet:

> Words strain,
> Crack and sometimes break, under the burden,
> Under the tension, slip, slide, perish,
> Decay with imprecision, will not stay in place,
> Will not stay still. ("Burnt Norton," V)

Words, as T. S. Eliot also said in another way, make up the mystical Body of Christ. Composing a work in words means the reorganization of one's internal life, where Christ is reborn as Logos. The universe, or the Book of Creatures, is made up of letters; and it is therefore waiting to be read. These ideas are at the basis of the seventeenth-century belief in the verbal, literary, and "significative" nature of all experience. Thus the verse epistles of both Donne and Jonson, and many single poems of Robert Herrick, adopt the *lexis* or word of the universe as text, of person as "volume" or "poem." Literary thinking, in this age, was metaphorical, where speaking is more than speaking, but *doing*, too. Names are not only referential but "essential" (see pp. 183–88, 196); and so, even in a secular context, Donne writes with no levity "of my name, in the window," while in sacred terms, Crashaw writes, "To the Name above Every Name": "In the Name / Of HIM who never sleeps, All Things that Are."

John Donne was one of the most gifted preachers of all time, and to grasp the theories that lie behind his understanding of human discourse is to know much of the substance and capacity of the sermon. Donne never excludes in principle the transitory "now" from his thinking, but there is a sense in which all things *mean* in the eternal Being of God; the spoken word for him is a Christian, even sacramental event in which the work of God is palpable. A reading of Donne's sermons and the sermons of many others whom he knew suggests that all preachers have a "theology of language." Our title is consequently both an observation and a requirement. One lesson of this volume teaches that man is but a voice (2.A.1) and that every minute of one's life is not only a preparation for but also a prophecy of the life to come. Donne declared in a letter near the end of his life that he wished to die in the pulpit; or, "if not that, yet that I might take my death in the Pulpit, that is, die the sooner by occasion of my former labours."[7] This is the statement of one whose career practiced on the materials of language, of one who also studied the eternal order rather than the temporal world.

Since Donne was a practitioner of language who tried to represent the immediacy of the Christian faith in a historically present time, his occupation is clearer when we remember the achievement and possibly the influence of two of his older contemporaries. Lancelot Andrewes (1555–1626), one of King James's favorite court preachers, is difficult to quote in small excerpts because the fabric of his sermons is so tightly woven and their texture so thick. This kind of richness led T. S. Eliot to praise Andrewes in a celebrated essay (in *For Lancelot Andrewes*, 1928), even to prefer Andrewes to Donne (a highly personal judgment). Yet Eliot forces us to make the comparison and to see the qualities of both preachers, different really in degree more than in kind.

In a prose that seems to stand still, Andrewes makes us see the Magi as if they were continuing their journey in this "very dead of winter." In his familiar *Sermon 15 of the Nativitie* of 1622 (well known from Eliot's use of it in *Journey of the Magi*), Andrewes preaches on a text from Matthew 11:1, 2: "Behold there came *Wise Men*, from the East . . .":

> Now, to *Venimus*, their *Comming* it selfe. And it followes well. For, it is not a *starr* only, but a *Lode-starr*: And, whither should *stella Ejus ducere*, but *ad Eum*? whither lead us, but to *Him*, whose the *starr is*? The *starr*, to the *Starr's Master* . . .
>
> It was no *summer Progresse*. A cold comming they had of it, at this time of the yeare; just, the worst time of the yeare, to take a journey, and specially a long journey, in. The waies deep, the weather sharp, the daies short, the sunn farthest off *in solstitio brumali*, the very dead of *Winter*. *Venimus*, We are come, if that be one; *Venimus*, We are (now) come, come at this time, that (sure) is another.[8]

The Incarnation never ceases in spite of time and place, a fundamental Christian theme that Andrewes's curious prose—unmoving, yet richly narrative—at its best well conveys. This theme is equally

7. See R. C. Bald, *John Donne: A Life* (Oxford, 1970), pp. 521–22.
8. *Sermons*, ed. G. M. Story (Oxford, 1967), pp. 108–9.

important in Donne, but his method of elaborating it seems generally more intimate and dramatic.

Thomas Playfere (1561?-1609), the Lady Margaret Professor of Divinity at Cambridge, cultivated a witty and yet expansive style that Donne more nearly approximates. In "Hearts Delight" (1593, Cambridge, 1603), he describes, for example, St. Peter, who

> seeing but a glimps of Christs glorie, upon mount Tabor, stood so astonished and amazed with it, that he was in a sort beside himselfe, when he was at that time beside Christ. Master, saies he, it is good for us to be here. As if he should have said, Now farewell Galilie, and all my goods: farewell fellow Disciples, and all my friends: farewell wife, and all the world: so I may injoy this heavenly sight, and be continually thus *delighted* in the Lord.[9]

The shift from the temporal world of man to the eternal one of the spirit, marked by the conditional "should have said" (a form that may be nearly obsolete in modern English) contains the idea of "stillness" akin to Andrewes, but especially of the personal, universal, and dramatic moment inherent in Donne's strong prophetic vision of the life that has been and is to come.

Within such an age of preaching, Donne flourished, learning from the examples around him, and assimilating other voices into his own. The many passages by Donne collected here reveal him at work inside a context of homiletic belief and practice. Our hope is that this volume will provide a place where students and scholars may discover for themselves the applicability of these passages to the interpretation of seventeenth-century devotional literature. Donne's own comment about interpretation being "not of *our rest* in the end, but of our labour in the way" (4:224–26) expresses the spirit in which we should approach this present work. Because Donne so obviously concerned himself with method in interpretation, one helpful direction for further study might compare what various poets of the seventeenth century said about it (for example, Herbert in "The H. Scriptures II" and Vaughan in the "H. Scriptures"); thus we might learn more about the different hermeneutic assumptions affecting individual writers and their works.

9. "Hearts Delight," p. 44. The "right style" of pulpit oratory was already an issue in Donne's time, and it became increasingly important in the later years of the century. The cultivation of a particular style—from "witty" to "plain," from "grand" to "low"—came to be associated with what seemed to be a suitable kind of subject. The principles of classical rhetoric that Augustine had Christianized led, on the one hand, to Donne's kind of eloquence, but they also reemerged, on the other hand, in the secular sermon of the Restoration and the eighteenth century. For one view of this subject, see Irène Simon, "The Reform of Pulpit Oratory in the Seventeenth Century," in her edition of *Three Restoration Divines: Barrow, South, Tillotson* (Paris, 1967), 1:1–73.

One misconception that this volume may dispel is the traditional idea that Christ alone is Logos. Donne makes clear that the whole Trinity is involved in the operation of the Word in the words of poetry and devotion (see pp. 22–29, 141–46). Father, Son, and Holy Ghost are, for the Anglican writer, related to the threefold operation of heart, mouth, and hand in the writing of poetry; as Vaughan puts it, the "glorious three" find "*Anty-types* in me" ("Trinity-Sunday"; and see Herbert's "Trinitie Sunday"). Donne argues that the Trinity is the first letter in the alphabet of the man who seeks to learn of God. We have been too long in finding the Son alone as the divine instrument in religious poetry. The Holy Ghost, Donne says, is "the soules Schoolmaster" (6 : 260), working in the faculty of memory.

The ideas expressed in Donne's sermons and represented by the passages given here are not so much original as eclectic. But what appears in this book represents seventeenth-century thought, borrowed from the past and individually fashioned. Although Donne frequently scorns the subtle "questions" of the "Schools" (the scholastic theology of the Middle Ages), he is, nevertheless, deeply influenced by them (see pp. 119–24, and also as an example in the poetry, Holy Sonnet 9, "What if this present were the worlds last night?"). The importance of scholastic logic to the devotional writing of the seventeenth century needs to be more thoroughly explored; for one sees its vocabulary and terms sprinkled in so much of the writing of the first half of the century. How many modern readers, indeed, understand what Herrick is saying in his two-line poem "God is not onely said to be / An *Ens*, but Supraentitie"?

The exercise of collecting, assimilating, and organizing these passages invited us to include some corroborative material. We had earlier thought that an appendix presenting what each of the principal Church Fathers mentioned by Donne had to say about language, grammar, logic, genre, and so on might be a useful addition to the book; but this is really a separate project. On the other hand, when Donne is reaching up to his most eloquent outbursts, he frequently invents words from Latin roots: he is creating language while at the same time he is creating *with* language. This has moved us to include at the back of the book a glossary of difficult terms and of words that might mislead the modern reader. More extended explanations are given in notes at the foot of the page. The biblical texts on which each sermon is based are all given at the end; but a simple textual reference occurs at the head of each selection in the volume, along with the date Donne preached the sermon at the end of the selection. A bibliography of works about Donne's sermons concludes the volume. Our aim at all times has been to mend the initial act of dividing and separating passages from whole sermons in order to create one coherent whole, and to avoid giving any impression that the volume is a compilation of "purple" passages.

We hope that this volume illuminates Donne's own priorities. From his many negative remarks about "extemporall" meditation and preaching, we may perhaps suppose that he would have approved this effort to describe his language systematically and "theologically." Writing, for Donne and for his age, was not accidental, or little considered; it was, of course, a self-conscious art. One is bound to remember always Donne's single most important point. Besides the idea that words apparel God and are His breath-spirit operating in us, that one point upon which all else pivots is the directive that we are all in the *debt* of writing. *Cantate*, sing; *Dicite*, speak, Donne urges. Upon momentary language, eternal life is predicated. Decisions about verse or prose cannot be casual, nor can any work or change of mood be ignored; for each decision has the utmost consequence in God's final pattern.

The Text

The text is that given in *The Sermons of John Donne*, ed. George R. Potter and Evelyn M. Simpson, 10 vols. (Berkeley: University of California Press, 1953–1962), by permission of the Regents of the University of California Press, with the following alterations: abbreviations such as the ampersand are spelled out ("et" or "and"); u/v and i/j are inverted in accordance with modern usage; a letter is supplied in such words as "refined" (from "refin'd"), where no separate syllable is intended; Donne's marginal notes have been moved to the foot of each page where they occur, and they are keyed in the text by complete alphabets, the letter appearing *before* the citation, in the style of the seventeenth century. Annotations by the editors are given as numbered footnotes. Donne's forms of citing books of the Bible are preserved where they are part of his own notes, but citations are otherwise regularized as "2. Reg. 6:27." Reference to the California edition is by volume and page.

Donne commonly quotes patristic and scriptural authorities in Latin, but he then immediately gives his own translation; in a few instances, we have given a note to clarify a point, but we have generally not attempted to comment on Donne's sources. The headings, which are by the present editors, are intended to help the reader recognize and remember the critical point being illustrated and to direct attention toward the unfolding of the theme of the whole volume.

1 The Speech of the Trinity

Introduction

We may appropriately begin with "logology," or the understanding of God's Word both through its manifestation and apprehension. The Word is infinitely expressive; and its creative action is conveyed through the three persons of the Trinity, on the one hand, and through man's eager response to go forth in joyful celebration, on the other. That God is the Word "implies a Communication, Gods goodnesse in speaking to us, and an obligation upon us, to speake to him" (8:119). Thus this chapter falls naturally into four sections, the first on God's speech, the second on Christ's language, the third on the eloquence of the Holy Ghost, and the last on the showing forth of the threefold Word by man's song, "who can *doe*, like the *Father*, who can *suffer* like the *Sonne*, who can *speake* like the *Holy Ghost*" (8:270–71). Donne himself best summarizes this whole concept in a passage near the opening of the last section, in a paraphrase of St. Basil, who "calls the holy Ghost the Word of God, because as the Son is the Word, because he manifests the Father unto us, so the holy Ghost is the Word, because he manifests the Son unto us, and enables us to apprehend, and apply to our selves, the promises of God in him . . . God, in all three Persons, is *Verbum*. . . . If the Lord open thy lips . . . let it be to shew forth his praise" (8:52).

For Donne the phenomenon of human speech cannot be separated from its paradigm—the language of God, who is always creating "with one word, with one *Fiat*." God made the world with a song, and He speaks to the world continuously in human history, both in its joyous and cataclysmic events. But alas, man is apt "to ascribe even Gods immediate and miraculous actions to naturall causes; apt to rest and determine in Nature, and leave out God" (6:218–19). If we are to understand Donne's perception of the poet and writer, we must also hear "the true harmony of the Spheares, which every man may heare"; we must believe with Donne that God speaks in the motions of these spheres as well as "in the seasons of the yeare, in the vicissitudes and revolutions of Church, and State, in the voice of Thunder, and lightnings, and other declarations of his power" (p. 20). Here are signs and sounds from every order, visible and invisible, physical and supernatural, in whatever language is clear, particular, and personal to each person's situation. In the long selection that closes the first section on God the Father's own speech, Donne makes use of the familiar image of the bell: "In every minute that strikes upon the *Bell*, is a syllable, nay a syllogisme from God. And, and in my *last Bell*, God shall speake too" (10:109–11). God speaks closely to each one of us in our own dialect, and since "all comes from Gods hand . . . by way of hand-writing, by way of letter, and instruction to us," then we can write back with an answer and give Him "reformation for his information" (8:305–6). Donne's lively and playful use of language illustrates what he has been describing—human words that embody and reflect their Creator's power.

The second member of the Trinity—the Son of God—is differently active in man's speech, being manifest in the Word in three directions, "sermo innatus" (the innate, or natural Word), "sermo illatus" (the "occasioned," or Incarnate Word), and "sermo prolatus" (the showing forth of the Word): "Let the word be Christ, so he is God; Let the word be for Christ, for his comming hither, so he is man; Let the word be of Christ, so the Scriptures make this God and man ours." So Christ is called Logos, Sermo, Verbum, Oratio: "the Word, Saying, Speaking" (8:179); and because we make up the mystical body of Christ with our own individual words, then Christ must be the source of our breath, and spirit, and life. "*Breath is speech*; but *Breath is life too*, and so *our life is his*" (4:254). Language or speech must therefore be the soul of religion, for "God came to us *in verbo*, In the word; for Christ is, The word that was made flesh. Let us, that are Christians, go to God so, too" (8:338). As God speaks to all creatures through His Word, the preacher can also speak directly to man; nevertheless, man may always speak to God through prayer.

One of Donne's late sermons, preached before Charles I in 1628, on the text from Psalms 6:6,7, takes up the sadness of human misery: "I am weary with my groaning; all the night make I my bed to swim, I water my couch with my teares. Mine age is consumed because of griefe; it waxeth old, because of all mine enemies." When Donne turns to the first part of the text in his sermon, he proceeds to study the particulars of the sighs and groans of the psalmist. To sigh and fall back in sadness is woeful, indeed; but to sigh and go forward, "to turne upon God, and to pursue this sorrow for our sins, then, in such sighes, *The Spirit of man returnes to God that gave it*" (8:197). In such a way are we called upon to make use of our suffering, and to speak through Christ to God.

The third section of this chapter describes "The Eloquence of the Holy Ghost." Whereas the language of God the Father resounds in the events of history, and the language of the Son in the words that we use when we call upon Him, the language of the Holy Ghost is the style of Scripture, and it is the language of teaching. Calling the Holy Ghost "the soules School-master," Donne speaks also of the "abundant . . . yet not luxuriant" style of the Holy Ghost in Scripture, "far from a penurious, but as far from a superfluous style too." The Holy Ghost uses hyperbole, too, such as we see in the text of the sermon quoted above: here David expresses the abundance of emotion in drowning, where penitential tears dissolve, macerate, and melt his bed. But finally, the destiny of the language of the Holy Ghost is the pulpit, where it continues to teach and give testimony: "The spirit of the Minister, is not so pure, as the spirit of God, but it is the chariot, the meanes, by which God will enter into you" (5:135). The preaching of the Word is thus blessed by God "with his institution, and ordinance"; the eloquence of the Spirit is in the gospel, but it can only be widely and well known in the pulpit where the preacher reflects the Word.

We have seen that the Holy Ghost is an author, but the persons of the Trinity, each with a different focus, urge us to respond, and require us as God's saints to "speak, utter, declare, publish the glory of God" (8:52). The emphasis and direction of this last section imposes on us what we might call a "verbal imperative"; since God in all three persons is verbal, so we must be, too. "*Dicite, Say unto God,* Publish, declare, manifest your zeale" (8:119). That God is the Word implies "a Communication, Gods goodnesse in speaking to us, and an obligation upon us, to speake to him." Since God did all, we must "second his *Faciamus*, with our *Dicamus*"—his making with our speaking. Such reciprocal and mutual action is expressed also in the terms "Descendamus" and "Ascendamus": "if we would have him come down . . . we should first goe up to him" (5:279). The theme of this final and fourth section of the chapter is action and celebration, "*To rejoyce*, and *to be glad*," and the publicness of worship, as in the singing of Psalms. It is described in terms of "commemoration," not of God's mysterious purposes in Himself, but of His glory, "of those things in which he hath declared, and manifested himselfe to us" (8:121). The words are from the fifth of Donne's Prebend sermons, on Psalm 66:3: "Say unto God, how terrible art thou in thy works! Through the greatnesse of thy power shall thine enemies submit themselves unto thee." The text provides the occasion for Donne's particular emphasis: "*Say*, speake, but *Dicite Deo*, Do this *to God*," who must be contemplated in His works, His actions, His scriptures. Through this kind of action, Donne implies, do we truly find God's essential power, the force of His decrees, and the speech of the Trinity.

A. God's Creative Speaking

1. Creation as Dixit *(2 Cor. 4:6)*

When as [a]*Dicere Dei est intelligere ejus practicum:* when God would produce his *Idaea*, his pre-conception into action, that action, that production was his *Dixit*, his saying. It is, as we say in the School,[1] *Actus indicativus practici intellectus*; Gods outward Declaration of an inward purpose by execution of that purpose, that [is] his *Dixit*, his saying. It is sufficiently expressed by *Rabbi Moses, In Creatione Dicta sunt voluntates*; In the act of Creation, the Will of GOD, was the Word of God; his Will that it should be, was his saying, Let it be. Of which it is a convenient example which is in the Prophet *Jonah*, [b]*The Lord spake unto the Fish, and it vomited Jonah upon the dry Land*; that is, God would have the Fish to do it, and it did it. God spake then in the Creation, but he spake *Ineffabiliter*, says St. *Augustine*, without uttering any sound. He spake, but he spake *Intemporaliter*, says that Father too, without spending any time in distinction of syllables. But yet when he spoke, *Aliquis adfuit*, as *Athanasius* presses it; surely there was some body with him; there was, says he. Who? *Verbum ejus adfuit, et adfuit Spiritus ejus*, says he, truly, the second Person in the Trinity, his Eternal Word; and the third Person, the Holy Ghost, were both there at the Creation, and to them he spoke. For, [c]*By the Word of the Lord were the heavens framed, and all the host of them; Spiritu oris ejus*, by that Spirit that proceeded from him, says *David*. [d]*The Spirit of God hath made me*; and, *By his Spirit he hath garnished the heavens*. So that, in one word, thou, who wast nothing, hast employed and set on work, the heart and hand of all the three Persons, in the blessed and glorious Trinity, Father, Son, and Holy Ghost, to the making of thee. (*1622*) 4:102

1. Donne refers to the Scholasticism of the Medieval Schools, to which he alludes more extensively, especially in selection number 6 below, with its "well known families," Thomists and Scotists, i.e., the followers of St. Thomas Aquinas (c.1225–1274) and Duns Scotus (c.1264–1308). In the Thomist system, knowledge and reason, more than love and the will, are emphasized; thus Aquinas teaches the primacy of the immutable mind of God that man *must* see, Scotus the will of God that man *may* see. See also Chap. 4, selection A.6 below.

a. Dionysius the Carthus[ian (1402–1471), theologian and mystic].
b. 2.10.
c. Ps. 33:6.
d. Job 33:4, 26:13.

2. Word from Nothing (Isa. 50:1)

With one *word, One Fiat, (Let there bee a world,)* nay with one *thought* of *God* cast toward it, (for *Gods* speaking in the *Creation*, was but a *thinking,) God* made all of *Nothing*. And is any one *rationall Ant*, (The wisest *Phylosopher* is no more) Is any *roaring Lyon*, (the most ambitious and devouring *Prince* is no more) Is any *hive of Bees*, (The wisest *Councels*, and *Parliaments* are no more) Is any of these so established, as that, that *God* who by a *word*, by a *thought*, made them of *nothing*, cannot by recalling that *word*, and withdrawing that *thought*, in sequestring his *Providence*, reduce them to *nothing* againe? (*1626*) 7:80

3. Fiat *and* Pereat *(2 Pet. 3:13)*

I consider, what *God* did with one word, with one *Fiat* he made all; And, I know, he can doe as much with another word; With one *Pereat*, he can destroy all;[2] As hee *spake, and it was done, he commanded and all stood fast*; so he can *speak*, and all shall bee *undone*; *command*, and all shall *fall in peeces*. (*1627*) 8:68

4. The World Began with Song (Judges 5:20)

This world begun with a Song, if the *Chalde Paraphrasts*,[3] upon *Salomons Song of Songs* have taken a true tradition, That assoone as *Adams* sinne was forgiven him, he expressed (as he cals it in that Song) *Sabbatum suum*, his Sabboth, his peace of conscience, in a Song; of which, we have the entrance in that *Paraphrase*. This world begun so; and so did the next world too, if wee count the beginning of that (as it is a good computation to doe so) from the comming of *Christ Jesus*: for that was expressed on Earth, in divers Songs; in the blessed *Virgins* Magnificat; *My soule doth magnifie the Lord*: In *Zacharies* Benedictus; *Blessed be the Lord God of Israel*; and in *Simeons*, Nunc dimittis,[4] *Lord, now lettest thou thy servant depart in peace*. This world began so, and the other; and when both shall joyne, and make up one world without end, it shall continue so in heaven, in that Song of the *Lamb*, [e] *Great and marveilous are thy workes, Lord God Almighty*,

2. *Fiat, Pereat*: "Let there be," "Let it be destroyed."
3. The Aramaic translation of the Scriptures, commonly printed in polyglot Bibles of the sixteenth and seventeenth centuries. See Evelyn M. Simpson on Donne's sources, *Sermons*, 10:312–16.
4. Magnificat . . . Benedictus . . . Nunc dimittis. See Luke 1:46, 68 and 2:29. The Magnificat and Nunc dimittis occur in the Order for Evening Prayer and the Benedictus for Morning Prayer in the Book of Common Prayer.

e. Apoc. 15:3.

just and true are thy wayes, thou King of Saints. And, to Tune us, to Compose and give us a Harmonie and Concord of affections, in all perturbations and passions, and discords in the passages of this life, if we had no more of the same *Musique* in the *Scriptures* (as we have the Song of *Moses* at the *Red Sea*, and many *Psalmes* of *David* to the same purpose) this Song of *Deborah* were enough, abundantly enough, to slumber any storme, to becalme any tempest, to rectifie any scruple of Gods slacknesse in the defence of his cause. (*1622*) 4:180

5. The Opus *of Creation (Job 36:25)*

Dost thou love learning, as it is expounded, dilated, by *Orators*? The Father of Orators[5] testifies, [f]*Nihil tam perspicuum*, there is nothing so evident, as that there is a soveraigne power, that made, and governes all. Dost thou love learning, as it is contracted, brought to a quintessence, wrought to a spirit, by *Philosophers*? the eldest of all them in that whole book, [g]*Quod Deus latens, simul et patens est*, testifies all that, and nothing but that, that as there is nothing so dark, so there is nothing so cleare, nothing so remote, nothing so neare us, as God. Dost thou love learning, as it is sweetned and set to musique by *Poets*? the King of the Poets testifies the same, [h]*Mens agitat molem, et magno se corpore miscet*; that is, a great, an universall spirit, that moves, a generall soule, that inanimates, and agitates every peece of this world. But *Saint Paul* is a more powerfull Orator, then *Cicero*, and he says, [i]*The Invisible things of God, are seen by things which are made*; and thereby man is made *inexcuseable*: *Moses* is an ancienter *Philosopher*, then *Trismegistus*; and his picture of God, is the Creation of the world. *David* is a better *Poet* then *Virgil*; and with *David, Coeli enarrant, the heavens declare the glory of God*; The power of *oratory*, in the force of perswasion, the strength of conclusions, in the pressing of *Philosophy*, the harmony of *Poetry*, in the sweetnesse of composition, never met in any man, so fully as in the Prophet *Esay*, nor in the Prophet *Esay* more, then where he says, [j]*Levate Oculos, Lift up your eyes, on high, and behold who hath created these things*; behold them, *therefore*, to

5. Donne may not be quoting a particular phrase here, but recalling a common expression, as in Cicero's *De Natura Deorum*, 3.4.11: "quid potest esse tam apertum, tamque perspicuum." Cf. also the phrase in Phillipic 7, "in re tam perspicua."

f. Cicero.
g. Trismeg. [Hermes Trismegistus, "thrice greatest," or Thoth, the Egyptian God believed to be the protector of knowledge. Donne is referring also to alchemy. See Chap. 4, selection A.6 below.]
h. Virgil [Aen. 6.747].
i. Rom. 1:20.
j. 40:26.

know that they are created, and to know who is their creator. All other authors we distinguish by *tomes*, by *parts*, by *volumes*; but who knowes the volumes of this Author; how many volumes of Spheares involve one another,[6] how many tomes[7] of Gods Creatures there are? Hast thou not room, hast thou not money, hast thou not understanding, hast thou not leasure, for great volumes, for the *bookes of heaven*, (for the *Mathematiques*) nor for the books of *Courts*, (the *Politiques*) take but the *Georgiques*, the consideration of the *Earth*, a farme, a garden, nay seven foot of earth, a grave, and that will be book enough. Goe lower; every *worme* in the grave, lower, every *weed* upon the grave, is an abridgement of all; nay lock up all doores and windowes, see nothing but *thy selfe*; nay let thy selfe be locked up in a close prison, that thou canst not see thy selfe, and doe but feel thy *pulse*; let thy pulse be intermitted, or stupefied, that thou feel not that, and doe but thinke, and a *worme*, a *weed*, thy *selfe*, thy *pulse*, thy *thought*, are all testimonies, that *All*, this *All*, and all the parts thereof, are *Opus*, a *work made*, and *opus ejus*, *his work*, made by *God*. (*1622*) 4:166–67

6. The Work and the Workman (Job 36:25)

That's the *object*, not onely the *work*, but the *workman*, *God* in the work; and the *meanes* is, that *man may see it*; that is, by that spectacle, he may see God; what of God? how much of God? Is it his *essence*? For that, the resolution of the *School* is sufficient; [k]*Nulla visio naturalis in terris*; no man can *see God* in this world, and *live*, but no man can see God in the next world, and dye, there *visio* is *beatitudo*, sight is salvation. Yet, *Nulla visio corporalis in Coelis*: These bodily eyes, even then, when they are glorified, shall not see the *Essence* of God: our mortal eyes do not see bodies here; they see no *substance*, they see onely *quantities*, and dimensions; our glorified eyes, shall see the *glory* shed out of God, but the very essence of God, those glorified bodily eyes shall not see: but the eyes of our soul, shal be so enlightned, as that they shal see God *Sicuti est*, even in his *essence*, which the best illumined and most sanctified men are very far from in this life. Now the *sight* of God in this text, is the *knowledge* of God, to *see* God, is but to *know*, that there is a God. And can man as a *natu-*

6. A play (and rhyme) on "volume" as book and as quantity, and "involve" as intricate and also enfolded.
7. That is, tombs or rooms, as well as books.

k. Durand[us (1230–1296), writer on canon law, author of *Rationale Divinorum Officiorum*, of which Donne owned a copy of the 1605 edition].

rall man, doe that? [l]See God so, as to know that there is a God? Can hee doe it? Nay can he chuse but doe it? The question hath divided the School; those two great, and well known families of the School, whom we call, *Thomists*, and *Scotists*: the first say, that this proposition, *Deus est*, is *per se nota*, evident in it selfe, and the others deny that; But yet they differ, but thus far, that *Thomas* thinks that it is so evident, that man cannot chuse but know it, though he resist it; The other thinks, in it selfe, it is but so evident, as that a man may know it, if he imploy his naturall faculties, without going any farther; thus much, indeed, thus little, they differ. Now the holy Ghost is the God of *Peace*, and doth so far reconcile these two, in this text, as that first in our reading, it is, *That man may see God*; and that *Scotus* does not deny; but in the *Originall*, in the *Hebrew*, it is *Casu*, and *Casu* is, *viderunt*: not, every man *may*, but every man *hath* seen God: Though it goe not absolutely, so far, as *Thomas*, every man *must*, no man can chuse but see God, yet it goes so far further then Scotus, (who ends in every man *may*) as that it says, every man *hath* seen God. So that our labour never lies in this, to prove to any man, that he *may* see God, but onely to remember him that he *hath* seen God: not to make him beleeve that there is a God, but to make him see, that he does beleeve it. (*1622*) 4:168–69

7. The Language of God in History (Acts 9:4)

He heares him *saying*, that is, He heares him so, as that he knowes what he sayes, so, as that he understands him; for, he that heares the word, and understands it not, is subject to that which Christ sayes, [m]*That the wicked one comes, and catches away that that was sowne*. S. *Augustine* puts himselfe earnestly upon the contemplation of the Creation, as *Moses* hath delivered it; he findes it hard to conceive, and he sayes, [n]*Si esset ante me Moses*, If *Moses* who writ this were here, *Tenerem eum, et per te obsecrarem*, I would hold him fast, and beg of him, for thy sake, O my God, that he would declare this worke of the Creation more plainly unto me. But then, sayes that blessed Father, *Si Hebraea voce loqueretur*, If *Moses* should speake Hebrew to mee, mine eares might heare the sound, but my minde would not heare the voyce; I might heare him, but I should not heare what he said. This was that that distinguished betweene S. *Paul*, and those who were in

l. Boverius fo[lio]. 14. [Boverius (1568–1638), Italian Capuchin, author of *Demonstrationes Symbolorum*.]

m. Matt. 13:19.

n. Confes[sions]. xi.3.

his company at this time; S. *Luke* sayes in this Chapter, [o]*That they heard the voyce*, and S. *Paul* relating the story againe, after sayes, [p]*They heard not the voyce of him that spoke to me*; they heard a confused sound, but they distinguished it not to be the voyce of God, nor discerned Gods purpose in it. In the twelfth of *John*, [q]*there came a voyce from Heaven*, from God himselfe, *and the people said, It thundred*. So apt is naturall man to ascribe even Gods immediate and miraculous actions to naturall causes; apt to rest and determine in Nature, and leave out God. The Poet chides that weaknesse, (as he cals it) to be afraid of Gods judgements, or to call naturall accidents judgements; *Quo morbo mentem concusse? timore Deorum*, sayes he; he sayes The Conscience may be over-tender, and that such timerous men, are sick of the feare of God; But it is a blessed disease The feare of God, and the true way to true health. And though there be a morall constancy that becomes a Christian well, not to bee easily shaked with the variations and revolutions of this world, yet it becomes him to establish his constancy in this, That God hath a good purpose in that action, not that God hath no hand in that action; That God will produce good out of it, not that God hath nothing to doe in it. The Magicians themselves were forced to confesse [r]*Digitum Dei*, The finger of God, in a small matter. Never thinke it a weakenesse, to call that a judgement of God, which others determine in Nature; Doe so, so far as works to thy edification, who seest that judgement, though not so far, as to argue, and conclude the finall condemnation of that man upon whom that judgement is fallen. Certainely, we were better call twenty naturall accidents judgements of God, then frustrate Gods purpose in any of his powerfull deliverances, by calling it a naturall accident, and suffer the thing to vanish so, and God be left unglorified in it, or his church unedified by it. Then we heare God, when we understand what he says; And therefore, as we are bound to bless God, that he speakes to us, and heares us speake to him, in a language which wee understand, [s]and not in such a strange language, as that a stranger who should come in and heare it, would thinke the Congregation mad; So also let us blesse him for that holy tendernesse, to be apt to feele his hand in every accident, and to discerne his presence in every thing that befals us. *Saul heard the voyce, saying*; He understood what it said, and by that, found that it was directed *to him*. (*1625*) 6:218–19

o. ver. 7.
p. Acts 22:9.
q. Ver. 28.
r. Exod. 8:19.
s. 1. Cor. 14:23.

8. God's Several Dialects (Phil. 3:2)

God multiplies his mercies to us, in his divers ways of speaking to us. [t]*Coeli enarrant*, says *David*, *The heavens declare the glory of God*; and not onely by showing, but by *saying*; there is a *language* in the heavens; for it is *enarrant*, a verball declaration; and, as it followes literally, *Day unto day uttereth speech*. This is the true harmony of the Spheares, which every man may heare. Though he understand no tongue but his owne, he may heare God in the motions of the same, in the seasons of the yeare, in the vicissitudes and revolutions of Church, and State, in the voice of Thunder, and lightnings, and other declarations of his power. This is Gods *English* to thee, and his *French*, and his *Latine*, and *Greek*, and *Hebrew* to others. God once confounded languages, that conspiring men might not understand one another; but never so, as that all men might not understand *him*. When the holy Ghost fell upon the Apostles, they spoke so, as that all men understood them, *in their owne tongues*. When the holy Ghost fell upon the waters, in the Creation, God spoke so, in his language of *Workes*, as that all men may understand them. For, in this language, the language of *workes*, the *Eye* is the *eare*, *seeing* is *hearing*. How often does the holy Ghost call upon us, in the Scriptures, *Ecce, quia os Domini locutum*, *Behold, the mouth of the Lord hath spoken it*? he calls us to *behold*, (which is the office of the *eye*) and that that we are to behold, is the *voice* of God, belonging to the eare; seeing is hearing, in Gods first language, the language of *works*. But then God translates himself, in particular *works*; *nationally*, he speaks in particular judgments, or deliverances to one *nation*; and, *domestically*, he speaks that language to a particular family; and so *personally* too, he speaks to every particular soul. God will speak unto me, in that voice, and in that way, which I am most delighted with, and hearken most to. If I be *covetous*, God will tel me that heaven is a pearle, a treasure. If cheerfull and affected with mirth, that heaven is all *Joy*. If ambitious, and hungry of preferment, that it is all *Glory*. If sociable, and conversable, that it is a *communion of Saints*. God will make a *Fever* speake to me, and tell me his minde, that there is no health but in *him*; God will make the *disfavour*, and frowns of *him* I depend upon, speake to me, and tell me his minde, that there is no safe dependence, no assurance but in *him*; God will make a *storme* at Sea, or a *fire* by land, speake to me, and tell mee his minde, that there is no perpetuity, no possession but in *him*; nay, God will make my *sinne* speake to me, and tell me his minde; even my sinne shall bee a Sermon, and a Catechisme to me;

t. Ps. 19:1, vulg. 18:2.

God shall suffer mee to fall into some such sinne, as that by some circumstances in the sinne, or consequences from the sinne, I shall be drawn to hearken unto him; and whether I heare *Hosannaes*, acclamations, and commendations, or *Crucifiges*, exclamations and condemnations from the world, I shall stil finde the voice and tongue of God, though in the mouth of the Devill, and his instruments. God is a declaratory God. The whole yeare, is, to his Saints, a continuall *Epiphany*, one day of manifestation. In every minute that strikes upon the *Bell*, is a syllable, nay a syllogisme from God. And, and in my *last Bell*, God shall speake too; that Bell, when it tolls, shall tell me I am going, and when it rings out, shall tell you I am gone into the hands of that God, who is the God of the living and not of the dead, for, they dye not that depart in him. [u] *Dives* pressed *Abraham* to send a preacher from the dead, to his brethren. This was to put God to a new language, when he had spoken sufficiently by *Moses*, and the *Prophets*. And yet, even in this language, the tongue of the dead, hath God spoken too. Saint *Hierome* says, [v] that that Prophet *Jonas*, who was sent to *Niniveh*, was the same *man*, whom, beeing then a *child*, and dead in his mothers house, the widow of *Zarepta's* house, *Elias* the Prophet raised to life againe; and so, God spoke to *Niniveh* in that language, in the tongue of the *dead*. But be that but *Problematicall*, wrapped up in a Traditionall, and Historicall faith, this is *Dogmaticall*, and irrefragable, that God hath spoken to the whole world in the tongue of the dead, in his Sonne *Christ Jesus*, the Lord of life, and yet the *first borne of the dead*. God is lothe to lose us, at worst, and therefore, did not, surely, reject us, before we were ill, (And that was our first) God hath drawn us to him, by manifesting his will, and our way in a law, and therefore, will not judge us at last, by any thing never revealed to us, (And that was our second) God holds us to him by these remembrances, these common manifestations in our text, *Videte, Cavete*, and therefore let no man that does not heare God speaking to him, in this present voice, despaire that hee shall never heare him, but hearken still, and in one language or other, perchance a *sicknesse*, perchance a *sinne*, hee shall heare him, for these are severall Dialects in Gods language, severall instruments in Gods Consort; And this is our third consideration, and the end of this first part, the Prohibition, the Commonefaction, *Videte, Cavete*. (*after 1625?*) 10:109–11

9. God's Hand and Letters ("Lord, who hath beleeved our report?")

All comes from Gods hand; and from his hand, by way of handwriting, by way of letter, and instruction to us. And therefore to as-

u. Luke 16:27. *v*. Proemium in Jonam. 1. Reg. 17.

cribe things wholy to nature, to fortune, to power, to second causes, this is to mistake the hand, not to know Gods hand; But to acknowledge it to be Gods hand, and not to read it, to say that it is Gods doing, and not to consider, what God intends in it, is as much a slighting of God, as the other. Now, in every such letter, in every judgement, God writes to the King; but it becomes not me to open the Kings letter, nor to prescribe the King his interpretation of that judgement. In every such letter, in every judgement God writes to the State; but I will not open their letter, nor prescribe them their interpretation of that judgement; God, who of his goodnesse hath vouchsafed to write unto them in these letters, of his abundant goodnesse interprets himselfe to their religious hearts. But then, in every such letter, in every judgement, God writes to me too; and that letter I will open, and read that letter; I will take knowledge that it is Gods hand to me, and I will study the will of God to me in that letter; and I will write back again to my God and return him an answer, in the amendment of my life, and give him my reformation for his information. (*1628*) 8:305–6

B. God's Word: His Son

1. The Word: Sermo *(1 Cor. 16:22)*

Christ is not defined, not designed by any name, by any word so often, as by that very word, *The Word, Sermo,* Speech. In man there are three kinds of speech; *Sermo innatus,* That inward speech, which the thought of man reflecting upon it selfe produces within, He thinks something; And then *Sermo illatus,* A speech of inference, that speech which is occasioned in him by outward things, from which he drawes conclusions, and determins; And lastly, *Sermo prolatus,* That speech by which he manifests himselfe to other men. We consider also three kindes of speech in God; and Christ is all three. There is *Sermo innatus,* His eternall, his naturall word, which God produced out of himselfe, which is the generation of the second Person in the Trinity; And then there is *Sermo illatus,* His word occasioned by the fall of *Adam,* which is his Decree of sending Christ, as a Redeemer; And there is also *Sermo prolatus,* His speech of manifestation and application of Christ, which are his Scriptures. The first word is Christ, the second, the Decree, is for Christ, the third, the Scripture, is of Christ. Let the word be Christ, so he is God; Let the word be for Christ, for his comming hither, so he is man; Let the word be of Christ, so the Scriptures makes this God and man ours. (*1621?*) 3:292

2. The Son: Logos, Sermo, Verbum, Oratio *(Acts 7:60)*

The duty in this Text is expressed and limited in speaking. *Cum dixisset, When hee had said this he fell a sleepe,* and truly so, literally so, in speaking, and no more, it stretches far: Many duties, in many great places consist in speaking; Ours doe so: And therefore, when Vices abound in matter of Manners, and Schismes abound in matter of Opinions, *Antequam dixerimus hoc,* till wee have said this, that is, that that belongeth to that duty, wee cannot sleepe *Stephen's* sleepe, wee cannot die in peace. The Judges duty lies much in this too, for hee is bound not only to give a hearing to a Cause, but to give an End, a Judgement in the Cause too: And so, for all them whose duty lies in speaking, from him who is to counsell his friend, to him who is to counsell his Master in the family (for *Job* professes that hee never refused the counsell of his Servant) *Antequam dixerint,* till they have said this, that is still, that that belongs to that duty, they cannot sleep *Stephen's* sleepe, they cannot die in peace: and when wee ascend to the consideration of higher Persons, they and wee speake not one language, for our speaking is but speaking, but with great Persons, *Acta Apothegmata,* their Apothegms are their Actions, and wee heare their words in their deeds. God, whose Image and Name they beare does so: If wee consider God; as a second Person in the Godhead, the Sonne of God, God of God, so God is *Logos, Sermo, Verbum, Oratio*; The Word, Saying, Speaking; But God considered primarily and in himself so, is *Actus purus,* all Action, all doing. In the Creation there is a *Dixit* in Gods mouth, still God sayes something; but evermore the *Dixit* is accompanied with a *Fiat,* Somthing was to be done, as well as said. The Apostles are Apostles in that capacity as they were sent to preach, that's Speaking; But, when wee come to see their proceeding, it is *in Praxi,* in the Acts of the Apostles. In those Persons whose duty lies in speaking, there is an *Antequam dixerint*; in those where it lies in Action, there is an *Antequam fecerint*; till that be said, and done, which belongs to their particular callings, they cannot sleepe *Stephen's* sleepe, they cannot die in peace. (*1628*) 8:179

3. Verbum Caro*: Christ's Testimony (1 John 5:7, 8)*

The second witnesse in heaven, is *verbum,* The *Word*: and that is a welcome message, for it is *Christ* himselfe: It is not so when the Lord sends a word; [w] *The Lord sent a word unto Jacob, and it lighted upon Israel;* there the word is a judgement, and an execution of the Judge-

w. Esa. 9:8.

ment: for that word, that signifies, a *word* there, in the same letters exactly signifies, a *pestilence*, a Calamity; It is a word, and a blow; but the word here, is *verbum caro*, that Word which for our sakes was made our selves. The word then in this place, is the second *person* in the Trinity, *Christ Jesus*, who in this Court of heaven, where there is no corruption, no falsification, no passion, but fair and just proceeding, is admitted to be a witnesse in his owne cause; It is Jesus, that testifies for Jesus now, when he was upon earth, and said, *If I should beare witnesse of my selfe, my witnesse were not true*, whether we take those words to be spoken, *per Conniventiam*, by an allowance, and concession, (It is not true, that is, I am content that you should not beleeve my witnesse of my selfe to be true) (as *Saint Cyrill* understands them) or whether we take them, *Humano more*, that Christ as a man, acknowledged truely, and as he thought, that in legall proceeding a mans owne testimony ought not to be beleeved in his owne behalfe, (as *Athanasius* and Saint *Ambrose* understand them) yet Christ might safely say as he did, [x]*Though I beare record of my selfe, yet my record is true*; why? *because I know whence I come, and whither I goe*. Christ could not be *Singularis testis*, a single witnesse; He was alwayes more then one witnesse, because he had alwayes more then *one nature*; God and man; and therefore Christ instructing *Nicodemus*, speakes plurally, [y]*we speake, that we know, we testifie that we have seene*, and you receive not *Testimonium nostrum*, our witnesse; he does not say *my witnesse*, but *ours*, because although a singular, yet he was a plurall person too.[8] (*1624?*) 5:141–42

4. Christ as Scripture (Mark 4:24)

You see Christs way, to them that came to heare him; [z]*Audiistis*, and *Audiistis*, This, and that you have heard others say; *Ego autem dico*; your Rule is, what I say; for Christ spoke Scripture; Christ was Scripture. As we say of great and universall Scholars, that they are *viventes Bibliothecae*, living, walking, speaking Libraries; So Christ was *loquens Scriptura*; living, speaking Scripture. Our Sermons are Text and Discourse; Christs Sermons were all Texts: Christ was the *Word*; not onely the Essentiall Word, which was alwayes with God, but the very written word too; Christ was the Scripture, and therefore, when he refers them to himselfe, he refers them to the Scriptures, for though

8. A play on number (tense) and on quality (singular as unique, plural as customary).

x. John 8:14.
y. John 3:11.
z. Matth. 5.

here he seem onely, to call upon them, to hearken to that which he spoke, yet it is in a word, of a deeper impression; for it is *Videte*; *See* what you hear. Before you preach any thing for my word, *see it, see it written,* see it in the body of the Scriptures. Here then lies the double obligation upon the Apostles, The salvation of the whole world lies upon your preaching of that, of *All* That, of *onely* That, which you hear from me now, And therefore, *take heed what you hear.* (*1627*) 7:400

5. Words: The Mystical Body of Christ (2 Cor. 1:3)

The Son of God, is Λόγος, *verbum, The word*; God made us with his word, and with our words we make God so farre, as that we make up the mysticall body of Christ Jesus with our prayers, with our whole liturgie, and we make the naturall body of Christ Jesus appliable to our soules, by the words of Consecration in the Sacrament, and our soules apprehensive, and capable of that body, by the word Preached. Blesse him therefore in speaking to him, in your prayers: Blesse him in speaking with him, in assenting, in answering that which he sayes to you in his word: And blesse him in speaking of him, in telling one another the good things that he hath done abundantly for you. [a]*I will blesse the Lord at all times*, sayes *David*. Is it at all times, sayes S. *Augustine, Cum circumfluunt omnia*, at all times, when God blesses mee with temporall prosperity? *Cum minus nascuntur, cum nata dilabuntur,* sayes that Father, when thy gaine ceases for the present, when that that thou hadst formerly got, wasts and perishes, and threatens penury for the future, still blesse thou the Lord, *Quia ille dat, ille tollit sed seipsum a benedicente se non tollit*; The Lord gives, and the Lord takes away, but the Lord never takes away himselfe from him that delights in blessing his name. Blesse, praise, speake; there is the duty. (*1621?*) 3:259–60

6. Christ as Style (1 Cor. 16:22)

Christ then is the style, the title of his Office; *Non Nomen, sed Appellatio, Christ* is not his Name, but his Addition. [b]*Unctus significatur,* sayes he, *et unctus non magis nomen, quam vestitus, calceatus; Christ* signifies but anointed, and anointed is no more a Name, then apparelled, or shod, is a name: So, as hee was apparelled in our flesh, and his apparell dyed red in his owne blood, so as he was shod to tread the Wine-presse for us, So he was *Christ*. That it is *Nomen Sacramenti,* as S. *Augustine* cals it, A mystery, is easily agreed to: for all the

a. Ps. 34:1.

b. Tertullian.

mysteries of all the Religions in the World, are but Milke in respect of this Bone, but Catechismes in respect of this Schoolepoint, but Alphabets in respect of this hard Style, God and Man in one person. (*1621?*) 3:297

7. Christ as Breath-Spirit-Life (Lam. 4:20)

Thus then he is our Breath; *our Breath is his; our speech* must be contained, not expressed in his dishonour; not in misinterpretations of his Actions; jealousies have often made women ill; incredulitie, suspiciousnesse, jealousie in the Subject, hath wrought ill effects upon Princes, otherwise not ill. We must *not speake ill;* but our duty is not accomplished in that abstinence, we must *speake well.*

. . . .

As then the Breath of our nostrils, our breath, is his, that is, *our speech,* first, in *containing* it, not to speak in his diminution; then in *uttering* it *amongst men;* to interpret fairly, and loially, his proceedings; and then in uttering it *to God,* in such prayers for the continuing thereof, as imply a thankfull acknowledgement of the present blessings, spirituall and temporall, which we enjoy now by him; So farre, *Breath is speech,* but *Breath is life too,* and so *our life is his.*

. . . .

[c]As then the breath of our nostrils, is expressed by this word in this Text, *Ruach, spiritus, speech,* and *life,* so it is his. When the breath of life was first breathed into man, there it is called by another word, *Neshamah,* and that is the *soule,* the immortall soule. (*1622*) 4:252, 254–55

8. Speech: The Soul of Religion (James 2:12)

Therefore, as gold is not *Merx,* but *pretium;* Gold is not ware, but the price of all ware; So speaking is not Doing, but yet fair speaking prepares an acceptation before, and puts a value after, upon the best actions. God hath made other Creatures *Gregalia,* sociable, besides man; Sheep, and Deer, and Pigeons, will flock, and herd, and troup, and meet together; but when they are met, they are not able to tell one another why they meet. Man onely can speak; silence makes it but a Herding: That that makes Conversation, is speech, *Qui datum deserit, respuiit datorem,* says *Tertullian.* He that uses not a benefit, reproaches his Benefactor. To declare Gods goodness, that hath enabled us to speak, we are bound to speak: speech is the Glue, the Cyment, the soul of Conversation, and of Religion too.

c. *Anima.* Gen. 2:7.

Now, your *conversation is in heaven*; and therefore *loquimini Deo*, first speak to him that is in heaven, speak to God. Some of the Platonique Philosophers thought it a profanation of God, to speak to God; They thought, that when our Thoughts were made Prayers, and that the Heart flowed into the Tongue, and that we had invested and appareled our Meditations with words, this was a kinde of Painting, and Dressing, and a superfluous diligence, that rather tasted of humane affections, then such a sincere service, as was fit for the presence of God; Onely the first conceptions, the first ebullitions and emanations of the soul, in the heart, they thought to be a fit sacrifice to God, and all verball prayer to be too homely for him. But God himself, who is all spirit, hath yet put on bodily lineaments, Head, and Hands, and Feet, yea and Garments too, in many places of Scripture, to appear, that is, to manifest himself to us: And when we appear to God, though our Devotion be all spiritual, as he is all spirit, yet let us put on lineaments and apparel upon our Devotions, and digest the Meditations of the heart, into words of the mouth. God came to us *in verbo*, In the word; for Christ is, The word that was made flesh. Let us, that are Christians, go to God so, too, That *the words of our mouth*, as well as *the Meditations of our heart*, may *be acceptable to him*. Surely, God loves the service of Prayer, or he would never have built a house for Prayer; And therefore we justly call Publique prayer, the Liturgy, *Service*: Love that place, and love that service in that place, *Prayer*. They will needs make us believe, that S. *Francis* preached to Birds, and Beasts, and Stones joyned with S. *Francis* in Prayer. God can speak to all things; that's the office of Preaching, to speak to others: But, of all, onely Man can speak to God; and that's the office of Prayer. It is a blessed conversation, to spend time in Discourse, in Communication with God. [d]God *went his way, as soon as he had left communing with Abraham*. When we leave praying, God leaves us: But God left not *Abraham*, as long as he had any thing to say to God; And we have always something to say unto him. He loves to hear us tell him, even those things which he knew before; his Benefits in our Thankfulness, And our sins in our Confessions, And our necessities in our Petitions. And therefore having so many Occasions to speak to God, and to speak of God, *David* ingeminates that, and his ingemination implies a wonder, *O that men would* (And it is strange if Men will not) *O that men would praise the Lord, and tell the wondrous works that he hath done for the sons of Men!* for, *David* determines not his precept in that, Be thankful unto him; for a Thankfulness may pass in private, But

d. Gen. 18:ult.

[e]*Be thankful unto him, and speak good of his name.* Glorifie him in speaking to him, in speaking of him, in speaking for him. (*1629*) 8:338–39

9. *Tau-Groan-Cross (Ps. 6:6, 7)*

To proceed then to the particulars in our first Part, *Quid factum*, What *David* did, first *Gemit*, He comes to sigh, to groane, to an outward declaration of a sense of Gods indignation upon him, till he had perfected his repentance. [f]*She sighed, and turned backward*, was Jerusalems misery. To sigh, and turne backward, to repent, and relapse, is a wofull Condition: But to sigh, and turne forward, to turne upon God, and to pursue this sorrow for our sins, then, in such sighes, [g]*The Spirit of man returnes to God that gave it;* As God breathed into man, so man breathes unto the nostrils of God *a savour of rest*, as it is said of *Noah*, an acceptable sacrifice, when he sighes for his sins. This sighing, this groaning, expressed in this word, *Anach, Gemitus*, is *Vox Turturis. Turtur gemit*; It is that voyce, that sound which the Turtle gives; [h]And we learne by Authors of Naturall Story, and by experience, *Turturis gemitus indicium veris*, The voyce of the Turtle is an evidence of the Spring; When a sinner comes to this voyce, to this sighing, there is a Spring of grace begun in him; Then *Vox Turturis audita in terra nostra*, sayes Christ to his Spouse, [i]*The voyce of the Turtle is heard in our Land*; And so he sayes to thy soule, This voyce of the Turtle, these sighs of thy penitent soul, are heard *in terra nostra*, in our Land, in the Kingdome of heaven.

And when he heares this voyce of this Turtle, these sighs of thy soule, then he puts thy name also into that List, which he gave to his Messenger, (in which Commission this very word of our Text, *Anach*, is used) [j]*Signabis signum super frontibus virorum suspirantium et gementium*, Upon all their fore-heads, that sigh and groane, imprint my mark; Which is ordinarily conceived by the Ancients to have been the letter *Tau*; of which though *Calvin* assigne a usefull, and a convenient reason, that they were marked with this letter *Tau*, which is the last letter of the Hebrew Alphabet, in signe, that though they were in estimation of the world, the most abject, and the outcasts thereof, yet God set his mark upon them, with a purpose to raise them; yet S. *Hierome*, and the Ancients for the most part assigne that for the reason, why they were marked with that letter, because that letter had the forme of the Crosse; Not for any such use, or power, as the

e. Ps. 100:4.
f. Lam. [1:8].
g. Eccles. 12:7.
h. Plin[y, Natural History]. 18.28.
i. Can. 2:12.
j. Ezek. 9:4.

Roman Church hath ascribed to that sign, but as in the Persecutions of the Primitive Church, the Martyrs at the stake, when a cry was raised, that they dyed for Treason, for Rebellion, for Sedition, and could not be heard, for the clamour, to cleare themselves, used then in the sight of all, who, though they could not heare them, could see them, to signe themselves with the Crosse, not to drive away devils, or to strengthen themselves against tentations by that signe, but by that signe to declare the cause of their death to be the profession of the Christian Religion, and not Treason, nor Sedition. And as we in our Baptisme have that Crosse imprinted upon us, not as a part of the Sacrament, or any piece of that armour, which we put on of spirituall strength, but as a protestation, whose Souldiers wee became: so God imprinted upon them, that sighed, and mourned, that *Tau*, that letter, which had the forme of the Crosse, that it might be an evidence, that all their crosses shall be swallowed in his Crosse, their sighs in his sighs, and their agonies in his. And therefore, Beloved, these sighs are too spirituall a substance, to be bestowed upon worldly matters; All the love, all the ambitions, all the losses of this world, are not worth a sigh; If they were, yet thou hast none to spare, for all thy sighs are due to thy sins; bestow them there. (*1628*) 8:197–98

C. The Eloquence of the Holy Ghost

1. The Holy Ghost: The Soul's Schoolmaster (John 14:26)

And this soul of the world is the Holy Ghost, who doth that office to the soule of every Christian, which the soul it self doth to every naturall man, informes him, directs him, instructs him, makes him be that he is, and do that he doth. And therefore as *Tertullian* cals Christ by the Holy Ghosts name, (for he calls Christ *Spiritum Dei*, because, as the office of our spirits is to unite the body and the soul, so Christ hath united God and man in one *Emanuel*) S. *Basil* gives the Holy Ghost Christs name, for he calls the Holy Ghost *Verbum Dei*, The word of God, because he undertakes the Pedagogy of the soul, to be the soules School-master, and to teach it as much of God as concernes it, that is, Christ crucified. Therefore when the Holy Ghost was first sent, he was sent but to testifie of Christ; At Christs Baptisme (which was his first sending) he was sent but to establish an assurance, and a beliefe, that that Christ was the Son of God, in whom he was well pleased; And this he did but as a witnesse, not as a Teacher; for the voice that wrought this, and taught this, came not from the Dove, not from the Holy Ghost, but from above; The Holy Ghost said nothing then. But when the Holy Ghost in performance of Christs promise in this Text, was sent as a Teacher, then he came in the form of Tongues, and they that received him, were thereby presently enabled to speak to others. . . .

Doth any man put his son to schoole, to learn what his Master thinks? The Holy Ghost is sent to Teach; he teaches by speaking; he speaks by his Ordinance, and Institution in his Church. All knowledge, and all zeale, that is not kindled by him, by the Holy Ghost, and kindled here, at first is all smoke, and then all flame; Zeale without the Holy Ghost, is at first, cloudy ignorance, all smoke; and after, all crackling and clambering flame, Schismaticall rage, and distemper. Here we, we that are naturally ignorant, we, that are naturally hungry of knowledge, are taught, a free School is opened unto us, and taught by him, by the Holy Ghost speaking in his Delegates, in his Ministers. (*1628*) 8:260–61

2. The Eloquence of Scripture (Phil. 3:2)

This is one of those places of Scripture, which afford an argument for *that*, which I finde often occasion to say, That there are not so *eloquent* books in the world, as the *Scriptures*. For there is not onely that *non refugit*, which *Calvin* speaketh of in this place, (*Non refugit in Organis suis Spiritus Sanctus leporem et facetias*, The *Holy Ghost* in his Instruments, (in those whose tongues or pens he makes use of) doth not forbid, nor decline elegant and cheerfull, and delightfull expression; but as God gave his Children a bread of *Manna*, that tasted to every man like that that he liked best, so hath God given us *Scriptures*, in which the plain and simple man may heare God speaking to him in his own plain and familiar language, and men of larger capacity, and more curiosity, may heare God in that Musique that they love best, in a curious, in an harmonious style, unparalleled by any. For, that also *Calvin* adds in that place, that there is no secular Authour, *Qui jucundis vocum allusionibus, et figuris magis abundat*, which doth more abound with perswasive *figures* of Rhetorique, nor with musicall *cadences* and *allusions*, and assimilations, and conformity, and correspondency of words to one another, then some of the *Secretaries of the Holy Ghost*, some of the authours of some books of the Bible doe. (*after 1625?*) 10:103

3. The Powerful Sweetness of the Words of God (Prov. 14:31)

These are such words, as if we were to consider the *words onely*, might make a *Grammar* Lecture, and a *Logick* Lecture, and a *Rhetorick* and *Ethick*, a *Philosophy* Lecture too; And of these foure Elements might a better Sermon then you are like to heare now, be well made. Indeed they are words of a large, of an extensive comprehension. And because *all the words* of the *Word of God*, are, in a great measure, so, that invites me to stop a little, as upon a short first part before the rest, or as upon a *long entrie* into the rest, to consider, not onely the *powerfulnesse* of the matter, but the *sweetnesse* and elegancy of *the words* of the Word of God in generall, before I descend to the particular words of this Text, *He that oppresseth the poore, etc.*

We may justly accommodate those words of *Moses*, to God the Father, [k]*What God is there in Heaven, or in Earth, that can doe according to thy workes?* And those words of *Jeremie*, to God the Sonne, [l]*Behold, and see, if there be any sorrow like unto my sorrow;* And those to the Holy Ghost which are in *Esay, Loquimini ad Cor, speake to the heart, speake comfortably to my People*, And those of Saint *John* too, [m]*A voyce of Thunder*, and after, *A voyce of seaven Thunders talking with me:* for, who can *doe*, like the *Father*, who can *suffer* like the *Sonne*, who can *speake* like the *Holy Ghost*? [n]*Eloquia Domini, eloquia casta*, saith *David, The words of the Lord are chaste words, sincere, pure words*, no drosse, no profanenesse, no such allay mingled with them; for, as it followeth there, *They are as silver tried and purified seaven times in the fire*. They are as *that silver*, that is so tried, and they are as *that fire* that trieth it. It is *Castum*, a *Pure* Word in it self, and then it is *powerfull* upon the Hearer too; [o]*Ignitum Eloquium tuum vehementer*, saith he, Thy word hath the vehement operation of fire; and *therefore, thy servant loveth it well*, as it followeth there; Therefore, because it *pierces*; But therefore especially, because it carrieth a *sweetnesse* with it. For, the *sting of the Serpent* pierces, and the *toothe of the Viper* pierces, but they carry *venenosam salivam*, a venimous and mischievous liquour with them. But [p]*Dulcia faucibus super Mel, Thy words are sweeter to my mouth, then Hony;* then Hony, it selfe. For, [q]*verba composita*, saith *Solomon*, chosen words, *studied*, premeditated words, *pleasing* words, (so we translate it) are *as a Hony-combe*. Now, in the Hony-combe, the Hony is collected and gathered, and dispensed, and distributed from the Hony-combe, And of this Hony-combe is wax, wax apt for *sealing*, derived too. The distribution of this Hony to the Congregation, The sealing of this Hony to the Conscience, is in the *outward Ordinance of God*, and in the labour of the *Minister*, and his conscionable fitting of himselfe for so great a service. But the *Hony-Combe* is not the *Hony*, The gifts of the man, is not the Holy Ghost. [r]*Jacob* laid this blessing

k. Deut. 3:24.
l. Lam. 1:12.
m. Apoc. 14:2; 10:3.
n. Ps. 12:6.
o. Ps. 119:140.
p. Ps. 103.
q. Prov. 16:24.
r. Gen. 49:21.

upon his sonne *Naphtali, Dabit Eloquia pulchritudinis*; That he should be a well-spoken, and a perswasive man. For, of a defect in this kinde, *Moses* complained, and so did *Esay*, and *Jeremie* did so too, when they were to be imployed in Gods service, *Moses* that he was of *uncircumcised*, *Esay* that he was of *unclean* lips, and *Jeremie* that he was a *Childe* and could not speak; and therefore this was a Blessing upon *Naphtali*, that hee should bee a well-spoken, and a perswasive man. (*1623*) 8:270–71

4. *The Gospel:* In Sermone *(1 Tim. 1:15)*

The Gospell then, that which is the Gospell to thee, that is, the assurance of the peace of Conscience, is grounded *in sermone*, upon the word; not upon imaginations of thine owne, not upon fancies of others, nor pretended inspirations, nor obtruded Miracles, but upon the word; and not upon a suspicious and questionable, not upon an uncertain or variable word, but upon this, that is *fidelis sermo, This is a faithfull saying*. It is true, that this Apostle seemes to use this phrase of speech, as an earnest asseveration, and a band for divers truths in other places: He saies sometimes, *This is a true saying*, and *This is a faithfull saying*, when he does not meane, that it is the word of God, but only intends to induce a morall certitude, when he would have good credit to be given to that which followes, he uses to say so, *fidelis sermo*, it is a true, *it is a faithfull saying:* But in all those other places where he uses this phrase, he speaks only of some particular duties, or some particular point of Religion; but here he speaks of the whole body of Divinity, of the whole Gospell, *That Christ is come to save Sinners*, and therefore more may be intended by this phrase here, then in other places: When hee speaks of that particular point, *The Resurrection*, he uses this phrase, [s]*It is a true saying; If we be dead with him we shall also live with him*; when he would invite men to godlinesse, even by the rewards which accompany it in this life, he uses this addition, this confirmation, [t]*For this is a true saying, and worthy to bee received*; when he gives a dignity to the function and office of the Ministery, he proposes it so, [u]*It is a true saying; If any man desire the Office of a Bishop, he desireth a good worke*; it is a worke, not an occasion and oportunity of ease. And lastly, when he provokes men to glorify God, by good works, he labors to be beleeved, by the same phrase still, *This is a true saying*, and these things I would thou shouldst affirme, [v]*That they which have beleeved in God, might be carefull to shew forth good*

s. 2. Tim. 2:11.
t. 1. Tim. 4:9.
u. 1. Tim. 3:1.
v. Tit. 3:8.

works. Till he have found faith, and beleefe in God, he never calls upon good works, he never calls them good; but when we have Faith, he would not have us stop nor determine there, but proceed to works too. It is a phrase which the Apostle does frequently, and almost proverbially use in these many places, but in all these places, upon particular and lesser occasions; but here, preparing the doctrine of the whole Gospell, this phrase admits a larger extent, That as it is grounded upon the Word, that is, we must have somthing to shew for it; so it is upon a faithfull word, upon that which is cleerly, and without the encumbrance of disputation, the infallible word of God; no traditionall word, no apocryphall word, but the cleere and faithfull word. Now of all the attributes, of all the qualities that can be ascribed to the word of God, this is most proper to it selfe, and most available, and most comfortable to us, that it is *fidelis*, a faithfull word; For, this being a word that hath principally respect and relation to the fidelity of God, it implies necessarily a Covenant, a Contract with us, which God hath bound himselfe faithfully to perform unto us; and therefore God calls his Covenant with *David* by this name, [w]*fideles misericordias David, An everlasting Covenant, even the sure mercies of* David. (*1618*) 1:294–95

5. The Abundant Style of the Holy Ghost (Ps. 90:14)

The Holy Ghost is an eloquent Author, a vehement, and an abundant Author, but yet not luxuriant; he is far from a penurious, but as far from a superfluous style too. And therefore we doe not take these two words in the Text, *To rejoyce*, and *to be glad*, to signifie meerely one and the same thing, but to be two beames, two branches, two effects, two expressings of this joy. We take them therefore, as they offer themselves in their roots, and first naturall propriety of the words. The first, which we translate *To rejoyce*, is *Ranan*; and *Ranan* denotes the externall declaration of internall joy; for the word signifies *Cantare*, To sing, and that with an extended and loud voyce, for it is the word, which is oftnest used for the musique of the Church, and the singing of Psalmes. (*1622?*) 5:287–88

6. The Hyperbole of the Holy Ghost (Ps. 6:6, 7)

And this may be some Embleme, some useful intimation, how hastily Repentance follows sinne; *Davids* sinne is placed, but in the beginning of the night, in the Evening, ([x]*In the evening he rose, and walked upon the Terase, and saw Bathsheba*) and in the next part of time, in

w. Esai. 55:3.

x. [2. Sam. 11:2.]

the night, he falls a weeping: no more between the sweetnesse of sinne, and the bitternesse of repentance, then between evening, and night; no morning to either of them, till the Sunne of grace arise, and shine out, and proceed to a Meridionall height, and make the repentance upon circumstance, to be a repentance upon the substance, and bring it to be a repentance for the sinne it selfe, which at first was but a repentance upon some calamity, that that sinne induced.

He wept then, and wept in the night; in a time, when he could neither receive rest in himselfe, which all men had, nor receive praise from others, which all men affect. And he wept *Omni nocte*; which is not onely *Omnibus noctibus*, sometime every night, but it is *Tota nocte*, cleane through the night; And he wept in that abundance, as hath put the Holy Ghost to that Hyperbole in *Davids* pen to expresse it, *Liquefecit stratum, natare fecit stratum*, it drowned his bed, surrounded his bed, it dissolved, it macerated, it melted his bed with that brine. Well; [y]*Qui rigat stratum*, he that washes his bed so with repentant teares, *Non potest in cogitationem ejus libidinum pompa subrepere:* Tentations take hold of us sometimes after our teares, after our repentance, but seldome or never in the act of our repentance, and in the very shedding of our teares; At least *Libidinum pompa*, The victory, the triumph of lust breaks not in upon us, in a bed, so dissolved, so surrounded, so macerated with such teares. Thy bed is a figure of thy grave; Such as thy grave receives thee at death, it shall deliver thee up to Judgement at last; Such as thy bed receives thee at night, it shall deliver thee in the morning: If thou sleepe without calling thy selfe to an account, thou wilt wake so, and walke so, and proceed so, without ever calling thy selfe to an account, till Christ Jesus call thee in the Clouds. It is not intended, that thou shouldest afflict thy selfe so grievously, as some over-doing Penitents, to put chips, and shels, and splints, and flints, and nayles, and rowels of spurres in thy bed, to wound and macerate thy body so. The inventions of men, are not intended here; But here is a precept of God, implied in this precedent and practice of *David*, That as long as the sense of a former sinne, or the inclination to a future oppresses thee, thou must not close thine eyes, thou must not take thy rest, till, as God married thy body and soule together in the Creation, and shall at last crowne thy body and soule together in the Resurrection, so they may also rest together here, that as thy body rests in thy bed, thy soule may rest in the peace of thy Conscience, and that thou never say to thy head, Rest upon this pillow, till thou canst say to thy soule, Rest in this repentance, in this peace. (*1628*) 8:202–3

y. Hieron.

7. The Spirit in Preaching (1 John 5:7, 8)

The first of these three upon earth, is the *Spirit*: which Saint *Augustine* understands of the spirit, the *soule* of Christ: For when Christ commended his spirit, into the hands of his Father, . . . this was a testimony, that he was *Verus Deus*, true God; And so says Saint *Augustine*, *Spiritus*, The Spirit, that is *anima Christi*, the soule of Christ, did testifie *De integritate Jesu*, all that belonged to Jesus, as he was God, and as he was *Man*. But this makes the witnesses in heaven, and the witnesses in earth all one; for the personall testimony of Christs *preaching*, and living, and dying, the testimony which was given by these three Persons of the Trinity, was all involved in the first rank of witnesses: Those three which are in heaven. Other later Men understand by the *Spirit* here the Spirit of every *Regenerate Man*; and that in the other heavenly witnesses, the spirit is *Spiritus sanctus*, the spirit that is holy in it selfe, the holy Ghost, and here it is *Spiritus sanctificatus*, that spirit of Man, which is made holy by the holy Ghost, according to that, [z] *The same spirit, beareth witnesse, with our spirit, that we are the children of God*. But in this sense, it is too particular a witnesse, too singular, to be intended here; for that speakes but to one Man, at once; The spirit therefore here is, *Spiritus oris*, the word of God, the *Gospell*; and the preaching, and ministration thereof. [a] *We are made Ministers of the New testament, of the spirit*, that *giveth life:* [b] *And if the ministration of death were glorious, how shall not the ministration of the spirit, be more glorious?* It is not therefore the Gospell meerly, but the *preaching* of the Gospell, that is this spirit. *Spiritus sacerdotis vehiculum Spiritus Dei*; The spirit of the Minister, is not so pure, as the spirit of God, but it is the chariot, the meanes, by which God will enter into you. The Gospell is the Gospell, at home, at your house; and there you doe well to read it, and reverence it, as the Gospell: but yet it is not *Spiritus*, it is not this Spirit, this first witnesse upon earth, but onely there, where God hath blessed it with his institution, and ordinance, that is, in the *preaching* thereof. (*1624?*) 5:145

D. The Showing Forth of the Word

1. Ut Dicant *(Rev. 4:8)*

Remember that when thou wast a child, and presented to God in Baptisme, God gave thee a tongue in other mens mouthes, and inabled thee, by them, to establish a covenant, a contract between thy

z. Rom. 8:16.
a. 2. Cor. 3:6.
b. Ibid. [8.]

soule, and him then. And therefore since God spake to thee, when thou couldst not heare him, in the faith of the Church; since God heard thee when thou couldst not speak to him, in the mouth of thy sureties; Since that God that created thee was *Verbum*, the Word, (for, *Dixit, et facta sunt*, God spake, and all things were made) Since that God that redeemed thee was *Verbum*, The Word, (for *The Word was made flesh*) Since that God that sanctified thee is *Verbum*, The Word, (for therefore S. *Basil* calls the holy Ghost *Verbum Dei, quia interpres Filii*, He calls the holy Ghost the Word of God, because as the Son is the Word, because he manifests the Father unto us, so the holy Ghost is the Word, because he manifests the Son unto us, and enables us to apprehend, and apply to our selves, the promises of God in him) since God, in all the three Persons, is *Verbum*, The Word to thee, all of them working upon thee, by speaking to thee, Be thou *Verbum* too, A Word, as God was; A Speaking, and a Doing Word, to his glory, and the edification of others. If the Lord open thy lips, (and except the Lord open them, it were better they were luted with the clay of the grave) let it be to shew forth his praise, and not in blasphemous, not in scurrile, not in prophane language. If the Lord open thy hand, (and if the Lord open it not, better it were manacled with thy winding sheet) let it be, as well to distribute his blessings, as to receive them. Let thy mouth, let thy hand, let all the Organs of thy body, all the faculties of thy soule, concurre in the performance of this duty, intimated here, and required of all Gods Saints, *Ut Dicant*, That they speak, utter, declare, publish the glory of God. For this is that Ingenuity, that Alacrity, which constitutes our first Branch. And then the second is the Assiduity, the constancy, the incessantnesse, *They rest not day nor night*. (*1627*) 8:52

2. Dicite *(Ps. 66:3)*

So far we have proceeded, and we come now to the Duty, as it is here more particularly expressed, *Dicite, Say unto God*, Publish, declare, manifest your zeale. Christ is *Verbum, The Word*, and that excludes silence; but Christ is also λόγος, and that excludes rashnesse, and impertinence in our speech. [c]*Inter caeteras Dei appellationes, Sermonem veneramur*, Amongst Gods other Names, we honour that, that he is *the Word*; That implies a Communication, Gods goodnesse in speaking to us, and an obligation upon us, to speake to him. For, Beloved, [d]That standing of the Sunne and Moone, which gave occasion to the drawing of so much blood of the Amorites, is, in the Originall,

c. Nazianz[en]. *d*. Josh. 10:12.

not *Siste Sol*, but *Sile Sol*; He does not bid the Sunne and Moone stand still, but he bids them say nothing, make no noise, no motion so. Be the Sunne the Magistrate, and be the Moone, the Church, *Si sileant*, if they be silent, command not, pray not, avow not Gods cause, the case is dangerous. [e]The *Holy Ghost* fell in *fiery tongues*, he inflamed them, and inflamed them to speake. Divers dumb men were presented to Christ; but if they were *dumb*, they were *deafe* too, and some of them *blinde*. Upon men that are dumb, that is, speechlesse in avowing him, God heaps other mischievous impediments too; Deafnesse, They shall not heare him in his word, and Blindnesse, They shall not see him in his works.

Dicite, Say, sayes *David*, Delight to speake of God, and with God, and for God; *Dicite*, say something. We told you, this was *Magis quam Cogitare*, That there was more required then to thinke of God. Consideration, Meditation, Speculation, Contemplation upon God, and divine objects, have their place, and their season; But this is more then that; And more then Admiration too; for all these may determine in extasies, and in stupidities, and in uselesse and frivolous imaginations. (*1627*) 8:119

3. Faciamus—Dicamus *(Ps. 90:14)*

This onely is charity, to doe all, all that we can. And something there is which every man may doe; There are Armies, in the levying whereof, every man is an absolute Prince, and needs no Commission, there are Forces, in which every man is his owne Muster-master, The force which we spoke of before, out of *Tertullian*, the force of prayer; In publique actions, we obey God, when we obey them to whom God hath committed the publique; In those things which are in our own power, the subsidies and contributions of prayer, God looks that we should second his *Faciamus*, with our *Dicamus*, That since he must doe all, we would pray him that he would doe it, And his *Descendamus*, with our *Ascendamus*, That if we would have him come down, and fight our battayls, or remove our calamities, we should first goe up to him, in humble and fervent prayer, That he would continue the Gospel where it is, and restore it where it was, and transfer it where it was never as yet heard; Charity is to doe all to all; and the poorest of us all can doe this to any.

. . . .

Now if we looke for this early mercy from God, we must rise betimes too, and meet God early. [f]God hath promised to give *Matutinam*

e. Acts 2:3. Matt. 12:22. Mark 7:32. *f.* Rev. 2:28.

stellam, the Morning-star; but they must be up betimes in the morning, that will take the Morning-star. He himselfe who is it, hath told us who is this Morning star; [g]*I Jesus am the bright and Morning starre.* God will give us Jesus; Him, and all his, all his teares, all his blood, all his merits; But to whom, and upon what conditions? That is expressed there, *Vincenti dabo, To him that overcommeth I will give the Morning-star.* Our life is a warfare, our whole life; It is not onely with lusts in our youth, and ambitions in our middle yeares, and indevotions in our age, but with agonies in our body, and tentations in our spirit upon our death-bed, that we are to fight; and he cannot be said to overcome, that fights not out the whole battell. If he enter not the field in the morning, that is, apply not himselfe to Gods service in his youth, If hee continue not to the Evening, If hee faint in the way, and grow remisse in Gods service for collaterall respects, God will overcome his cause, and his glory shall stand fast, but that man can scarce be said to have overcome.

It is the counsell of the Wise man, [h]*Prevent the Sunne to give thanks to God, and at the day-spring pray unto him.* You see still, how these two duties are marshalled, and disposed; First Praise, and then Prayer, but both early: And it is placed in the Lamentations, as though it were a lamentable negligence to have omitted it, [i]*It is good for a man, that he beare his yoake in his youth.* Rise as early as you can, you cannot be up before God; no, nor before God raise you: Howsoever you prevent this Sunne, the Sunne of the Firmament, yet the Sonne of Heaven hath prevented you, for without his preventing Grace you could not stirre. Have any of you slept out their Morning, resisted his private motions to private Prayer at home, neglected his callings so? (*1622?*) 5:279, 281

4. God's Answering (Ps. 65:5)

In this Consideration, (Gods proceeding with us in the Christian Church) this observation meets us first, That Gods conversation with us there, is called an *Answering;* (*He shall answer us*) Now if we looke that God should answer us, we must say something to God; and our way of speaking to God, is by petition, by prayer. If we present no petition, if we pray not, we can looke for no answer, for we aske none. [j]*Esaias is very bold,* (saith S. *Paul*) *when he sayes, That God was found of them that sought him not, and made manifest to them that asked not after him;* Yet though it were boldly said, it was truly said; so early, and so powerfull is Gods preventing grace towards us. So it is a very

g. Rev. 22:16.
h. Wisd. 16:28.
i. Lam. 3:27.
j. Rom. 10:20.

ordinary phrase amongst the Prophets, *God answered, and said* thus, and thus, when the Prophet had asked nothing of God. But here we are upon Gods proceeding with man in the Christian Church; and so, God answers not, but to our petitions, to our prayers. In a Sermon, God speaks to the Congregation, but he answers onely that soule, that hath been with him at Prayers before. A man may pray in the street, in the fields, in a fayre; but it is a more acceptable and more effectuall prayer, when we shut our doores, and observe our stationary houres for private prayer in our Chamber; and in our Chamber, when we pray upon our knees, then in our beds. But the greatest power of all, is in the publique prayer of the Congregation.

. . . .

Gods blessing here, in the Christian Church, (for, to that we limit this consideration) is, that here *He will answer us*; Therefore, here we must ask; Here, our asking is our communion at Prayer: And therefore they that undervalue, or neglect the prayers of the Church, have not that title to the benefit of the Sermon; for though God doe speake in the Sermon, yet hee answers, that is, applies himselfe, by his Spirit, onely to them, who have prayed to him before. . . . Petition God at prayers, and God shall answer all your petitions at the Sermon. There we begin, (if wee will make profit of a Sermon) at Prayers; And thither wee returne againe, (if we have made profit by a Sermon) in due time, to prayers. For, [k]that is S. *Augustines* holy Circle, in which hee walkes from Prayers to the Sermon, and from the Sermon, next day to Prayers againe. *Invocat te fides mea*, sayes he to God; Here I stand or kneele in thy presence, and in the power of faith, to pray to thee. But where had I this faith, that makes my prayer acceptable? *Dedisti mihi per ministerium Praedicatoris*; I had it at the Sermon, I had it, saith he, by the ministery of the Preacher; but I had it therefore, because thy spirit prepared me by prayer before; And I have it therefore, that is, to that end, that I might returne faithfully to prayers againe. As hee is *The God of our salvation*, (that is, As he works in the Christian Church) *he answers us*: If we aske by prayer, he applies the Sermon; And, *He answers by terrible things, in righteousnesse*. (*1627*) 7:311–13

5. Cantare *(Ps. 90:14)*

There remaines yet a third Part, what this Prayer produces, and it is joy, and continual joy, *That we may rejoyce and be glad all our dayes*. The words are the Parts, and we invert not, we trouble not the Order;

k. Confes. l.1. c.1.

the Holy Ghost hath laid them fitliest for our use, in the Text it selfe, and so we take them. First then, the gaine is joy. Joy is Gods owne Seale, and his keeper is the Holy Ghost; wee have many sudden ejaculations in the forme of Prayer, sometimes inconsiderately made, and they vanish so; but if I can reflect upon my prayer, ruminate, and returne againe with joy to the same prayer, I have Gods Seale upon it. And therefore it is not so very an idle thing, as some have misimagined it, to repeat often the same prayer in the same words; Our Saviour did so; he prayed a third time, and in the same words; This reflecting upon a former prayer, is that that sets to this Seale, this joy, and if I have joy in my prayer, it is granted so far as concernes my good, and Gods glory. It hath beene disputed by many, both of the Gentiles, with whom the Fathers disputed, and of the Schoolemen, who dispute with one another, *An sit gaudium in Deo, de semet,* Whether God rejoyce in himselfe, in contemplation of himselfe, whether God be glad that he is God: But it is disputed by them, onely to establish it, and to illustrate it, for I doe not remember that any one of them denyes it. It is true, that *Plato* dislikes, and justly, that salutation of *Dionysius* the Tyran to God. *Gaude, et servato vitam Tyranni jucundam*; that he should say to God, Live merrily, as merrily as a King, as merrily as I doe, and then you are God enough; to imagine such a joy in God, as is onely a transitory delight in deceivable things, is an impious conceit. But when, as another Platonique sayes, [l] *Deus est quod ipse semper voluit,* God is that which hee would be, If there be something that God would be, and he be that, If *Plato* should deny, that God joyed in himself, we must say of *Plato* as *Lactantius* does, *Deum potius somniaverat, quam cognoverat, Plato* had rather dreamed that there was a God, then understood what that God was. *Bonum simplex,* sayes S. *Augustine,* To be sincere Goodnesse, Goodnesse it selfe, *Ipsa est delectatio Dei,* This is the joy that God hath in himselfe, of himselfe; And therefore sayes *Philo Judaeus, Hoc necessarium Philosophiae sodalibus,* This is the tenent of all Philosophers, (And by that title of Philosophers, *Philo* alwaies meanes them that know and study God) *Solum Deum vere festum agere,* That only God can be truly said to keepe holy day, and to rejoyce.

This joy we shall see, when we see him who is so in it, as that he is this joy it selfe. But here in this world, so far as I can enter into my Masters sight, I can enter into my Masters joy. I can see God in his Creatures, in his Church, in his Word and Sacraments, and Ordinances; Since I am not without this sight, I am not without this joy.

l. Plotinus.

Here a man may [m]*Transilire mortalitatem*, sayes that Divine Morall man; I cannot put off mortality, but I can looke upon immortality; I cannot depart from this earth, but I can looke into Heaven. So I cannot possesse that finall and accomplished joy here, but as my body can lay downe a burden or a heavy garment, and joy in that ease, so my soule can put off my body so far, as that the concupiscencies thereof, and the manifold and miserable encumbrances of this world, cannot extinguish this holy joy. And this inchoative joy, *David* derives into two branches, *To rejoyce*, and *to be glad*. (*1622?*) 5:286–87

6. Commemoration (Ps. 66:3)

God had conceived in himselfe, from all eternity, certaine Idea's, certaine patterns of all things, which he would create. But these Idea's, these conceptions produced not a creature, not a worme, not a weed; but then, *Dixit, et facta sunt*. God spoke, and all things were made. Inward speculations, nay, inward zeale, nay, inward prayers, are not full performances of our Duty. God heares willingliest, when men heare too; when we speake alowd in the eares of men, and publish, and declare, and manifest, and avow our zeale to his glory.

It is a duty, which in every private man, goes beyond the *Cogitare*, and the *Admirari*; but yet not so far as to a *Facite*, in the private man. Private men must thinke piously, and seriously, and speake zealously, and seasonably of the cause of God. But this does not authorize, nor justifie such a forwardnesse in any private man, as to come to actions, though he, in a rectified conscience, apprehend, that Gods cause might be advantaged by those actions of his. [n]For, matter of action requires publique warrant, and is not safely grounded upon private zeale. When *Peter*, out of his own zeale, drew his sword for Christ, *Nondum manifeste conceperat Evangelium patientiae*, He was not yet well instructed in the patience of the Gospel; Nay, he was submitted to the sentence of the law, out of the mouth of the supreme Judge, [o]*All they that take the sword* (that take it before it be given them by Authority) *shall perish by the sword*. The first law, that was given to the new world, after the Flood, was against [p]*the eating of blood*. God would not have man so familiar with blood. And the second commandement, was against *the shedding of blood*, ([q]*Who so sheddeth mans blood, by man shall his blood be shed*.) Nay, not onely where *Peter* was over-forward of himself, to defend Christ by armes, but where *John* and *James* were too vehement, and importunate upon Christ, to give

m. Seneca.
n. Origen.
o. Matt. 26:52.
p. Gen. 9:4.
q. Gen. 9:6.

them leave to revenge the wrong done to him upon the Samaritans, ([r] *Wilt thou that we command fire to come down from heaven, and consume them?*) Christ rebukes them, and tells them, *They knew not of what spirit they were;* that is, of what spirit they ought to be. They knew, sayes S. *Hierome*, they had no power of their own; They goe to him who had; And they doe not say, *Domine jube*, Lord doe thou doe it; but, Thou shalt never appeare in it, never be seene in it, onely let us alone, and we will revenge thee, and consume them. Though they went no farther then this, yet this rash, and precipitate importunity in *James* and *John*, as well as that hasty comming to action in *Peter*, was displeasing to Christ; *Dicite*, speake; so far goes the duty of this Text; Speake by way of Counsell, you that are Counsellors to Princes, And, by way of Exhortation, you that are Preachers to the people; but leave the *Facite*, matter of action, to them in whose hearts, and by whose hands, and thorough whose commandments God works.

We are yet in our first, in our Historicall part, Commemoration; and there we made it, (in our distribution and paraphrase) our next step, what we are to commemorate, to employ this *Dicite*, this speaking upon; and it is upon Gods works; (*Say unto God, how terrible art thou in thy works*!) So that the subject of our speech, (let it bee in holy Conferences, and Discourses, let it be in Gods Ordinance, Preaching) is not to speake of the unrevealed Decrees of God, of his internall, and eternall purposes in himselfe, but of his works, of those things in which he hath declared, and manifested himselfe to us. God gave not alwayes to his Church, the Manifestation of the pillar of Fire, but a pillar of Cloud too; And, though it were a Cloud, yet it was a Pillar; In a holy, and devout, and modest ignorance of those things which God hath not revealed to us, we are better settled, and supported by a better Pillar, then in an over-curious, and impertinent inquisition of things reserved to God himselfe, or shut up in their breasts, of whom God hath said, *Ye are gods*. God would not shew *all himselfe* to *Moses*, as well as he loved him, and as freely as he conversed with him, [s] He shewed him but *his hinder parts*. Let that be his Decrees then, when in his due time they came to execution; for then, and not till then, they are works. [t] And God would not suffer *Moses* his body to be seene, when it was dead, because then it could not speake to them, it could not instruct them, it could not direct them in any duty, if they transgressed from any. God himselfe would not be spoken to by us, but as hee speaks of himselfe; and he speaks in his works. And as among men, some may Build, and some may Write, and wee call both by one

r. Luke 9:[54,] 55.
s. Exod. 33:23.
t. Deut. 34:6.

name, (wee call his Buildings, and wee call his Books, his Works) so if wee will speake of God, this World which he hath built, and these Scriptures which he hath written, are his Works, and we speak of God in his Works, (which is the commandement of this Text) when we speak of him so, as he hath manifested himselfe in his miracles, and as hee hath declared himselfe in his Scriptures; for both these are his Works. There are Decrees in God, but we can take out no Copies of them, till God himself exemplifie them, in the execution of them; The accomplishing of the Decree is the best publishing, the best notifying of the Decree. But, of his Works we can take Copies; for, his Scriptures are his Works, and we have them by Translations and Illustrations, made appliable to every understanding; All the promises of his Scriptures belong to all. And, for his Miracles, (his Miracles are also his Works) we have an assurance, That whatsoever God hath done for any, he will doe againe for us.

. . . .

And so we have done with all those pieces, which in our paraphrasticall distribution of the text, at beginning, did constitute our first, our Historicall part, *Davids* retrospect, his commemoration of former blessings; In which he proposes a duty, a declaration of Gods goodnesse, *Dicite*, publish it, speake of it; He proposes Religious duties, in that capacity, as he is King; (Religion is the Kings care) He proposes, by way of Counsaile to all; by way of Commandment to his owne Subjects; And by a more powerfull way, then either counsaile or Commandment, that is, by Example, by doing that himselfe, which he counsailes, and commands others to doe. *Dicite, Say*, speake; It is a duty more then thinking, and lesse then doing; Every man is bound to speake for the advancement of Gods cause, but when it comes to action, that is not the private mans office, but belongs to the publique, or him, who is the Publique, *David* himselfe, the King. The duty is Commemoration, *Dicite, Say*, speake, but *Dicite Deo*, Do this *to God*; ascribe not your deliverances to your Armies, and Navies, by Sea, or Land; no, nor to Saints in Heaven, but to God onely. Nor are ye called upon to contemplate God in Essence, or in his Decrees, but in his *works*; In his Actions, in his Scriptures; In both those you shall find him *terrible*, that is, Reverend, majesticall, though never tyrannicall, nor cruell. (*1627*)   8:120–22, 125–26

2 The Word Transcribed into Art

Introduction

Donne believed that an essential part of man is made up of sound, and he plays on the Hebrew words for mankind that imitate sound. There is *Ish*, the name for "mankind" first used in the Scriptures (Gen. 2:24), a word derived "a sonitu," from its sound, signifying "nothing but a *sound*, a voyce, a word" (2:200). Or as Donne says in the selection that opens this chapter, man "begins the noise himselfe, when he comes crying into the world," and in another place "our very Laws presume, that if he be alive, he will cry, and if he be not heard [to] cry, conclude him to be born dead" (2:79). Donne compares *Ish* with *Enosh*, another name "elegantly used by David" to express the misery and oblivion of man, whose name shall be forgotten (see Psalms 8:4 and 9:20); and Donne also invokes *Gheber*, a word derived from "greatness"; yet man is great only to be stricken down, afflicted and made into Adam, the fourth name of man expressive of his earthly nature. All of these words for man (or mankind) thus express his fall, his aspiration, and his dependence upon God's Word, which calls him to a true, not an empty sound and voice.

As we move from the general principle that shows man's crying out for the words of his voice, we turn toward the *veni vocare*, the mission of Christ—"I came to call"—in spoken (and written) art, the form of our payment to God: "He came to save by calling us, as an eloquent and a perswasive man draws his Auditory, but yet imprints no necessity upon the faculty of the will" (1:313). Our bonds are therefore untied in order to set free our good and creative actions; but a debt remains, expressed in the ordinances and obligations of our first disobedience and fall. The *chirographum* (handwriting, or else the deed itself) tells of this relationship, "as a *writing*, but not a writing onely in the nature of a peece of *Evidence*, to plead our inheritance by, but a writing in the nature of a Copy, to learne by . . . not onely to tell us *what he* did, but *how we* should do so too" (10:196). Herein lies a ritual, in which we all are actors, that dramatizes the struggle between Christ and Satan, with man caught between the opposing sides.

Poetry, as a central part of our lives, helps to give shape to our soul's destiny. Since our communication with God is (or should be) marked by constant devotion, so poetic devotion must not be made up of "interjections" or "parentheses" that can be forgotten or omitted: "They erre equally, that make a God of Necessity, and that make a God of Contingency . . . Gods service is no extemporall thing" (9:303–4). Neither is this mortal life a "parenthesis," for "upon every minute of this life, depend millions of yeares in the next." Consequently, art expressed as praise and prayer is one measure of our life's sojourn—a sojourn that is soon finished, yet endless, containing all of eternity. The life of man finds its speech in art—in the Word of God—at the meeting place where expressive sound has a harmony that is both human and divine.

Because Donne cannot think of the relationship between God and man apart from the Word and the words of human art, his considerations of life and death are permeated with literary metaphors: "the *letters* in this *Alphabet* of our life"; a well made "sentence" whose first part "peeces wel with the last, and never respects, never hearkens after the *parenthesis* that comes betweene" (10:241). Devotion must necessarily be poetic since it is celebrated in God's Word, "as the voyce of the Seraphim in *Esay*, thrice repeated, Sanctus, sanctus, sanctus, Holy, holy, holy" (6:125), a reverence that refers to the heart, the tongue, and the hand—a lesser trinity that reflects the greater one. Donne summarizes this idea in a metaphor: "Christ places a tongue in the hands; Actions speake; . . . There is not onely a tongue, but a Trumpet, in every good worke." Donne returns us finally to the mutual and reciprocal action between God and man, where calling is the equivalent of contemplation, feeling of wishing or desiring.

But many dangers lurk within this connection between God the Word and man the sound and performer. No part of man is more rebellious than his tongue—and Donne gives the text from Luke 16:24, "Father Abraham, have mercy upon me . . . and coole my tongue." That organ which is so useful in praising God "no man can tame" (James 3:8), and it is always likely to speak falsely by praising the self, by suggesting that the beauty of a poem comes from the self rather than from the gracious meeting of man and God in sound and Word. Donne is evidently recalling the admonition that learning and art may be deceiving, that "art is suspicious" in some circumstances. The idea is common in his time: George Herbert reflects it throughout *The Temple*, as in "Jordan" (1), "May no lines passe, except they do their dutie / Not to a true, but painted chair?"; or Milton in Christ's rejection of the wisdom and eloquence of Athens in *Paradise Regained* (4.286–364). This concept is aptly summarized in these lines attributed to St. Augustine and frequently quoted in the seventeenth century: "The pious and devout, though unlearned, went to heaven, whilest other men, trusting to their learning, disputed it quite away." The reason rectified by nature—by the natural soul—provides the antidote; the right measure lies in "the testimony of our owne naturall soule" and in the poets that St. Paul cites, who say "We are the offspring of God" (Acts 17:28). Apollo must give way to the Holy Ghost, and the nine muses to the twelve Apostles. "To end all," we find Donne saying finally in this section of warnings, "embrace Fundamental, Dogmatical, evident Divinity. . . . And it begins with . . . Belief in God, and not in man, nor traditions of men" (4:144).

From the origin and range of poetry, and then to its limitations, we turn at last to its special possibilities. Calling preachers "Trumpets, and Trumpetors" of the Word, Donne describes the *musicum carmen*, the love-song between God and man, which when rightly made is the music of salvation declared in the gospel. "Religious preaching is a grave exercise," Donne observes (with a pun), "but not a sordid, not a barbarous, not a negligent" (2:170). The Scriptures contain an abundance of tropes and figures, set in a style that is diligent, artificial, in large part musical, metrical, and in measured composition or verse; and at important times, God gives instruction in song, especially when He wants to be certain that His Law is remembered (see Deut. 31:19–22). Preaching may be corrective, and offer "a present inchoation [that is, commencement or beginning] of the joyes of heaven." This "religious preaching" replaces the ancient oratory of praise, so often artificial and inappropriate to the subject who really deserved an "increpation" or rebuke. Now unworthy men can be shown that they are fallen and yet be urged to arise again, "and that's the richest gain, that we can get" (5:201).

In a further passage, which reminds us of "The Canonization," Donne speaks of the process by which the words of Elihu, a "natural" man, are "canonized" into the Word of God: "*Every man may see it* [that is, the natural man], *Man may behold it afar off*" (4:163). Thus the words of secular writers may be sanctified and inserted into the book of God. Donne continues to urge us toward a rectified conscience, toward seeing God now, and in this time. Every man shall see light in his salvation, and so may go in peace; in every desire of the heart is a meeting with God. All is motion, and yet fixity, with the sealing of truths by "Selah" and "Amen," expressed in the "two blessed Monosyllables," "*Pray*" and "*Stay*": "To ascend to God, To attend Gods descent to us, is the Motion, and Rest of a Christian; . . . all Motion is for Rest" (5:363). Donne treats every aspect of the poetry and the language of God and man with earnest affection, even to the "shutting up" of all metrical compositions: the best and most forceful impression must be left by the end; "the whole frame of the Poem is a beating out of a piece of gold, but the last clause is as the impression of the stamp, and that is it that makes it currant" (6:41), not false or counterfeit, but valuable and true.

A. The Premises of Poetry

1. Man as Sound (Gen. 1:26)

One name of Man is *Ish*; and that they derive *a Sonitu*; Man is but a voice, but a sound, but a noise, he begins the noise himselfe, when he comes crying into the world; and when he goes out, perchance friends celebrate, perchance enemies calumniate him, with a diverse voice, a diverse noise. A melancholique man, is but a groaning; a sportfull man, but a song; an active man, but a Trumpet; a mighty man, but a thunderclap: Every man but *Ish*, but a sound, but a noyse. Another name is *Enosh*. *Enosh* is meer Calamity, misery, depression. It is indeed most properly Oblivion. And so the word is most elegantly used by *David*, [a]*Quid est homo?* where the name of man, is *Enosh*: And so, that which we translate *What is man, that thou art mindefull of him?* is indeed, *What is forgetfulnesse, that thou shouldest remember it?* That thou shouldest thinke of that man, whom all the world hath forgotten? First, man is but a voice, but a sound. But because fame, and honour may come within that name of a sound, of a voice; therefore he is overtaken with another dampe: man is but oblivion: his fame, his name shall be forgotten. One name man hath, that hath some taste of greatnesse, and power in it, *Gheber*, And yet, I that am that man, says the Prophet, (for there that name of man *Gheber* is used) [b]*I am the man, that hath seen affliction, by the rod of Gods wrath*. Man, *Ish*, is so miserable, as that he afflicts himselfe, cryes, and whines out his own time. And man, *Enosh*, so miserable, as that others afflict him, and bury him in ignominious oblivion; And man, that is *Gheber*, the greatest, and powerfullest of men, is yet but that man, that may possibly, nay that may justly see affliction by the rod of Gods wrath, and from *Gheber* be made *Adam*, which is the fourth name of man, indeed the first name of man, the name in this text, and the name to which every man must refer himselfe, and call himselfe by, Earth, and red Earth. (*1629*) 9:61–62

a. Ps. 8:4. *b.* Lam. 3:1.

2. Veni Vocare *(1 Tim. 1:15)*

He was able to redeem man, He was sent to redeem man, He did redeem man; How? *Servavit*, He came to save. And here also is that word, which as we said before, is above expressing; for the word which we content our selves with, To save, implies but a preserving from falling into ruine; but we were absolutely fallen before. The word signifies *salutem dare, medici*, and it signifies *salutem esse*; and Christ is truly both, both the Physitian and the Physick. But how is it ministred? we see his method is in St. *Matthew* [c] *veni vocare*, I came to call: his way is a voice now, *vocat non cogit*; God doth but call us he does not constrain us, He does not drive us into a pound; He cals us as Birds do their young, and he would gather us as a Hen doth her Chickins. It is true there is a *Trahit*, but there is no *cogit*; [d] *no man comes to me*, saies Christ, *except the Father draw him*, But, *non inviti trahimur, non inviti credimus*, saies St. *Augustine*, God draws no man against his will, no man believes in God against his will, *non adhibitur violentia sed voluntas exitatur*, saies the same Father, God only excites and exalts our will, but he does not force it: He makes use of that of the Poet, *Trahit sua quemque voluptas*, our carnal desires draw us, but this drawing is not a constraining; for then we should not be commanded to resist them, nor to fight against them, for no man will bid me do so against a Cannon bullet that comes with an inevitable, and irresistible violence now, [e] *habet sensus suas voluptates, et animus deseritur a suis?* shall our carnal affections draw us, though they do not force us, and shall not Grace do the same office too? shall we still trust to such a power, or such a measure of that Grace, at last, as that we shall not be able to resist, but shall convert us whether we will or no, and never concur willingly with Gods present grace? [f] *Draw me, and I will run after thee*, saies the Spouse: she was called before, now she awakens; and she does not say draw me, and so I shall be screwed up unto thee, and lay all upon the force of grace, but draw me and I will run; she promises an application and concurrence on her part. So then *venit salvare*, is *venit vocare*, He came to save by calling us, as an eloquent and a perswasive man draws his Auditory, but yet imprints no necessity upon the faculty of the will; so works Gods calling of us in his word. God expresses it fully in the Prophet, *I taught* Ephraim *to go*; we are not able to go, to rise, to move without him; But how did he teach him? I took them by their arms; God made use of their faculties, which faculties are the limbs of the Soul: so he enlightned their understanding, and he rectified their will; but still

c. 9:13.
d. John 6:44.
e. August[ine].
f. Cant. 1:4.

their understanding, and their will. I drew them saies God there; But how, and with what? *With cords of man* saies he, and with bands of love; *with the cords of man*, the voice of the Minister, and the power which Gods Ordinance hath infused into that, and with the band of love, that is, of the Gospel so proposed unto us: and as it is added there, *I took off the yoke from their jaws, and I laid meat before them*: God takes off our yoke, the weight of our sins, and the indisposition of our natural infirmities, and he laies meat before us, the Word and the Sacraments in his Church. So that his *venit salvare*, is *venit solvere*; *solvere*, that is, to pay our debt, in his death, and *solvere*, that is, to unty our bands, and by his grace to make our natural faculties, formerly bound up in a corrupt inhability, to do so, now able to concurre with him, and cooperate to good actions. (*1618*) 1:312–13

3. The Chirograph of Debt (James 2:12)

Let no man make you afraid of secret purposes in God, which they have not, nor you have not seen; for, that by which you shall be judged, is the Law; that Law, which was notified, and published to you. The Law alone were much too heavy, if there were not a superabundant ease and alleviation in that hand, that Christ Jesus reaches out to us. O consider the weight and the ease; and for pity to such distrustful souls, and for establishment of your owne, stop your devotions a little, upon this consideration: first, there is *Chirographum*, [g] a handwriting of Ordinances against me; a Debt, an Obligation contracted by our first Parents, in their disobedience, and falne upon me. And even that (be it but Originall sin) is shrewd evidence; there's my first charge. But, *Deletum est*, sayes the Apostle there; that's blotted, that's defaced, that cannot be sued against me, after Baptisme: Nay, *Sublatum, cruci affixum*, it is cancelled, it is nailed to the Crosse of Christ Jesus, it is no more sin; in it self it is; but to me, to condemnation, it is not: here's my charge, and my discharge for that. But yet there is a heavier evidence, *Pactum cum inferno*, as the Prophet *Esay* speaks, [h]*I have made a covenant with death, and with Hell I am at an agreement*; that is, says S. *Gregory*, *Audacter Indefinenter peccamus, et diligendo, amicitiam profitemur:* We sin constantly, and we sin continually, and we sin confidently; and we finde so much pleasure and profit in sin, as that we have made a league, and sworn a friendship with sin; and we keep that perverse, and irreligious promise, over-religiously; and the sins of our youth flow into other sins, when age disables us for them. But yet there is a *Deletum est*, in this case too; our covenant with death is disanulled (sayes that Prophet) when we

g. [Col. 2:] 14. *h.* 28:15.

are made partakers of the death of Christ, in the blessed Sacrament. Mine actuall sins lose their act, and mine habituall sins fall from me as a habit, as a garment put off, when I come to that: there's my charge, and my discharge for that. But yet there is worse evidence against me, then either this *Chirographum*, the first hand-writing of *Adams* hand, or then this *pactum*, this contract of mine own hand, actuall and habituall sin (for of these, one is washed out in water, and the other in blood, in the two Sacraments). But then there is *Lex in Membris*, sayes the Apostle, [i]*I finde a law, that when I would do good, evil is present with me.* Sin assisted by me, is now become a tyrant over me, and hath established a government upon me; and there is a law of sin, and a law in my flesh, which after the water of Baptism taken, and the water of penitent teares given; after the blood of Jesus Christ taken, and mine own blood given (that is, a holy readiness at that time, when I am made partaker of Christs death, to die for Christ) throwes me back, by relapses into those repented sins. This put the Apostle to that passionate exclamation, *O wretched man that I am!* And yet he found a deliverance, even from the body of this death, through Jesus Christ his Lord: that is, a free, an open recourse and access to him in all oppressions of heart, in all dejections of spirit. Now, when this *Chirographum*, this bond of *Adams* hand, Original sin, is cancelled upon the Cross of Christ; And this *Pactum*, this bond of mine own hand, actual sins, washed away in the blood of Christ; and this *Lex in membris*, this disposition to relapse into repented sins (which, as a tide that does certainly come every day, does come every day in one form or other) is beaten back, as a tide by a bank, by a continual opposing the merits and the example of Christ Jesus, and the practise of his fasting, and such other medicinall disciplines, as I find to prevaile against such relapses; when by this blessed means, the whole Law, against which I am a trespasser, is evacuated, will God condemn me for all this, and not by a Law? (*1629*) 8:346–48

4. A Chirograph to Use and Write (Lam. 3:1)

Beloved, the death of Christ is given to us, as a *Hand-writing*; for, when Christ naild that *Chirographum*, [j]that first hand-writing, that had passed between the Devill and us, to his Crosse, he did not leave us out of debt, nor absolutely discharged, but he laid another *Chirographum* upon us, another Obligation arising out of his death. His death is delivered to us, as a *writing*, but not a writing onely in the nature of a peece of *Evidence*, to plead our inheritance by, but a writ-

i. Rom. 7:21. *j.* Col. 2:14.

ing in the nature of a Copy, to learne by; It is not onely given us to reade, but to write over, and practise; Not onely to tell us *what he* did, but *how we* should do so too.

All the evills and mischiefes that light upon us in this world, come (for the most part) from this, [k]*Quia fruimur utendis*, because we thinke to injoy those things which God hath given us onely to *use*. God hath given us a *use* of things, and we set our hearts upon them. And this hath a proportion, an assimilation, an accommodation in the death of Christ. God hath proposed *that* for our *use*, in this world, and we think to enjoy it; God would have us doe it over again, and we think it enough to know that Christ hath done it already; God would have us *write* it, and we doe onely *read* it; God would have us *practise* the death of Christ, and we do but *understand* it. The *fruition*, the enjoying of the death of Christ, is reserved for the next life; To this life belongs the *use* of it; that use of it, to *fulfill his sufferings in our bodies*, by bearing the afflictions and tribulations of this life. (*after 1625?*) 10:196

5. Devotion No Interjection (Ps. 32:5)

God is the Rocke of our salvation; God is no Occasionall God, no Accidentall God; neither will God be served by Occasion, nor by Accident, but by a constant Devotion. Our communication with God must not be in Interjections, that come in by chance; nor our Devotions made up of Parentheses, that might be left out. They erre equally, that make a God of Necessity, and that make a God of Contingency: They that with the Manichees, make an ill God, a God that forces men to do all the ill that they doe, And they that with the Epicures, make an idle God, an indifferent God, that cares not what is done; God is not Destiny; Then there could be no reward, nor punishment: but God is not Fortune neither, for then there were no Providence. If God have given reason onely to Man, it were strange that Man should exercise that reason, in all his Morall and Civill actions, and onely do the acts of Gods worship casually; To go to Court, to Westminister, to the Exchange, for ends, and to come to Church, by chance, or for company, or for some collaterall respects, that have no relation to God, Not to thinke of our Confession, till the Priest have called upon us, to say after him, *We have erred and straied from thy wayes like lost sheepe,*[1] To come for Absolution, [l]as *Nebuchadnezzar* came to *Daniel*, for the in-

1. Donne recalls the priest's admonition in the Book of Common Prayer (in the Order of Morning and of Evening Prayer) that we should "humbly confess our sins"; he quotes part of the opening of the general confession, after which the priest gives pardon and absolution.

k. August. *l*. Dan. 2:3.

terpretation of his Dreame, who did not onely not understand his Dreame, but not remember it, *Somnium ejus fugit ab eo*, He did not onely not know what his Dreame meant, but hee did not know what his Dreame was. Not to consider the nature of Confession, and Absolution, not to consider the nature of the sins we should confesse, and be absolved of, is a stupidity against *Davids* practise here; *Dixit*, He said, he meditated, he considered, Gods service is no extemporall thing. But then *Dixit*, He resolved too, for so the word signifies, Consideration, but Resolution upon it; And then, that he Resolved, he Executed. (*winter 1624–1625?*) 9:303–4

6. Life No Parenthesis (1 Pet. 1:17)

This life is not a Parenthesis, a Parenthesis that belongs not to the sense, a Parenthesis that might be left out, as well as put in. More depends upon this life then so: upon every minute of this life, depend millions of yeares in the next, and I shall be glorified eternally, or eternally lost, for my good or ill use of Gods grace offered to me this houre. Therefore where the Apostle sayes of this life, *Peregrinamur a Domino*, [m] *We are absent from the Lord*, yet he sayes, *We are at home in the body*: This world is so much our home, as that he that is not at home now, he that hath not his conversation in heaven here, shall never get home. And therefore even in this Text, our former Translation[2] calls it *Dwelling*; That which we reade now, *passe the time of your sojourning*, we did reade then, *passe the time of your dwelling*; for this, where we are now, is the suburb of the great City, the porch of the triumphant Church, and the Grange, or Country house of the same Landlord, belonging to his heavenly Palace, in the heavenly Jerusalem. Be it but a sojourning, yet thou must pay God something for thy sojourning, pay God his rent of praise and prayer; and be it but a sojourning, yet thou art bound to it for a time; Though thou sigh with *David*, [n] *Heu mihi, quia prolongatus incolatus*, woe is me that I sojourne so long here, Though the miseries of thy life make thy life seeme long, yet thou must stay out that time, which he who tooke thee in, appointed, and by no practice, no not so much as by a deliberate wish, or unconditioned prayer, seeke to be delivered of it: Because thy time here is such a sojourning as is quickly at an end, and yet

2. A reference to the Geneva Bible (1560), which gives *dwelling* for *sojourning* (the King James version). Donne plays with the double sense of *παροικία* (*πάροικας*), a dwelling of one who dwells (or sojourns): *ἐν φόβῳ τὸν τῆς παροικίας ὑμῶν χρόνον ἀναστράφήτε.*

m. 2. Cor. 5:6. *n.* Ps. 120:5.

such a sojourning as is never at an end, (for our endlesse state depends upon this) fear him, who shall so certainly, and so soone be a just Judge of it. (*1621?*) 3:288

7. The Alpha and Omega of Life (Job 13:15)

Our whole life is but a *parenthesis*, our *receiving* of our soule, and *delivering* it back againe, makes up the perfect sentence; Christ is *Alpha* and *Omega*, and our *Alpha* and *Omega* is all we are to consider.

Now, for all the *letters* in this *Alphabet* of our life, that is, for all the various accidents in the course thereof, we cannot study a better booke, then the person of *Job*. His first letter, his *Alpha*, we know not, we know not his *Birth*; His last letter, his *Omega*, we know not, we know not his *Death*: But all his other letters, His *Children*, and his *riches*, we read over and over againe, How he *had* them, how he *lost* them, and how he *recovered* them. By which though it appeare that those temporall things doe also belong to the care and provision of a godly man, yet it appears too, that neither his first care, nor his last care appertaines to the things of this world, but that there is a *Primum quaerite*, something to be sought for before, The *kingdome* of God; and there is a *Memorare novissima*, something to be thought on after, The *Joyes of heaven*; And then, *Caetera adjicientur*, says Christ, All other cares are allowable by way of *Accessary*, but not as *principall*.[3]

This world then is but an *Occasionall* world, a world onely to be used; and that but so, *as though we used it not*: The next world is the world to be *enjoyed*, and that so, as that we may *joy* in nothing by the way, but as it directs and conduces to that end. (*1620*) 3:188

8. The Sentence of Life and Death (Ps. 68:20)

Our *criticall* day is *not* the *very day* of our *death*: but the whole course of our life. I thanke him that *prayes* for me when my bell tolles, but I thank him much more that *Catechises mee*, or *preaches* to mee, or *instructs mee how to live. Fac hoc et vives, there's* my securitie, the mouth of the *Lord hath sayd it, doe this and thou shalt live:* But *though I doe it*, yet *I shall dye too*, dye a bodily, a naturall death. But *God* never mentions, never seems to consider that death, the bodily, the naturall death. *God* doth not say, Live well and thou shalt dye well, that is, an easie, a quiet death; But *live well here*, and thou shalt *live well for ever*. As the first part of a sentence peeces wel with the last, and never respects, never hearkens after the *parenthesis* that comes

3. In the legal sense, an accessory is one who aids in the offense of the principal or actual perpetrator.

betweene, so doth a *good life* here flowe into an *eternall life*, without any consideration, what *manner* of *death* wee dye. (*1631*) 10:241

9. Heart, Mouth, Hand (1 Cor. 12:3)

For this voice, wherein thou saiest *Dominus Jesus, The Lord Jesus*, must be, as the voyce of the Seraphim in *Esay*, thrice repeated, [o]*Sanctus, sanctus, sanctus, Holy, holy, holy*; our hearts must say it, and our tongue, and our hands too, or else we have not said it. For when a man will make Jesus his companion, and be sometimes with him, and sometimes with the world, and not direct all things principally towards him; when he will make Jesus his servant, that is, proceed in all things, upon the strength of his outward profession, upon the colour, and pretence, and advantage of Religion, and devotion, would this man be thought to have said *Jesum Dominum, That Jesus is the Lord?* [p]*Why call ye me Lord, Lord, and doe not the things I speake to you?* saies Christ; Christ places a tongue in the hands; Actions speake; and *Omni tuba clarior per opera Demonstratio*, sayes S. *Chrysostome*, There is not onely a tongue, but a Trumpet, in every good worke. When Christ sees a disposition in his hearers, to doe according unto their professing, then only he gives allowance to that that they say, [q]*Dicitis me Dominum, et bene dicitis*, You call me Lord, and you doe well in doing so, doe ye therefore, as I have done to you. To call him Lord, is to contemplate his Kingdome of power, to feele his Kingdome of grace, to wish his Kingdome of glory. It is not a *Domine usque quo*, Lord how long before the Consummation come, as though we were weary of our warfare: It [is] not a [r]*Domine si fuisses, Lord if thou hadst beene here, our brother had not died*, as *Martha* said of *Lazarus*, as though, as soon as we suffer any worldly calamity, we should thinke Christ to be absent from us, in his power, or in his care of us; It is not a [s]*Domine vis mandemus, Lord wilt thou that we command fire from Heaven to consume these Samaritans*, as though we would serve the Lord no longer, then he would revenge his owne and our quarrel; for, (that we may come to our last part) to that fiery question of the Apostles, Christ answered, *You know not of what spirit you are*; It is not the Spirit of God, it is not the Holy Ghost, which makes you call Jesus the Lord onely to serve your own ends, and purposes; and *No man can say, that Jesus is the Lord, but by the Holy Ghost*. (*1624?*) 6:125–26

o. Esay 6:3.
p. Luke 6:46.
q. John 13:13.
r. John 11:21.
s. Luke 9:54.

B. The Caveat: The Limitations and Dangers of Art

1. Blasphemy: The Rebellious Tongue (Matt. 12:31)

Blasphemy, as it is a contumelious speech, derogating from any man, that good that is in him, or attributing to any man, that ill that is not in him, may be fastned upon any man. For the most part it is understood a sin against God, and that directly; and here, by the manner of Christ expressing himselfe, it is made the greatest sin; *All sin*, even *blasphemy*. And yet, a drunkard that cannot name God, will spue out a blasphemy against God: A child that cannot spell God, will stammer out a blasphemy against God: If we smart, we blaspheme God, and we blaspheme him if we be tickled; If I lose at play, I blaspheme, and if my fellow lose, he blasphemes, so that God is alwayes sure to be a loser. An Usurer can shew me his bags, and an Extortioner his houses, the fruits, the revenues of his sinne; but where will the blasphemer shew mee his blasphemy, or what hee hath got by it? The licentious man hath had his love in his armes, and the envious man hath had his enemy in the dust, but wherein hath the blasphemer hurt God?

[t]In the Schoole we put it for the consummation of the torment of the damned, that at the Resurrection, they shall have bodies, and so be able, even verbally, to blaspheme God; herein we exceed the Devill already, that we can speake blasphemously. There is a rebellious part of the body, that *Adam* covered with figge leaves, that hath damned many a wretched soule; but yet, I thinke, not more then the tongue; And therefore the whole torment that *Dives* suffered in hell, is expressed in that part, [u]*Father Abraham, have mercy upon me, and send Lazarus, that he may dip the tip of his finger in water, and coole my tongue*. The Jews that crucified God, will not sound the name of God, and we for whom he was Crucified, belch him out in our surfets, and foame him out in our fury: An Impertinent sin, without occasion before, and an unprofitable sin, without recompense after, and an incorrigible sin too; for, almost what Father dares chide his son for blasphemy, that may not tell him, Sir I learnt it of you? or what Master his servant, that cannot lay the same recrimination upon him? How much then do we need this extent of Gods mercy, that he will forgive *sin*, and *all sin*, and even this sin of *blasphemy*, and (which is also another addition) *blasphemy against the Son*. (*162?*) 5:82–83

t. Aquin. 2.2. q.13. ar.4.

u. Luke 16:24.

2. "Art is suspicious" (Rom. 8:16)

The holy Ghost will fulfill his owne law, [v] *In ore duorum, In the mouth of two witnesses.* Sometimes our spirit bears witnesse of some things appertaining to the next world, without the testimony of the holy Ghost. *Tertullian* in that excellent Book of his, *De testimonio Animae,* Of the testimony which the soule of man gives of it selfe to it selfe, where he speaks of the soule of a naturall, an unregenerate man, gives us just occasion to stop a little upon that consideration. If, sayes he, we for our Religion produce your own Authors against you, (he speaks to naturall men, secular Philosophers) and shew you out of them, what Passions, what Vices even they impute to those whom you have made your Gods, then you say, they were but *Poetae vani,* Those Authors were but vaine, and frivolous Poets; But when those Authors speake any thing which sound against our Religion, then they are Philosophers, and reverend and classique Authors. And therefore, sayes he, I will draw no witnesse from them, *Perversae foelicitatis, quibus in falso potius creditur, quam in vero,* Because they have this perverse, this left-handed happinesse, to be beleeved when they lye, better then when they say true. *Novum testimonium adduco,* saies he; I wayve all them, and I call upon a new witnesse: A witnesse, *Omni literaturi notius,* More legible then any Character, then any text hand, for it is the intimation of mine owne soule, and conscience; and *Omni Editione vulgatius,* More publique, more conspicuous then any Edition, any impression of any Author, for Editions may be called in, but who can call in the testimony of his owne soule? He proceeds, *Te simplicem, et Idioticum compello,* I require but a simple, an unlearned soule, *Qualem te habent, qui te solam habent,* Such a soule, as that man hath, who hath nothing but a soule, no learning; *Imperitia tua mihi opus est, quoniam aliquantulae peritiae tuae nemo credit;* I shall have the more use of thy testimony, the more ignorant thou art, for, in such cases, Art is suspicious, and from them who are able to prove anything, we beleeve nothing; And therefore, saies he, *Nolo Academiis, bibliothecis instructam,* I call not a soule made in an University, or nursed in a Library, but let this soule come now, as it came to me in my Mothers wombe, an inartificiall, an unexperienced soule; And then, (to contract *Tertullians* Contemplation) he proceeds to shew the notions of the Christian Religion, which are in such a soule naturally, and which his spirit, that is, his rectified reason, rectified but by nature, is able to infuse into him. And certainly, some of that, which is proved by the testimony mentioned in this text, is proved by the testimony of

v. [Deut. 17:6.]

our owne naturall soule, in that Poet whom the Apostle cites, that said, [w]*Genus ejus, We are the off-spring of God.* (*1622?*) 5:68–69

3. Apollo and the Holy Ghost (John 16:8, 9, 10, 11)

As God begun all with judgement, (for he made all things in measure, number, and waight) as he proceeded with judgement, in erecting a judiciall seat for our direction, and correction, the Church, [x]so he shall end all with judgement, The finall, and generall judgement, at the Resurrection; which he that beleeves not, beleeves nothing; not God; for, [y]*He that commeth to God* (that makes any step towards him) *must beleeve, Deum remuneratorem*, God, and God in that notion, as he is a Rewarder; Therefore there is judgement. But was this work left for the Holy Ghost? Did not the naturall man that knew no Holy Ghost, know this? Truly, all their fabulous Divinity,[4] all their Mythology, their Minos, and their Rhadamantus, tasted of such a notion, as a judgement. And yet the first planters of the Christian Religion found it hardest to fixe this roote of all other articles, *That Christ should come againe to judgement.* Miserable and froward men! They would beleeve it in their fables, and would not beleeve it in the Scriptures; They would beleeve it in the nine Muses, and would not beleeve it in the twelve Apostles; They would beleeve it by Apollo, and they would not beleeve it by the Holy Ghost; They would be saved Poetically, and fantastically, and would not reasonably, and spiritually; By Copies, and not by Originals; by counterfeit things at first deduced by their Authors, out of our Scriptures, and yet not by the word of God himself. Which *Tertullian* apprehends and reprehends in his time, when he sayes, *Praescribimus adulteris nostris,* Wee prescribe above them, which counterfeit our doctrine, for we had it before them, and they have but rags, and those torn from us. *Fabulae immissae, quae fidem infirmarent veritatis,* They have brought part of our Scriptures into their Fables; that all the rest might seem but Fables too. *Gehennam praedicantes et judicium, ridemur, decachinnamur,* They laugh at us when we preach of hell, and judgement, *Et tamen Elysii campi fidem praeoccupaverunt,* And yet they will needs be beleeved when they talk of their Elysian fields. *Fideliora nostra, quorum imagines fidem inveniunt,* Is it not safer trusting to our substance, then their shadows; To our doctrine of the judgement, in the Scriptures, then their allusions in their Poets? (*1626*) 7:233–34

4. Fictional belief, here described in terms of Minos and Rhadamanthus (see *Aeneid* 6), who, with Aeacus, because of their just lives on earth, were judges of the dead.

w. Acts 17:28.
x. Sap. 11[:20].
y. Heb. 11:16.

4. A Warning Against Learning (Deut. 12:30)

What is curiosity? [z]*Qui scire vult ut sciat,* He that desires knowledge only that he may know, or be known by others to know; he who makes not the end of his knowledge the glory of God, he offends in curiosity, says that Father; But that is only in the end. But in the way to knowledge there is curiosity too; In seeking such things as man hath no faculty to compass, unrevealed mysteries; In seeking things, which if they may be compassed, yet it is done by indirect means, by Invocation of Spirits, by Sorcery; In seeking things which may be found, and by good means, but appertain not to our profession; all these ways men offend in curiosity. It is so in us, in Church-men, *si Iambos survemus, et metrorum silvam congerimus,* If we be over-vehemently affected or transported with Poetry, or other secular Learning. And therefore St. *Hierom* is reported himself to have been whipt by an Angel, who found him over-studious in some of *Cicero's* Books. This is curiosity in us, and it is so in you, if when you have sufficient means of salvation Preached to you in that Religion wherein you were Baptized, you enquire too much, too much trouble your self with the Religion of those, from whose superstitions you are already by Gods goodness rescued; remember that he who desired to fill himself with the husks, was the Prodigal. It was Prodigality, and a dangerous expence of your constancy, to open your self to temptation, by an unnecessary enquiring into impertinent controversies. We in our profession may embrace secular Learning, so far as it may conduce to the better discharge of our duties, in making the easier entrance, and deeper impression of Divine things in you: You may inform your selves occasionally, when any scruple takes hold of you, of any point of their Religion. But let your study be rather to live according to that Religion which you have, then to enquire into that from which God hath delivered you; for that's the looking back of *Lots* wife, and the distemper and distaste of the children of *Israel,* who remembered too much the *Egyptian* diet. If you will enquire whether any of the Fathers of the Primitive Church did at any time pray for any of the dead, you shall be told (and truly) that *Augustine* did, that *Ambrose* did; but you shall not so presently be told how they deprehended themselves in an infirmity, and collected and corrected themselves ever when they were so praying. If you enquire whether any of them speak of Purgatory, you shall easily finde they do; but not so easily, in what sense; when they call the calamities of this life, or when they call the general Conflagration of the world, Purgatory. If you enquire after Indulgences,

z. Augustine.

you may finde the name frequent amongst them; but not so easily finde when and how the Relaxations of Penances publickly enjoyned, were called Indulgences; nor how, nor when Indulgences came to be applyed to souls departed. If thou enquire without a *Melius Inquirendum*, without a through Inquisition (which is not easie for any man who makes it not his whole study and profession) thou maist come to think holy men have prayed for the dead, why may not I? Holy men speak of Purgatory and Indulgences, why should I abhor the names or the things? And so thou maist fall into the first snare, it hath been done, therefore it may be done; and into another after, It may be done, therefore it must be done: When thou art come to think that some men are saved that have done it, thou wilt think that no man can be saved except he do it: From making infirmities excusable necessary (which is the bondage the Council of *Trent* hath laid upon the world)[5] to make Problematical things, Dogmatical; and matter of Disputation, matter of Faith; to bring the University into *Smithfield*, and heaps of Arguments into Piles of Faggots.[6] If thou enquire further then thy capacity enables thee, further then thy calling provokes thee; How do those Nations serve their gods? thou maist come to say, as the Text says, in the end, *Even so will I do also*.

To end all, embrace Fundamental, Dogmatical, evident Divinity; That is expressed *in Credendis*, in the things which we are to believe in the Creed. And it begins with *Credo in Deum*, Belief in God, and not in man, nor traditions of men. And it is expressed *in petendis*, in the things which we are to pray for in the Lords Prayer; and that begins with *Sanctificetur nomen tuum, Hallowed be thy Name*, not the name of any. (*1622*) 4:142–44

C. Possibilities, Style, and Form

1. Musicum carmen *(Ezek. 33:32)*

God shall send Prophets, Trumpets, and Trumpetors, that is, preachers of his word, and not the word of men; and they shall be heard willingly too; for as they are *Tubae*, Trumpets, so they shall be *musicum carmen*, acceptable musick to them that hear them.

5. The Nineteenth Ecumenical Council met in Trent, Italy, from 1545–1563. As an embodiment of the ideals of the Counter Reformation, its numerous decrees dealt with many aspects of Roman Catholic doctrine and order, including the interpretation of judgment and merit, which Donne, *inter alia*, strikes at here.

6. To render the university, with its manifold disputations, into a single, specialized, and vulgar market (Smithfield); to transform the complications of arguments into well-ordered bundles of sticks (faggots).

They shall be so, first *In re,* in their matter, in the doctrine which they preach. The same trumpet that sounds the alarm (that is, that awakens us from our security) and that sounds the Battail (that is, that puts us into a colluctation with our selves, with this world, with powers and principalities, yea into a wrastling with God himself and his Justice) the same trumpet sounds the Parle too, calls us to hearken to God in his word, and to speak to God in our prayers, and so to come to treaties and capitulations for peace; and the same trumpet sounds a retreat too, that is, a safe reposing of our souls in the merit, and in the wounds of our Saviour Christ Jesus. And in this voice they are *musicum carmen,* a love-song (as the text speaks) in proposing the love of God to man, wherein he loved him so, as that he gave his onely begotten Son for him. God made this whole world in such an uniformity, such a correspondency, such a concinnity of parts, as that it was an Instrument, perfectly in tune: we may say, the trebles, the highest strings were disordered first; the best understandings, Angels and Men, put this instrument out of tune, God rectified all again, by putting in a new string, *semen mulieris,* the seed of the woman, the *Messias*: And onely by sounding that string in your ears, become we *musicum carmen,* true musick, true harmony, true peace to you. If we shall say, that Gods first string in this instrument, was Reprobation, that Gods first intention, was, for his glory to damn man; and that then he put in another string, of creating Man, that so he might have some body to damn; and then another of enforcing him to sin, that so he might have a just cause to damne him; and then another, of disabling him to lay hold upon any means of recovery: there's no musick in all this, no harmony, no peace in such preaching. But if we take this instrument, when Gods hand tuned it the second time, in the promise of a *Messias,* and offer of the love and mercy of God to all that will receive it in him; then we are truly *musicum carmen,* as a love-song, when we present the love of God to you, and raise you to the love of God in Christ Jesus: for, for the musick of the Sphears, whatsoever it be, we cannot hear it; for the decrees of God in heaven, we cannot say we have seen them; our musick is onely that salvation which is declared in the Gospel to all them, and to them onely, who take God by the right hand, as he delivers himself in Christ.

So they shall be musick *in re,* in their matter, in their doctrine; and they shall be also *in modo,* in their manner of presenting that doctrine. Religion is a serious thing, but not a sullen; Religious preaching is a grave exercise, but not a sordid, not a barbarous, not a negligent. There are not so eloquent books in the world, as the Scriptures: Accept those names of Tropes and Figures, which the Grammarians and Rhetoricians put upon us, and we may be bold to say, that in all their Authors, Greek and Latin, we cannot finde so high, and so lively examples, of those Tropes, and those Figures, as we may in the Scriptures: whatsoever hath justly delighted any man in any mans writings, is exceeded in the Scriptures. The style of the Scriptures is a diligent, and an artificial style; and a great part thereof in a musical, in a metrical, in a measured composition, in verse. The greatest mystery of our Religion, indeed the whole body of our Religion, the coming, and the Kingdome of a *Messias*, of a Saviour, of Christ, is conveyed in a Song, in the third chapter of *Habakkuk*: and therefore the Jews say, that that Song cannot yet be understood, because they say the *Messiah* is not yet come. His greatest work, when he was come, which was his union and marriage with the Church, and with our souls, he hath also delivered in a piece of a curious frame, *Solomons* Song of Songs. And so likewise, long before, when God had given all the Law, he provided, as himself sayes, a safer way, which was to give them a heavenly Song of his owne making: for that Song, he sayes there, he was sure they would remember. (*1619*) 2:169–71

2. Epideictic Oratory and Preaching (Micah 2:10)

There was such a tendernesse, amongst the orators, which were used to speake in the presence of the people, to the Romane Emperors, (which was a way of *Civill preaching*) that they durst not tell them then their duties, nor instruct them, what they should doe, any other way then by saying, that they had done so before; They had no way to make the Prince wise, and just, and temperate, but by a false praising him, for his former acts of wisedom, and justice, and temperance, which he had never done; and that served to make the people beleeve, that the Princes were so; and it served to teach the Prince, that he ought to be so. And so, though this were an expresse, and a direct flattery, yet it was a collaterall increpation too; And on the other side, our later times have seen another art, another invention, another workmanship, that when a great person hath so abused the favour of his Prince, that he hath growne subject to great, and weighty increpations, his owne friends have made *Libells* against him, thereby to lay some light aspersions upon him, that the Prince might thinke, that this comming with the malice of a *Libell*, was the worst that could be said of him: and so, as the first way to the Emperors, though it were a direct flattery, yet it was a *collaterall Increpation* too, so this way, though it were a direct increpation, yet it was a *collaterall flattery* too. If I should say of such a congregation as this with acclamations and showes of much joy, Blessed company, holy congregation, in which there is no pride at all, no vanity at all, no prevarication at all, I could be thought in that, but to convey an increpation, and a rebuke mannerly, in a wish that it were so altogether. If I should say of such a congregation as this, with exclamations and show of much bitternesse, that they were sometimes somewhat too worldly in their owne businesse, sometimes somewhat too remisse, in the businesses of the next world, and adde no more to it, this were but as a plot, and a *faint libelling*, a publishing of small sinnes to keep greater from being talked of: slight increpations are but as *whisperings*, and work no farther, but to bring men to say, Tush, no body hears it, no body heeds it, we are never the worse, nor never the worse thought of for all that he says. And loud and bitter increpations, are as a *trumpet*, and work no otherwise, but to bring them to say, Since he hath published all to the world already, since all the world knowes of it, the shame is past, and we may goe forward in our ways againe. Is there then no way to convey an increpation profitably? *David* could find no way; [a]*Vidi praevaricatores et tabescebam*, says he, *I saw the transgressors, but I languished and consumed away with griefe, because they would not keep the law*; he could not mend them, and so impaired himselfe with his compassion: but God hath provided a way here, to convey, to imprint this increpation, this rebuke, sweetly, and succesfully; that is, by way of counsaile: by bidding them *arise*, he chides them for falling, by presenting the exaltation and exultation of a peacefull conscience, he brings them to a foresight, to what miserable distractions, and distortions of the soule, a habite of sinne will bring them to. If you will take knowledge of Gods fearfull judgements no other way, but by hearing his mercies preached, his *Mercie is new every morning*, and his dew falls every evening; and morning, and evening we will preach his mercies unto you. If you will beleeve a *hell* no other way, but by hearing the joyes of heaven presented to you, you shall heare enough of that; we will receive you in the morning, and dismisse you in the evening, in a religious assurance, in a present inchoation of the joyes of heaven. It is Gods way, and we are willing to pursue it; to shew you that you are Enemies to Christ, *we pray you in Christs stead, that you would be reconciled to him*; to shew you, that you are faln, we pray you to *arise*, and *si audieritis*, if you hear us so, if any way, any means, convey this rebuke, this sense into you, [b]*Si audieritis, lucrati sumus fratrem, If you hear, we have gained a brother*; and that's the richest gain, that we can get, if you may get salvation by us. (*1621 or 1623?*) 5:200–201

a. Ps. 119:158.

b. Matt. 18:15.

3. Elihu: A Secular Poet (Job 36:25)

The words are the words of *Elihu*; *Elihu* was one of *Jobs* friends, and a meer *naturall* man: a man not captivated, not fettered, not enthralled, in any *particular forme* of *Religion*, as the *Jewes* were; a man not macerated with the *feare of God*; not infatuated with any preconceptions, which *Nurses*, or *Godfathers*, or *Parents*, or *Church*, or *State* had infused into him; not dejected, not suppled, not matured, not entendred, with *crosses* in this world, and so made apt to receive any impressions, or follow any *opinions* of *other men*, a *meer naturall man*; and in the meer use of meer *naturall reason*, this man sayes of God in his works, *Every man may see it, Man may behold it afar off*. It is the word of a naturall man; and the *holy Ghost* having canonized it, sanctified it, by inserting it into the booke of *God*, it is the word of *God* too. Saint *Paul* cites sometimes the words of *secular Poets*, and approves them; and then the words of those Poets, become the word of *God; Elihu* speakes, a *naturall man*, and *God* speakes, in *canonizing* his words; and therefore when we speake to *godly* men, we are sure to be believed, for *God* sayes it; if we were to speake to *naturall* men onely, we might be believed, for *Elihu*, a *naturall* man, and *wise in his generation*, sayes it, that for *God* in his *works Every man may see it, man may behold it afar off*. (*1622*) 4:163

4. Manifestation: Jacob's Nunc *(Gen. 32:10)*

But that hath been Gods abundant and overflowing goodness, ever to succor the infirmity of Man, with sensible and visible things; with the pillars in the Wilderness; with the Tabarnacle after; and with the Temple and all the mysterious, and significative furniture thereof after all. So God leaves not *Jacob* to the general knowledge, that the Angels of God protect Gods Children, but he manifested those Angels unto him, *Occurrerunt ei*, the Angels of God met him. The word of God is an infalible guide to thee, But God hath provided thee also visible, and manifest assistants, the Pillar his Church, and the Angels his Ministers in the Church. The Scripture is thine onely *Ephod*, but *Applica Ephod*, apply it to thee by his Church, and by his visible Angels, and not by thine own private interpretation.

This was *Jacobs nunc;* now, when he was returned, returned upon Gods Commandement; upon Gods Commandement pursued, and testified by Angels, and Angels visibly manifested; now, he could take a comfort in the contemplation of his fortune, of his estate, to see, that he was two bands. Here's a great change; we see his vowe; and we see how far his wishes extended at his going out; [c]*If God will give me*

c. Gen. 28:20[, 21].

bread to eate, and cloathes to put on, so that I come againe unto my fathers house in safety, then shall the Lord be my God. In which vow is included all the service that he could exhibite, or retribute to God. Now his staffe is become a sword; a strong Army; his one staff now is multiplyed. (*1618*) 1:283

5. Now Is the Time for God (Ps. 32:6)

In a word, then is a fit time of finding God, whensoever thy conscience tells thee he calls to thee; for, a rectified conscience is the word of God; If that speake to thee now this minute, now is thy time of finding God. That *Now,* that I named then, that minute is past; but God affords thee another *Now;* he speaks againe, he speaks still, and if thy conscience tell thee that he speaks to thee, now is that time. This word of God, thy conscience will present unto thee, but that one condition, which *Moses* presented to Gods people, and that is, [d]*That thou seeke the Lord with all thy heart, and all thy soule.* It is a kinde of denying the Infinitenesse of God, to serve him by pieces, and ragges; God is not Infinite to me, if I thinke a discontinued service will serve him. It is a kinde of denying the Unity of God, to joyne other gods, Pleasure, or Profit with him. (*winter 1624–1625?*) 9:327

6. Epiphany: The Now of Holy Action (Luke 2:29, 30)

To be able to conclude to your selves, that because you have had a Christmas-day, a manifestation of Christs birth in your soules, by the Sacrament, you shall have a whole Good-Friday, a crucifying, and a *consummatum est*, a measure of corrections, and joy in those corrections, tentations, and the issue with the tentation; And that you shall have a Resurrection, and an Ascension, an inchoation, and an unremoveable possession of heaven it self in this world; Make good your Christmas day, that Christ by a worthy receiving of the Sacrament, be born in you, and he that dyed for you, will live with you all the yeare, and all the yeares of your lives, and inspire into you, and receive from you at the last gasp, this blessed acclamation, *Lord now lettest thou thy servant, etc.*[7]

The end of all digestions, and concoctions is assimilation, that that meate may become our body. The end of all consideration of all the actions of such leading and exemplar men, as *Simeon* was, is assimilation too; That we may be like that man. Therefore we shall make it a first part, to take a picture, to give a character of this man, to consider how *Simeon* was qualified and prepared, matured and disposed to

7. The Song of Simeon, or the Nunc dimittis.

d. Deut. 4:29.

that confidence, that he could desire to depart in peace, intimated in that first word, *Now;* now, that all that I look for is accomplished; And farther expressed in the first word of the other clause, *For, for mine eyes have seen thy salvation*; *Now, now* the time is fulfilled; *For, for mine eyes have seen.* And then enters the second part, what is the greatest happinesse that can be well wished in this world, by a man well prepared, is, that he may depart in peace; *Lord now lettest thou, etc.* And all the way, in every step that we make, in his light, (in *Simeons* light) we shall see light; we shall consider, that that preparation, and disposition, and acquiescence, which *Simeon* had in his Epiphany, in his visible seeing of Christ then, is offered to us in this Epiphany, in this manifestation and application of Christ in the Sacrament; And that therefore every penitent, and devout, and reverent, and worthy receiver, hath had in that holy action his *Now*, there are all things accomplished to him, and his *For, for his eyes have seen his salvation*; and so may be content, nay glad *to depart in peace.* (*1626*) 7:280–81

7. The Hieroglyphic Y: A Stem and Two Beams (Matt. 6:21)

Of this Noble Body of Divinity, one fair Limb is in this Text, *Where your treasure is, there will your heart be also.* Immediately before, our blessed Saviour had forbidden us the laying up of *Treasure in this world*, upon this Reason, That *here moths and rust corrupt, and thieves break in, and steal.* There, the reason is, because the *Money* may be lost; but here, in our Text it is, because the *Man* may be lost: *for where your Treasure is, there your Heart will be also:* So that this is equivalent to that, [e]*What profit to gain the whole world, and loose a mans own soul?* Our Text therefore stands as that Proverbial, that Hieroglyphical Letter, *Pythagoras* his Y;[8] that hath first a stalk, a stem to fix it self, and then spreads into two Beams. The stem, the stalk of this Letter, this Y, is in the first word of the Text, that Particle of argumentation, *For*: Take heed where you place your Treasure: for it concerns you much, where your Heart be placed; and, *where your Treasure is, there will your Heart be also.* And then opens this Symbolical, this Catechistical Letter, this Y, into two Horns, two Beams, two Branches; one broader, but on the left hand, denoting the Treasures of this World; the other narrower, but on the right hand, Treasure laid up for the World to come. Be sure ye turn the right way: for, *where your Treasure is, there will your Heart be also.*

. . . .

8. The upsilon is called the Pythagorean letter because Pythagoras used it to teach the divergent paths of good and evil.

e. Matt. 16:26.

God requires the heart, the whole man, all the faculties of that man: for onely that that is intire, and indivisible, is immovable; and that that God calls for, and we seek for, in this stem of *Pythagoras* his Symbolical Letter, is this immovableness, this fixation of the heart. (*1629*) 9:174, 176

8. Selah *and* Amen: *Hyperbolical Attestation (Ps. 32:3, 4)*

To end all; all this, the Holy Ghost by the pen of *David*, seales with the last word of this Text, *Selah*. A word of uncertain sense, and signification; for the Jews themselves do not know exactly, and certainly what it signifies; but deriving this *Selah*, from *Selal*, which signifies *Attollere, To lift up*, they think it to be but a Musicall note, for the raising of the voyce, at that part of the Psalme, where that word is used; as, indeed the word is never used in the Bible, but in the Psalmes, and [f]twice in one Chapter, in the Prophet *Habakkuk*, which is a Musicall, a Metricall Chapter. In the Latine Translation, and in the Arabique Translation of the Psalmes it is cleane left out, because they were not sure how to translate it aright. But, to speak upon the best grounds in the Grammar of that language, and upon best Authority too, the word signifies a Vehement, a Patheticall, a Hyperbolicall asseveration, and attestation, and ratification of something said before. Such, in a proportion, as our Saviours *Amen, Amen* is, *Verily, verily I say unto you;* Such, as S. *Pauls fidelis Sermo*, with which he seales so many truths, is, *This is a faithfull saying*; Such, as that Apostles *Coram Domino* is, with which he ratifies many things, *Before the Lord I speak it;* and such, as *Moses* his *Vivo ego*, and *Vivit Dominus, As I live saith the Lord*, and *As the Lord liveth*. And therefore, though God be in all his words, *Yea, and Amen*, no word of his can perish in it selfe, nor should perish in us, that is, passe without observation, yet, in setting this seal of *Selah* to this Doctrine, he hath testified his will that he would have all these things the better understood, and the deeplier imprinted, That if a man conceale and smother his sins, *Selah*, Assuredly, God will open that mans mouth, and it shall not shew forth his praise, but God will bring him, *Ad rugitum*, to fearfull exclamations out of the sense of the affliction, if not of the sin; *Selah*, Assuredly, God wil shiver his bones, shake his best actions, and discover their impurity; *Selah*, assuredly, God will suffer to be dried up all his moysture, all possibility of repentant teares, and all interest in the blood of Christ Jesus; *Selah*, Assuredly, Gods hand shall be heavy upon him, and he shall not discerne it to be his hand, but shall attribute all to false causes, and so place all his comfort in false remedies; Hee shall leave out God all

f. Heb. 3:3, 9.

day, and God shall leave out him all night, all his everlasting night, in which he shall never see day more. *Selah*, Assuredly, Verily, Amen, *Fidelis Sermo*, This is a faithfull, an infallible Truth, *Coram Domino*, Before the Lord, *Vivit Dominus*, as the Lord liveth, as *Moses*, as *Christ*, as S. *Paul* testifie their, *David* testifies his Doctrine, All between God and man is conditionall, and where man will not be bound, God will not be bound neither; if man invest a habit and purpose of sinning, God will study a judgement against that man, [g] and doe that, even in Israel, which shall make all our eares to tingle, and all our hearts to ake; Till that man repent, God will not, and when he does, God will repent too; For, though God be not Man, that he can repent, yet that God, who for Mans sake became Man, for our sakes, and his owne glory, will so farre become Man againe, as upon Mans true repentance, to repent the Judgements intended against that Man. (*winter 1624–1625?*) 9:294–95

9. Blessed Monosyllables: Pray and Stay (Ps. 6:2, 3)

Any degree of wearinesse of attending the Lords leisure, arising in thee, suppresse it, overcome it, with more and more petitions, and that which God did by way of Commandement, in the first Creation, doe thou by way of prayer, in this thy second Creation; First he said, *Fiat Lux, Let there be light:* Pray thou, that he would enlighten thy darknesse. God was satisfied with that light for three daies, and then he said, *Fiant luminaria, Let there be great lights*; Blesse God for his present light, but yet pray that hee will inlarge that light which he hath given thee; And turne all those his Commandments into prayers, till thou come to his *Faciamus hominem, Let us make man according to our own Image*; Pray that he will restore his Image in thee, and conforme thee to him, who is [h] *the Image of the invisible God*, our Lord and Saviour Christ Jesus. He did his greatest work upon thee, before time was, thine Election; And he hath reserved the consummation of that work, till time shall be no more, thy Glorification: And as for thy Vocation he hath taken his own time, (He did not call thee into the world in the time of the Primitive Church, nor, perchance, call thee effectually, though in the Church, in the dayes of thy youth) So stay his time for thy Sanctification, and, if the day-spring from on high have visited thee, but this morning, If thou beest come to a *fiat lux* but now, that now God have kindled some light in thee, hee may come this day seaven-night to a *fiant luminaria*, to multiply this light by a more powerfull meanes. If not so soone, yet still remember, that it was God that made the Sun stand still to Joshuah, as well as to run his race as

g. 1. Sam. 3:11.

h. Coloss. 1:15.

a Giant to *David*; And God was as much glorified in the standing still of the Sun, as in the motion thereof; And shall be so in thy Sanctification, though it seeme to stand at a stay for a time, when his time shall be to perfect it, in a measure acceptable to thee. Nothing is acceptable to him, but that which is seasonable; nor seasonable, except it come in the time proper to it: And, as S. *Augustine* sayes, *Natura rei est, quam indidit Deus*, That is the nature of every thing, which God hath imprinted in it, So that is the time for every thing, which God hath appointed for it. *Pray*, and *Stay*, are two blessed Monosyllables; To ascend to God, To attend Gods descent to us, is the Motion, and the Rest of a Christian; And as all Motion is for Rest, so let all the Motions of our soule in our prayers to God be, that our wills may rest in his, and that all that pleases him, may please us, therefore because it pleases him; for therefore, because it pleases him, it becomes good for us, and then, when it pleases him, it becomes seasonable unto us, and expedient for us. (*1623?*) 5:362–63

10. Closure: The Stamp on All (Ps. 6:8, 9, 10)

David makes it his first worke, to stay Gods anger in a deprecatory prayer, but he stayes not upon that long, he will not prescribe his Physitian, what he shall prescribe to him, but leaves God to his own medicines, and to his own methode. But then the Postulatory prayer, what he begs of God, employes six verses: as well to shew us, that our necessities are many; as also that if God doe not answer us, at the beginning of our prayer, our duty is still to pursue that way, to continue in prayer. And then the third part of the Psalme, which is the Gratulatory part, his giving of thanks, is, shall we say deferred, or rather reserved to the end of the Psalme, and exercises onely those three verses which are our Text. Not that the duty of thankesgiving is lesse then that of prayer; for if we could compare them, it is rather greater; because it contributes more to Gods glory, to acknowledge by thanks, that God hath given, then to acknowledge by prayer, that God can give. But therefore might *David* be later and shorter here, in expressing that duty of thanks, first, because being reserved to the end, and close of the Psalme, it leaves the best impression in the memory. And therefore it is easie to observe, that in all Metricall compositions, of which kinde the booke of Psalmes is, the force of the whole piece, is for the most part left to the shutting up; the whole frame of the Poem is a beating out of a piece of gold, but the last clause is as the impression of the stamp, and that is it that makes it currant. (*1623*) 6:41

3 Grammar and Theology

Introduction

The Logos, or the Word made flesh and incarnate among men, expresses God's creative power and activity. While the Word freely comes to us, we must at the same time open our hearts to it and make way for a new enlargement of wisdom and strength. As the Word is imprinted on our souls, so are we enabled to speak. Imbued with the instrument of creation, speech puts on artistic and prophetic dress, and the preacher or poet can possess the means to call on people everywhere, to sound the trumpet that brings men together for sacred celebration.

Having discovered concrete and artistic shape, the Word demands special refinement so that it can be widely apprehended. The laws governing human discourse must therefore be understood as a divine grammar, where no feature of arrangement or form is too small for contemplation and analysis, where no word or even syllable is able to escape an exacting test for rightness, just measure, and truth. Since God speaks through the Logos, it follows that each man who would hear the Word must also recognize the discrete tones in the divine register. Donne's insistent desire to find the meaning of words and to examine their relationships and his inclination to wring texts of their secrets may be understood in this light. Like his older contemporary Lancelot Andrewes, who proceeded in a similar way, the close inspection of words aimed not so much to show off learning and wittiness as to get closer to God's own voice.

The selections of this chapter illustrate Donne's concern for the study of language in all its particulars. Since "nothing is to be neglected as little [in language]," we should approach the relationship between grammar and theology with "no levity." First of all, we learn that grammar is an indispensable discipline with which to analyze the relationship between man and God: "God blesses man *Dative* . . . *Optative* . . . *Vocative*," that is, God acts upon man by sending His goodness *to* him, by working as if in the dative or indirect case, with grace and the free gifts of His Spirit; God acts in the optative mood by desiring good for man; and He acts in the vocative mood by calling and speaking directly to man. Even sin is grammatical: "beyond speaking sins, and crying sins . . . there is a *Quia*, a Reason." Donne says elsewhere that "the Devils grammar is . . . to apply Actives to Passives; where he sees an inclination, to subminister a temptation. . . . And God's grammar is to *change* Actives into Passives: where a man delights in cursing, to make that man accursed" (7 : 367). The idea of sin waiting voraciously upon our desires in order to translate them into actions is implicit in all Donne says in the passages quoted here; for in order to make translation possible, we come at last "to sin Grammatically, to tie sins together in construction, in a Syntaxis, in a chaine, and dependance, and coherence upon one another" (1 : 225).

Donne is convinced that the structure of most relationships can be analyzed through grammar acting as a prism, and that an investigation of grammar is integral to an understanding of the divine Logos. Tense, mood, and voice in verb structure is of particular interest to him: God's judgments are conditional, God's idiom is imperative. In his own analyses of biblical texts, he is also most careful with adverbs of time, such as *nunc* and *tunc*, now and then, for with them he is able to explore the usual time planes and watch them blur and fuse into each other. We see God by His light now and later, in and out of time, according to the light which flows from Him, but which also dwells essentially in Him.

Donne returns frequently to this theme of the conflation of tenses: the Holy Ghost is indifferent to present, future, or past, for "whatsoever he hath done, and will doe, hee is alwayes ready to doe at the present." In closely considering Hebrew—the language, Donne frequently says, in which God spoke—we come closer to an understanding of His thought. By an analogy with Hebrew grammar, Donne urges that the Creator is not singular but plural, "so manifold are the beames, and emanations that flow out from him"; that there is no present tense in the language which God speaks, but that there is a binding identity between the past and the future; and that God's language lacks superlatives and must resort to circumlocutions—and thus God becomes the King or the Sun.

What Donne believes about grammar is closely related to what he believes about logic. Logic appears, for instance, as the "*quia*" of argumentation in grammatical structure; but this particle of argumentation, "for," is extremely important as well to Donne's thinking about prayer. All prayer must have a *quia* (or a "for") to ground it in reason. A brief look at the Holy Sonnets reveals how frequently Donne turns to that "for" wherever there is a pivotal point: "for I / Except you'enthrall mee" (10, Grierson 14); "For I have sinn'd" (7, Grierson 11); and so on. "How" and "Why," the "dangerous monosyllables," are the tools of sophistry that defeat us in the Devil. Again, we can find these single words working at crucial places in Donne's poetry: "Why are wee by all creatures waited on?," Donne begins one of his Holy Sonnets (8, Grierson 12); or, "How shall my mindes white truth to them [faithful souls] be try'd?" (Additional Sonnets, 4; Grierson 8).

The Christian graduates from school to university when he moves from grammar to logic, but even then Donne continues his insistence on the "imperative" idiom of God, "that is *Logos* it self." Perhaps the best summary of the Word, in the terms of God's grammar, is the Lord's Prayer. With its seven petitions—the perfect and infinite number—it makes a circle of praise, "and a circle is infinite too." Prayer and praise are the same; they draw on words, but they lead beyond, yet back to man and the instruments of his discourse and holy desire.

A. The Grammar of Devotion

1. The Grammar of Blessing (2 Cor. 1:3)

There is not a better Grammar to learne, then to learne how to blesse God, and therefore it may be no levity, to use some Grammar termes herein. God blesses man *Dative*, He gives good to him; man blesses God *Optative*, He wishes well to him; and he blesses him *Vocative*, He speaks well of him.[1] For, though towards God, as well as towards man, reall actions are called blessings, ([a] *so Abigail* called the present which she brought to *David*, *A blessing*, and so *Naaman* called that which he offered to *Elisha*, *A blessing*) though reall sacrifices to God, and his cause, sacrifices of Almes, sacrifices of Armes, sacrifices of Money, sacrifices of Sermons, advancing a good publique cause, may come under the name of blessing, yet the word here, Εὐλογία, is properly a blessing in speech, in discourse, in conference, in words, in praise, in thanks. (*1621?*) 3:258–59

2. Sin: Grammatical, Logical, Rhetorical (Ps. 55:19)

Sinful thoughts produced into actions, are speaking sins; sinful actions continued into habits, are crying sins. There is a sin before these; a speechless sin, a whispering sin,[2] which no body hears, but

1. The dative expresses indirect action or giving, that is, God gives something (good) *to* man; the optative denotes a verb form that expresses desire; the vocative indicates address or invocation.

2. Donne's interesting description of these sins appears again in a sermon of 1627 (on Isaiah 65:20), *Sermons*, 7:361. See John Cosin, *A Collection of Private Devotions*, also of 1627, where the conceit is elaborated in a "Form of Confession" (ed. P. G. Stanwood, Oxford, 1967, p. 238).

a. 1. Sam. 25:27. 2. Kings 5:15.

our own conscience; which is, when a sinful thought or purpose is born in our hearts, first we rock it, by tossing, and tumbling it in our fancies, and imaginations, and by entertaining it with delight and consent, and with remembring, with how much pleasure we did the like sin before, and how much we should have, if we could bring this to pass; And as we rock it, so we swathe it, we cover it, with some pretences, some excuses, some hopes of coveraling it; and this is that, which we call *Morosam delectationem*, a delight to stand in the air and prospect of a sin, and a loathness to let it go out of our sight. Of this sin S. *Gregory* sayes nothing in this place, but onely of actual sins, which he calls *speaking*; and of habitual, which he calls *crying sins*. And this is as far, as the Schools, or the Casuists[3] do ordinarily trace sin; To find out *peccata Infantia*, speechless sins, in the heart; *peccata vocatia*, speaking sins, in our actions; And *peccata clamantia*, crying and importunate sins, which will not suffer God to take his rest, no nor to fulfil his own Oath, and protestation: He hath said, *As I live, I would not the death of a sinner*; and they extort a death from him. But besides these, Here is a farther degree, beyond speaking sins, and crying sins; beyond actual sins and habitual sins; here are *peccata cum ratione*, and *cum disputatione*; we will reason, we will debate, we will dispute it out with God, and we will conclude against all his Arguments, that there is a *Quia*, a Reason, why we should proceed and go forward in our sin.

. . . .

We hear Witnesses, and we suborn Witnesses against God; and we do more; we proceed by Recriminations, and a cross Bill, with a *Quia Deus*, because God does as he does, we may do as we do; Because God does not punish Sinners, we need not forbear sins. Whilst we sin strongly, by oppressing others, that are weaker, or craftily by circumventing others that are simple, This is but *Leoninum*, and *Vulpinum*, that tincture of the Lyon, and of the Fox, that brutal nature that is in us. But when we come to sin, upon reason, and upon discourse, upon Meditation, and upon plot, This is *Humanum*, to become the Man of Sin, to surrender that, which is the Form, and Essence of man, Reason, and understanding, to the service of sin. When we come to sin wisely and learnedly, to sin logically, by a *Quia*, and an *Ergo*, that, Because God does thus, we may do as we do, we shall come to sin through all the Arts, and all our knowledge, To sin Grammatically, to tie sins together in construction, in a Syntaxis, in a chaine, and dependance, and coherence upon one another: And to sin Historically,

3. Generally referring to those who deliberate over cases of moral conscience.

to sin over sins of other men again, to sin by precedent, and to practice that which we had read: And we come to sin Rhetorically, perswasively, powerfully; and as we have found examples of our sins in History, so we become examples to others, by our sins, to lead and encourage them, in theirs; when we come to employ upon sin, that which is the essence of man, Reason, and discourse, we will also employ upon it, those which are the properties of man onely, which are, To speak, and to laugh; we will come to speak, and talk, and to boast of our sins, and at last, to laugh and jest at our sins; and as we have made sin a Recreation, so we will make a jest of our condemnation. (*1617*) 1:224–26

3. The Letters and Grammar of Understanding (Ps. 32:8)

It is my soule that sayes to mine eye, *faciam te videre*, I will make thee see, and my soule that sayes to mine eare, *faciam te audire*, I will make thee heare, and without that soule, that eye and eare could no more see nor heare, then the eyes and eares of an Idol; so it is my God that sayes to my soule, *faciam te intelligere*, I will make thee understand. And therefore as thou art bound to infinite thankesgivings to God, when he hath brought thee to faith, to forget not thy tribute by the way, to blesse and magnifie him, if he have enlarged thy desire of understanding, and thy capacity of understanding, and thy meanes of understanding; for, as howsoever a man may forget the order of the letters, after he is come to reade perfectly, and forget the rules of his Grammar, after he is come to speake perfectly, yet by those letters, and by that Grammar he came to that perfection; so, though faith be of an infinite exaltation above understanding, yet, as though our understanding be above our senses, yet by our senses we come to understand, so by our understanding we come to beleeve. 9:357

4. Grammar—School; Logic—University (James 2:12)

The Law was a Schoolmaster. The Jews were as School-boys, always spelling, and putting together Types and Figures; which things typified and figured, how this Lamb should signifie *Christ*, how this fire should signifie a *holy Ghost*. The Christian is come from school to the University, from Grammar to Logick, to him that is *Logos* it self, the Word; to apprehend and apply Christ himself; and so is at more liberty then when he had onely a dark law, without any comment, with the natural man; or onely a dark comment, that is, the Law, with a dimme light, and ill eys, as the Jews had: for though the Jew had the liberty of a Law, yet they had not the law of Liberty. (*1629*) 8:351

B. Salvation: Verb, Tense, Mood, Voice

1. God's Judgments: Conditional (Matt. 18:7)

In this, beloved, consists our comfort, that all Gods *vae's* and *Amens*, all judgments, and all his executions are *Conditionall*; There is a *Crede et vives*, Beleeve and thou shalt live; there is a *Fac hoc et vives*, doe this and thou shalt live; If thou have done otherwise, there is a *Converte et vives*, turne unto the Lord and thou shalt live; If thou have done so, and fallen off, there is a *Revertere et vives*, returne againe unto the Lord, and thou shalt live. How heavy so ever any of Gods judgements be, yet there is always roome for *Davids* question, [b]*Quis scit*, who can tell whether God will be gracious unto mee? What better assurance could one have, then *David* had? The Prophet *Nathan* had told *David* immediately from the mouth of God, *this child shall surely dye*, and ratified it by that reason, *because thou hast given occasion to the enemies of the Lord to blaspheme*, this child shall surely dye, yet *David* fasted, and wept, and said, *who can tell whether the Lord will be gratious unto me, that the child may live?* There is always roome for *Davids* question, *Quis scit, who can tell?* Nay there is no roome for it, as it is a question of diffidence and distrust; every man may and must know, that whatsoever any Prophet have denounced against any sinne of his, yet there are conditions, upon which the Lord will be gracious and thy soule shall live. (*1620?*) 3:165

2. God's Active Part in Man's Passive Understanding (Ps. 32:8)

Though then some later Expositors have doubted of the person, who doth this Office, *To Instruct*, who this *I* in our Text is, because the Hebrew word *Le David*, is as well *Davidis*, as *Davidi*, An Instruction from *David*, as an Instruction to *David*, and so the Catechist may seeme to be *David*, and no more; yet since this Criticisme upon the word, *Le David*, argues but a possibility that it may, and not a necessity that it must be so, wee accompany S. *Hierome*, and indeed the whole body of the Fathers, in accepting this Instruction from God himselfe, it is no other then God himselfe that sayes, *I will instruct thee, etc.* No other then God himselfe can undertake so much as is promised in this text. For here is first, a rectifying of the understanding, *I will instruct thee*, and in the Originall there is somewhat more then our Translation reaches to; It is there, *Intelligere faciam te, I will make thee understand*. Man can instruct, God onely can make us understand. And then it is *Faciam te*, I will make Thee, Thee understand;

b. 2. Sam. 12:22.

The worke is the Lords, The understanding is the mans: for God does not worke in man, as the Devill did in Idols, and *In Pythonissis*, and *In Ventriloquis*, in possest persons, who had no voluntary concurrence with the action of the Devill, but were meerely Passive; God works so in man, as that he makes man worke too, *Faciam Te*, I will make Thee understand; That that shall be done shall be done by mee, but in Thee; the Power that rectifies the act is Gods, the Act is mans. (*winter 1624–1625?*) 9:351–52

3. Clamor Hortatorius *(1 Thess. 4:17)*

The dead heare not Thunder, nor feele they an Earth-quake. If the Canon batter that Church walls, in which they lye buryed, it wakes not them, nor does it shake or affect them, if that dust, which they are, be thrown out, but yet there is a voyce, which the dead shall heare; [c] *The dead shall heare the voyce of the Son of God*, (sayes the Son of God himself) *and they that heare shall live*; And that is the voyce of our Text. It is here called a clamour, a vociferation, a shout, and varied by our Translators, and Expositors, according to the origination of the word, to be *clamor hortatorius*, and *suasorius*, and *jussorius*, A voyce that carries with it a penetration, (all shall heare it) and a perswasion, (all shall beleeve it, and be glad of it) and a power, a command, (all shall obey it.) Since that voyce at the Creation, *Fiat*, Let there be a world, was never heard such a voyce as this, *Surgite mortui*, Arise ye dead. That was spoken to that that was meerely nothing, and this to them, who in themselves shall have no cooperation, no concurrence to the hearing or answering this voyce. (*1622*) 4:69

4. Dicta *vs.* Facta Ecclesiae *(Job 19:26)*

It is the Christian Church, that hath delivered to us the article of the resurrection. Nature says it not, Philosophy says it not; it is the language and the Idiotisme of the Church of God, that the resurrection is to be beleeved as an article of faith. For, though articles of faith be not *facta Ecclesiae*, they are *dicta Ecclesiae*, though the Church doe not *make* articles, yet she *declares* them. In the Creation, the way was, *Dixit et facta sunt*, God spake, and so things were made; In the Gospell, the way is, *Fecit, et dicta sunt*, God makes articles of faith, and the Church utters them, presents them. (*1620?*) 3:94–95

5. Commandments, Lord's Prayer, Creed: Declaratory (Mark 16:16)

So that when all is done, the Ten Commandements, which is the sum of all that we are to doe; The Lords Prayer, which is the summe of

c. John 5:25.

all that we are to ask; and the Apostles Creed, which is the summe of all that wee are to beleeve, are but declaratory, not introductory things; The same things are first written in mans heart, though dimly and sub-obscurely, and then the same things are extended, shed in a brighter beame, in every leafe of the Scripture; And the same things are recollected againe, into the Ten Commandements, into the Lords Prayer, and into the Apostles Creed, that we might see them al together, and so take better view and hold of them. (*1622?*) 5:247–48

6. The Grammar of Forgiveness: Future Tense (Matt. 12:31)

There is then forgivenesse for *sin*, for *all sin*, even for blasphemy, for *blasphemy against the Son*, but it is *In futuro remittetur, It shall be forgiven*. It is not *Remittebatur*, It was forgiven; Let no man antidate his pardon, and say, His sins were forgiven in an Eternall Decree, and that no man that hath his name in the book of life, hath the addition, sinner; that if he were there from the beginning, from the beginning he was no sinner. It is not, in such a sense, *Remittebatur*, It was forgiven; nor it is not *Remittitur*, that even then, when the sin is committed, it is forgiven, whether the sinner think of it or no, That God sees not the sins of his Children, That God was no more affected with *Davids* adultery, or his murder, then an indulgent Father is to see his child do some witty waggish thing, or some sportfull shrewd turne. It is but *Remittetur*, Any sin *shall be*, that is, may be *forgiven*, if the meanes required by God, and ordained by him, be entertained. If I take into my contemplation, the Majesty of God, and the uglinesse of sin, If I devest my selfe of all that was sinfully got, and invest my self in the righteousnesse of Christ Jesus, (for else I am ill suted, and if I clothe my self in Mammon, the righteousnesse of Christ is no Cloke for that doublet) If I come to Gods Church for my absolution, and the seale of that reconciliation, the blessed Sacrament, *Remittetur*, by those meanes ordained by God any sin shall be forgiven me. But if I relie upon the *Remittebatur*, That I had my *Quietus est* before hand, in the eternall Decree, or in the *Remittuntur*, and so shut mine eyes, in an opinion that God hath shut his, and sees not the sins of his children, I change Gods Grammar, and I induce a dangerous solecisme, for, it is not They were forgiven before they were committed, nor They are forgiven in the committing, but, They shall be, by using the meanes ordained by God, they may be. (*1623?*) 5:84–85

C. Great Things of Small: Prepositions, Adverbs, Pronouns

1. "Nothing is to be neglected as little" (Gen. 1:26)

I know it is a good rule, that *Damascen* gives, *Parva, parva non sunt, ex quibus magna proveniunt:* Nothing is to be neglected as little, from which great things may arise. If the consequence may be great, the thing must not be thought little. No *Jod* in the Scripture shall perish; therefore no *Jod* is superfluous.[4] If it were superfluous, it might perish. Words, and lesse particles then words have busied the whole Church. In the Councell of *Ephesus*,[5] where Bishops in a great number excommunicated Bishops in a greater, Bishop, against Bishop, and Patriarch, against Patriarch; in which case, when both parties had made strong parties in Court, and the Emperor forbare to declare himselfe, on either side for a time, he was told, that he refused to assent to that, which six thousand Bishops had agreed in: the strife was but for a word, whether the Blessed Virgin might be called *Deipara*, the mother of God, for *Christipara*, the mother of Christ, (which Christ all agree to be God) *Nestorius*, and all his party agreed with *Cyrill*, that she might be. In the Councell of *Chalcedon*, the difference was not so great, as for a word composed of syllables. It was but for a syllable, whether *Ex*, or *In*. The Heretiques condemned then, confessed Christ, to be *Ex duabus naturis*, to be composed of two natures, at first; but not to be *in duabus naturis*, not to consist of two natures after: and for that *In*, they were thrust out. In the councell of *Nice*, it was not so much as a syllable made of letters. For it was but for one letter; whether *Homoousion*, or *Homoiousion*,[6] was the issue. Where the question hath not been of divers words, nor syllables, nor letters, but onely of the place of words; what tempestuous differences have risen? How much *Sola fides* and *fides sola*, changes the case? Nay, where there hath been no quarrell for precedency, for transposing of words, or syllables, or letters; where there hath not been, so much as a letter in question; how much doth an accent vary a sense? An interrogation, or no interrogation will make it directly contrary. All Chris-

4. See Matt. 5:18: "Till heaven and earth pass, one jot [ἰῶτα, "i," the smallest letter] or one tittle [the dot over the *i*] shall in no wise pass from the law, till all be fulfilled."

5. The Third General Council of the Church was summoned in 431 to settle the Nestorian controversy, the teaching that there are two separate persons in Christ, the one divine, the other human, a notion in conflict with the Creed of Nicea (325). Cyril of Alexandria was the chief opponent of Nestorius, whose doctrine the council condemned.

6. *Homoousion* describes the equality or same essence of the three persons of the Trinity; *homoiousion* is opposed to this principle, and it describes "the greatest *Heresie* that ever was," i.e., Arianism. See the following selection.

tian expositors read those words of *Cain*, [d] *My sin is greater then can be pardoned*, positively; and so they are evident words of desperation. The Jews read them with an interrogation, *Are my sinnes greater, then can be pardoned?* And so they are words of compunction, and repentance. The prophet *Micah* says, that [e] *Bethlehem* is a small place; the Evangelist Saint *Matthew* says [f] no small place. An interrogation in *Micahs* mouth reconciles it; Art thou a small place? amounts to that, thou art not. Sounds, voices, words must not be neglected. For, Christs forerunner *John Baptist* qualified himselfe no otherwise: He was but a voice. And Christ himselfe is *Verbum*; the Word, is the name, even of the Sonne of God. (*1629*) 9:70–72

2. Prepositions and Heresies (Ps. 11:3)

There have been *Verball Heresies*, and *Heresies* that were but *Syllabicall*; little *Praepositions* made *Heresies*; not onely *State-praepositions*, Precedencies, and Prerogatives of *Church* above *Church*, occasioned great *Schismes*, but *Literall Praepositions*, *Praepositions* in *Grammar*, occasioned great *Heresies*. That great *Heresie* of the *Acephali*,[7] against which *Damascene* bendes himselfe in his Booke, *De Natura Composita*, was grounded in the *Praeposition, In;* They would confesse *Ex*, but not *In*, That *Christ* was made *of* two Natures, but that hee did not consist *in* two Natures. And wee all know, what differences have beene raysed in the *Church*, in that one poynt of the *Sacrament*, by these three Prepositions, *Trans*, *Con*, and *Sub*.[8] There have beene great *Heresies*, but *Verball*, but *Syllabicall*; and as great, but *Litterall*; The greatest *Heresie* that ever was, that of the *Arrians*, was but in one Letter.[9] So then, in *Heresie*, there is nothing to bee called little, nothing to bee suffered. (*1625*) 6:247

3. In Via, *not* Citra *or* Contra *(Ps. 32:8)*

A Christian hath no Solstice, no highest point, where he may stand still, and goe no farther; much lesse hath hee any Aequator, where

7. The Achephali were a Monophysite sect, that is, those who held that there is but a single divine nature in the person of Christ, rather than a double nature, both divine and human. Donne alludes to their contention over certain crucial terms against which St. John of Damascus (c.675-c.749) argued in his most important work, properly known as Πηγὴ γνώσεως.

8. *Trans*substantiation, *con*substantiation, and *sub*stance, terms in eucharistic theology used to define the nature of the consecrated elements.

9. That is, *homoiousion* rather than *homoousion*, the letter being the "jot" or iota, referred to in note 4 above. Donne plays on *Litterall* and *Letter* (from Latin *littera*). To take a word in its primary sense is to study its letter(s).

d. Gen. 4:13.
e. 5:2.
f. 2:6.

dayes and nights are equall, that is, a liberty to spend as much time ill, as well, as many houres in sinfull pleasures, as in religious exercises. [g]*Quicquid citra Deum est, via est, nec immorandum in ea*; Hee doth not say, *praeter Deum*, much lesse *contra Deum*; For whatsoever is against God, nay, whatsoever is besides God, is altogether out of the way; But *citra Deum*, on this side of God: Till we come to God in heaven, all our best is but our way to him. All the zeale of gathering knowledge, all the growth of faith, all the practise of sanctification, is but *via*, the way; and *non immorandum in ea*; since wee have here a promise of Gods assistance in it, in the way, we are sure there is an obligation upon it, as upon a duty, in this way, humbly, and patiently, and laboriously to walke towards him, without stopping upon any thing in this world. (*winter 1624–1625?*) 9:365

4. Nunc *and* Tunc *(1 Cor. 13:12)*

These two termes in our Text, *Nunc* and *Tunc*, *Now* and *Then*, *Now in a glasse, Then face to face*, Now in part, Then in perfection, these two secular termes, of which, one designes the whole Age of this world from the Creation, to the dissolution thereof (for, all that is comprehended in this word, *Now*) And the other designes the everlastingnesse of the next world, (for that incomprehensiblenesse is comprehended in the other word, *Then*) These two words, that design two such Ages, are now met in one Day; in this Day, in which we celebrate all Resurrections in the roote, in the Resurrection of our Lord and Saviour Christ Jesus, blessed for ever. For the first Term, *Now* (*Now in a glasse, now in part*) is intended most especially of that very act, which we do now at this present, that is, of the Ministery of the Gospell, of declaring God in his Ordinance, of Preaching his word; (*Now*, in this Ministery of his Gospell, *we see in a glasse, we know in part*) And then the *Then*, the time of *seeing face to face*, and *knowing as we are knowne*, is intended of that time, which we celebrate this day, the day of Resurrection, the day of Judgement, the day of the actuall possession of the next life. So that this day, this whole Scripture is fulfilled in your eares; for now, (now in this Preaching) you have some sight, and then, (Then when that day comes, which (in the first roote thereof) we celebrate this day) you shall have a perfect sight of all; *Now we see through a glasse, etc.*

That therefore you may the better know him, when you come *to see him face to face, then*, by having *seen him in a glasse now*, and that your seeing him now in his Ordinance, may prepare you to see him

g. August[ine].

then in his Essence, proceed we thus in the handling of these words. First, That there is nothing brought into comparison, into consideration, nothing put into the balance, but the sight of God, the knowledge of God; It is not called a better sight, nor a better knowledge, but there is no other sight, no other knowledge proposed, or mentioned, or intimated, or imagined but this; All other sight is blindnesse, all other knowledge is ignorance; And then we shall see how there is a twofold sight of God, and a twofold knowledge of God proposed to us here; A sight, and a knowledge here in this life, and another manner of sight, and another manner of knowledge in the life to come: For, here we see God *In speculo, in a glasse*, that is, by reflexion, And here we know God *In aenigmate*, sayes our Text, *Darkly*, (so we translate it) that is, by obscure representations, and therefore it is called a *Knowledge but in part*; But in heaven, our sight is *face to face*, And our knowledge is *to know, as we are knowne*.

For our sight of God here, our Theatre, the place where we sit and see him, is the whole world, the whole house and frame of nature, and our *medium*, our *glasse*, is the Booke of Creatures, and our light, by which we see him, is the light of Naturall Reason. And then, for our knowledge of God here, our Place, our Academy, our University is the Church, our *medium*, is the Ordinance of God in his Church, Preaching, and Sacraments; and our light is the light of faith. Thus we shall finde it to be, for our sight, and for our knowledge of God here. But for our sight of God in heaven, our place, our Spheare is heaven it selfe, our *medium* is the Patefaction, the Manifestation, the Revelation of God himselfe, and our light is the light of Glory. And then, for our knowledge of God there, God himself is All; God himself is the place, we see Him, in Him; God is our *medium*, we see Him, by him; God is our light; not a light which is His, but a light which is He; not a light which flowes from him, no, nor a light which is in him, but that light which is He himself. (*1628*) 8:219–20

5. *God's* Quando *and* Ubi *(John 10:22)*

As it diminishes not, prejudices not *Gods Eternitie*, that wee give him his *Quando*, certaine times of Invocation, *God* is not the lesse *yesterday, and to day, and the same for ever*, because wee meet here to day, and not yesterday, so it diminishes not, prejudices not *Gods Ubiquitie* and *Omnipresence*, that wee give him his *Ubi*, certaine places for Invocation. Thats not the lesse true, that [h] *the most High dwells not in Temples made with handes*, though *God* accept at our hands our dedi-

h. Acts 7:48.

cation of certaine places to his service, and manifest his working more effectually, more energetically in those places, then in any other. For when we pray, *Our Father which art in Heaven,* It is not (sayes *Saint Chrysostome*) that wee deny him to bee heere, where wee kneele when we say that Prayer, but it is that we acknowledge him to be there, where he can graunt, and accomplish our prayer. It is as *Origen* hath very well expressed it, *Ut in melioribus mundi requiramus Deum*: That still wee looke for *God* in the best places; looke for him, as he heares our petitions, here, in the best places of this world, in his House, in the Church; looke for him as he graunts our petition, in the best place of the next world, at the right hand, and in the bosome of the *Father*. When *Moses* sayes that [i] *the word of* God *is not beyond Sea,* he addes, *It is not so beyond Sea, as that thou must not have it without sending thither*. When he sayes there, *it is not in heaven,* he adds, *not so in heaven, as that one must goe up, before hee can have it*. The word of *God,* is beyond Sea, the true word, truly preached in many true *Churches* there, but yet we have it here, within these Seas too; *God* is in Heaven, but yet hee is here, within these walles too. (*1623*) 4:369

6. How and Why: Dangerous Monosyllables (Gen. 17:24)

It is a Dangerous and Infectious *Monosillable, How* or *Why*: If I will aske a *reason,* why God commands such a thing; first, *Periculosum est,* It is Dangerous; for, I have nothing to answer me, but mine owne *reason,* and that affords not Lead enough, nor Line enough, to sound the depth of Gods proceedings, nor length enough, nor strength enough to reach so farre, and therefore I may mistake the reason, and goe upon false grounds. So *Periculosum est,* It is a Dangerous question, and a lost question, because I can have no certaine answer; and it is an *infectious* question too, for here is one coale of the Devils fire, of his pride, kindled in me; as the Devil said, *Similis ero Altissimo, I will be like the Highest,* and see whether I may not stand by my selfe, without any Influence from God, without any Dependance upon God: so, in our case, I will be so farre equall to God, as that I will measure his actions by my reason, and not doe his Commandements till I know *why* he commanded them: And then, when the infection is got into a House, who can say, it shall end here in this Person, and kill no more; or it shall end this weeke, and last no longer? So if that *infectious inquisition,* that *Quare,* (*Why* should God command this or this particular?) be entred into me, all my *Humilitie* is presently infected, and I shall looke for a reason, why God made a world, or why he made a

i. Deut. 30:13.

world no sooner than 6000. yeares agoe,[10] and why he saves *some*, and why *but* some,[11] and I shall examine God upon all the *Interrogatories* that I can frame, upon the *Creed* (why I should believe a Sonne of a Virgin without a Man, or believe the Sonne of God to descend into Hell) Or frame upon the *Pater Noster*, (why I should worship such a God, that must be prayed to, *not to leade me into tentation*) Or frame upon the *Ten Commandements*, why after all is done and heapt, for any sinfull action, yet I should be guilty of all, for coveting in my heart another mans horse or house. And therfore *Luther* pursues it farther, with words of more vehemence, *Odiosa et exitialis vocula, Quare*, It is an Execrable and Damnable Monosillable, *Why*; it exasperates God, it ruines us: For, when we come to aske a reason of his actions, either we doubt of the *goodnesse* of God, that he is not so carefull of us, as we would be; or of his *power*, that he cannot provide for us, so well as we could doe; or of his *wisdome*, that he hath not grounded his Commandements so well as we could have advised him: whereas Saint *Augustine* saies justly, *Qui rationem quaerit voluntatis Dei, aliquid majus Deo quaerit*, He that seekes a reason of the will of God, seekes for something greater then God. It was the Devill that opened our eies in Paradise, it is our parts to shut them so farre, as not to gaze upon Gods secret purposes. [j]God guided his Children as well by a *Pillar of Cloud*, as by a *Pillar of Fire*, and both, Cloud and Fire, were equally Pillars: There is as much strength in, and as safe relying upon some ignorances, as some knowledges; for God provided for his people, as well in *this*, that he *hid Moses body* from them, as that he revealed other Mysteries to them, by him. All is well summed and collected by Saint *Augustine, Dominus cur jusserit, viderit; faciendum est a serviente, quod jusserit*: *Why* God commands any thing, God himselfe knowes; our part is, not to enquire *why*, but to doe *what* he commands. (*1625*) 6:188–89

7. *"For": Particle of Argumentation (Ps. 38:2)*

First then, this particle of *connexion* and *argumentation, For*, which begins our text, occasions us, in a first part, to consider, that such an impatience in affliction, as brings us toward a *murmuring* at Gods proceedings, and almost to a calling of God to an account, in inordi-

10. Donne follows one popular tradition of biblical chronology (of the Septuagint version) that puts six thousand years between the creation of Adam and the birth of Christ.

11. Donne refers to the Calvinist doctrine of limited atonement, or absolute predestination, whereby some are saved and some are damned even before the Fall.

j. [Exod. 13:21.]

nate expostulations, is a leaven so kneaded into the nature of man, so innate a tartar, so inherent a sting, so inseparable a venim in man, as that the holyest of men have scarce avoided it in all degrees thereof. (*1618*) 2:51–52

8. Deus Noster: *God of the Church (Ps. 144:15)*

And this appropriates him so neare to us, as that hee is thereby *Deus noster*. For, it is not enough to finde *Deum*, a God; a great and incomprehensible power, that sits *in luce*, in light, but *in luce inaccessibili*, in light that we cannot comprehend. A God that enjoyes his owne eternity, his owne peace, his owne blessedness, but respects not us, reflects not upon us, communicates nothing to us. But it is a God, that is *Deus noster*; Ours, as we are his creatures; ours, as we are like him, made to his image; ours, as he is like us, in assuming our nature; ours, as he hath descended to us in his Incarnation; and ours, as we are ascended with him in his glorification: So that wee doe not consider God, as our God, except we come to the consideration of God in Christ, God and man. It is not enough to find *Deum*, a God in generall, nor to find *Deum meum*, a God so particularly my God, as that he is a God of my making: That I should seeke God by any other motions, or know God by any other notions, or worship God in any other fashions, then the true Church of God doth, for there he is *Deus noster*, as hee is received in the unanime consent of the Catholique Church. (*1620*) 3:87

9. David's Possessive: Appropriation of Repentance (Ps. 6:6, 7)

Howsoever therefore you exclude dangerous names, doe not upon colour of that, exclude necessary things: Howsoever you have delivered your selves to the mercy of God, and he hath delivered a seale of his mercy to you, inwardly in his Spirit, outwardly in his Sacrament, yet there are *Amarae sagittae ex dulci manu Dei*, (as *Nazianzen* calls afflictions after repentance) Sharp arrowes out of the sweet hand of God; Corrections, by which God intends to establish us in that spirituall health, to which our repentance, by his grace, hath brought us: Remember still, that this which *David* did for the present, and that which he promised he would doe for the future, both together made up the reason of his prayer to God, by which he desired God in the former verses, to *returne* to him, to *deliver* his soule, and to *save* him; He had had no reason, no ground of his prayer, though he had done something already, if he had not proposed to himselfe something more to be done: There is a preparation before, and there is a preservation after required at our hands, if wee studie a perfect recovery, and cure of our soules. And as S. *Gregory* notes well, there is a great deale of force in *Davids* Possessive, in his word of appropriation, *Meus, lectus meus*, and *Oculus meus*, It is his bed that he washed, and they are his eyes that washed it: He bore the affliction himselfe, and trusted not to that which others had suffered by way of Supererogation. Sometimes, when the children of great persons offend at Schoole, another person is whipped for them, and that affects them, and works upon a good nature; but if that person should take Physick for them in a sicknesse, it would doe them no good: Gods corrections upon others, may worke by way of example upon thee; but because thou art sick for physicke, take it thy selfe. Trust not to the treasure of the Church; neither the imaginary treasure of the Church of Rome, which pretends an inexhaustible mine of the works of other men, to distribute and bestow; No, nor to the true treasure of the true Church, that is, Absolution, upon Confession, and Repentance; No, trust not to the merits of Christ himselfe, in their application to thee, without a *Lectus tuus*, and an *Oculus tuus*, except thou remember thy sins in thy bed, and poure out thy teares from thine eyes, and fulfill the sufferings of Christ in thy selfe. (*1628*) 8:216–17

10. Possessives of Work and Faith (Matt. 5:16)

I cannot alwaies call the works that I do, my works; for sometimes God works them, and sometimes the devill: Sometimes God works his owne worke, [k]*The Lord will do his worke, his strange worke, and bring to passe his act, his strange act*. Sometimes he works my works, [l]*Thou Lord hast wrought all our workes in us*. In us, and in all things else, [m]*Operatur omnia in omnibus*, he worketh all in all. And all this in all these, [n]*Secundum consilium voluntatis suae*, After the counsaile of his owne will; for, [o]*I will worke, and who shall let it?* But for all this his generall working, his enemy works in us too. [p]*That which I doe, I allow not*, saies the Apostle; nay, *I know it not*; for, saies he, [q]*what I hate, that I doe. And, if I doe that I would not doe, it is no more I that doe it, but sin that dwelleth in me*. Yet, for all this diverse, this contrary working, as S. *Augustine* sayes of the faculty of the will, *Nihil tam nostrum, quam voluntas*, there is nothing so much our owne, as our will before we worke, so there is nothing so much our owne, as our workes, after they are done. They stick to us, they cleave to us; whether as fomentations to nourish us, or as corrasives, to gnaw upon us, that lyes in the

k. Esay 28:21.
l. Esay 26:12.
m. 1. Cor. 12:6.
n. Ephes. 1:11.
o. Esay 43:11.
p. Rom. 7:15.
q. ver. 20.

nature of the worke; but ours they are; and upon us our works work. Our good works are more ours, then our faith is ours. Our faith is ours as we have received it, our worke is ours, as we have done it. Faith is ours, as we are possessors of it, the work ours, as we are doers, actors in it. Faith is ours, as our goods are ours, works, as our children are ours. And therefore when the Prophet *Habakkuk* saies, [r]*Fide sua, The just shall live by his faith*, that particle *His*, is a word of possession, not a word of Acquisition; That God hath infused that faith into him, and so it is his, not that he hath produced that faith in himselfe. His faith must save him; his own, and not anothers, not his parents faith, though he be the son of holy parents, not the Churches faith, (if he be of yeares) though he be within the covenant, but his own personall faith; yet not his so, as that it grew in him, or was produced in him, by him, by any plantation, or semination of his own. And therefore S. *Paul* [s] in citing that place of *Habakkuk* (as he doth cite it three severall times) in all those places leaves out that particle of propriety, and acquisition, *his*, and still sayes, *The just shall live by faith*, and he sayes no more. (*1622 or 1623?*) 10:87–88

D. Singular and Plural in God and His Church

1. Creator Not Singular (Deut. 25:5)

From the beginning God intimated a detestation, a dislike of *singularity*; of beeing *Alone*. The first time that God himselfe is named in the Bible, in the first verse of *Genesis*, hee is named *Plurally, Creavit Dii, Gods*, Gods in the plurall, Created Heaven and Earth. God, which is but *one*, would not appeare, nor bee presented *so alone*, but that hee would also manifest more persons. As the *Creator* was not *Singular*, so neither were the *creatures*; First, he created *heaven and earth*; both together; which were to be the generall parents, and out of which were to bee produced all other creatures; and then, he made all those other creatures plurally too; *Male, and Female created hee them*; And when he came to make *him*, for whose sake (next to his glory) he made the whole world, *Adam*, he left not *Adam alone*, but joyned an *Eve* to him; Now, when they were *maried*, we know, but wee know not when they were *divorced*; we heare when *Eve* was made, but not when shee *dyed*; The husbands death is recorded at last, the wives is not at all. So much detestation hath God himselfe, and so little memory would hee have kept of any singularity, of being alone. The union of Christ to the whole Church is not expressed by any

r. Heb. 2:4. *s.* Rom. 1:17. Gal. 3:11. Heb. 10:38.

metaphore, by any figure, so oft in the Scripture, as by this of *Mariage*: and there in that union with Christ to the whole Church, neither husband, nor wife can ever die; Christ is immortall as hee is *himselfe*, and immortall, as hee is the *head* of the Church, the *Husband* of that wife: for that wife, the Church is immortall too; for as a Prince is the same Prince, when he fights a battaile, and when hee triumphs after the victory: so the militant, and the triumphant Church is the same Church. (*1624*) 6:81–82

2. Plural God: Trinity (Gen. 1:26)

First then we looke towards our East, the fountaine of light, and of life. There this world beganne; the Creation was in the east. And there our next world beganne too. There the gates of heaven opened to us; and opened to us in the gates of death; for, our heaven is the death of our Saviour, and there he lived, and dyed there, and there he looked into our west, from the east, from his Terasse, from his Pinacle, from his exaltation (as himselfe calls it) the Crosse. The light which arises to us, in this east, the knowledge which we receive in this first word of our text, *Faciamus, Let us*, (where God speaking of himselfe, speakes in the Plurall) is the manifestation of the Trinity; the Trinity, which is the first letter in his Alphabet, that ever thinks to read his name in the book of life; The first note in his Gammut, that ever thinks to sing his part, in the Quire of the Triumphant Church. Let him have done as much, as all the Worthies; and suffered as much as all Natures Martyrs, the penurious Philosophers; let him have known as much, as they that pretend to know *Omne scibile*, all that can be known; nay, and *In-intelligibilia, In-investigabilia*, (as *Tertullian* speakes) ununderstandable things, unrevealed decrees of God; let him have writ as much, as *Aristotle* writ, or as is written upon *Aristotle*, which is multiplication enough: yet he hath not learnt to spel, that hath not learnt the Trinity; not learnt to pronounce the first word, that cannot bring three Persons into one God. (*1629*) 9:50–51

3. Elohim: *Plural Word (Apoc. 7:9)*

Religion is not a *melancholy*; the spirit of God is not a *dampe*; the Church is not a *grave*: it is a *fold*, it is an *Arke*, it is a *net*, it is a *city*, it is a *kingdome*, not onely a house, but a house that hath *many mansions* in it: still it is a *plurall* thing, consisting of *many*: and very good *grammarians* amongst the *Hebrews*, have thought, and said, that that *name*, by which God notifies himself to the world, in the very beginning of *Genesis*, which is *Elohim*, as it is a *plurall word* there, so it hath no *singular*:[12] they say we cannot name God, but *plurally*: so sociable, so communicable, so extensive, so derivative of himself, is God, and so manifold are the beames, and the emanations that flow out from him.

. . . .

There is but one God; but yet was that one God ever *alone*? There were more *generations* (infinitely infinite) before the world was made, then there have been *minutes*, since it was made: all that while, there were no *creatures*; but yet was God alone, any one minute of al this? was there not alwais a *Father* and a *Son*, and a *holy Ghost*? And had not they, always an acquiescence in one another, an exercise of *Affection*, (as we may so say) a love, a delight, and a complacency towards one another? So, as that the Father could not be without the *Son* and the *holy Ghost*, so as neither *Sonne*, nor *holy Ghost* could be without the *Father*, nor without one another; God was from all eternity collected into *one God*, yet from all eternity he derived himselfe into *three persons*: God could not be so alone, but that there have been three persons, as long as there hath been one God. (*1624*) 6:152–53

4. Faciamus *in Creation: Father, Son, and Holy Ghost (Cant. 3:11)*

In the Creation of man, in that one word, *Faciamus, let Us make man*, God gave such an intimation of the *Trinity*, as that we may well enlarge, and spread, and paraphrase that one word, so farre, as to heare therein, a councell of all the *three Persons*, agreeing in this gracious designe upon Man, *faciamus*, let us make him; *make* him, and *mend* him, and make him *sure*: I, the Father, will make him by my power; if he should fall, Thou the Sonne shalt repayr him, re-edify him, *redeem* him; if he should distrust, that this Redemption belonged not to him, Thou, the *Holy Ghost*, shalt apply to his particular soule, and conscience, this *mercy* of mine, and this *merit* of the Sonnes; and so let *us make him*. (*1625*) 6:280

5. Plural God: Distinctive (Gen. 1:26)

This Seal then, this impression, this notion of the Trinity being set upon us, in the first Creation, in this first plurall word of our text, *Faciamus, Let us*, (for Father, Sonne, and holy Ghost made man) and this seale being re-imprinted upon us, in our second Creation, our Regeneration, in Baptisme, (Man is Baptized *In the name of the Father, of*

12. See Gen. 1:1, Bara Elohim, "God created," where the word for God (*Elohim*) is a plural form, but *bara*, the verb of which Elohim is the subject, is in the singular. See selection number 5 below. Evelyn Simpson writes an extended note on this famous crux in *Sermons*, 10:329–30.

the Sonne, and of the holy Ghost) This notion of the Trinity being our distinctive Character, from *Jew* and Gentile; This being our specifique forme: why does not this our forme, this soule of our Religion denominate us? why are we not called *Trinitarians*, a name that would embrace the profession of all the Persons, but onely Christians, which limits, and determines us upon one?

. . . .

Here then God notified the Trinity; and here first, for though we accept an intimation of the Trinity, in the first line of the Bible, where *Moses* joynes a plurall name, *Elohim*, with a singular Verbe, *Bara*; and so in construction it is *Creavit Dii*, Gods created heaven, and earth: yet, besides that, that is rather a mysterious collection, then an evident conclusion of a plurality of Persons, though we read that in that first verse, before this in the twenty sixth, yet *Moses* writ that, which is in the beginning of this chapter, more then two thousand years after God spake this,[13] that is in our text: so long was Gods plurall, before *Moses* his plurall; Gods *Faciamus*, before *Moses Bara Elohim*. So that in this text, beginnes our Catechisme. Here we have, and here first the saving knowledge of the Trinity. (*1629*) 9:54, 57

6. *First Person Singular vs. First Person Plural in God (Rom. 8:16)* [That we are the Children of God]

This part hath also two branches; First, That the Testimony concernes our selves, *We are*; And then, That that which we are is this, *We are the Children of God*. And in the first branch, there will be two twiggs, two sub-considerations; *Wee*, A personall appropriation of the grace of God to our selves, *We are*, we are now, a present possession of those Graces. First, consider we the Consolation in the particle of appropriation, *Wee*. In the great Ant-hill of the whole world, I am an Ant; I have my part in the Creation, I am a Creature; But there are ignoble Creatures. God comes nearer; In the great field of clay, of red earth, that man was made of, and mankind, I am a clod; I am a man, I have my part in the Humanity; But Man was worse than annihilated again. When Satan in that serpent was come, as *Hercules* with his club into a potters shop, and had broke all the vessels, destroyed all mankind, And the gracious promise of a Messias to redeeme all mankind, was shed and spread upon all, I had my drop of that dew of Heaven, my sparke of that fire of heaven, in the universall promise, in which I was involved; But this promise was appropriated after, in

13. Donne follows traditional chronology; and Moses reflects in his plural usage God's plural creation.

a particular Covenant, to one people, to the Jewes, to the seed of *Abraham*. But for all that I have my portion there; for all that professe Christ Jesus are by a spirituall engrafting, and transmigration, and transplantation, in and of that stock, and that seed of *Abraham*; and I am one of those. But then, of those who doe professe Christ Jesus, some grovell still in the superstitions they were fallen into, and some are raised, by Gods good grace, out of them; and I am one of those; God hath afforded me my station, in that Church, which is departed from Babylon.

Now, all this while, my soule is in a cheerefull progresse; when I consider what God did for Goshen in Egypt, for a little parke in the midst of a forest; what he did for Jury, in the midst of enemies, as a shire that should stand out against a Kingdome round about it: How many Sancerraes he hath delivered from famins, how many Genevaes from plots, and machinations against her; all this while my soule is in a progresse: But I am at home, when I consider Buls of excommunications, and solicitations of Rebellions, and pistols, and poysons, and the discoveries of those; There is our *Nos, We*, testimonies that we are in the favour, and care of God; We, our Nation, we, our Church; There I am at home; but I am in my Cabinet at home, when I consider, what God hath done for me, and my soule; There is the *Ego*, the particular, the individuall, I. This appropriation is the consolation, *We are*; But who are they? or how are we of them? *Testimonium est clamor ipse*, sayes S. *Chrysostome* to our great advantage, Even this, that we are able *to cry Abba, Father, by the Spirit of Adoption*, is this testimony, *that we are his Children*; if we can truly do that, that testifies for us. (*1622?*) 5:70–71

7. Mercy: Collective and Distributive (John 10:10)

The manner of expressing the mercy of God, in the frame and course of Scriptures, expresses evermore the largenesse of that mercy. Very often, in the Scriptures, you shall finde the person suddenly changed; and when God shall have said in the beginning of a sentence, I will shew mercy unto them, them, as though he spoke of others, presently, in the same sentence, he will say, my loving kindnesse will I not draw from thee; not from thee, not from them, not from any; that so whensoever thou hearest of Gods mercy proposed to them, to others, thou mightest beleeve that mercy to bee meant to thee, and whensoever they, others heare that mercy proposed to thee, they might beleeve it to be meant to them. . . . God is a plurall God, and offers himselfe to all, collectively; God is a singular God, and offers himselfe to every man, distributively. So also is it said there, *Nominibus suo, He cals his sheepe by their names*; It is *names* in the plurall, and *theirs*, in the singular: whatsoever God proposes to any, he intends to all. (*1629?*) 9:140

8. Plural Concepts of the Church (1 Thess. 5:16)

The Key of *David* openeth and no man shutteth; the Spirit of comfort shineth upon us, and would not be blown out. Monasterie, and Ermitage, and Anchorate, and such words of singularitie are not *Synonyma* with those plurall words *Concio, Coetus, Ecclesia, Synagoga et Congregatio*,[14] in which words God delivereth himselfe to us. A Church is a Company, Religion is Religation, a binding of men together in one manner of Worship; and Worship is an exteriour service; and that exteriour service is the *Venite exultemus*, to come and rejoyce in the presence of God. (*1623?*) 10:219

E. Hebrew: The Language in Which God Spake

1. Hebrew: No Present Tense (Ps. 63:7)

That language in which God spake to man, the Hebrew,[15] hath no present tense; They forme not their verbs as our Westerne Languages do, in the present, *I heare*, or *I see*, or *I reade*, But they begin at that which is past, *I have seene* and *heard*, and *read*. God carries us in his Language, in his speaking, upon that which is past, upon that which he hath done already; I cannot have better security for present, nor future, then Gods former mercies exhibited to me. *Quis non gaudeat*, sayes S. *Augustine*, Who does not triumph with joy, when hee considers what God hath done? *Quis non et ea, quae nondum venerunt, ventura sperat, propter illa, quae jam tanta impleta sunt?* Who can doubt of the performance of all, that sees the greatest part of a Prophesie performed? (*1625*) 7:62

2. God Speaks in Future, Not Present Tense (Ps. 64:10)

In the Hebrew there is no Present tense; In that language wherein God spake, it could not be said, *The upright in heart, Are praised*; Many times they are not. But God speaks in the future; first, that he may still keepe his Children in an expectation and dependance upon him, (you shall be, though you be not yet) And then, to establish them in

14. A monastery, a hermitage, an "anchorate" are places for individual seclusion in contrast with such religious communities as *concio* (assembly), *coetus* (league), *ecclesia* (church), *synagoga* (synagogue), and *congregatio* (congregation).

15. See Evelyn Simpson's discussion of Donne's Hebrew sources and of his knowledge of Hebrew in *Sermons*, 10:306–12, 329–44.

an infallibility, because he hath said it, (I know you are not yet, but comfort your selves, I have said it, and it shall be.) As the Hebrew hath no Superlatives, because God would keepe his Children within compasse, and in moderate desires, to content themselves with his measures, though they be not great, and though they be not heaped; so, considering what pressures, and contempts, and terrors, the upright in heart are subject to, it is a blessed reliefe, That they have a future proposed unto them, That they shall be praised, That they shall be redeemed out of contempt. This makes even the Expectation it selfe as sweet to them, as the fruition would be. This makes them, that when *David* sayes, [t]*Expecta viriliter*, Waite upon the Lord with a good courage; Waite, I say, upon the Lord; they doe not answer with the impatience of the Martyrs under the Altar, [u]*Usquequo*, How long, Lord, wilt thou defer it? But they answer in *Davids* owne words, [v]*Expectans expectavi*, I have waited long, And, [w]*Expectabo nomen tuum*, still I will waite upon thy Name; I will waite till the Lord come. (*1626*) 7:252–53

3. Holy Ghost's Indifference to Verb Tense (Ps. 32:7)

Wee enter into these considerations, with this observation, That as God himselfe is eternall and cannot bee considered in the distinction of times, so hath that language in which God hath spoken in his written word, the Hebrew, the least consideration of Time of any other language. Evermore in expressing the mercies of God to man, it is an indifferent thing to the holy Ghost whether he speak in the present, or in the future, or in the time that is past: what mercies soever he hath given us, he will give us over againe; And whatsoever he hath done, and will doe, hee is alwayes ready to doe at the present. (*winter 1624–1625?*) 9:335

4. Hebrew: Time Confounded (1 Tim. 1:15)

As in the former branch the Gentils the Heathens are our adversaries, they deny the *veniet*, that a Messias is to come at all; so in this, the Jews are our enemies, they confess the *veniet*, a future comming, but they deny the *venit*, that this Messias is come yet. In that language in which God spoke to man there is such an assurance intimated, that whatsoever God promises shall be performed; that in that language ordinarily in the Prophets, the times are confounded, and when God is intended to purpose or to promise any thing in the future, it is very often expressed in the time past; that which God

t. Ps. 27:14.
u. Rev. 6:10.
v. Ps. 40:1.
w. Ps. 52:9.

means to do, he is said to have done; future, and present, and past is all one with God: But yet to man it is much more, that Christ is come, then that he would come; not but that they who apprehended faithfully his future comming, had the same salvation as we, but they could not so easily apprehend it as we: God did not present so many handles to take hold of him in that promise, that he would come, as in the performance, that he was come. They had most of these handles that lived with him, and saw him, and heard him; but we that come after, have more then they which were before them, we have more in the history then they had in the Prophets. (*1618*) 1:305

5. Interrelation of Past Praise and Future Prayer (Ps. 90:14)

The Book is Praise, the parts are Prayer. The name changes not the nature; Prayer and Praise is the same thing: The name scarce changes the name; Prayer and Praise is almost the same word; As the duties agree in the heart and mouth of a man, so the names agree in our eares; and not onely in the language of our Translation, but in the language of the holy Ghost himselfe, for that which with us differs but so, Prayer, and Praise, in the Originall differs no more then so, *Tehillim*, and *Tephilloth*.

And this concurrence of these two parts of our devotion, Prayer and Praise, that they accompany one another, nay this co-incidence, that they meet like two waters, and make the streame of devotion the fuller; nay more then that, this identity, that they doe not onely consist together, but constitute one another, is happily expressed in this part of the Prayer, which is our Text; for that which in the Originall language is expressed in the voice of Prayer, *O satisfie us, etc.* in the first Translation, that of the Septuagint, is expressed in the voice of praise, *Saturasti, Thou hast satisfied us*; The Original makes it a Prayer, the Translation a Praise. And not to compare Original with Translation, but Translation with Translation, and both from one man, we have in S. *Hieroms* works two Translations of the Psalmes; one, in which he gives us the Psalmes alone; another, in which he gives them illustrated with his notes and Commentaries. And in one of these Translations he reads this as a Prayer, *Reple nos, O fill us early with thy mercie*, and in the other he reads it as a Praise, *Repleti sumus, Thou hast filled us, etc*. Nay, not to compare Originall with Translation, nor Translation with Translation, but Originall with Originall, the holy Ghost with himselfe, In the Title of this Psalme, (and the Titles of the Psalms are Canonicall Scripture) the holy Ghost calls this Psalme a *Prayer*, and yet enters the Psalme, in the very first verse thereof, with praise and thanksgiving, *Lord, thou hast been our dwell-*

ing place in all generations. And such is the constitution and frame of that Prayer of Prayers, That which is the extraction of all prayers, and draws into a summe all that is in all others, That which is the infusion into all others, sheds and showres whatsoever is acceptable to God, in any other prayer, That Prayer which our Saviour gave us, (for as he meant to give us all for asking, so he meant to give us the words by which we should ask) As that Prayer consists of seven petitions, and seven is infinite, so by being at first begun with glory and acknowledgement of his raigning in heaven, and then shut up in the same manner, with acclamations of power and glory, it is made a circle of praise, and a circle is infinite too, The Prayer, and the Praise is equally infinite. Infinitely poore and needy man, that ever needst infinite things to pray for; Infinitely rich and abundant man, that ever hast infinite blessings to praise God for.

Gods house in this world is called the house of Prayer; but in heaven it is the house of Praise: No surprisall with any new necessities there, but one even, incessant, and everlasting tenor of thanksgiving.

. . . .

If we compare these two incomparable duties, Prayer, and Praise, it will stand thus, Our Prayers besiege God, (as *Tertullian* speakes, especially of publique Prayer in the Congregation, *Agmine facto obsidemus Deum*) but our praises prescribe in God, we urge him, and presse him with his ancient mercies, his mercies of old; By Prayer we incline him, we bend him, but by praise we bind him; our thanks for former benefits, is a producing of a specialty, by which he hath contracted with us for more. In Prayer we sue to him, but in our Praise we sue him himselfe; Prayer is as our petition, but Praise is as our Evidence; In that we beg, in this we plead. God hath no law upon himselfe, but yet God himselfe proceeds by precedent: And whensoever we present to him with thanksgiving, what he hath done, he does the same, and more againe. Neither certainly can the Church institute any prayers, more effectuall for the preservation of Religion, or of the State, then the Collects for our deliverances, in the like cases before: And when he heares them, though they have the nature of Praise onely, yet he translates them into Prayers, and when we our selves know not, how much we stand in need of new deliverances, he delivers us from dangers which we never suspected, from Armies and Navies which we never knew were prepared, and from plots and machinations which we never knew were brought into Consultation, and diverts their forces, and dissipates their counsels with an untimely abortion. And farther I extend not this first part of Prayer in generall, in which, to that which you may have heard often, and usefully of the duty and dignity of Prayer, I have only added this, of the method and elements thereof, that prayer consists as much of praise for the past, as of supplication for the future. (*1621?*) 5:270–72

6. God's Language: No Superlative (Isa. 7:14)

So, for temporall things, we know the most that man can have; for we know all the world; but for Gods mercy, and his spirituall graces, as that language in which God spake, the Hebrew, hath no superlative, so, that which he promises, in all that he hath spoken, his mercy hath no superlative; he shewes no mercy, which you can call his Greatest Mercy, his Mercy is never at the highest; whatsoever he hath done for thy soule, or for any other, in applying himselfe to it, he can exceed that. Onely he can raise a Tower, whose top shall reach to heaven: The Basis of the highest building is but the Earth; But though thou be but a Tabernacle of Earth, God shall raise thee peece by peece, into a spirituall building; And after one Story of Creation, and another of Vocation, and another of Sanctification, he shall bring thee up, to meet thy selfe, in the bosome of thy God, where thou wast at first, in an eternall election. (*1624*) 6:174–75

7. Superlative: "Of God" (Prov. 22:11)

As it is frequent and ordinary in the Scriptures, when the Holy Ghost would express a *superlative*, the highest degree of any thing, to express it, by adding the name of God to it (as when *Saul* and his company were in such a dead sleep, as that *David* could take his Spear, and pot of water from under his head, It is called, *Tardemath Jehovah, sopor Domini, The sleep of the Lord,* The greatest sleep that could possess a man; and so in many other places, *fortitudo Domini*, and *timor Domini*, signifie the greatest strength, and the greatest fear that could fall upon a man) so also doth the Holy Ghost often descend from God, to God's Lieutenant; and as to express superlatives, he does sometimes use the name of *God*; so doth he also sometimes use the name of *King*. For, *Reges sunt summi Regis defluxus* (says that Author, who is so antient, that no man can tell when he was, *Trismegistus*) God is the *Sun*, and Kings are *Beams*, and emanations, and influences that flow from him. Such is the manner of the Holy Ghost expressing himself in *Esai.* [x]*Tyrus shall be forgotten seventy years, according to the years of one King*; that is, during the time of any one mans life, how happy and fortunate soever. And so also the miserable and wretched estate of the wicked, is likewise expressed, [y]*His hope shall be rooted out of his*

x. Esay 23:15. *y.* Job 18:14.

dwelling, and shall drive him to the King of fears; that is, to the greatest *despair*; *ad Regem interituum* (says the *Vulgar*) to the greatest *destruction* that can be conceived. So that in this first sense, *Amicitia Regis*, the Kings friendship that is promised here, (*The King shall be his friend*) is a superlative friendship, a spreading, a delating, an universal friendship. He that is thus qualified, all the world shall love him. (*1616*) 1:210–11

8. "Of the Lord" (Lam. 3:1)

It is ordinary in the Scriptures, that when the Holy Ghost would expresse a superlative, or the highest degree of any thing, to expresse it, by adding to it, the name of God. So, in many places, *fortitudo Domini*, and *timor Domini*, The power of the Lord, and the fear of the Lord, doe not import that power which is in the Lord, nor that fear which is to be conceived by us of the Lord, but the power of the Lord, and the fear of the Lord denote the greatest power, and the greatest fear that can be conceived. As in particular, when *Saul* and his company were in such a dead sleep, as that *David* could enter in upon them, and take his speare, and his pot of water from under his head, this is there called [z] *sopor Domini, the sleep of the Lord was upon him*, the heaviest, the deadliest sleep that could be imagined. So may these Afflictions in our Text be conceived to bee exalted to a *superlative* heighth, by this addition, that *They*, and *the Rod*, and *the wrath*, are said to be *His, The Lords*. But this cannot well be the sense, nor the direct proceeding, and purpose of the Holy Ghost, in this place, because where the addition of the name of God constitutes a superlative, that name is evidently and literally expressed in that place, as *fortitudo Dei, sopor Dei*, and the rest; But here, the name of God is onely by implication, by illation, by consequence; All necessary, but yet but *illation*, but *implication*, but *consequence*. (*1623?*) 10:201

z. 1. Sam. 26:12.

4 Logic and the Son

Introduction

In the previous chapter, the selections illustrated Donne's interest in grammar and its connection with theology, where the syntactic arrangement of words tries dimly to reflect the divine wisdom, where perfect patterns unfold ceaselessly and without number. Now we are to learn better that in God's mind the relationships that men struggle to proclaim in words exist in natural harmony. With us there is always the searching for the sources of grammar in formal logic, as we move hopefully from the school of grammar to the university of logic; but with God, logic radiates through every design, as "Bright effluence of bright essence increate" (*Paradise Lost,* 3.6). In Donne's words, "God is *Logos, speech* and *reason*: He declares his will by his *Word* . . . and he proceeds *Logically*" (5 : 103). The Logos *is* logic, and "*religion* is *reason* and *Logique*." Donne playfully describes this double role, which in fact is also single, with a *therefore*: "therefore God seales his promises with a *Quia*, a reason, an assurance" (5 : 104). God acts out of reason and for a reason, because he contains all reason and all logic.

Sometimes Donne speaks disparagingly of the "Schools" and the "Schoolmen," but he frequently refers to the medieval universities and to their great scholastic representatives, St. Thomas Aquinas, St. Bonaventure, and Duns Scotus, explicitly mentioning them, or their teaching, over one hundred times in the sermons. While Donne might take exception to some of their formulations and show impatience with their tendency to systematize all the data of faith, he could agree with those of them whose fundamental adherence to the right and faculty of reason might acquire and test the knowledge of faith: "Whosoever lives according to rectified Reason, which is the Law of nature, he is a Christian" (4 : 119). Knowledge is thus a help to salvation, and it teaches us that "Christ is Reason," that the Holy Ghost leads us to rest upon this Reason, and saves us from "tentations of Recidivation" (our inclination to backslide and fall into apostasy). Even as the angels "are not defective in their best part," that is, in their reason, so also must we exalt "that which is best in us naturally" (10 : 46).

Reason must be used in matters of religion: the authority of the

Church, while founded on Scripture, needs also to be tested by reason; the mysteries of faith are no less secret because reason tries to apprehend them. Nevertheless, Donne warns, the importance of the reason must not lead to its exaltation above the unsearchable judgments of God. Indeed, the extent of all our knowledge is like the earth in a great sea of profound and wide ignorance: "we are ignorant of more things then we know" (8:256). Yet our prayers are anchored in reason, expressed in such connectives as *for* and *but*. Thus "for thine is the Kingdom" is a form of prayer given to us by Christ in terms of the reason, *Quia tuum*. Here again Donne skillfully plays on the double sense of reason—as principle and explanation, as knowledge and wit, as cause and effect.

Like rhetoric and eloquence, logic also carries many hazards. There is the perverse *quia* of sin, when we argue a cause—never assigning the right one—for our sin. Such is the reasoning that imputes sin to innate disposition: "we make our sin our Nature: we impute it to our Station, to our Calling, to our Course of life" (1:226). Moreover, man's nature is such that his logic "strayes into superstition and idolatry." Thus in both "Naturall Logique" and in "Naturall Religion" opportunities lurk for error, for unreliability, and above all for uncharitableness.

Donne makes particular use of scholastic terminology: in the spirit of the Schools and with their language, he carries on the philosophical inquiry begun by Aristotle and continued by Aquinas and his followers. "How," "Why," "For," and "Therefore" are conjunctions that reveal logical, and often legitimate, relationships. Earlier we saw Donne writing of these "Dangerous and Infectious," these "Execrable and Damnable" monosyllables (pp. 81–82), of the *how* and *why* that can clog discourse and reason. Here the same *how* and *why* are called "dangerous, and deadly Monosyllables"; but context rules the fitness of these words. Corruption or inconsistency accompanies the terms, on the one hand, but also right reason, on the other, where we may justly ask after God's special purposes toward us, when "it becomes us to aske, and to know the reason" (5:206). One then should reach beyond the reason to its relief; having discovered why God's judgement falls as it does, a man must go next to the remedy—the *tamen*: "I am fallen, *yet* turn to the Lord."

Donne is fascinated by the possibilities implicit in the connective *for*, with its grammatical and logical significance. In preaching on the text from Colossians 1:19, 20, "For, it pleased the father, that in him should all fulnesse dwell," Donne observes that *For* is "a particle of connexion . . . of argumentation . . . a seale of all that was said from that place" (4:283). The word looks back and it looks forward, showing whence we have come and whither we are to proceed through an "illation," or inference and conclusion; indeed, "we are to trace the reason of our redemption intimated in that first word, *For*" (4:284). Even the angel of the resurrection "argues" logically, with "He is not here, *for* he is risen." Finally, on the text "Therefore, let all the house of Israel know assuredly, that God hath made that same Jesus, whom ye have crucified, both Lord and Christ" (Acts 2:36), Donne underlines the crucial importance of *Therefore*: "And so his Resurrection is become an argument, and an assurance of our Resurrection too" (4:346).

Much of what Donne says about logic in his sermons we might name "common sense." In calling conscience a syllogism, he means that a man has true knowledge when his own conscience, through practice and "conversation," tells him how to conclude. Yet conscience is a science, that is, a means to knowledge; "it is knowledge, and more"—a *practical* syllogism. Having declared this much, Donne also reveals more of his logic, evidently learned from scholastic theology and from his own legal study at the Inns of Court. Thus demonstration is the most powerful proof; a syllogism must be formed from agreed-upon premises; conclusions may not safely be drawn out of single instances, for "singularity" (or a unique instance) is only a kind of "halfe-proofe"; and so on. Throughout his discussions of grammatical logic, Donne regularly attaches a wide, even spiritual significance to words and their functions, especially the little words that reveal relationships, where "*And* . . . is as a ligament, as a sinew, to connect and knit together that glorious body of Gods preventing grace, and his subsequent grace" (9:312).

When Donne speaks specifically about *relation*, he sounds most of all like a man of the "Schools," which say that "God could not be a father without a Son, nor the Holy Ghost *Spiratus sine spirante*" (inspired without being inspired). Relation, indeed, forms the special area for discussion in most medieval and Renaissance arguments about the sacraments and the Trinity, and Donne is obviously influenced by them. The premise of relation states that one cannot have a sign without something being signified; relation distinguishes between essence and substance (*Ens* and *Substantia*), as in God and the Son who are separate, yet one. Similarly, God's way is described as *positive* (suggesting completeness, or having unconditional form, reminiscent of the old grammatical term that expresses simple quantity, without qualification, comparison, or relation to increase or diminution); man's way is called *privative* (tending toward removal, or, in grammar, the expressing of privation or negation). This chapter on relationships fitly ends with a passage that offers an inaccessible conclusion, where all our representations of God—or of man—end in the light of faith: "substraction" or addition of color or fancied shape may be helpful in depicting God, but toward the greatest mystery, "the expressing of the distinction of the Persons in the Trinity" (8:54), nothing may be done.

A. Reason and the Image of God

1. Logos *and Logic (Rev. 7:17)*

God leaves no way of satisfaction unperformed unto us; sometimes he workes upon the phantasie of Man; as in those often *Visions*, which he presented to his Prophets in *dreames*; sometimes he workes upon the *senses*, by preparing objects for them; [a] So he filled the Mountaine round about with horses, and chariots, in defence of *Elisha*; but alwayes he workes upon our *reason*; he bids us feare no judgment, he bids us hope for no mercy, except it have a *Quia, a reason*, a foundation, in the Scriptures. For God is *Logos, speech* and *reason*: He declares his will by his *Word*, and he proves it, he confirmes it; he is *Logos*, and he proceeds *Logically*. It is true, that we have a *Sophistry*, which as farre as concernes our owne destruction, frustrates his Logique; If *Peter* make a *Quia*, a reason why his fellowes could not bee drunke, [b] *Because it was but nine a Clocke*, wee can find Men that can overthrow that reason, and rise drunke out of their beds; If Christ make a *Quia*, a reason against *fashionall*, and *Circumstantiall christians*, that doe sometimes some offices of religion, out of custome, or company, or neighborhood, or necessity, because [c] *no man peeceth an old garment with new cloth, nor puts new wine into old vessells*, yet since S. *Augustine* says well, *Carnalitas vetustas, gratia novitas*, our carnall delights, are our old garments, and those degrees and beames of grace, which are shed upon us, are the new, we do peece this old with this new, that is, long habits of sin, with short *repentances*, flames of *concupiscence*, with little sparks of *remorse*; and into old *vessells*, (our sin-worne *bodies*) we put in once a year, some drops, of *new wine*, of the *bloud of our Saviour Christ Jesus*, in the *Sacrament*, (when we come to his *table*, as to a *vintage*, because of the season, and we *receive* by the *Almanack*, because it is *Easter*) and this new wine so taken in, *breakes the vessells*, (as Christ speakes in that similitude) And his breaking shall be, as the [d] *breaking of a Potters pot, which is broken*

a. 2. Reg. 6:27.
b. Act 2:15.
c. Matt. 9:16, 17.
d. Esay 30:14.

without pity, and in the breaking thereof is not found a shard, to take fire at the hearth, nor to take water out of the pit; No way in the Church of God, to repaire that Man, because he hath made either a *Mockery*, or at best, but a *Civill action* of Gods institution in the Church. To conclude this, all sin is but fallacy and *Sophistry*; *Religion* is *reason* and *Logique*; The devill hides, and deludes, Almighty God demonstrates and proves: That fashion of his goes through all his precepts, through all his promises, which is in *Esay*, [e]*Come now, and let us reason together*; that which was in *Job*, is abundantly in God, [f]*That he did not contemne the judgment of his servant, nor of his maid, when they did contend with him. Nec decet Dei judicium quicquid habere affine tyrannidi*, we may not think that here is any thing in God, like a *Tyran*; and it is a Tyrannicall proceeding, as to give no reason of his cruelties, so to give no assurance of his benefits; and therefore God seales his promises with a *Quia*, a reason, an assurance. (*1624–1625?*) 5:103–4

2. "Christ is Reason" (2 Cor. 4:6)

Ignorance then is not our Usher into this presence, *to shew us the face of Christ Jesus*: almost in every one of the ancient Fathers, you shall find some passages, wherein they discover an inclination to that opinion, that before Christ came in the manifestation of his Gospel (for, since that coming, every man is bound to see him there) many Philosophers, men of knowledge, and learning, were saved without the knowledge of Christ. *Christus Ratio*, says one of them, well, (for *Logos*, is *Ratio*, and not only *Verbum*, as it is ordinarily translated) Christ is Reason, rectified Reason; and *secundum Rationem vixerunt, Christiani semper*, says he, Whosoever lives according to rectified Reason, which is the Law of nature, he is a Christian; and therefore, when that Father, *Justin Martyr*, who had been before a Philosopher amongst the Gentiles, came to be a Preacher amongst the Christians, he never left off his Philosophers habit, because that gave an impression of his learning, and an estimation by it. That knowledge was a help to salvation, the Ancients thought: but that is a new Doctrine, that men should make a title to God, by being ignorant. (*1622*) 4:119

3. The Holy Ghost and Reason (Micah 2:10)

We are bidden to *rise*: that is, to leave our bed, our habit of sin; and then not to be idle, when we are up, but to *depart*; not onely to depart from the *Custome*, but from *tentations* of *Recidivation*; and not onely that, but to *depart* into *another way*, a habit of Actions, contrary to our former Sins. And then, all this is pressed, and urged upon us, by a

e. Esay 1:18.

f. Job 31:13.

Reason; The Holy Ghost appears not like a ghost in one sodain glance, or glimmering, but he testifies his presence, and he presses the businesse, that he comes for; And the reason that he uses here, is, *Quia non requies,* because otherwise we lose the *Pondus animae,* the weight, the ballast of our soule, *rest,* and peace of Conscience: for howsoever there may be some rest, some such shew of Rest, as may serve a carnall man a little while, yet, sayes our Text, it is not *your Rest,* it conduces not to that Rest, which God hath ordained for you, whom he would direct to a better Rest. That Rest, (*your Rest*) is not here; not in that, which is spoken of here; not in your lying still, you must rise from it; not in your standing still, you must *depart* from it; *your Rest is not here*: but yet, since God sends us away, because our Rest is not here, he does tacitly direct us thereby, where there is Rest. (*1621 or 1623?*) 5:199

4. Reason and Angels (Apoc. 7:2, 3)

Now as the Angels are not defective in their best part, their Reason, and therefore do their office in assisting us, so also let us exalt our best part, our Reason too, to reverence them with a care of doing such actions onely as might not be unfit for their presence. Both Angels and we have the Image of God imprinted in us; the Angels have it not *in summo,* though they have it *in tuto*; They have it not in the highest degree, ([g] for so Christ onely is *the Image of the invisible God*) but they have it in a deep impression, so as they can neither lose it, nor deface it. We have this Image of God so as that we cannot lose it, but we may, and doe deface it; *Uri potest, non exuri*; The Devil hath this Image in him, and it cannot be burnt out in hell; for it is imprinted in the very naturall faculties of the soule. But if we consider how many waters beat upon us in this world to wash off this Image, how many rusty and habituall sins gnaw upon us, to eat out this Image, how many files pass over our souls in calamities, and afflictions, in which though God have a purpose, *Resculpere imaginem,* to re-engrave, to refresh, to polish this Image in us, by those corrections, yet the devill hath a harsh file too, that works a murmuring, a comparing of our sinnes with other mens sinnes, and our punishments with other mens punishments, and at last, either a denying of Providence, (That things so unequally carried cannot be governed by God) or a wilfull renouncing of it in Desperation, That his Providence cannot bee resisted, and therefore it is all one what wee doe, If wee consider this, wee had need looke for Assistants.

Let us therefore looke first to that which is best in us naturally, that

g. Colos. 1:15. Bern[ard]. August[ine].

is, Reason; For if we lose that, our Reason, our Discourse, our Consideration, and sinke into an incapable and barren stupidity, there is no footing, no subsistence for grace. All the vertue of Corne is in the seed; but that will not grow in water, but onely in the earth: All the good of man, considered supernaturally, is in grace; but that will not growe in a washy soule, in a liquid, in a watery, and dissolute, and scattered man. Grace growes in reason; In that man, and in that minde, that considers the great treasure, what it is to have the Image of God in him, naturally; for even that is our earnest of supernaturall perfection. And this Image of God, even in the Angels, being Reason, and the best act of rectified Reason, The doing of that for which they were made, It is that which the Angels are naturally inclined to doe, to be alwayes present for the assistance of man; for therefore they are Angels. And since they have a joy at the Conversion of a sinner, and every thing affects joy, and therefore they indeavour our Conversion, yea, since they have an increase of their knowledge by being about us, (for, S. *Paul* sayes, [h]*That he was made a Preacher of the Gospel, to the intent that Angels might know, by the Church, the manifold wisedome of God*) And every thing affects knowledge, these Saints of God upon earth, intended in our Text, might justly promise themselves a strong and a blessed comfort, and a happy issue in all tribulations, by this Scripture, if there were no more intended in it, but onely the assistance of Angels; *I saw an Angel.* (*1623?*) 10:46–47

5. Reason and the Judgments of God (Eccles. 8:11)

First then, in handling the perversness of assigning Reasons for sins, we forbid no man the use of Reason in matters of Religion. As S. *Augustine* says, *Contra Scripturam, nemo Christianus,* No man can pretend to be a Christian, if he refuse to be tryed by the Scriptures: And, as he adds, *Contra Ecclesiam nemo pacificus,* No man can pretend to love order and Peace, if he refuse to be tryed by the Church: so he adds also, *Contra Rationem nemo sobrius,* No man can pretend to be in his wits, if he refuse to be tryed by Reason. He that believes any thing because the Church presents it, he hath Reason to assure him, that this Authority of the Church is founded in the Scriptures: He that believeth the Scriptures, hath Reasons that govern and assure him that those Scriptures are the Word of God. Mysteries of Religion are not the less believed and embraced by Faith, because they are presented, and induced, and apprehended by Reason.

But this must not enthrone, this must not exalt any mans Reason so

h. Eph. 3:10.

far, as that there should lie an Appeal, from Gods Judgements to any mans reason: that if he see no reason, why God should proceed so, and so, he will not believe that to be Gods Judgement, or not believe that Judgement of God, to be just: For, of the secret purposes of God, we have an Example what to say, given us by Christ himself, [i] *Ita est, quia complacuit; It is so, O Father, because thy good pleasure was such.* (*1616*) 1:169

6. The Case Against Ignorance (John 14:26)

The Schooles have made so many Divisions, and sub-divisions, and re-divisions, and post-divisions of Ignorance, that there goes as much learning to understand ignorance, as knowledg. One, much elder then al they, and elder (as some will have it) then any but some of the first Secretaries of the Holy Ghost in the Bible, that is *Trismegistus*, hath said as much as all, *Nequitia animae Ignorantia*, Ignorance is not only the drousinesse, the sillinesse, but the wickednesse of the soule: Not onely dis-estimation in this world, and damnification here, but damnation in the next world, proceeds from ignorance. And yet, here in this world, knowledge is but as the earth, and ignorance as the Sea; there is more sea than earth, more ignorance than knowledge; and as if the sea do gaine in one place, it loses in another, so is it with knowledge too; if new things be found out, as many, and as good, that were knowne before, are forgotten and lost. What Anatomist knowes the body of man thorowly, or what Casuist the soule? What Politician knowes the distemper of the State thorowly; or what Master, the disorders of his owne family? Princes glory *in Arcanis*, that they have secrets which no man shall know, and, God knowes, they have hearts which they know not themselves; Thoughts and purposes indigested fall upon them and surprise them. It is so in naturall, in morall, in civill things; we are ignorant of more things then we know; And it is so in divine and supernaturall things too; for, for them, the Scripture is our onely light, and of the Scripture, S. *Augustine* professes, *Plura se nescire quam scire*, That there are more places of Scripture, that he does not, then that he does understand. (*1628*) 8:255–56

7. Prayer and Reason (Luke 23:24)

But the Affections of our Saviour are not inordinate, nor irregular. He hath a *For*, for his Prayer: *Forgive them, for, etc*. And where he hath not this *For*, as in his Praier in his agony, he quickly interrupts the violence of his request, with a But, *Father, let this cup passe;* but *not*

i. Matt. 11:26.

my will: In that form of Prayer which himself taught us, he hath appointed a *for*, on Gods part, which is ever the same unchangeable: *For thine is the Kingdome*; Therefore supplications belong to thee: *The power, Thou openest thy hand and fillest every living thing*: *The Glory*, for thy Name is glorified in thy grants. But because on our part, the occasions are variable, he hath left our *for*, to our religious discretion. For, when it is said, James 4. *You lust and have not, because you aske not;* it followeth presently, *You aske and misse, because you aske amisse*. It is not a fit *for*, for every private man, to aske much means for he would doe much good. I must not pray, Lord put into my hands the strength of Christian Kings, for out of my zeale, I will imploy thy benefits to thine advantage, thy Souldiers against thine enemies, and be a bank against that Deluge, wherewith thine enemy the Turk threatens to overflow thy people. I must not pray, Lord fill my heart with knowledge and understanding, for I would compose the Schismes in thy Church, and reduce thy garment to the first continuall and seemlesse integrity; and redresse the deafnesses and oppressions of Judges, and Officers. But he gave us a convenient scantling for our *fors*, who prayed, Give me enough, for I may else despair, give me not too much, for so I may presume. Of Schoolmen, some affirm Prayer to be an act of our will; for we would have that which we aske. Others, of our understanding;[1] for by it we ascend to God, and better our knowledge, which is the proper aliment and food of our understanding; so, that is a perplexed case. But all agree, that it is an act of our Reason, and therefore must be reasonable. (*1621 or 1622?*) 5:236–37

8. Prayer Must Have a Quia *(Ps. 6:2, 3)*

First then, how imperfect, how weak soever our prayers be, yet still if it be a prayer, it hath a *Quia*, a Reason, upon which it is grounded. It hath in it, some implied, some interpretative consideration of our selves, how it becomes us to aske that, which wee doe ask at Gods hand, and it hath some implied, and interpretative consideration of God, how it conduces to Gods glory to grant it: for, that prayer is very farre from faith, which is not made so much as with reason; with a consideration of some possibility, and some conveniency in it. *Every man that sayes Lord, Lord, enters not into heaven*; Every *Lord, Lord*, that is said, enters not into heaven, but vanishes in the ayre. A prayer must be with a serious purpose to pray; for else, those fashionall and customary prayers, are but false fires without shot, they batter not

1. Aquinas is of the first sort (will), Scotus of the second (understanding). See Chap. 1, selection A.1 above.

heaven; It is but an Interjection, that slips in; It is but a Parenthesis, that might be left out, whatsoever is uttered in the manner of a prayer, if it have not a *Quia*, a Reason, a ground for it. And therefore, when our Saviour Christ gave us that forme of prayer, which includes all, he gave us in it a forme of the reason too, *Quia tuum, For thine is the Kingdome, etc.* It were not a prayer, to say, *Adveniat Regnum, Thy Kingdome come,* if it were not grounded upon that faithfull assurance, that God hath a Kingdome here; Nor to say *Sanctificetur nomen, Hallowed be thy name,* If he desired not to be glorified by us; Nor to aske *daily bread*, nor *forgivenesse of sins*, but for the *Quia potestas*, Because he hath all these in his power. We consider this first accesse to God, *Miserere mei, Have mercy upon me,* to be but a kind of imperfect prayer, but the first step; but it were none at all, if it had no reason, and therefore it hath this, *Quia infirmus, Because I am weake.* (*1623?*) 5:345–46

B. The Dangers of Reason

1. The Perverse Quia *of Sin (Ps. 55:19)*

Now amongst the manifold perversnesses and incongruities of this artificial sinning, of sinning upon Reason, upon a *quia*, and an *ergo*, of arguing a cause for our sin; this is one, That we never assigne the right cause: we impute our sin to our Youth, to our Constitution, to our Complexion; and so we make our sin our Nature: we impute it to our Station, to our Calling, to our Course of life; and so we make our sin our Occupation: we impute it to Necessity, to Perplexity, that we must necessarily do that, or a worse sin; and so we make our sin our Direction. We see the whole world is [j]*Ecclesia malignantium*, a Synagogue, a Church of wicked men; and we think it a Schismatical thing, to separate our selves from that Church, and we are loth to be excommunicated in that Church; and so we apply our selves to that, we do as they do, with the wicked we are wicked; and so we make our sin our Civility. And though it be some degree of injustice, to impute all our particular sins, to the devil himself, after a habit of sin hath made us [k]*spontaneos daemones*, devils to our selves; yet we do come too near an imputing our sins to God himself, when we place such an impossibility in his Commandments, as makes us lazie, that because we cannot do all, therefore we will do nothing; or such a manifestation and infallibility in his Decree, as makes us either secure, or desperate; and say, The Decree hath saved me, therefore I can take no

j. Ps. 26:5.

k. Chrysost[om].

harm; or, The Decree hath damned me, therefore I can do no good. No man can assigne a reason in the Sun, why his body casts a shadow: why all the place round about him, is illumined by the Sun, the reason is in the Sun; but of his shadow, there is no other reason, but the grosness of his own body: why there is any beam of light, any spark of life, in my soul, he that is the Lord of light and life, and would not have me die in darkness, is the onely cause; but of the shadow of death, wherein I sit, there is no cause, but mine own corruption. And this is the cause, why I do sin; but why I should sin, there is none at all. (*1617*) 1:226–27

2. The Fallacy of Natural Logic (Acts 28:6)

The first words of our Text carry us necessarily so far back, as to see from what they changed; And their periods are easily seene; Their *Terminus a quo*, and their *Terminus ad quem*, were these; first, that he was a *Murderer*, Then that he was a *God*. An error in Morality; They censure deeply upon light evidence: An error in Divinity; They transfer the Name and estimation of a God, upon an unknowne Man. Place both the errors in Divinity; (so you may justly do) And then there is an error in Charity, a hasty and inconsiderate condemning; And an error in faith, a superstitious creating of an imaginary God. Now, upon these two generall Considerations will this Exercise consist; first, that it is naturall Logique,[2] an argumentation naturally imprinted in Man, to argue, and conclude thus, Great calamities are inflicted, therefore God is greatly provoked; These men of Malta were but naturall men, but *Barbarians*, (as S. *Luke* cals them) and yet they argue, and conclude so; Here is a judgement executed, therefore here is evidence, that God is displeased. And so far they kept within the limits of humanity and piety too; But when they descended hastily and inconsiderately, to particular, and personall applications, This judgement upon this man is an evidence of his guiltinesse in this offence, then they transgressed the bounds of charity; That because a Viper had seised *Pauls* hand, *Paul* must needs be a murderer.

And then when we shall have passed thorough those things, which belong to that first Consideration, which consists of these two Propositions, That to conclude so, God strikes, therefore he is angry, is naturall, but hastily to apply this to the condemnation of particular persons, is uncharitable, we shall descend to our second Consideration,

2. Donne plays with the terms *natural, naturally*. *Natural*—innately given ("natural Logique"), lacking enlightenment (natural man), normally connected with some inherent characteristic (that God is angry is "natural"), and so on, with shades of different senses being subtly interrelated throughout this passage.

to see what they did, when they changed their minds, *They said, He is a God*. And, as in the former part, we shall have seen, That there is in man a naturall Logique, but that strays into uncharitablenesse; So in this we shall see, That there is in man a naturall Religion, but that strayes into superstition and idolatry; Naturally man is so far from being devested of the knowledge and sense of God, from thinking that there is no God, as that he is apt to make more Gods then he should, and to worship them for Gods, whom he should not. These men of Malta were but Naturall men, but *Barbarians*, (sayes S. *Luke*) yet they were so far from denying God, as that they multiplied Gods, and because the Viper did *Paul* no harme, they change their minds, and say, *He is a God*.

And from these two generall considerations, and these two branches in each, That there is in man a Naturall Logique, but that strayes into Fallacies; And a Naturall Religion, but that strayes into Idolatry, and Superstition, we shall derive, and deduce unto you, such things as we conceive most to conduce to your edification, from this knot, and summary abridgement of this Story, *Then they changed their minds, and said, He is a God*.

. . . .

And farther we carry not your consideration upon this first branch of our first Part, Naturally man hath this Logique, to conclude, where God strikes, God is angry; when God is angry, he will strike: But God never strikes in such anger, but with relation to sin. These men of Malta, naturall men, did so, and erred not in so doing; They erred when they came to particulars, to hasty and inconsiderate applications, for that is uncharitablenesse, and constitutes our second branch of this part. (*1629*) 8:313–14, 316–17

C. Logical Conjunctions: How, Why, For, Therefore

1. How and Why: Appropriate to God's Particular Purposes (Micah 2:10)

Now, we noted it to be a particular degree of Gods mercy, that he insisted upon it, that he pressed it, that he urged it with a reason; doe thus says God, *for*, it stands thus with you. It is always a boldnesse, to aske a reason of those decrees of God, which were founded, and established onely in his owne gratious will, and pleasure; In those cases, [1]*Exitiales voculae, cur et quomodo*; to aske, *why* God elected some, and *how* it can consist with his goodnesse, to leave out others, there the

1. Luther.

how, and *why* are dangerous, and deadly Monosyllables. But of Gods particular purposes upon us, and revealed to us, which are so to be wrought and executed upon us, as that we our selves have a fellow-working, and co-operation with God, of those, it becomes us to aske, and to know the reason. When the Angell *Gabriel* promised such unexpected blessings to *Zachary*, *Zachary* askes, [m]*whereby shall I know this?* and the Angel does not leave him unsatisfied. When that Angel promises a greater miracle to the blessed Virgin *Mary*, she says also, *Quomodo, how shall this be?* and the Angel settles, and establishes the assurancc in her: Whatsoever we are bid to beleeve, whatsoever we are bid to doe, God affords us a reason for it, and we may try it by reason, but because that sinner, whom in this text, he speakes to, *to arise and depart*, is likely to stand upon false reasons, against his rising, to murmur, and ask *Cur* or *quomodo*, *why* should I arise, since me thinkes I lye at my ease, *how* shall I arise, that am already at the top of my wishes? God who is loath to lose any soule, that he undertakes, followes him with this reason, *Quia non requies, Arise, and depart, for here is not your rest*. (*1621 or 1623?*) 5:206–7

2. Necessity and Quia; Tamen *(Micah 2:10)*

And this vexation hath another heavy weight upon it, in this little word, *for*; for this drawes a Curtain between the face of God, and them: this locks a dore between the Court of mercy, and them, when God presents his judgements with such an assurednesse, such a resolution, as leaves no hope in their heart, that God will alter it, no power in themselves to solicite God to a pardon, or a reprieve; but as he was led [n]*as a foole to the stocks*, when he hearkened to pleasant sins before, so he is led *as an oxe to the slaughter*, when he hears of Gods Judgements now; his own Conscience prevents God, and tels him, there is a *for*, a reason, a necessity, an irrecoverablenesse in his condemnation. God had iterated, and multiplied this *Quia*, this *for*, oftentimes in their ears: This Prophet was no upstart, no sodain, no transitory Man, to passe through the streets with a *Vae, Vae, Wo, wo unto this City*, and no more; but he prophecied constantly, during the reign of *three Kings*, of *Jotham*, *Ahaz*, and *Hezekiah*: [o]He was no suspitious Man out of his singularity; but he prophecied jointly with *Isaiah*, without separation, and he held the communion of his fellow-Prophets; He was no particular man, (as many Interpreters have taken it) so, as that he addressed his prophecies upon *Judah* onely; but he extended it to all, to all the Tribes. It is not a prophecy limited to *Idolatry*, and

m. Luke 1:18.
n. Prov. [7:22.]
o. Mic. 1:1.

the sins against the first Table, but to robbery, and murder, and fornication, and oppression, and the sins between *Man*, and *Man*: It is not a timorous prophecy, directed onely to persons, whom a low fortune, and a miserable estate, or a sense of sin, and a wounded Conscience, had depressed, and dejected, but principally bent upon rulers and Magistrates, and great persons. So that no Man hath a *Quia* against this *Quia*, a *for* against this *for*, to say, we need not heed him, for he is an upstart, a singular person, and all these his threatnings are rather *Satyricall*, then *Propheticall*, or Theologicall; but this thunderbolt, this *Quia*, this reason, why these judgements must necessarily fall upon them, fell upon them with so much violence, as that it stupefied with the weight, and precluded all wayes of escape. These be the heaviest Texts that a Man can light upon in the Scriptures of God, and these be the heaviest Commentaries, that a Man can make upon these Texts, that when God wakens him and raises him from his dream, and bed of sin, and pleasure, and raises him with the voice of his judgements, he suffers him to read to the *Quia*, but not to come to the *Tamen*; He comes to see reason why that Judgement must fall, but not to see any remedy. His inordinate *Melancholy*, and halfe desperate sadnesse carries his eye, and mind upon a hundred places of Commination, of threatning in the Prophets, and in them all he finds quickly that *Quia*, This curse must fall upon me, for I am faln into it; but he comes not to the *Tamen*, to that reliefe, *yet turn to the Lord, and he will turne to thee*. (*1621 or 1623?*) 5:191–92

3. "For" of Argumentation: A Seal (Col. 1:19, 20)

The whole journey of a Christian is in these words; and therefore we were better set out early, then ride too fast; better enter presently into the parts, then be forced to passe thorow them too hastily. First then wee consider the Collation and Reference of the Text, and then the Illation, and Inference thereof. For, the Text looks back to all that was said from the twelfth verse. For, the first word of the text, [*For*] which is a particle of connexion, as well as of argumentation, is a seale of all that was said from that place. And then, the Text looks forward to the 23 *verse* where all these blessings are sealed to us, with that Condition, *If ye continue setled in the Gospell*. This is the Collation, the Reference of the text; for the Illation, and Inference, the first clause thereof, [*For, it pleased the Father, that in him should all fulnesse dwell*] presents a double Instruction; First, that we are not bound to accept matters of Religion, meerely without all reason, and probable inducements; And secondly, with what modesty we are to proceed, and in what bounds we are to limit that inquisition, that search of Reason in matters of that nature. When the Apostle presents to us here, the great mystery of our reconciliation to God, he, in whose power it was not to infuse faith into every reader of his Epistle, proceeds by reason. He tels us, [p]*That the Father hath translated us into the Kingdome of his deare Son, the Son of his love.* That were well, if we were sure of it; If our consciences did not accuse us, and suggest to us our owne unworthinesse, and thereby an impossibility of being so translated. Why no, sayes the Apostle, there is no such impossibility now, For, [q]*Now we have Redemption, and forgivenesse of sinnes.* Who should procure us that? [r]*If a man sin against God, who shall plead for him?* What man is able to mediate, and stand in the gap between God and man? You say true, sayes the Apostle, no man is able to doe it; and therefore, [s]*He that is the Image of the invisible God, he by whom all things were created, and by whom all things consist, he hath done it.* Hath God reconciled me to God; And reconciled me by way of satisfaction? (for, that I know his justice requires) What could God pay for me? What could God suffer? God himselfe could not; and therefore God hath taken a body that could. [t]*And as he is the Head of that body,* he is passible, so he may suffer; And, as he is the first born of the dead, he did suffer; so that he was defective in nothing; not in Power, as God, not in passibility, as man; for, *Complacuit; It pleased the Father, that in him, All fulnesse* (a full capacity to all purposes) *should dwell.* Thus farre we are to trace the reason of our redemption, intimated in that first word, *For.* And then, we are to limit and determine our reason in the next, *Quia complacuit,* because it was his will, his pleasure to proceed so, and no otherwise. Christ himselfe goes no farther then so, in a case of much strangenesse, [u]*That God had hid his mysteries from the wise, and revealed them unto babes;* This was a strange course, but *Ita est, quia,* Even so, Father, for so it seemed good in thy sight. I would faine be able to prove to my selfe that my redemption is accomplished; and therefore I search the Scriptures; and I grow sure that Christ hath redeemed the world; and I search the Scriptures again, to finde what marks are upon them, that are of the participation of that Redemption, and I grow to a religious, and modest assurance, that those marks are upon me. I finde reasons to prove to me, that God does love my soule; but why God should love men better then his own Son, or why God should love me better then other men, I must end in the reason of the text, *Quia complacuit,* and in the reason of Christ himself, *Ita est, quia,* It is so, O Father, because thy good pleasure was it should be so. (*1622*) 4:283–85

p. v. 13.
q. v. 14.
r. 1. Sam. 2:25.
s. v. 15.
t. v. 18.
u. Matt. 11:25.

4. *"For" and the Logic of the Resurrection (Matt. 28:6)*

First; this *For,* (*for he is risen*) this particle of argumentation, the angel opposes prophetically, and by way of prevention, both against that heresie of Rome, That the body of Christ may be in divers places at once, by the way of Transubstantiation, and against that dream of the Ubiquetaries,[3] That the body of Christ must necessarily be in all places at once, by communication of the divine Nature. For, if the Angel argue fairely, logically, sincerely, (*He is not here, for he is risen*) then there is no necessity, there is no possibility of this omni-presence, or this multi-presence, for then the Angels argument might have been denied, and they might have replyed, What though he be risen, he may be here too, for he may be in divers places; But the Angel concludes us in this *for,* He cannot be here, for he is risen; Because he is risen, he cannot be here in the Sepulchre, so, as that you may embalm his body, Because he is ascended, he cannot be here, here in the Sacrament, so, as you may break or eat that body. (*1630*) 9:201–2

5. *"Therefore" (Acts 2:36)*

The first word of the Text, must be the last part of the Sermon, *therefore*; Therefore let all know it. Here is something necessary to be knowne, And the Meanes by which we are to know it; And these will be our two parts; *Scientia, et Modus,* Knowledge, and the way to it; For, *Qui testatur de scientia, testatur de modo scientiae,* is a good rule in all Laws, He that will testifie any thing upon his knowledge, must declare how he came by that knowledge. So then, what we must conclude, and upon what premisses, what we must resolve, and what must lead us to that resolution, are our two stages, our two resting places: And to those two, our severall steps are these; In the first, *Let all the house of Israel know, etc.* we shall consider first, The Manner of S. *Peter,* (for the Text is part of a Sermon of S. *Peters*) in imprinting this Knowledge in his Auditory; which is, first, in that Compellation of love and honour, *Domus Israel, The house of Israel*: But yet, when hee hath raised them to a sense of their dignity, in that attribute, he doth not pamper them with an overvalue of them, he lets them know their worst, as well as their best, Though you be the house of Israel, yet it is you that have crucified Christ Jesus, *That Jesus, whom ye have*

3. In eucharistic theology, especially Roman Catholic, transubstantiation teaches that the bread and wine are converted in their *substance* into the Body and Blood of Christ, only the *accidents* (or their appearance) remaining. "Ubiquetaries" describes Luther and many of his followers, ubiquitarianism being the doctrine that Christ in his human nature is everywhere present; thus He must necessarily be present in the Eucharist.

crucified; And from this his Manner of preparing them, we shall passe to the Matter that he proposes to them: When he had remembred them what God had done for them (*You are the house of Israel*) and what they had done against God, (*You have crucified that Jesus*) He imparts a blessed message to them all, *Let all know it:* Let them know it, and know it assuredly; He exhibits it to their reason, to their naturall understanding, And what? The greatest mystery, the entire mystery of our salvation, *That that Jesus is both Lord, and Christ*; But he is made so; Made so by God; Made both; Made Christ, that is, anointed, embalmed, preserved from corruption, even in the grave, And madc Lord by his triumph, and by being made Head of the Church, in the Resurrection, and in the Ascension: And so, that which is the last step of our first stage, (*That that Jesus is made Lord, as well as he is made Christ*) enters us upon our second stage, The meanes by which we are to know, and prove all this to our selves; [v]*Therefore*, sayes the Text, *let all know it*; wherefore? why, because God hath raised him, after you had crucified him; Because *God hath loosed the bands of death, because it was impossible that he should be holden by death*; Because *Davids* prophecy of a deliverance from the grave is fulfilled in him, Therefore let all know this to be thus. So that the Resurrection of Christ is argument enough to prove, that Christ is made Lord of all; And if he be Lord, he hath Subjects, that do as he does; And so his Resurrection is become an argument, and an assurance of our Resurrection too. (*1623*) 4:345–46

D. Common Sense and Grammatical Logic

1. Conscience and Syllogism (John 14:20)

How then is Christ in us? Here the question *De modo*, How it is, is lawfull: for, he hath revealed it to us. It is, by our obedience to his inspiration, and by our reverent use of those visible meanes, which he hath ordained in his Church, his Word and Sacraments: As our flesh is in him, by his participation thereof, so his flesh is in us, by our communication thereof; And so is his divinity in us, by making us partakers of his divine nature, and by making us one spirit with himself, which he doth at this Pentecost, that is, whensoever the holy Ghost visits us with his effectuall grace: for this is an union, in which, Christ in his purpose hath married himself to our souls, inseparably, and *Sine solutione vinculi*, Without any intention of divorce on his part: . . . If either we take the bed of licentiousnesse, or the board of volup-

v. ver. 23, 24, 25, 26, 27.

tuousnesse, or if when we eat and drink, or sleep or wake, we do not all to the glory of God, if we separate, he will divorce.

If then we be thus come to this knowledge, let us make *Ex scientia conscientiam*, Enlarge science into conscience: for, *Conscientia est Syllogismus practicus*, Conscience is a Syllogisme that comes to a conclusion; Then only hath a man true knowledge, when he can conclude in his own conscience, that his practise, and conversation hath expressed it. (*1630?*) 9:248

2. *Conscience and Science (2 Cor. 4:6)*

It was the Devils first advantage, knowledge, *The Serpent was wiser then any beast*: It is so still; Satan is wiser then any man in natural, and in Civil knowledge. 'Tis true, he is a Lyon too; but he was a Serpent first; and did us more harm as a Serpent, then as a Lyon. But now, as Christ Jesus hath nailed his hand-writing, which he had against us, to the Cross, and thereby cancelled his evidence; so in his descent to hell, and subsequent acts of his glorification, he hath burnt his Library, annihilated his wisdom, in giving us a wisdome above his craft; he hath shined in our hearts by the knowledge of his Gospel.

Measure not thou therefore the growth and forwardness of thy Child, by how soon he could speak, or go; how soon he could contract with a man, or discourse with a woman: but how soon he became sensible of that great contract which he had made with Almighty God, in his Baptism: how soon he was able to discharge those sureties, which undertook for him, then, by receiving his confirmation, in the Church: how soon he became to discern the Lords Spirit, in the preaching of his Word, and to discern the Lords body, in the Administration of the Sacrament. A Christian Child must grow, as Christ when he was a Child, [w] *in wisdom and in stature*: first, *in wisdom*, then *in stature*. Many have been taller at sixteen, then ever Christ was; but not any so learned at sixty, as he when he disputed at twelve. *He grew in favour*, says that Text, *with God and Man*; first, with God, then with man. Bring up your children in the knowledge and love of God; and good, and great men, will know, and love them too.

It is a good definition of ill love, that St. *Chrysostom* gives, that it is *Animae vacantis passio*, a passion of an empty soul, of an idle mind. For fill a man with business, and he hath no room for such love. It will fit the love of God too, so far, as that that love must be *in anima vacante*: at first, when the soul is empty, disencumbered from other studies, disengaged in other affections, then to take in the knowledge, and the love of God; for, *Amari nisi nota non possunt*, says St. *Augustine*

w. Luc. 2:52.

truely; however we may slumber our selves with an opinion of loving God; certainly we do not, we cannot love him, till we know him; and therefore hear, and read, and meditate, and confer, and use all means whereby thou mayst increase in knowledge. *If ye know these things, happy are ye if ye do them,* says Christ; you are not happy till you do them; that's true: but ye can never do them, till ye know them. Zeal furthers our salvation; but it must be *Secundum scientiam,* Zeal according to knowledge. Works further our salvation; but not works done in our sleep, stupidly, casually, nor erroniously, but upon such grounds as fall within our knowledge to be good. Faith most of all furthers and advances our salvation; but a man cannot believe that which he does not know. Conscience includes science; it is knowledge, and more; but it is that first. It is, as we express it in the School, *Syllogismus practicus*. I have a good Conscience in having done well; but I did that upon a former knowledge, that that ought to be done. (*1622*) 4:120–22

3. Demonstration: Most Powerful Proof (Matt. 19:17)

But in such doubtful cases in other mens actions, when it appeares not evidently, whether it were well, or ill done, where the balance is eaven, alwayes put you in your charity, and that will turne the scale the best way. Things which are in themselves, but mis-interpretable, doe not you presently mis-interpret, you allow some graines to your gold, before you call it light: allow some infirmities to any man, before you call him ill.

. . . .

Of all proofes, Demonstration is the powerfullest: when I have just reason to think my superiours would have it thus, this is Musique to my soul; When I heare them say they would have it thus, this is Rhetorique to my soule; When I see their Laws enjoyne it to be thus, this is Logick to my soul; but when I see them actually, really, clearely, constantly do thus, this is a Demonstration to my soule, and Demonstration is the powerfullest proofe: The eloquence of inferiours is in words, the eloquence of superiours is in action. (*1625*) 6:226–27

4. Fancy and Opinion (John 16:8, 9, 10, 11)

As it must not be only a fancy, an imagination, but an opinion, (in which, though there be not a *Certo*, yet there is a *Potius*, Though I be not sure, yet I doe rather thinke it) so we consider *Contraria opinantem,* That it must be an opinion contrary to something that we are sure of; that is, to some received article, or to some evident religious duty; contrary to religion, as religion is matter of faith, or as religion is matter of obedience, to lawfull Authority. Though fancies grow to be opinions, that men come to thinke they have reasons for their opinions, and to know they have other men on their side, in those opinions; yet, as long as these are but opinions of a little too much, or a little too little, in matter of Ceremony and Circumstance, as long as they are but deflectings, and deviations upon collaterall matters, no foundation shaked, no corner-stone displaced, as long as they are but preteritions, not contradictions, but omissions, not usurpations, they are not worthy of a reproofe, of a conviction, and there may be more danger then profit in bringing them into an over-vehement agitation. Those men whose end is schisme, and sedition, and distraction, are brought so neare their owne ends, and the accomplishment of their owne desires, if they can draw other men together by the eares: As some have all they desire, if they can make other men drunke, so have these if they can make sober men wrangle.

They must be Opinions, not fancies, and they must have a contrariety, an opposition to certaine truths, and then they must be held, persisted in, before it be fit to give a reproofe, either by calling in question, or by confutation. As some men are said to have told a lye so often, as that at last, they beleeve it themselves, so a man admits sometimes an opinion to lodge so long, as that [x]*Transit in intellectum*, It fastens upon his understanding, and that that he did but think before, now he seems to himself to know it, and he beleeves it. And then, [y]*Fides si habet haesitationem, infirma est*, As that faith that admits a scruple is weake, and so, without scruple he comes peremptorily to beleeve it. But so, *Opinio si habet assertionem, temeraria est*, When that which is but an opinion comes to be published and avowed for a certaine, and a necessary truth, then it becomes dangerous; And that growes apace; for scarcely does any man beleeve an opinion to be true, but he hath a certaine appetite and itch to infuse it into others too.

Now when these pieces meet, when these atomes make up a body, a body of Error, that it come to an Opinion, a halfe-assurance, and that in some thing contrary to foundations, and that it be held stiffely, publiquely persisted in, then enters this reproofe; but yet even then reproofe is but *Syllogismus*, it is but an argument, it is but convincing, it is not destroying; it is not an Inquisition, a prison, a sword, an axe, a halter, a fire; It is a syllogisme, not a syllogisme, whose *major* is this, Others, your Ancestors beleeved it, and the *minor* this, We that are your Superiours beleeve it, *Ergo* you must, or else be banisht or burnt. With such syllogismes the Arians abounded, where they pre-

x. Bernard. *y*. Idem.

vailed in the Primitive Church, and this is the Logique of the Inquisition of Rome. But our syllogisme must be a syllogisme within our Authors definition, when out of some things which are agreed on all sides, other things that are controverted, are made evident and manifest. (*1625?*) 6:318–19

5. No Conclusions from One Example (Acts 9:4)

It is not safe concluding out of single Instances. It is true, that if a soure, and heavy, and severe man, will adde to the discomforts of a disconsolate soule, and in that souls sadnesse, and dejection of spirit, will heap up examples, that God hath still suffered high-minded sinners to proceed and to perish in their irreligious wayes, and tell that poore soule, (as *Jobs* company did him) It is true, you take God aright, God never pardons such as you, in these cases, these singular, these individuall examples, That God hath done otherwise once, have their use. One instance to the contrary destroys any peremptory Rule, no man must say, God never doth it; He did it to *Saul* here, He did it to the Theife upon the Crosse. But to that presumptuous sinner, who sins on, because God shewed mercy to One at last, we must say, a miserable Comforter is that Rule, that affords but one example. Nay, is there one example? The Conversion of *Saul* a Persecutor, and of the Theife upon the Crosse, is become [z]*Proverbium peccatorum*, The sinners proverb, and serves him, and satisfies him in all cases. But is there any such thing? Such a story there is, and it is as true as Gospel, it is the truth of Gospel it selfe; But was this a late Repentance? Answer S. *Cyril*, *Rogo te frater*, Tell me, Beloved, Thou that deferrest thy Repentance, doest thou do it upon confidence of these examples? *Non in fine, sed in principio conversus latro*, Thou deludest thine owne soule; The Theife was not converted at last, but at first; As soone as God afforded him any Call, he came; And at how many lights hast thou winked? And to how many Cals hast thou stopped thine eares, that deferrest thy repentance? Christ said to him, *Hodie mecum eris, This day thou shalt be with me in paradise*; when thou canst finde such another day, looke for such another mercy; A day that cleft the gravestones of dead men; A day that cleft the Temple it selfe; A day that the Sunne durst not see; A day that saw the soule of God (may we not say so, since that Man was God too) depart from Man; There shall be no more such dayes; and therefore presume not of that voyce, *Hodie*, This day thou shalt be with me, if thou make thy last minute that day, though Christ, to magnifie his mercy, and his glory, and to take away

z. Gregor.

all occasion of absolute desperation, did here, under so many disadvantages call, and draw S. *Paul* to him. (*1625*) 6:208–9

6. Singular Not Judicial (Job 14:18)

For, though in the exposition of Scriptures, singularity alwaies carry a suspition with it, singularity is *Indicium*, (as we say in the Law) some kind of evidence, It is *Semi-probatio*, a kind of halfe-proofe against that man, that holds an opinion, or induces an interpretation different from all other men; yet as these which we call *Indicia*, in the Law, worke but so, as that they may bring a man to his oath, or, in some cases, to the rack, and to torture, but are not, alone sufficient to condemne him; So if we finde this singularity in any man, we take from thence just occasion to question and sift him, and his Doctrine, the more narrowly, but not only upon that, presently to condemne him. For this was S. *Augustines* case; S. *Augustine* induced new Doctrines, in divers very important points, different from all that had written before him; but, upon due examination, for all his singularity, the Church hath found reason to adhere to him, in those points, ever since his reasons prevailed. (*1629*) 8:357

7. Always vs. Conditional (Exod. 4:13)

First then, our first Consideration constitutes that Proposition, *Ordinary Duties*, arising out of the Evidence of Gods Word, require a present Execution. There are Duties that binde us *semper*, and *Ad semper*, as our Casuists speak; we are Alwayes bound to doe them, and bound to doe them Alwayes; that is, Alwayes to produce *Actus elicitos*, Determinate acts, Successive and Consecutive Acts, conformable to those Duties; whereas in some other Duties, we are onely bound to an Habituall disposition, to doe them in such and such necessary cases; And those Actions of the later sort, fall *in Genere Deliberativo*, we may consider Circumstances, before we fall under a necessity of doing them; that is, of doing them Then, or doing them Thus: Of which kind, even those great duties of Praying, and Fasting are; for we are alwayes bound to Pray, and alwayes bound to Fast; but not bound to fast alwayes, nor alwayes to pray. But for Actions of the first kind, such as are the worshipping of God, and the not worshipping of Images; such as are the sanctifying of Gods Sabbaths, and the not blaspheming of his Name, which arise out of cleare and evident commands of God; they admit no Deliberation, but require a present Execution. (*1627*) 8:133–34

8. Surely vs. Conditional (Ps. 62:9)

It is in doctrines and opinions, as it is in designes and purposes; *Goe to,* (sayes the Prophet, by way of reprehension) *Goe to, you that say, we will goe to such a City, and trade thus and thus there, etc*. So, goe to, you that pronounce upon every invention, and Tradition of your own, a *Quicunque vult salvus esse,* Whosoever will be saved, must beleeve this, and clogge every problematicall proposition with an *Anathema,* Cursed be he, Excommunicated he that thinks the contrary to this; Goe to, you that make matters of faith of the passions of men. So also, goe to, you that proceed and continue in your sinnes, and say, Surely I shall have time enough to repent hereafter. Goe to, you that in a spirituall and irreligious melancholy and diffidence in Gods mercy, say, Surely the Lord hath locked up his mercy from me, surely I shall never see that Sunne more, never receive, never feele beame of his mercy more, but passe through this darknesse into a worse. This word, *surely,* in such cases, in such senses, is not your mothers tongue, not thc language of the Christian Church. She teaches you, to condition all in Christ; In him you are enabled to doe all things, and without him nothing. But absolutely, unconditionally, this *surely* is appropriated to the propositions, to the assertions of God himselfe; And some of those follow in this text. (*1625*) 6:302

9. Conjunction "And": Connection of Grace (Ps. 32:5)

This is a wide doore, and would let out Armies of Instructions to you; but we will shut up this doore, with these two leaves thereof, The fulnesse of Gods Mercy, *He forgives the sin and the punishment*; And the seasonablenesse, the acceleration of his mercy, in this expression in our text, that *Davids* is but *Actus inchoatus,* He sayes *he will confesse,* And Gods is *Actus consummatus, Thou forgavest,* Thou hadst already forgiven the iniquity, and punishment of my sin. These will be the two leaves of this doore; and let the hand that shuts them be this *And,* this Particle of Connection which we have in the text, *I said, And thou didst*. For though this Remission of sin be not presented here as an effect upon that cause of *Davids* Confession, (It is not delivered in a *Quia,* and an *Ergo,* Because *David* did this, God did that; for mans wil leads not the will of God, as a cause, who does all his acts of mercy for his mercies sake) yet though it be not an effect, as from a cause, yet it is at least as a consequent from an occasion, so assured, so infallible, as let any man confesse as *David* did, and he shall be sure to be forgiven as *David* was. For though this forgiveness be a flower of mercy, yet the roote growes in the Justice of God; [a]If wee acknowledge our sin, he is faithfull and just to forgive us our sin; It growes out of his faithfulnesse, as he hath vouchsafed to binde himselfe by a promise, And out of his Justice, as he hath received a full satisfaction for all our sins. So that this Hand, this *And*, in our Text, is as a ligament, as a sinew, to connect and knit together that glorious body of Gods preventing grace, and his subsequent grace; if our Confession come between and tie the knot, God, that moved us to that act, will perfect all. (*winter 1624–1625?*) 9:312

E. Formal Logic: Relation and Privation

1. The Logic of "Relation" (Prov. 22:11)

King and subjects are Relatives, and cannot be considered in execution of their duties, but together. The greatest Mystery in Earth, or Heaven, which is *the Trinity*, is conveyed to our understanding, no other way, then so, as they have reference to one another *by Relation*, as we say in the Schools; for, God could not be a father without a Son, nor the Holy Ghost *Spiratus sine spirante*.[4] As in Divinity, so in Humanity too, *Relations* constitute one another, King and subject come at once and together into consideration. Neither is it so pertinent a consideration, which of them was made for others sake, as that they were both made for Gods sake, and equally bound to advance his glory. (*1617*) 1:184

2. Relation: Father Implies a Son (Gen. 1:26)

When we professe God, in the Creed, by way of beleefe, *Credo in Deum*, I beleeve in God, in the same article we professe him to be a Father too, *I beleeve in God the Father Almighty*: And that notion, the Father, necessarily implies a second Person, a Sonne: And then we professe him to be *maker of heaven, and earth:* And in the Creation, the holy Ghost, the Spirit of God, is expresly named. So that we doe but exercise reason, and nature, in directing our selves upon God. We exercise not faith, (and *without faith it is impossible to please God*) till we come to that, which is above nature, till we apprehend a Trinity. We know God, we beleeve in the Trinity. The Gentiles multiplyed Gods.

4. "Spirit without spiration," referring to the procession of the Holy Spirit in the Godhead.

a. 1. John 1:9.

There were almost as many Gods as men, that beleeved in them. And I am got out of that thrust, and out of that noise, when I am come into the knowledge of one God: But I am got above staires, got into the Bedchamber, when I am come to see the Trinity, and to apprehend not onely, that I am in the care of a great, and a powerfull God, but that there is a Father, that made me, a Sonne that Redeemed me, a holy Ghost, that applies this good purpose of the Father, and Sonne, upon me, to me. The root of all is God. But it is not the way to receive fruits, to dig to the root, but to reach to the boughs. I reach for my Creation to the Father, for my Redemption to thc Sonne, for my sanctification to the holy Ghost: and so I make the knowledge of God, a Tree of life unto me; and not otherwise. Truly it is a sad Contemplation, to see Christians scratch and wound and teare one another, with the ignominious invectives, and uncharitable names of Heretique, and Schismatique, about Ceremoniall, and Problematicall, and indeed but Criticall, verball controversies: and in the meane time, the foundation of all, the Trinity, undermined by those numerous, those multitudinous Anthills of *Socinians*,[5] that overflow some parts of the Christian world, and multiply every where. And therefore the Adversaries of the Reformation, were wise in their generation, when to supplant the credit of both those great assistants of the Reformation, *Luther*, and *Calvin*, they impute to *Calvin* fundamentall error, in the Divinity of the second Person of the Trinity, the Sonne; And they impute to *Luther*, a detestation of the very word Trinity, and an expunction thereof, in all places of the Liturgy, where the Church had received that word. They knew well, if that slander could prevaile against those persons, nothing that they could say, could prevaile upon any good Christians. But though in our *Doctrine* we keep up the Trinity aright; yet, God knowes, in our *Practise* we doe not. I hope it cannot be said of any of us, that he beleeves not the Trinity, but who amongst us thinkes of the Trinity, considers the Trinity? Father and Sonne doe naturally imply, and induce one another; and therefore they fall oftner into our consideration. (*1629*) 9:52–53

3. Relation: Three Kinds (Ephes. 5:25, 26, 27)

Almighty God ever loved *unity*, but he never loved *singularity*; God was always *alone* in heaven, there were no *other Gods*, but he; but he was never *singular*, there was never any time, when there were not *three persons* in heaven; *Pater et ego unum sumus*; The *father and I are*

5. Donne reserves his condemnation for "true heretiques," the anti-Trinitarians who followed Socinus (especially Sozzini, d. 1604), and who formed a tradition distinct from post-Trentine Rome or reformed protestantism.

one, says Christ: one in *Essence*, and one in *Consent*; our *substance* is the same, and our *will* is the same; but yet, *Tecum fui ab initio*, says Christ, in the person of *Wisdome*, I was with thee, disposing all things, at the Creation. As then God seemes to have been eternally delighted, with this eternall generation, (with persons that had ever a relation to one another, *Father*, and *Sonne*) so when he came to the Creation of this lower world, he came presently to those three relations, of which the whole frame of this world consists; of which, (because the principall foundation, and preservation of all States that are to continue, is *power*) the first relation was between *Prince* and *Subject* when God said to Man, [b]*Subjicite et dominamini*, subdue and govern all Creatures; The second relation was between *husband* and *wife*, when *Adam* said, [c]*This now is bone of my bone, and flesh of my flesh*; And the third relation was between *parents* and *children*, when *Eve* said, [d]*that she had obtained a Man by the Lord*, that by the plentifull favour of God, she had conceived and borne a sonne: from that time, to the dissolution of that frame, from that beginning to the end of the world, these three relations, of *Master* and *Servant*, *Man* and *Wife*, *Father* and *Children*, have been, and ever shall be the materialls, and the elements of all society, of families, and of Cities, and of Kingdomes. (*1624?*) 5:113–14

4. Ens *and* Substantia *(Matt. 19:17)*

We see that God, as soon as he saw that any thing was good, he said so, he uttered it, he declared it, first of the Light, and then of other creatures: God would be no author, no example of smothering the due praise of good actions. For, surely that man hath no zeale to goodnesse in himself, that affords no praise to goodnesse in other men.

But Christs purpose was also, that this praise, this recognition, this testimony of his goodnesse, might be carried higher, and referred to the only true author of it, to God. So the Priests and the Elders come to *Judith*, and they say to her, [e]Thou art the exaltation of Jerusalem, thou art the great glory of Israel, thou art the rejoycing of our Nation, thou hast done all these things by thy hand; And all this was true of *Judith*, and due to *Judith*; and such recognitions, and such acclamations God requires of such people, as have received such benefits by such instruments: For as there is Treason, and petty-treason, so there is Sacriledge, and petty-sacriledge; and petty-sacriledge is to rob Princes and great persons of their just praise. But then, as we must confer this upon them, so must they, and we, and all transfer all upon

b. Gen. 1:28.
c. 2:23.
d. 4:1.
e. Judith 15:8.

God: for so *Judith* proceeds there, with her Priests and Elders, Begin unto my God, with Timbrels, sing unto the Lord with Cymbals, exalt him, and call upon his name. So likewise *Elizabeth* magnifies the blessed Virgin *Mary*, [f]*Blessed art thou amongst women*: And this was true of her, and due to her; and she takes it to her self, when she sayes there, *From henceforth all Generations shall call me blessed*; but first, she had carried it higher, to the highest, *My soule doth magnifie the Lord, and my spirit doth rejoyce in God my Saviour*. In a word, Christ forbids not this man to call him good, but he directs him to know in what capacity that attribute of goodnesse belonged to him, as he was God: That when this man beleeved before that Christ was good, and learnt from him now, that none was good but God, he might by a farther concoction, a farther rumination, a farther meditation of this, come in due time to know that Christ was God; And this was his Method.

Now this leads us into two rich and fragrant fields; this sets us upon the two Hemispheares of the world; the Western Hemispheare, the land of Gold, and Treasure, and the Eastern Hemispheare, the land of Spices and Perfumes; for this puts us upon both these considerations, first, that nothing is essentially good, but God, (and there is the land of Gold, centricall Gold, viscerall Gold, gremiall Gold, Gold in the Matrice and womb of Gold, that is, Essentiall goodnesse in God himself) and then upon this consideration too, That this Essentiall goodnesse of God is so diffusive, so spreading, as that there is nothing in the world, that doth not participate of that goodnesse; and there is the land of Spices and Perfumes, the dilatation of Gods goodnesse. So that now both these propositions are true, First, That there is nothing in this world good, and then this also, That there is nothing ill: As, amongst the Fathers, it is in a good sense, as truly said, *Deus non est Ens, Deus non est substantia*, God is no Essence, God is no substance, (for feare of imprisoning God in a predicament) as it is said by others of the Fathers, that there is no other Essence, no other Substance but God. (*1625*) 6:230–31

5. God's Positive, Man's Privative (Acts 7:60)

When God placed *Adam* in the world, God enjoyned *Adam* to fill the world, to subdue the world, and to rule the world; when God placed him in Paradise, He commanded him to dress Paradise, and to keep Paradise; when God placed his children in the land of promise, he enjoyned them to fight his battails against Idolatry, and to destroy

f. Luke 1:42.

Idolators; to every body some errand, some task for his glory; and thou commest from him into this world, as though he had said nothing to thee at parting, but go and do as thou shalt see cause, go and do as thou seest other men do, and serve me so far, and save thine own Soul so far, as the times, and the places, and the persons, with whom thou doest converse, will conveniently admit. Gods way is positive, and thine is privative: God made every thing something, and thou makest the best of things, man, nothing; and because thou canst not annihilate the world altogether, as though thou hadst God at an advantage, in having made an abridgment of the world in man, there in that abridgment thou wilt undermine him, and make man, man, as far as thou canst, man in thy self nothing. He that qualifies himself for nothing, does so; He whom we can call nothing, is nothing: this whole world is one intire creature, one body; and he that is nothing may be excremental nailes, to scratch and gripe others, he may be excremental hairs for ornament, or pleasurableness of meeting; but he is no limb of this intire body, no part of Gods universal creature, the world. Gods own name is *I am*: *Being*, is Gods name, and nothing is so contrary to God as to be nothing. Be something, or else thou canst do nothing; and till thou have said this, saies our text, that is, done something in a lawful calling, thou canst not sleep *Stephens* sleep, not die in peace. *Sis aliquid*, propose something, determine thy self upon something, be, profess something, that was our first; and then our second consideration is, *hoc age*, do seriously, do scedulously, do sincerely the duties of that calling. (*1628*) 8:177–78

6. Representation by Subtraction and Addition (Rev. 4:8)

For the Trinity it self, it is *Lux*, but *Lux inaccessibilis*; It is light, for a child at Baptisme professes to see it; but then, it is so inaccessible a light, as that if we will make naturall reason our *Medium*, to discerne it by, it will fall within that of *David*, [g] *Posuit tenebras latibulum suum*, God hath made darknesse his secret place; God, as God, will be seen in the creature; There, in the creature he is light; light accessible to our reason; but God, in the Trinity, is open to no other light, then the light of faith. To make representations of men, or of other creatures, we finde two wayes; Statuaries have one way, and Painters have another: Statuaries doe it by Substraction; They take away, they pare off some parts of that stone, or that timber, which they work upon, and then that which they leave, becomes like that man, whom they would represent: Painters doe it by Addition; Whereas the cloth, or table

g. Ps. 18:11.

presented nothing before, they adde colours, and lights, and shadowes, and so there arises a representation. Sometimes we represent God by Substraction, by Negation, by saying, God is that, which is not mortall, not passible, not moveable: Sometimes we present him by Addition; by adding our bodily lineaments to him, and saying, that God hath hands, and feet, and eares, and eyes; and adding our affections, and passions to him, and saying, that God is glad, or sorry, angry, or reconciled, as we are. Some such things may be done towards the representing of God, as God; But towards the expressing of the distinction of the Persons in the Trinity, nothing. (*1627*) 8:54

5 Voice and Character— The Revelation of Self

Introduction

Donne's understanding of character is closely linked to his idea that poetry expresses religious devotion. Because Christ puts on manhood through His incarnation, we are able to put on the new man through the regeneration which He has thus made possible. At the center of our souls' destiny, where human and divine can meet, we may dress ourselves in Christ's garment. Thus, as His servants and His sons, we are to be distinguished by the signs of Christianity, by having the same nature and substance as the son has of the father. To put on a garment, however, is but the first stage of dressing; the second stage is to put on a person, to grow into our inheritance as the sons of God, when "we shall every one be so accepted, as if every one of us were *all Mankind*" (5 : 159–60), as if we were indeed He. In becoming a wholly new person, we are also giving prophetic voice to the changes to come and which will have been made; for life is lived in the future perfect tense where whatever is looked for is accomplished. In one of his Holy Sonnets, Donne describes this "rite of reclothing," using similarly typological ideas:

> And *Jacob* came cloth'd in vile harsh attire
> But to supplant, and with gainfull intent:
> God cloth'd himselfe in vile mans flesh, that so
> Hee might be weake enough to suffer woe. (7, Grierson 11)

Here the expectation is at once a hope and a fulfillment.

This concept of the newly revealed self, based upon the common nature of man and Christ, is vital to Donne's thinking about affliction. Since God comprehends all, the misery of age may be the result of indulgence in youth; but God's judgments, while often unsearchable, can never be unjust. And the one who complains of the pain attendant upon the Christian life is not alone, for he shares his pain with Christ, and with all the members of the Church. The connection of man with Christ expresses a dependency and implies a community of believers, for "God hath made all *mankinde* of *one blood*, and all *Christians* of *one calling*" (2:122). The idea is identical with the sentiment expressed in the famous passage of *Devotions Upon Emergent Occasions* (Meditation 17): "No man is an island . . . because I am involved in mankind . . . never send to know for whom the bell tolls; it tolls for thee." Since we all are concerned with the sins and the grief of other men, the self reveals itself in others.

We have seen before (p. 48) that Christ "came to save by calling us." Donne has defined the eloquence of the divine mission as it may be expressed in art. Now he examines the role of Christ's voice and His calling in the formation of human character. Through Christ, God gives His voice to us, "and that's his errand, and purpose in coming" (7:144). This is the miracle of the Word: man knows God's voice weakly through internal desire and the created world, and even more powerfully through miracles; but all these signs are ineffectual without the animating voice of the Word. Saul is the type of those who are saved by the calling voice: "Here then is the first step of *Sauls* cure, and of ours, That there was not onely a word, the Word, Christ himselfe, a Son of God in heaven, but a Voyce" (6:217).

St. John the Baptist, who was "all voice" ("the voice of him that cries in the wilderness"), is a central figure in Donne's description of character. "Man is but a voice" at the beginning of his life, "when he comes crying into the world" (p. 47); but voice forms words, and these are the forerunners of deeds. Right action (or "rectified Nature") grows out of the voice that is calling, bringing news, and preaching. John Baptist is so striking a figure because he espoused the word without himself being the Word. He is like the preacher who brings the congregation together not to hear his own voice, but the voice of his calling. Donne's evident delight in playing on words and on Christian paradoxes is typical; his vision is always double, but not blurred or confused, and his habits of mind reflect the ease with which he and his seventeenth-century contemporaries apprehended everywhere "divided and distinguished worlds," separate yet one. The bringing together of *occurrere* and *vocare*, to meet and to call, expresses this duality—two actions from different directions that end in the same place, like the riding westward (in "Goodfriday, 1613") only to see the "sun" rising in the east. Thus do we learn of the uniqueness of man's own "calling"—his voice and his vocation, for he alone among the creatures knows that "Christ is *verbum*. The word; not A word, but The word: the Minister is *Vox*, voyce; not A voyce, but The voyce, the voyce of that word" (2:172).

Voice is a phenomenon not only of the here and now—a voice leading the sheep in the paths of righteousness—but also it is the sound that will be heard at the end of time. This voice "carries with it a penetration, (all shall heare it) and a perswasion, (all shall beleeve it, and be glad of it) and a power, a command, (all shall obey it)" (4:69–72). In its last clamorous sound, this voice is that of the Archangel of the general Resurrection. As the power of this voice had once gathered souls together, it will then "recollect their scattered dust, and recompact their ruined bodies." Voice is at once an agent of redemption and of resurrection. "The Trumpet of God is his loudest Instrument"; with it He declares His word, unfolds each person's character, and reveals each self. But with the kind of metamorphosis that is frequent in Donne, God's trumpet really becomes man himself; the preacher-poet is the one who hears and plays the celestial harmonies, who is "wrought upon."

A. To Put on the Person of Christ: Redefining Self

1. Induere Personam *(Gal. 3:27)*

But this act of Christ, this redemption makes us onely *servants*; *servi a servando*, we are servants to him, that preserved, and saved us, is the derivation of the *Law*. But the *application* of this redemption (which is the *putting on of Christ*,) makes us *sons*; for we are not to put on Christ, onely as a *Livery*, to be distinguished by externall marks of *Christianity*; but so, as the sonne puts on his father; that we may be of the same nature and substance as he; and that God may be in us, [a]*Non tanquam in denario*, not as the King is in a peece of coine, or a medall, but *tanquam in filio*, as he is in his sonne, in whom the same nature both humane, and Royall doth reside.

There is then a double *Induere*, a twofold clothing; we may *Induere*, 1. *Vestem*, put on a garment; 2. *Personam*, put on a person. We may put on Christ so, as we shall be *his*, and we may put him on so, as we shall be *He*.

. . . .

And from this (which is *Induere vestem*,) from this putting on Christ as a garment, we shall grow up to that perfection, as that we shall *Induere personam*, put on *him*, his person; That is, we shall so appeare before the Father, as that he shall take us for his owne Christ; we shall beare his name and person; and we shall every one be so accepted, as if every one of us were *all Mankind*; yea, as if we were *he* himselfe. He

a. Aquin.

shall find in all our bodies his *woundes*, in all our mindes, his *Agonies*; in all our hearts, and actions his *obedience*. And as he shall doe this by imputation, so really in all our Agonies, he shall send his Angels to minister unto us, as he did to *Elias*; In all our tentations he shall furnish us with his Scriptures to confound the Tempter, as he in person, did in his tentation, and in our heaviest tribulation, which may extort from us the voice of diffidence, *My God, My God, why hast thou forsaken me?* He shall give us the assurance to say, *In manus tuas etc. Into thy hands O Lord have I commended my spirit*, and there I am safe; He shall use us in all things, as his sonne; and we shall find restored in us, the Image of the whole Trinity, imprinted at our creation; for by this Regeneration, we are adopted by the Father in the bloud of the Sonne by the sanctification of the holy Ghost. (*1624?*) 5:158–60

2. To Put on the Garment of Christ (Deut. 12:30)

We say in Logick, *Substantia non suscipit magis et minus*, Substantial and fundamental points of Religion (and obedience to Superiors is amongst those) do not ebb and flow; they binde all men, and at all times, and in all cases. [b]*Induite Dominum Jesum*, says the Apostle, *Put ye on the Lord Jesus*, and keep him on, put him not off again. Christ is not only the Stuff, but the Garment ready made; he will not be translated and turned, and put into new fashions, nor laid up in a Wardrobe, but put on all day, all the days of our life; though it rain, and rain blood; how foul soever any persecution make the day, we must keep on that Garment, the true profession of Christ Jesus; follow not these men in their severity, to exclude men from salvation in things that are not fundamental, nor in their facility to disguise and prevaricate in things that are. (*1622*) 4:142

3. Our Afflictions Are God's (Lam. 3:1)

Then is an Affliction properly *Gods Affliction*, when thou in thy *Conscience* canst impute it to none but God. When thou disorderest thy body with a *surfeit*, nature will submit to sicknesse; When thou wearest out thy selfe with *licentiousnesse*, the sin it self will induce infirmities; When thou transgressest any law of the State, the *Justice of the State* will lay hold upon thee. And for the Afflictions that fall upon thee in these cases, thou art able to say to thy selfe, that they would have falne upon thee, though there had been *no God*, or though God had had *no rod* about him, no anger in him; Thou knowest in particular, *why*, and *by whose*, or *by what means*, these Afflictions

b. Rom. 13:14.

light upon thee. But when thou shalt have thy Conscience clear towards such and such *men*, and yet those men shall goe about to oppresse thee, when thou labourest uprightly in thy calling, and yet doest not prosper, when thou studiest the Scriptures, hearkenest to Sermons, observest Sabbaths, desirest conferences, and yet receivest not satisfaction, but still remainest under the torture of scruples and anxieties, when thou art in S. *Pauls* case, [c]*Nihili conscius*, That thou knowest nothing by thy selfe, and yet canst not give thy selfe peace, Though all Afflictions upon Gods children, be from *him*, yet, take knowledge that *this* is from *him*, more intirely, and more immediately, and that God remembers something in thee, that thou hast forgot; And, as that fit of an Ague, or that pang of the Gout, which may take thee to day, is not necessarily occasioned by that which thou hast eaten to day, but may be the effect of some former disorder, so the affliction which lights upon thee in thine age, may be inflicted for the sinnes of thy youth. Thy affliction is *his*, The Lords; And the Lord is infinite, and comprehends all at once, and ever finds something in thee to correct, something that thou hast done, or something that thou wouldest have done, if the blessing of that correction had not restrained thee. And therefore, when thou canst not pitch thy affliction upon any *particular sinne*, yet make not thy selfe so just, as that thou make God unjust, whose Judgements may be unsearchable, [d]but they cannot be unjust. (*after 1624?*) 10:202–3

4. Mankind of One Blood (Ps. 38:4)

But if I have no interest in the sins of other men, by any occasion ministred by me, yet I cannot chuse but feel a weight, a burthen of a holy anguish, and compassion and indignation, because every one of these sins inflict a new wound upon my Saviour, when my Saviour says to him, that does but injure me, *Why persecutest thou me*, and feels the blow upon himselfe, shall not I say to him that wounds my Saviour, *Why woundest thou me*, and groane under the weight of my brothers sin, and my Fathers, my Makers, my Saviours wound? If a man of my blood, or allyance, doe a shamefull act, I am affected with it; If a man of my calling, or *profession*, doe a scandalous act, I feel my self concerned in his fault; God hath made all *mankinde* of *one blood*, and all *Christians* of *one calling*, and the sins of every man concern every man, both in that respect, that *I*, that is, *This nature*, is in that man that sins that sin; and *I*, that is, *This nature*, is in that Christ, who is wounded by that sin. (*1618*) 2:122

c. 1. Cor. 4:4. *d.* August[ine].

B. Redemption: The Role of Voice

1. Vocare: *Christ's Errand (Matt. 9:13)*

And then the Errand, and purpose for which he came, is *vocare*, he came *to call*: It is not, *Occurrere*, That he came to meet them, who were upon the way before; for no man had either disposition in himself, or faculty in himself, neither will nor power to rise and meet him, no nor so much as to wish that Christ would call him, till he did call him: He came not *occurrere*, to meet us; but yet he came not *cogere*, to compel us, to force us, but onely *vocare*, to call us, by his Word, and Sacraments, and Ordinances, and lead us so; and that's his errand, and purpose in coming. And from that, we shall come to the persons upon whom his coming works: where we have first a Negative, a fearful thing in Christs lips; and then an Affirmative, a blessed seal in his mouth: first, an Exclusive, a fearful banishment out of his Ark; and then an Inclusive, a blessed naturalization in his Kingdom: *Non justos, I came to call, not the righteous, but sinners*. And then lastly, we have, not as before, his general intention and purpose, To call; but the particular effect and operation of this calling upon the godly, it brings them *to repentance*. (*1626*) 7:144

2. God Gives His Voice to Those He Saves (Matt. 3:17)

And it is necessary to all us, to have this meanes of understanding and beleeving, to heare. Therefore God gives to all that shall be saved, *vocem*, his voyce. We consider two other wayes of imprinting the knowledge of God in man; first in a darke and weake way, the way of Nature, and the book of Creatures; and secondly, in that powerfull way, the way of Miracles. But these, and all between these, are uneffectuall without the Word. When *David* sayes of the Creatures, [e] *There is no speech nor language, where their voyce is not heard*, (the voyce of the Creature is heard over all) S. *Paul* commenting upon those words, says, [f] *They have heard, All the world hath heard*; but what? The voyce of the Creature; now that is true, so much all the world had heard then, and does heare still: But the *hearing* that S. *Paul* intends there, is such a hearing as begets *faith*, and that the voyce of Creature reaches not to. The voyce of the Creature alone, is but a faint voyce, a low voyce; nor any voyce, till the voyce of the Word inanimate it; for then when the Word of God hath taught us any mystery of our Religion, then the booke of Creatures illustrates, and establishes, and cherishes

e. Psal. 19:3.

f. Rom. 10:18.

that which we have received by faith, in hearing the Word: As a stick bears up, and succours a vine, or any plant, more precious then it selfe, but yet gave it not life at first, nor gives any nourishment to the root now: so the assistance of reason, and the voyce of the Creature, in the preaching of Nature, works upon our faith, but the roote, and the life is in the faith it selfe. (*1624*) 6:142–43

3. Saul's Cure: He Heard a Voice (Acts 9:4)

First, he affords him a call, *A voyce*. *Saul* could not see; Therefore he deales not upon him by visions. He gives a voyce; and a voyce that he might heare; God speaks often, when we doe not heare; He *heard it*, and *heard it saying*; Not a voyce only, but a distinct, and intelligible voyce; and *saying unto him*, that is, appliable to himselfe; and then, that that the voyce said to him, was, *Saul, Saul, why persecutest thou me?* We are unequall enemies, Thou seest I am too hard for thee, *Cur tu me?* why wilt thou, thou in this weakenesse oppose me? And then, we might be good friends, Thou seest I offer parly, I offer treaty, *Cur tu me?* Why wilt thou oppose me, me that declare such a disposition to be reconciled unto thee? In this so great a disadvantage on thy part, why wilt thou stirre at all? In this so great a peaceablenesse on my part, why wilt thou stirre against me? *Cur tu me? Why persecutest thou me?*

First then, God speakes: For, beloved, we are to consider God, not as he is in himselfe, but as he works upon us: The first thing that we can consider in our way to God, is his Word. Our Regeneration is by his Word; that is, by faith, which comes by hearing; [g]*The seed is the word of God*, sayes Christ himselfe; Even the seed of faith.

. . . .

Here then is the first step of *Sauls* cure, and of ours, That there was not onely a word, the Word, Christ himselfe, a Son of God in heaven, but a Voyce, the word uttered, and preached; Christ manifested in his Ordinance: *He heard a voyce*. (*1625*) 6:216–17

4. John Baptist: All Voice; Words and Deeds (James 2:12)

John Baptist was all voice, yet *John Baptist* was a fore-runner of Christ. The best words are but words, but they are the fore-runners of Deeds: but Christ himself, as he was God himself, is *Purus Actus*, all Action, all Doing. Comfortable words are good cordials; They revive the spirits, and they have the nature of such occasional physick:[1] but

1. Medicine taken for a particular occasion, whose value is limited or temporary.

g. Luke 8:11.

Deeds are our food, our dyet, and that that constantly nourishes us. [h]*Non verbo*, says the Apostle; Let us not love in word, nor in tongue; but in Deed, and in Truth. Not that we may not love in words; but that our Deeds are the true seals of that love, which was also love, when it was in words.

. . . .

The instrument and Organ of Nature was the eye; The Natural Man finds God in that he sees, in the Creature. The Organ of the Law, which exalted, and rectified Nature, was the Hand; *Fac hoc et vives*; perform the law, and thou shalt live. So also, the Organ of the Gospel is the Ear, for faith comes by hearing; But then the Organ of faith it self, is the Hand too; A Hand that lays hold upon the Merits of Christ, for my self; and a Hand that delivers me over to the Church of God, in a holy life, and exemplary Actions, for the edification of others. (*1628*) 8:341–43

5. Preaching and Calling (Matt. 9:13)

But Christs end being meerly spiritual, to constitute a Church, *Non venit Occurrere*, as he came not to meet man, man was not so forward; so he came not to compel man, to deal upon any that was so backward; for, *Venit vocare, He came to call.*

Now, this *calling*, implies a voice, as well as a Word; it is by the Word; but not by the Word read at home, though that be a pious exercise; nor by the word submitted to private interpretation; but *by the Word preached*, according to his Ordinance, and under the Great Seal, of his blessing upon his Ordinance. So that *preaching* is this *calling*; and therefore, as if Christ do appear to any man, in the power of a miracle, or in a private inspiration, yet he appears but in weakness, as in an infancy, till he speak, till he bring a man to the hearing of his voice, in a setled Church, and in the Ordinance of preaching: so how long soever Christ have dwelt in any State, or any Church, if he grow speechless, he is departing; if there be a discontinuing, or slackning of preaching, there is a danger of loosing Christ. *Adam* was not made in Paradise, but brought thither, called thither: the sons of *Adam* are not born in the Church, but called thither by Baptism; [i]*Non Nascimur sed re-nascimur Christiani*; No man is born a Christian, but called into that state by regeneration. And therefore, as the Consummation of our happiness is in that, that we shall be called at last, into the Kingdom of Glory, in the *Venite Benedicti, Come ye blessed, and enter into your Masters joy*. (*1626*) 7:157

h. 1. John 3:18.

i. August[ine].

C. The Uniqueness of Human Voice

1. Man's Name from "Crying" (Ps. 38:3)

But the first name, by which God called man in generall, *mankinde,* is *Ish,* [j]*Therefore shall a man leave his Father, etc.* And *Ish,* is but *a sonitu, a rugitu*: Man hath his name from *crying,* and the occasion of *crying, misery,* testified in his entrance into the world, for he is *born crying*; and our very Laws presume, that if he be alive, he will cry, and if he be not heard cry, conclude him to be born dead. (*1618*) 2:79

2. Vox Dicens *(Matt. 3:17)*

There must be something heard; for, take the largest Spheare, and compasse of all other kinds of proofes, for the mysteries of Religion, which can be proposed, Take it first, at the first, and weakest kinde of proofe, at the book of creatures, (which is but a faint knowledge of God, in respect of that knowledge, with which we must know him) And then, continue this first way of knowledge, to the last, and powerfullest proofe of all, which is the power of miracles, not this weake beginning, not this powerfull end, not this *Alpha* of Creatures, not this *Omega* of miracles, can imprint in us that knowledge, which is our saving knowledge, nor any other meanes then a voyce; for this knowing is beleeving, And, *how should they beleeve, except they heare?* sayes the Apostle. It must be *Vox, A voyce,* And *Vox de coelis, A voyce from heaven*: For, we have had *voces de terra,* voyces of men, who have indeed but diminished the dignity of the Doctrine of the Trinity, by going about to prove it by humane reason, or to illustrate it by weak and low comparisons; And we have had *voces de Inferis,* voyces from the Devill himselfe, in the mouthes of many Heretiques, blasphemously impugning this Doctrine; Wee have had *voces de profundis,* voyces fetched from the depth of the malice of the Devill, Heretiques; And *voces de medio,* voyces taken from the ordinary strength of Morall men, Philosophers; But this is *vox de Excelsis,* onely that voyce that comes from Heaven, belongs to us in this mystery: And then lastly, it is *vox dicens, a voyce saying,* speaking, which is proper to man, for nothing speaks but man; It is Gods voyce, but presented to us in the ministery of man; And this is our way; To behold, that is, to depart from our own blindnesse, and to behold a way, that is shewed us; but shewed us in the word, and in the word of God, and in that word of God, preached by man. (*1624*) 6:133–34

j. Gen. 2:24.

3. Vox Clamantis *(Ezek. 33:32)*

John Baptist hath other great names; even the name of *Baptist*, is a great name, when we consider whom he baptized; him, who baptized the Baptist himself, and all us, in his own blood. So is his name of *Preacher*, the fore-runner of Christ (for in that name he came before him, who was before the world:) so is his *Propheta*, that he was a Prophet, and then, more then a Prophet; and then, the greatest among the sons of women; these were great names, but yet the name that he chose, is *Vox clamantis, The voyce of him that cryes in the wilderness*. What names and titles soever we receive in the School, or in the Church, or in the State; if we lose our voice, we lose our proper name, our Christian name. But then, *John Baptists* name is not A voyce, Any voyce, but The voyce: in the Prophesie of *Esay*, in all the four Evangelists, constantly, The voyce. Christ is *verbum*. The word; not A word, but The word: the Minister is *Vox*, voyce; not A voyce, but The voyce, the voyce of that word, and no other; and so, he is a pleasing voyce, because he pleases him that sent him, in a faithfull executing of his Commission, and speaking according to his dictate; and pleasing to them to whom he is sent, by bringing the Gospel of Peace and Reparation to all wounded, and scattered, and contrite Spirits. (*1619*) 2:172

D. Resurrection: The Role of Voice

1. The Last Judgment (John 5:28, 29)

The benefit then in our Text, the Resurrection, is by him; but it is limited thus, It is by hearing him, *They that are in their Graves shall heare, etc*. So it is in the other Resurrection too, the spirituall resurrection, *v*. 25. There, they must *heare* him, that will live. In both resurrections, That in the Church, now, by Grace, And that in the Grave hereafter, by Power, it is said, *They shall heare him*. They shall, which seemes to imply a necessity, though not a coaction; But that necessity, not of equall force, not equally irresistible in both: In the Grave, *They shall*; Though they be dead, and senslesse as the dust, (for they are dust it selfe) though they bring no concurrence, no cooperation, *They shall heare*, that is, They shall not chuse but heare. In the other resurrection, which is, in the Church, by Grace, in Gods Ordinance, *They shall heare too*, that is, There shall be a voice uttered so, as that they may heare, if they will, but not whether they will or no, as in the other case, in the grave. Therefore when God expresses his gathering of his Church, in this world, it is [k]*Sibilabo et congregabo, I will hisse, or chirpe for them, and so gather them*: He whispers in the voyce of the Spirit, and he speaks a little louder, in the voice of a man; Let the man be a *Boanerges*, a Son of thunder, never so powerfull a speaker, yet no thunder is heard over all the world. But for the voyce that shall be heard at the Resurrection, [l]*He shall send his Angels, with a great sound of a Trumpet*; A great sound, such as may be made by a Trumpet, such as an Angell, all his Angels can make in a Trumpet, and more then all that, [m]*The Lord himselfe shall descend from Heaven*, and that, *with a shout, and with the voice of an Archangel*, that is, saies S. *Ambrose*, of Christ himselfe, *And in the Trumpet of God*, that is also, Christ himselfe.

So then, you have the Person, Christ; The meanes, A Voyce, And the powerfulnesse of that voyce, in the Name of an Archangell, which is named but once more in all the Scriptures: And therefore, let no man, that hath an holy anhelation and panting after the Resurrection, suspect that he shall sleepe in the dust, for ever; for, this is a voyce that will be heard, he must rise. Let no man, who because he hath made his course of life like a beast, would therefore be content his state in death might be like a beast too, hope that he shall sleepe in the dust, for ever, for this is a voice, that must be heard, *And all that heare shall come forth, they that have done good, etc.* (*1625*) 6:276–77

2. The Reintegrating Voice (1 Thess. 4:17)

[n]*The dead shall heare the voyce of the Son of God*, (sayes the Son of God himself) *and they that heare shall live*; And that is the voyce of our Text. It is here called a clamour, a vociferation, a shout, and varied by our Translators, and Expositors, according to the origination of the word, to be *clamor hortatorius*, and *suasorius*, and *jussorius*, A voyce that carries with it a penetration, (all shall heare it) and a perswasion, (all shall beleeve it, and be glad of it) and a power, a command, (all shall obey it.) Since that voyce at the Creation, *Fiat*, Let there be a world, was never heard such a voyce as this, *Surgite mortui*, Arise ye dead. That was spoken to that that was meerely nothing, and this to them, who in themselves shall have no cooperation, no concurrence to the hearing or answering this voyce.

The power of this voyce is exalted in that it is said to be the *voyce of the Archangel*. Though legions of Angels, millions of Angels shall be employed about the Resurrection, to recollect their scattered dust,

k. Zecha. 10:8.
l. Matt. 24:31.
m. 1. Thes. 4:16.
n. John 5:25.

and recompact their ruined bodies, yet those bodies so recompact, shall not be able to heare a voyce. They shall be then but such bodies, as they were when they were laid downe in the grave, when, though they were intire bodies, they could not heare the voice of the mourner. But this voyce of the Archangel shall enable them to heare; The Archangel shall re-infuse the severall soules into their bodies, and so they shall heare that voyce, *Surgite mortui*, Arise ye that were dead, and they shall arise. And here we are eased of that disputation, whether there be many Archangels, or no, for, if there be but one, yet this in our text, is he, for, it is not said, [o]In the voyce of *An Archangell*, but of *The Archangell*; if not the Onely, yet he who comprehends them all, and in whom they all consist, Christ Jesus.

And then, the power of this voyce is exalted to the highest in the last word, that it is, *Tuba Dei, The Trumpet of God*. For, that is an Hebraisme, and in that language, it constitutes a superlative, to adde the name of God to any thing. As in *Sauls* case, when *David* surprised him, in his dead sleepe, it is said, that [p]*Sopor Domini, The sleepe of the Lord was upon him*, that is, the heaviest, the deadest sleepe that could be imagined, so here, *The Trumpet of God* is the loudest voice that we conceive God to speake in.

. . . .

Yet thou must heare this voice of the Archangell in the Trumpet of God. The Trumpet of God is his loudest Instrument; and his loudest Instrument is his publique Ordinance in the Church; Prayer, Preaching, and Sacraments; Heare him in these; In all these; come not to heare him in the Sermon alone, but come to him in Prayer, and in the Sacrament too. For, except the voyce come in the Trumpet of God, (that is, in the publique Ordinance of his Church) thou canst not know it to be the voyce of the Archangell.

. . . .

And as the Apostle saies here, [q]This we say unto you, by the word of the Lord, that thus the last resurrection shall be accomplished by Christ himselfe, so, this we say to you, by the Word of the Lord, (by the harmony of all the Scriptures) thus, and no other way, By the pure word of God, delivered and applied by his publique Ordinance, by Hearing, and Beleeving, and Practising, under the Seales of the Church, the Sacraments, is your first resurrection from sin, by grace, accomplished. So have you then those three branches, which constitute our first part; That they that are dead before us, shall not be prevented by us, but they shall rise first; That they shall be raised by the

o. Colos. 1:16.
p. 1. Sam. 26:12.
q. ver. 15.

power of Christ, that is, the power of God in Christ; That that power, working to their resurrection, shall be declared in a mighty voyce, the voyce of the Archangell, in the Trumpet of God. And then, then when they who were formerly dead, are first raised, and raised by this Power, and this power thus declared, then shall we, we who shall be then alive and remaine, be wrought upon. (*1622?*) 4:69–72

6 *Human Personality and the Faculties of the Soul*

Introduction

In the early fifth century, St. Augustine wrote *De Trinitate,* an immensely important work that was to affect the course of Western theology and profoundly influence Donne's own thinking about human personality. According to Augustine (writing especially in book 8), the triune God (Father, Son, and Holy Spirit) is mirrored in the faculties of man as reason (understanding), memory, and will. Donne elaborates on this psychological analogy with the other trinities implicit in heaven, earth, and self: "We have found a *Trinity* in heaven"; and then the three witnesses of spirit, water, and blood (of preaching, baptism, and communion) make up a trinity on earth. The third trinity in ourselves is expressed by reason, memory, and will; but faith, hope, and charity regenerate and reeestablish "a new Trinity in us" (5:148–49). Thus we have a trinity of trinities—nine "witnesses" in all.

In the selections shown here, Donne continues to see and to describe everything in terms of trinities. From the Father (*Principium,* or the all powerful) proceeds the Son and the Holy Ghost. So also in human personality, understanding and will proceed from memory—"discourse and ratiocination," a kind of recollection akin to reason, the least corrupted and most rectifiable of man's capacities: "when the mind hath produced a thought, that mind . . . produce[s] a will"; then the understanding is clarified, "and that understanding leads our will. And nearer then this . . . we cannot goe, to the proceeding of the holy Ghost" (5:64–65). The Power of the Father, the Wisdom of the Son, and the Goodness (or Love) of the Holy Ghost are the particular qualities of the Deity that reflect themselves in personality. Much of what Donne says about the faculties of the soul is predicated on his seeing the mirror of God in the world of man; for knowledge precedes love, even as understanding precedes will: "It is impossible to love any thing till we know it: First our Understanding must present it as *Verum,* as a Knowne truth, and then our Will imbraces it as *Bonum,* as Good, and worthy to be loved" (8:222).

The human faculty on which Donne lays greatest stress is, of course, the memory, since it is the easiest to correct and to cultivate: "Truly the Memory is . . . the Holy Ghosts Pulpit that he [the preacher] preaches in. . . . The Memory is as the conclusion of a Syllogisme, which being inferred upon true propositions, cannot be denied: He that remembers Gods former blessings, concludes infallibly upon his future" (8:261–62). Donne concludes this point with firm emphasis: "Christ places the comfort of this Comforter, the Holy Ghost, in this, that he shall work upon that pregnant faculty, the Memory." Salvation itself is but the art of memory: the understanding "requires long and cleer instruction," and the will is "the blindest and boldest faculty" (2:235). Thus an ignorant man, or a blind man, has all the instruction he needs in the simple remembering of the mercies and goodness of God that are "new every morning" (2:74).

In the third section of this chapter, we see Donne make use of another common division of man into body, soul, and spirit. First of all, the body is described in terms of original sin, with its temptations of pride and idolatry. Donne distinguishes between the *natural* man whose gift from God is the eye, who *sees* God in the creature, and the *Christian* man whose gift is the ear, who *hears* God in His Word. But when we are "under water," or drowned in sin, then both sight and sound are perverted and give false report. The soul is subject to deprivation, too, when, beyond the carnality of the flesh, a "diseased" man comes to suspect God's mercy and ends in misery and despair. Donne aims to bring together body and soul in a compromise, for "*plenty* is a misery, and *mortification* is a misery too" (2:63–64). Here is a "riddling" condition, where enjoyment of the good things of this world may lead to "unwieldy flesh," and yet the very hunger and fasting the body needs may produce a life of Fridays, and a continuous Lent. The answer is to put off temptations and provocations steadily, and "continue in those means, which may advance our repentance." In one of his most eloquent passages, Donne commends God's love, which receives any soul that seeks a cure and does not merely "squeaze the wound of Christ Jesus" without letting the blood fall upon his own hurt.

But Donne's aim is to show how the different capacities of man may be brought together; and so we learn that man's spirit is that middle nature between his body and his soul. Preaching on the words of St. Paul (commonly called "the Apostle"), "For now is our salvation nearer then when we believed" (Rom. 13:11), Donne considers the three terms, salvation, nearness, and believing as central to a description of the bridging work of the spirit. Salvation has its internal work or operation in man by uniting and applying "the faculties of the soul to the organs of the body." Then there is the nearness, "which is the effectual working of Grace" (2:262), and its exaltation; having been brought to such a height of holiness, man is able at last to reach still further, even beyond belief. Finally, in that realm of "the souls bloud" (George Herbert's phrase in "Prayer I"), prayer—the aspiration of belief—is something understood. "The Image of God is imprinted in the soule," Donne says, "and that gives him his conformity to Angels" (5:355; and see "Aire and Angels" in the *Songs and Sonets*). While the three faculties of man can be studied separately, yet there is enough confusion among them to render distinction obscure, quite enough to "vex one's bones."

In the final section, on "Salvation and the Natural Faculties," Donne evokes the crown of glory that man shall at the last receive, when "I" (who speak for mankind) "the same body, and the same soul, shall be recompact again, and be identically, numerically, individually the same man" (3:109–10). In the kind of direct speech to his congregation that is frequent in the sermons, Donne declares that "I cannot say, you cannot say so perfectly, so entirely now, as at the Resurrection, *Ego*, I am here; I, body and soul; I, soul and faculties." These words come from the concluding passage, and they aptly describe man's potentialities amidst his present limitations. We have learned, or realized, that the understanding of man is limited before the incomprehensibleness of God in spite of his sacrifice, his search, and the willingness of God to speak in man's language through the Scriptures—and through the preacher of the Word. Yet growth in the knowledge of God is not progressive, but instantaneous: "God shall Create us all Doctors in a minute" (p. 174), and in that time, when the universal subject of knowledge is the knowledge of the glory of God, then even the Scriptures themselves shall be taken away, and the preacher shall have no more to speak.

This chapter on human capacity, personality, and limitation, in spite of its often spoken or implied celebration of reason (or rectified nature), and with its confusion of categories, moves to proclaim the mystical joy of seeing God face to face. Donne is like his much older contemporary Richard Hooker (1554–1600), whose influence is as unmistakable as it is also subtle. Throughout his vast work, *Of the Laws of Ecclesiastical Polity* (1593, 1597), even in the long stretches that appeal so strongly to reason in their detailed and technical analyses of religious disputes, there runs an abiding sense of devotion that qualifies the claims of reason and of all human authority. In book 5, for example, at the end of his discussion of Christ's presence in the Blessed Sacrament, Hooker passes beyond argument into prayer:

> What these elementes are in them selves it skilleth not, it is enough that to me which take them they are the bodie and blood of Christ, his promise in witnes hereof sufficeth, his word he knoweth which way to accomplish, why should any cogitation possesse the minde of a faithfull communicant but this, *O my God thou art true, O my soule thou art happie?* (ed. W. Speed Hill, Cambridge, Mass., 1977, 5.67.12 [in Folger Library edition of the *Works,* 2:343])

Donne expresses a similar joy as he goes out, on behalf of us all, to "receive the crown of glory which shall not fade."

A. Trinitarian Theory

1. Three Trinities: Earth, Heaven, Self (1 John 5:7, 8)

If we remaine vessells of anger, and of dishonour still, we are under the [a]*vae vobis Hypocritis: woe unto you Hypocrites, that make cleane onely the outside of your Cuppes and Platters.* That baptize, and wash your owne, and your childrens bodies, but not their mindes with instructions. When we shall come to say [b]*Docuisti in plateis, we have heard thee preach in our streets,* we have continued our hearing of thy Word, when we say *Manducavimus coram te,* we have eate in thy presence, at thy table, yea [c]*Manducavimus te,* we have eaten thee thy selfe, yet for all this outward show of these three witnesses, of *Spirit,* and *Water,* and *bloud, Preaching,* and *Baptisme* and *Communion,* we shall heare that fearfull disclaiming from Christ Jesus, *Nescio vos,* I know not whence you are. But these witnesses, he will always heare, if they testifie for us, that Jesus is come unto us; for the *Gospell,* and the *preaching* thereof, is as the deed that conveys *Jesus* unto us; the *water,* the *baptisme,* is as the *Seale,* that assures it; and the *bloud,* the *Sacrament,* is the *delivery* of Christ into us; and this is *Integritas Jesu,* the entire, and full possession of him.

To this purpose therefore, as we have found a *Trinity* in heaven, and a *Trinity* in earth, so we must make it up a Trinity of Trinities, and finde a *third Trinity* in our selves. God created one *Trinity* in us; (the observation, and the enumeration is Saint *Bernards*) which are those *three faculties* of our soule, the *reason,* the *memory,* the *will;* That Trinity in us, by another Trinity too, (by *suggestion* towards sin, by *delight*

a. Mat. 23:25.
b. Luke 13:26.
c. Ibid.

in sinne, by *consent* to sinne) is fallen into a third Trinity; The *memory* into a weaknesse, that that comprehends not *God*, it glorifies him not for benefits received; The *reason* to a blindenesse, that that discernes not what is *true*; and the *will* to a perversnesse, that that wishes not what's *good*; But the goodnesse of God, by these three witnesses on earth regenerates, and reestablishes a new Trinity in us, *faith*, and *hope*, and *charity*; Thus farre that devout Man carries it; And if this new Trinity, *faith*, and *hope*, and *charity*, witnesse to us *Integritatem Christi*, all the worke of Christ, If *my faith* testifie to me, that Christ is sealed to my soule; and my *hope*, testifie, that at the Resurrection, I shall have a perfect fruition in soule, and body, of that glory which he purchased for every beleever; and my *charity* testifies to the world, that I labour to make sure that salvation, by a good life, then there's a *Trinity* of *Trinities*, and the *six* are made *nine* witnesses: There are three in heaven that testifie that this is done for all Mankinde, Three in the Church that testifie, this may be done for me, and three in my soule, that testifie, that all this is applied to me; and then the verdict, and the Judgement must necessarily goe for me. (*1624?*) 5:148–49

2. The Father: Principium *and Power (Ps. 2:12)*

Though those three Attributes of God, Power, and Wisedome, and Goodnesse, be all three in all the three Persons of the Trinity, (for they are all (as we say in the Schoole) *Co-omnipotentes*, they have all a joynt-Almightinesse, a joynt-Wisdome, and a joynt-Goodnesse) yet, because the Father is *Principium*, The roote of all, Independent, not proceeding from any other, as both the other Persons do, and Power, and Soveraignty best resembles that Independency, therefore we attribute Power to the Father: And because the Son proceeds *Per modum intellectus*, (which is the phrase that passes through the Fathers, and the Schoole) That as our understanding proceeds from our reasonable soule, so the second Person, the Son, proceeds from the Father, therefore we attribute Wisdome to the Son: And then, because the Holy Ghost is said to proceed *Per modum voluntatis*,[1] That as our soule (as the roote) and our understanding, proceeding from that soule, produce our will, and the object of our will, is evermore *Bonum*, that which is good in our apprehension, therefore we attribute to the Holy Ghost, Goodnesse. (*1621?*) 3:327–28

1. Literally, *Per modum intellectus* means in a discerning (ratiocinative) mode, *Per modum voluntatis* in a voluntary mode. Donne alludes to the Trinitarian doctrine of the Western Church, which distinguishes the Holy Ghost (or Spirit) from the two persons of the Father and the Son, whence proceeds the spiration of the Holy Ghost. Donne expands his thinking on this point in the following passage.

3. Proceeding: Creation, Son, Holy Ghost (Rom. 8:16)

But by what manner comes he [the Holy Ghost] from them [the Father and Son]? By proceeding. That is a very generall word; for, Creation is proceeding, and so is Generation too: Creatures proceed from God, and so doth God the Son proceed from God the Father; what is this proceeding of the holy Ghost, that is not Creation, nor Generation? [d]*Exponant cur et quomodo Spiritus pulsat in arteriis, et tum in processionem Spiritus sancti inquirant:* When they are able clearly, and with full satisfaction to tell themselves how and from whence that spirit proceeds, which beats in their pulse, let them inquire how this Spirit proceeds from the Father and the Sonne. And let them think till they be mad, and speak till they be hoarce, and reade till they be blind, and write till they be lame, they must end with S. *Augustine, Distinguere inter Processionem, et Generationem, nescio, non valeo, non sufficio,* I cannot distinguish, I cannot assigne a difference between this Generation, and this Proceeding. We use to say, they differ *principio,* That the Son is from the Father alone, the holy Ghost from both: but when this is said, that must be said too, That both Father and Son are but one beginning. We use to say, They differ *ordine,* because the Son is the second, and the holy Ghost the third person; but the second was not before the third in time, nor is above him in dignity.

There is *processio corporalis,* such a bodily proceeding, as that that which proceeds is utterly another thing then that from which it proceeds: frogs proceed (perchance) of ayre, and mise of dust, and worms of carkasses; and they resemble not that ayre, that dust, those carkasses that produced them. There is also *processio Metaphysica,* when thoughts proceed out of the minde; but those thoughts remaine still in the mind within, and have no separate subsistence in themselves: And then there is *processio Hyperphysica,* which is this which we seek and finde in our soules, but not in our tongues, a proceeding of the holy Ghost so from Father and Son, as that he remaines a subsistence alone, a distinct person of himselfe. This is as far as the Schoole can reach, *Ortu, qui relationis est, non est a se; Actu, qui personae est, per se subsistit:* Consider him in his proceeding, so he must necessarily have a relation to another, Consider him actually in his person, so he subsists of himselfe. And *De modo,* for the manner of his proceeding, we need, we can say but this, As the Son proceeds *per modum intellectus,* (so as the mind of man conceives a thought) so the holy Ghost proceeds *per modum voluntatis;* when the mind hath produced a thought,

d. Nazianz[en].

that mind, and that discourse and ratiocination produce a will; first our understanding is setled, and that understanding leads our will. And nearer then this (though God knows this be far off) we cannot goe, to the proceeding of the holy Ghost. (*1622?*) 5:64–65

4. Love as the Holy Ghost (Prov. 22:11)

Love, in Divinity, is such an attribute, or such a notion, as designs to us one person in the Trinity; and that person who communicates, and applies to us, the other two persons, that is, *The Holy Ghost*: So that, as there is no *power*, but with relation to the *Father*, nor *wisdom* but with relation to the *Son*, so there should be no *love* but in the *Holy Ghost*, from whom comes this pureness of heart, and consequently the love of it necessarily: For, the love of this pureness is part of this pureness it self, and no man hath it, except he love it. All love which is placed upon lower things, admits satiety; but this love of this pureness, always grows, always proceeds: It does not onely file off the rust of our hearts, in purging us of old habits, but proceeds to a daily polishing of the heart, in an exact watchfulness, and brings us to that brightness, [e] *Ut ipse videas faciem in corde, et alii videant cor in facie*, That thou maist see thy face in thy heart, and the world may see thy heart in thy face; indeed, that to both, both heart and face may be all one: Thou shalt be a Looking-glass to thy self, and to others too.

The highest degree of other love, is the love of woman: Which love, when it is rightly placed upon one woman, it is dignified by the Apostle with the highest comparison, [f] *Husbands love your wives, as Christ loved his Church:* And God himself forbad not that this love should be great enough to change natural affection, [g] *Relinquet patrem*, (for this, a man shall leave his Father) yea, to change nature it self, *caro una*, two shall be one. Accordingly *David* expresses himself so, in commemoration of *Jonathan*, [h] *Thy love to me was wonderful, passing the love of women:* A love above that love, is wonderful. (*1617*) 1:199

5. Goodness: The Holy Ghost (Matt. 12:31)

Goodnesse is the Attribute of the Holy Ghost; If you have Greatness, you may seeme to have some of the Father, for Power is his: If you have Wisdome, you may seeme to have some of the Son, for that is his: If you have Goodnesse, you have the Holy Ghost, who shall lead you into all truth. And Goodnesse is, To be good and easie in receiving his impressions, and good and constant in retaining them, and good and diffusive in deriving them upon others: To embrace the Gospel, to

e. Augustine.
f. Ephes. 5:25.
g. Gen. 2:24.
h. 2. Sam. 1:26.

hold fast the Gospel, to propagate the Gospel, this is the goodnesse of the Holy Ghost. And to resist the entrance of the Gospel, to abandon it after we have professed it, to forsake them, whom we should assist and succour in the maintenance of it, This is to depart from the goodnesse of the Holy Ghost: and by these sins against him, to come too neare the sin, the irremissible sin, in which the calamities of this world shall enwrap us, and deliver us over to the everlasting condemnation of the next. (*1623?*) 5:95

6. The Holy Ghost: Christ's Ambassador and Will (John 16:8, 9, 10, 11)

And there is our first comfort, in knowing that Christ is God; for, he were an Intruder for that which is past, no Redeemer, he were a weak Saviour for the future, an insufficient Mediator, a silenced Advocate, and a Judge that might be misinformed, if he were not God. And though he were God, he might be all these to my discomfort, if there were not a holy Ghost to make all these offices comfortable unto me. To be a Redeemer and not a Saviour, is but to pay my debts, and leave me nothing to live on. To be a Mediator, a person capable by his composition of two natures, to intercede between God and man, and not to be my Advocate, is but to be a good Counsellor, but not of counsell with me; To be a Judge of quick and dead, and to proceed out of outward evidence, and not out of his bosome mercy, is but an acceleration of my conviction; I were better lie in Prison still, then appeare at that Assize; better lye in the dust of the grave for ever, then come to that judgement. But, as there is *Mens in anima,* There is a minde in the soule, and every man hath a soule, but every man hath not a minde, that is, a Consideration, an Actuation, an Application of the faculties of the soule to particulars; so there is *Spiritus in Spiritu,* a Holy Ghost in all the holy offices of Christ, which offices, being, in a great part, directed upon the whole world, are made comfortable to me, by being, by this holy Spirit, turned upon me, and appropriated to me; for so, even that name of Christ, which might most make me afraid, The name of Judge, becomes a comfort to me. To this purpose does S. *Basil* call the holy Ghost, [i] *Verbum Dei, quia interpres filii:* The Son of God is the word of God, because he manifests the Father, and the Holy Ghost is the word of God, because he applies the Son. Christ comes with that loud Proclamation, [j] *Ecce auditum fecit,* Behold the Lord hath proclaimed it, to the end of the world, *Ecce Salvator,* and *Ecce Merces,* Behold his Salvation, Behold thy Reward, (This is his publication in the manifest Ordinances of the Church) And then the Holy Ghost whispers to thy soule, as thou standest in the Congrega-

i. Basil.

j. Esay 62:11.

tion, in that voyce that he promises, [k]*Sibilabo populum meum,* I will hisse, I will whisper to my people by soft and inward inspirations. Christ came to tell us all, [l]*That to as many as received him, he gave power to become the Sons of God,* The Holy Ghost comes to tell thee, that thou art one of them. The Holy Ghost is therefore *Legatus,* and *Legatum Christi,* He is Christs Ambassadour sent unto us, and he is his Legacy bequeathed unto us by his Will; his Will made of force by his death, and proved by his Ascension. (*1625?*) 6:314–15

B. The Mirror of the Trinity in Personality

1. Power, Wisdom, Goodness: Memory, Understanding, Will (Gen. 1:26)

In Nature then, man, that is, the soule of man hath this Image of God, of God considered in his Unity, intirely, altogether, in this, that this soule is made of nothing, proceeds of nothing. All other creatures are made of that pre-existent matter, which God had made before, so were our bodies too; But our soules of nothing. Now, not to be made at all, is to be God himselfe: Onely God himselfe was never made. But to be made of nothing; to have no other parent but God, no other element but the breath of God, no other instrument but the purpose of God, this is to be the Image of God. For this is nearest to God himselfe, who was never made at all, to be made of nothing. And then man, (considered in nature) is otherwise the nearest representation of God too. For the steppes, which we consider are four; First, *Esse,* Beeing; for some things have onely a beeing, and no life, as stones: Secondly, *Vivere,* Living; for some things have life, and no sense, as Plants: and then, thirdly, *Sentire,* Sense; for some things have sense, and no understanding. Which understanding and reason, man hath with his Beeing, and Life, and Sense; and so is in a nearer station to God, then any other creature, and a livelier Image of him, who is the root of Beeing, then all they, because man onely hath all the declarations of Beeings.

. . . .

For as there are three Persons in the Essence of God: so there are three faculties in the Soule of man. The Attributes, and some kind of specification of the Persons of the Trinity are, Power to the Father, Wisedome to the Sonne, and Goodnesse to the holy Ghost. And the three faculties of the Soule have the Images of these three.

. . . .

So then in this first naturall faculty of the soule, the Understanding, stands the Image of the first Person, the Father, Power: and in the sec-

k. Zach. 10:8. *l.* John 1:12.

ond faculty which is the Will, is the Image, the Attribute of the second Person, the Sonne, which is Wisdome: for wisdome is not so much in knowing, in understanding, as in electing, in choosing, in assenting. No man needs goe out of himselfe, nor beyond his owne legend, and the history of his owne actions for examples of that, that many times we know better, and choose ill wayes. Wisdome is in choosing, in Assenting. And then, in the third faculty of the soule, the Memory, is the Image of the third person, the holy Ghost, that is, Goodnesse. For to remember, to recollect our former understanding, and our former assenting, so far as to doe them, to Crowne them with action, that's true goodnesse. The office, that Christ assignes to the holy Ghost, and the goodnesse, which he promises in his behalfe is this, [m]that he shall bring former things to our remembrance. The wiseman places all goodnesse in this faculty, the memory: properly nothing can fall into the memory, but that which is past, and yet he says, [n]*Whatsoever thou takest in hand, remember the end, and thou shalt never doe amisse.* The end cannot be yet come, and yet we are bid to remember that. *Visus per omnes sensus recurrit,* says Saint *Augustine.* As all senses are called sight, in the Scriptures, (for there is *Gustate Dominum,* and *Audite,* and *Palpate*; Taste the Lord, and heare the Lord, and feele the Lord, and still the *Videte,* is added, taste, and see the Lord) so all goodnesse is in remembring, all goodnesse, (which is the Image of the holy Ghost) is in bringing our understanding and our assenting into action.

. . . .

The attribute of the first Person, the Father, is Power, and none but a Christian hath power over those great Tyrants of the world, Sinne, Satan, Death, and Hell. For thus my Power accrues and growes unto me. First, [o]*Possum Judicare,* I have a Power to Judge; a judiciary, a discretive power; a power to discerne between a naturall accident, and a Judgement of God, and will never call a Judgement, an accident; and between an ordinary occasion of conversation and a tentation of Satan. [p]*Possum judicare,* and then *Possum resistere,* which is another act of power. When I finde it to be a tentation, I am able to resist it: and [q]*Possum stare,* (which is another) I am able, not onely to withstand, but to stand out this battell of tentations to the end; And then [r]*Possum capere,* that which Christ proposes for a tryall of his Disciples, Let him, that is able to receive it, receive it, I shall have power to receive the gift of continency, against all tentations of that kinde. Bring it to the highest act of power, that with which Christ tryed his

m. Joh. 14:26.
n. Ecclus. 7:36.
o. 1. Cor. 6:55.
p. Ephe. 6:13.
q. Ibid.
r. Mat. 19:12.

strongest Apostles, [s]*Possum bibere calicem,* I shall be able to drinke of Christs Cup; even to drinke his bloud, and be the more innocent for that, and to powre out my bloud, and be the stronger for that. [t]*In Christo omnia possum,* there's the fulness of Power, in Christ I can doe all things, I can want, or I can abound, I can live, or I can die. And yet there is an extension of Power, beyond all this, in this [u]*Non possum peccare,* being borne of God in Christ, I cannot sinne. This that seemes to have a name of impotence, *Non possum,* I cannot, is the fullest omnipotence of all, I cannot sinne; not sinne to death; not sinne with a desire to sinne; not sinne, with a delight in sinne; but that tentation, that overthrowes another, I can resist, or that sinne, which being done, casts another into desperation, I can repent. And so I have the Image of the first Person, the Father, in Power.

The Image of the second Person, whose Attribute is Wisdome, I have in this, that Wisdome being the knowledge of this world, and the next, I embrace nothing in this world, but as it leads me to the next. For, thus my wisdome, my knowledge growes. First, [v]*Scio cui credidi,* I know whom I have beleeved in: I have not mislaid my foundation; my foundation is Christ; and then [w]*Scio non moriturum;* my foundation cannot sinke, I know that [x]*Christ being raised from the dead, dies no more;* againe *Scio quod desideret Spiritus,* I know what my spirit, enlightened by the Spirit of God, desires; I am not transported with illusions, and singularities of private spirits. And as in the Attribute of Power, we found an omnipotence in a Christian, so in this, there is an omniscience, [y]*Scimus, quia omnem Scientiam habemus;* there's all together; *We know that we have all knowledge,* for all Saint *Pauls* universall knowledge was but this, *Jesum Crucifixum,* [z]*I determined not to know any thing, save Jesus Christ, and him crucified;* and then, the way by which he would proceed, and take degrees in this Wisdome, was *Stultitia praedicandi,* the way that God had ordained, [a]when the world by Wisedome knew not God, it pleased God by the foolishnesse of preaching to save them that beleeve. These then are the steps of Christian Wisedome, my foundation is Christ, of Christ I enquire no more, but fundamentall doctrines, him Crucified, and this I apply to my selfe, by his ordinance of Preaching. And in this wisdome, I have the Image of the Second Person.

And then, of the third also in this, that his Attribute beeing Goodnesse, I, as a true Christian, call nothing good, that conduces not to

s. Matt. 20:22.
t. Phil. 4:13.
u. 1. John 3:9.
v. 2. Tim. 1:12.
w. Rom. 6:9.
x. 8:27.
y. 1. Cor. 8:1.
z. 2:2.
a. 1:21.

the glory of God in Christ Jesus, nor any thing ill, that drawes me not from him. Thus I have an expresse Image of his Goodnesse, that [b]*Omnia cooperantur in bonum*, all things worke together for my good, if I love God. I shall thanke my fever, blesse my poverty, praise my oppressor, nay thanke, and blesse, and praise, even some sinne of mine, which by the consequences of that sinne, which may be shame, or losse, or weakenesse, may bring me to a happy sense of all my former sinnes; and shall finde it to have been a good fever, a good poverty, a good oppression, yea a good sinne. [c]*Vertit in bonum*, says *Joseph* to his brethren, you thought evill, but God meant it unto good; and I shall have the benefit of my sinne, according to his transmutation, that is, though I meant ill, in that sinne, I shall have the good, that God meant in it. [d]*There is no evill in the City, but the Lord does it*; But, if the Lord doe it, it cannot be evill to me. [e]I beleeve that I shall see *Bona Dei*, the goodnesse of the Lord, in the land of the living, that's in heaven; but *David* speakes also of *Signum in bonum*, shew me a token of good, and God will shew me a present token of future good, an inward infallibility, that this very calamity shall be beneficiall, and advantageous unto me. And so, as in Nature I have the Image of God, in my whole soule, and of all the three Persons, in the three faculties thereof, the Understanding, the Will, and the Memory, so in Grace, in the Christian Church, I have the same Images, of the Power of the Father, of the Wisedome of the Sonne, of the Goodnesse of the holy Ghost, in my Christian profession: And all this we shall have in a better place, then Paradise, where we considered it in nature, and a better place then the Church, as it is Militant, where we considered it in grace, that is, in the kingdome of heaven, where we consider this Image in glory. (*1629*) 9:82–89

2. Knowledge Precedes Love (1 Cor. 13:12)

The first act of the will, is love, sayes the Schoole; for till the will love, till it would have something, it is not a will. But then, [f]*Amare nisi nota non possumus*; It is impossible to love any thing till we know it: First our Understanding must present it as *Verum*, as a Knowne truth, and then our Will imbraces it as *Bonum*, as Good, and worthy to be loved. Therefore the Philosopher[2] concludes easily, as a thing that admits no contradiction, That naturally, all men desire to know, that they may love. But then, as the addition of an honest man, varies

2. Aristotle.

b. Rom. 8:28.
c. Gen. 50:20.
d. Amos 3:6.
e. Psal. 27:13.
f. Aug[ustine].

the signification, with the profession, and calling of the man, (for he is an honest man at Court, that oppresses no man with his power; and at the Exchange he is the honest man, that keeps his word; and in an Army, the Valiant man is the honest man) so the Addition of learned and understanding, varies with the man: The Divine, the Physitian, the Lawyer are not qualified, nor denominated by the same kinde of learning. But yet, as it is for honesty, there is no honest man at Court, or Exchange, or Army, if he beleeve not in God; so there is no knowledge in the Physitian, nor Lawyer, if he know not God. Neither does any man know God, except he know him so, as God hath made himselfe known, that is, *In Christ*. Therfore, as S. *Paul* desires to know nothing else, so let no man pretend to know any thing, but *Christ Crucified*; that is, Crucified for him, made his. In the eighth verse of this Chapter he sayes, *Prophesie shall faile, and Tongues shall faile, and Knowledge shall vanish*; but this knowledge of God in Christ made mine, by being Crucified for me, shall dwell with me for ever. And so from this generall consideration, All sight is blindnesse, all knowledge is ignorance, but of God, we passe to the particular Consideration of that twofold sight and knowledge of God expressed in this Text, *Now we see through a glasse, etc.*

First then we consider, (before we come to our knowledge of God) our sight of God in this world, and that is, sayes our Apostle, *In speculo, we see as in a glasse*. But how doe we see in a glasse? Truly, that is not easily determined. The old Writers in the Optiques said, That when we see a thing in a glasse, we see not the thing itselfe, but a representation onely; All the later men say, we doe see the thing it selfe, but not by direct, but by reflected beames. It is a uselesse labour for the present, to reconcile them. This may well consist with both, That as that which we see in a glasse, assures us, that such a thing there is, (for we cannot see a dreame in a glasse, nor a fancy, nor a Chimera) so this sight of God, which our Apostle sayes we have *in a glasse*, is enough to assure us, that a God there is. (*1628*) 8:222–23

3. Memory: The Pulpit of the Holy Ghost (John 14:26)

They had wont to call Pictures in the Church,[3] the lay-mans book, because in them, he that could not reade at all, might reade much. The ignorantest man that is, even he that cannot reade a Picture, even a blinde man, hath a better book in himself; In his own memory he may reade many a history of Gods goodnesse to him. *Quid ab initio*, How it was in the beginning, is Christs Method; To determine things according to former precedents; And truly the Memory is oftner the

3. Church windows.

Holy Ghosts Pulpit that he preaches in, then the Understanding. How many here would not understand me, or not rest in that which they heard, if I should spend the rest of this houre in repeating, and reconciling that which divers authors have spoken diversly of the manner of Christs presence in the Sacrament, or the manner of Christs descent into Hell, or the manner of the concurrence, and joynt-working of the grace of God, and the free-will of man, in mens actions? But is there any man amongst us that is not capable of this Catechisme, Remember to morrow but those good thoughts which you have had within this houre, since you came hither now: Remember at your last houre, to be but as good as you are this minute; I would scarce ask more in any mans behalf, then that he would alwayes be as good, as at some times he is; If he would never sink below himself, I would lesse care, though he did not exceed himself: If he would remember his own holy purposes at best, he would never forget God; If he would remember the comfort he had in having overcome such a tentation yesterday, he would not be overcome by that tentation to day. The Memory is as the conclusion of a Syllogisme, which being inferred upon true propositions, cannot be denied: He that remembers Gods former blessings, concludes infallibly upon his future. Therefore Christ places the comfort of this Comforter, the Holy Ghost, in this, that he shall work upon that pregnant faculty, the Memory; *He shall bring* things *to your remembrance*; And then, *Omnia, All those things which I have said unto you.* (*1628*) 8:261–62

4. Memory and Salvation (Ps. 38:3)

That plurall word *nos*, which was used by God, in the making of Man, when God said *Faciamus, Let us, us make man, according to our image*, as it intimates a plurality, a concurrence of all the Trinity in our making, so doth it also a *plurality in that image of God*, which was then imprinted in us; As God, one *God* created us, so wee have a soul, *one soul*, that represents, and is some image of that one God; As the three Persons of the *Trinity* created us, so we have, in our one soul, a *threefold impression* of that image, and, as Saint *Bernard* calls it, *A trinity from the Trinity*, in those *three faculties* of the soul, the *Understanding*, the *Will*, and the *Memory*.

. . . .

It was a *seal* upon a *seal*, a seal of *confirmation*, it was a *sacrament* upon a *sacrament*, when in instituting the *sacrament* of his *body and his bloud*, Christ presented it so, [g]*Doe this in remembrance of me. Memorare novissima*, remember the *last* things, and *fear* will keep

g. Luc. 22:19.

thee from sinning; *Memorare praeterita*, remember the *first* things, what God hath done for thee, and *love*, (love, which, mis-placed, hath transported thee upon many sins) love will keep thee from sinning. *Plato* placed *all learning* in the memory; wee may place *all Religion* in the memory too: All knowledge, that seems new to day, says *Plato*, is but a remembring of *that*, which your soul knew before. All instruction, which we can give you to day, is but the remembring you of the mercies of God, which have been *new every morning*. Nay, he that hears no Sermons, he that reads no Scriptures, hath the Bible without book; He hath a *Genesis* in his *memory*; he cannot forget his *Creation*; He hath an *Exodus* in his memory; he cannot forget that God hath delivered him, from some kind of *Egypt*, from some oppression; He hath a *Leviticus* in his memory; hee cannot forget, that God hath proposed to him some Law, some rules to be observed. He hath *all* in his memory, even to the *Revelation*; God hath *revealed* to him, *even at midnight alone*, what shall be his portion, in the next world; And if he dare but remember that nights communication between God and him, he is well-near learned enough. There may be enough in *remembring our selves*; but sometimes, that's the hardest of all; many times we are farthest off from our selves; most forgetfull of our selves. It was a narrow enlargement, it was an addition that diminished the sense, when our former Translators added that word, *themselves*; [h] *All the world shall remember themselves*; there is no such particularity, as *themselves*, in that text; But it is onely, as our later Translators have left it, *All the world shall remember*, and no more;[4] Let them remember what they will, what they can, let them but remember thoroughly, and then as it follows there, *They shall turn unto the Lord, and all the kindreds of the Nations shall worship him*. Therefore *David* makes *that* the key into this Psalme; *Psalmus ad Recordationem*, A *Psalm for Remembrance*. (*1618*) 2:72–74

5. Memory: The Way to God (Eccles. 12:1)

Here then the holy-Ghost takes the neerest way to bring a man to God, by awaking his memory; for, for the understanding, that requires long and cleer instruction; and the will requires an instructed understanding before, and is in it self the blindest and boldest faculty; but if the memory doe but fasten upon any of those things which God hath

4. The reference is to Coverdale, whose translation of the Psalms (1535) is retained in the Book of Common Prayer (1549), and to the Geneva Bible (1559, 1560), on the one hand, and to the King James translation (the "Authorized Version," 1603), on the other.

h. Ps. 22:27.

done for us, it is the neerest way to him. Remember therefore, and remember now, though the Memory be placed in the hindermost part of the brain, defer not thou thy remembring to the hindermost part of thy life, but doe that now *in die*, in the day, whilst thou hast light, now *in diebus*, in the days, whilst God presents thee many lights, many means; and *in diebus juventutis*, in the days of thy youth, of strength, whilst thou art able to doe that which thou purposest to thy self; And as the word imports, *Bechurotheica, in diebus Electionum tuarum*, in the dayes of thy choice, whilst thou art able to make thy choyce, whilst the Grace of God shines so brightly upon thee, as that thou maist choose the way, and so powerfully upon thee, as that thou maist walke in that way. Now, *in this day*, and *in these dayes* Remember first the Creator, That all these things which thou laborest for, and delightest in, were created; made of nothing; and therfore thy memory looks not far enough back, if it stick only upon the Creature, and reach not to the Creator, Remember the Creator, and remember thy Creator; and in that, first that he made thee, and then what he made thee; He made thee of nothing, but of that nothing he hath made thee such a thing as cannot return to nothing, but must remain for ever; whether happy or miserable, that depends upon thy *Remembring thy Creator now in the dayes of thy youth*.

. . . .

And therefore God in giving the law, works upon no other faculty but this, [i] *I am the Lord thy God which brought thee out of the land of Egypt*; He only presents to their memory what he had done for them. And so in delivering the Gospel in one principal seal thereof, the sacrament of his body, he recommended it only to their memory, *Do this in remembrance of me*. This is the faculty that God desires to work upon; And therefore if thine understanding cannot reconcile differences in all Churches, if thy will cannot submit it self to the ordinances of thine own Church, go to thine own memory; for as St. *Bernard* calls that the stomach of the soul, we may be bold to call it the Gallery of the soul, hanged with so many, and so lively pictures of the goodness and mercies of thy God to thee, as that every one of them shall be a catachism to thee, to instruct thee in all thy duties to him for those mercies: And as a well made, and well placed picture, looks alwayes upon him that looks upon it; so shall thy God look upon thee, whose memory is thus contemplating him, and shine upon thine understanding, and rectifie thy will too.

. . . .

i. Exod. 20[:2].

He created thee, *ex nihilo*,[5] he gave thee a being, there's matter of exaltation, and yet all this from nothing; thou wast worse then a worm, there's matter of humiliation; but he did not create thee *ad nihilum*, to return to nothing again, and there's matter for thy consideration, and study, how to make thine immortality profitable unto thee; for it is a deadly immortality, if thy immortality must serve thee for nothing but to hold thee in immortal torment. To end all, that being which we have from God shall not return to nothing, nor the being which we have from men neither. As St. *Bernard* sayes of the Image of God in mans soul, *uri potest in gehenna, non exuri*, That soul that descends to hell, carries the Image [of] God in the faculties of that soul thither, but there that Image can never be burnt out, so those Images and those impressions, which we have received from men, from nature, from the world, the image of a Lord, the image of a Counsailor, the image of a Bishop, shall all burn in Hell, and never burn out; not only these men, but these offices are not to return to nothing; but as their being from God, so their being from man, shal have an everlasting being, to the aggravating of their condemnation. And therefore *remember thy Creator*, who, as he is so, by making thee of nothing, so he will ever be so, by holding thee to his glory. (*1619*) 2:235, 237, 247

C. Body, Soul, and Spirit

1. Original Sin (Gen. 17:24)

Tu qui vas figuli,[6] sayes the Apostle; whensoever any disputation against a commandement of God, arises in Gods children, the Spirit of God smothers that spirit of Rebellion with that, *Tu qui vas figuli*, wilt thou who art but the vessell, dispute with the potter, that fashioned thee? If *Abraham* had any such doubts, of a *frivolousnesse* in so base a seale, of an *obscenity* in so foule a seale, of an *incommodiousnesse* in so troublesome a seale, of a *needlesnesse* in so impertinent a seale; if he had these doubts, no doubt but his forwardnesse in obeying God, did quickly oppose these reasons to those, and overcome them: That *that* part of the body is the most rebellious part; and that therefore, onely that part *Adam* covered, out of shame, for all the other parts he could rule: [j]*Ad hominis inobedientiam redarguendam*,

5. That is, *creatio ex nihilo*, the doctrine which teaches that God created everything, including man, out of nothing; but before the creation, according to medieval and Scholastic theology, things existed as ideas in the mind of God.
6. See Rom. 9:20–21.

j. August[ine].

sua inobedientia quodammodo caro testimonium perhibet, to reproach Mans rebellion to *God, God* hath left one part of Mans body, to rebell against him; for though the seeds of this rebellion be dispersed through all the body, yet, *In illa parte magis regnat additamentum Leviathan,* sayes Saint *Bernard,* the spawns of *Leviathan,* the seed of sinne, the leven of the Devil, abounds and reignes most in that part of the body; it is *sentiva peccati,* saies the same Father, the *Sewar* of all sinne; not onely because all sinne is derived upon us, by *generation,* and so implyed, and involved in *originall sinne;* but because, almost all other sinnes have relation to *this:* for, *Gluttony* is a preparation to this sinne in our selves; *Pride* and *excesse* is a preparation to it, in others, whom we would enveigle and allure, by our bravery; *Anger* and malice inclines us to pursue this sinfull and inordinate love, quarrelsomly, so, as, that *then,* we doe not quarrell for wayes, and walls in the street,[7] but we quarrell for our way to the Devil; and when we cannot go fast enough to the Devil, by wantonnesse in the chamber, we will quarrell with him, who hinders us of our Damnation, and find a way, to go faster in the field, by *Duells,* and unchristian *Murder,* in so foule a cause, as unlawfull lust. In this rebellious part, is the root of all sinne, and therefore did that part need this stigmaticall marke of Circumcision, to be imprinted upon it. Besides, (for the Jewes in particular) they were a Nation prone to *Idolatry,* and most, upon this occasion, if they mingled themselves with Women of other Nations: And therefore, *Dedit est signum, ut admoverentur de generatione pura,* saies Saint *Chrysostome, God* would be at the cost even of a *Sacrament,* (which is the greatest thing that passes between *God* and *Man* next to his *Word*) to defend them thereby against dangerous alliances, which might turne their hearts from *God; God* imprinted a marke in that part, to keep them still in mind of that law, which forbade them *foraigne Marriages,* or any company of *strange Women:* [k]*Custodia pietati servandae; ne macularent paternam Nobilitatem,* lest they should degenerate from the Nobility of their race, *God* would have them carry this memoriall about them, in their flesh. And *God* foresaw that extreme Idolatry, that grosse Idolatry, which that Nation would come to, and did come to, [l]*when Maachah* the Mother of *Asa* worshipped that Idol, which Saint *Hierome* calls *Belphegor,* and is not fit to be named by us; and therefore, in foresight of that Idolatry, *God* gave this marke, and this mutilation upon this part. If *Abraham* were surprized with any suggestions, any *half-reasons* against this commandement, he might quickly recollect himself, and

7. Clear and protected passages.

k. Theodor[et]. *l.* 1. Reg. 15:13.

see, that Circumcision was first, [m]*Signum memorativum, et monimentum isti foederis,* it was a signe of the *Covenant* between *God* and *Abraham*; the *Covenant* was the *Messias*, who being to come, by a carnall continuance of *Abrahams* race, the signe and seale was conveniently placed in that part. And that was, secondly, *Signum representativum*, it represented *Baptisme*, [n]*In Christ you are circumcised*, saies the Apostle, *in that you are buried with him, through Baptisme:* And then, that was *Signum Distinctivum*; for, besides that it kept them from *Idolatry*, as the Greeks called all Nations, whom they despised, *Barbares, Barbarians*, so did the Jewes, *Incircumcisos, Uncircumcised:* And that was a great threatning in the Prophet, [o]*Thou shalt die the death of the Uncircumcised*; that is, without any part in the everlasting promise, and Covenant. But yet, the principall dignity of this Circumcision, was, that it was *Signum figurativum*, it prefigured, it directed to that Circumcision of the heart; [p]*Circumcise the foreskin of your heart, for the Lord your God is God of Gods, and Lord of Lords*. And for all the other reasons that could be assigned, of *Remembrance*, of *Representation*, of *Distinction, Caret ubique ratione Judaica carnis Circumcisio*, (sayes *Lactantius*) *Nisi quod est Circumcisionis figura, quae est Cor Mundum:* The Jewish Circumcision were an absurd and unreasonable thing, if it did not intimate and figure the Circumcision of the heart: And that is our Second part of this Exercise: But before we come to that, we are to say a word of the fourth branch of this part, That as there is no *Quare* to be made nor admitted against God, (which was our first part) If Man, out of his infirmity, doe fall into *that*, (which was our Second) God provides and furnishes them with Reasons against those Reasons, (which was our third.) And then, *God* rewards their fighting of that battaile, (which is his owne worke) with victories, and crownes, and blessings here. (*1625*) 6:191–93

2. *Eye and Ear (Ps. 38:4)*

The Organ that God hath given the naturall man, is the *eye*; he sees God in the creature. The Organ that God hath given the Christian, is the *ear*; he hears God in his Word. But when we are under water, both senses, both Organs are vitiated, and depraved, if not defeated. The habituall, and manifold sinner, sees nothing aright; Hee sees a *judgement*, and cals it an *accident*. He hears nothing aright; He hears the Ordinance of *Preaching* for salvation in the next world, and he calls it an invention of the State, for subjection in this world. And as under

m. Gen. 17[:10].
n. Colos. 2[:11–12].
o. Ezek. 28[:10].
p. Deut. 10[:16].

water, every thing seems distorted and crooked, to man, so does man himself to God, who sees not his own Image in that man, in that form as he made it. [q]When *man hath drunk iniquity like water*, then, [r]*The flouds of wickednesse shall make him afraid*; The water that he hath swum in, the sin that he hath delighted in, shall appear with horrour unto him. As God threatens the pride of *Tyrus*, [s]*I shall bring the deep upon thee, and great waters shall cover thee*, That, God will execute upon this sinner; And then, upon every drop of that water, upon every affliction, every tribulation, he shall come to that fearfulnesse, [t]*Waters flowed over my head*; then said I, *I am cut off;* Either he shall see nothing, or see no remedy, no deliverance from desperation. Keep low these waters, as waters signifie *sin*, and God shall keep them low, as they signifie *punishments*; [u]And his Dove shall return to the Ark with an Olive leaf, to shew thee that the waters are abated; he shall give thee a testimony of the return of his love, in his Oyle, and Wine, and Milk, and Honey, in the temporall abundances of this life. And, [v]*si impleat Hydrias aqua*, if he doe fill all your vessels with water, with water of bitternesse, that is, fill and exercise all your patience, and all your faculties with his corrections, yet he shall doe that, but to *change your water into wine*, as he did there, he shall make his very Judgements, Sacraments, conveyances and seals of his mercy to you, though those manifold sins be got over your heads, as a roof, as a noise, as an overflowing of waters. (*1618*) 2:114

3. Carnality of the Soul (Ps. 38:3)

Saint *Basil* will needs have us leave the obvious, and the naturall signification of this, *Bones*; for, *Habet et anima ossa sua*, says he, The soule hath Bones, as well as the body, and there shall be no Rest in those Bones. Such a signification is applyable to the Flesh, as well as the Bones; The flesh may signifie the *lower faculties* of the soule, or the weaker works of the higher faculties thereof; There may bee a Carnality in the understanding; a concupiscence of disputation, and controversie in unnecessary points. [w]*Requirit quod sibi respondere nequit*, The mind of a curious man delights to examine it selfe upon Interrogatories, which, upon the Racke, it cannot answer, and to vexe it selfe with such doubts as it cannot resolve. *Sub eo ignara deficit, quod prudenter requirit*; Wee will needs shew wit in moving subtile questions, and the more ignorance, in not being able to give our selves sat-

q. Job 15:16.
r. Ps. 18:4.
s. Ezek. 26:19.
t. Lam. 3:54.
u. Gen. 8:8.
v. Joh. 2:7.
w. Grego[ry].

isfaction. [x]But not onely *seditions*, and *contentions*, but *Heresies* too, are called workes of the *flesh*; howsoever men thinke themselves wittie, and subtile, and spirituall in these wranglings, yet they have carnall respects, they are of the flesh, and there is no soundnes in them. But beyond this carnality in matters of Opinions, in points of a higher nature, this diseased man in our Text, comes to trouble in his Bones, S. *Basils spirituall bones*: Hee shall suspect his Religion, suspect his Repentance, suspect the Comforts of the Minister, suspect the efficacy of the Sacrament, suspect the mercy of God himselfe. Every fit of an Ague is an Earth-quake that swallows him, every fainting of the knee, is a step to Hell; every lying down at night is a funerall; and every quaking is a rising to judgment; every bell that distinguishes times, is a passing-bell, and every passing-bell, his own; every singing in the ear, is an Angels Trumpet; at every dimnesse of the candle, he heares that voice, *Fool, this night they will fetch away thy soul*; and in every judgement denounced against sin, he hears an *Ito maledicte* upon himselfe, *Goe thou accursed into hell fire*. And whereas such meditations as these, might sustaine a rectified soule, as Bones, in this sinner, *despaire* shall have sucked out all the marrow of these Bones, and so there shall bee no *soundnesse in his flesh, no rest in his bones*. And so have you this sicke sinner dissected and anatomized; Hee hath not onely his portion in misery that lies upon all mankinde, which was our first branch, but in the heavyest of all, sickenesse, which was a second, and then a third sicknesse spread over all, *no soundnesse*, nor rest in that sicknesse, which was a fourth consideration, *No soundnesse in his flesh*, in his weaker faculties and operations, *No rest in his bones*, no acquiescence in his best actions, with which we end this first part. In which, wee consider sinfull man, in *himself*, and so all is desperate; But in the second, where we find him upon the consideration of the cause of all these distresses, That it is from the Contemplation of the anger of God, *There is no soundnesse in my flesh, because of thine Anger*, there wee shall finde a way offered to him, that may, if hee pursue it aright, bring him to a Reparation, to a Redintegration; for, if hee look upon the Anger of God in a right line, it will shew him, that as that Anger is the cause of his Calamities, so his sinnes are the cause of that Anger. (*1618*) 2:84–85

4. Body and Soul (Ps. 38:2)

I must have this body with me to heaven, or else salvation it self is not perfect; And yet I cannot have this body thither, except as S. *Paul* did his, [y]*I beat down this body*, attentuate this body by mortification;

x. Gal. 5:20. *y*. 1. Cor. 9 *ult*.

Wretched man that I am, who shall deliver me from this body of death? I have not body enough for my body, and I have too much body for my soul; not body enough, not bloud enough, not strength enough, to sustain my self in *health*, and yet body enough to destroy my soul, and frustrate the grace of God in that miserable, perplexed, riddling condition of man; sin makes the body of man miserable, and the remedy of sin, *mortification*, makes it miserable too; If we enjoy the good things of this world, [z] *Duriorem carcerem praeparamus*, wee doe but carry an other wall about our prison, an other story of unwieldy flesh about our souls; and if wee give our selves as much *mortification* as our body needs, we live a life of *Fridays*, and see no *Sabbath*, we make up our years of *Lents*, and see no other *Easters*, and whereas God meant us *Paradise*, we make all the world a *wildernesse*. Sin hath cast a curse upon all the creatures of the world, they are all worse then they were at first, and yet we dare not receive so much blessing, as is left in the creature, we dare not eat or drink, and enjoy them. The *daughters* of Gods quiver, and the *sons* of his quiver, the arrows of *tentation*, and the arrows of *tribulation*, doe so stick in us, that as he lives miserably, that lives in *sicknes*, and he as miserably, that lives in *physick*: so *plenty* is a misery, and *mortification* is a misery too; plenty, if we consider it in the *effects*, is a *disease*, a continuall sicknes, for it breeds diseases; And *mortification*, if we should consider it without the *effects*, is a disease too, a continuall hunger, and fasting; and if we consider it at best, and in the effects, mortification is but a *continuall physick*, which is misery enough.

They stick, and they *stick fast; alte infixae*; every syllable aggravates our misery. Now for the most part, experimentally, we know not whether they stick fast or no, for we never goe about to pull them out: these arrows, these tentations, come, and welcome: we are so far from offering to pull them out, that we fix them faster and faster in us; we assist our tentations: yea, we take preparatives and fomentations, we supple our selves by *provocations*, lest our flesh should be of proof against these arrows, that death may enter the surer, and the deeper into us by them. And he that does in some measure, soberly and religiously, goe about to draw out these arrows, yet never consummates, never perfects his own work; He pulls back the arrow a little way, and he sees *blood*, and he feels *spirit* to goe out with it, and he lets it alone: He forbears his sinfull companions, a little while, and he feels a *melancholy* take hold of him, the spirit and life of his life decays, and he falls to those companions again. Perchance he rushes out the arrow with a sudden, and a resolved vehemence, and he

z. Basil.

leaves the head in his body: He forces a divorce from that sinne, he removes himself out of distance of that tentation; and yet he surfets upon cold meat, upon the sinfull remembrance of former sins, which is a dangerous rumination, and an unwholesome chawing of the cud; It is not an ill derivation of repentance, that *poenitere* is *poenam tenere*; that's true repentance, when we continue in those means, which may advance our repentance. [a]When *Joash* the King of *Israel* came to visit *Elisha* upon his sick bed, and to consult with him about his war, *Elisha* bids the King smite the ground, and he smites it thrice, and ceases: Then the man of God was angry, and said, *Thou shouldst have smitten five or sixe times, and so thou shouldst have smitten thine enemies, till thou hadst consumed them*. Now, how much hast thou to doe, that hast not pulled at this arrow at all yet? Thou must pull thrice and more, before thou get it out; Thou must *doe*, and *leave undone* many things, before thou deliver thy selfe of that arrow, that sinne that transports thee. [b]One of these arrows was shot into Saint *Paul* himselfe, and it stuck, and stuck fast; whether an arrow of *tentation*, or an arrow of *tribulation*, the Fathers cannot tell; And therefore, wee doe now, (not inconveniently) all our way, in this exercise, mingle these two considerations, of tentation, and tribulation. Howsoever Saint *Paul* pulled thrice at this arrow, and could not get it out; *I besought the Lord thrice*, says he, *that it might depart from mee*. But yet, *Joash* his thrice striking of the ground, brought him some victory; Saint *Pauls* thrice praying, brought him in that provision of *Grace*, which God cals *sufficient for him*. Once pulling at these arrows, a slight consideration of thy sins will doe no good. Do it *thrice*; testifie some true desire by such a diligence; Doe it now as thou sitt'st, doe it again at the *Table*, doe it again in thy *bed*; Doe it *thrice*, doe it in thy *purpose*, do it in thine *actions*, doe it in thy *constancy*; Doe it thrice, within the wals of thy *flesh*, in thy self, within the wals of thy *house* in thy family, and in a holy and *exemplar conversation* abroad, and God will accomplish *thy work*, which is *his work* in thee; And though the arrow be not utterly pulled out, yet it shall not fester, it shall not *gangrene*; Thou shalt not be cut off from the body of Christ, in his Church here, nor in the Triumphant Church hereafter, how fast soever these arrows did stick upon thee before. [c]God did not refuse *Israel* for her wounds, and bruises, and putrefying sores, though from the sole of the foot, to the crown of the head, but because those wounds were not closed, nor bound up, nor suppled with ointments, therefore he refused her. God shall not refuse any soul, because it hath been shot

a. 2. Reg. 13:18,19.
b. 2. Cor. 12:7.
c. Esa. 1:6.

with these arrows; Alas, God himself hath set us up *for a mark*, says *Job*, and so says *Jeremy*, [d]*against these arrows*. But that soul that can pour out flouds of tears, for the losse, or for the absence, or for the unkindnes, or imagination of an unkindness of a friend, mis-beloved, beloved a wrong way, and not afford one drop, one tear, to wash the wounds of these arrows, that soul that can squeaze the wound of Christ Jesus, and spit out his bloud in these blasphemous execrations, and shed no drop of this bloud upon the wounds of these arrows; that soul, and only that soul, that refuses a cure, does God refuse; not because they fell upon it, and stook, and stook fast, and stook long, but because they never, never went about to pull them out; never resisted a tentation, never lamented a transgression, never repented a recidivation. (*1618*) 2:63–65

5. Meeting of Body and Soul: A Church (Gen. 28:16, 17)

Now of those divers gates, which *God* opens in this life, those divers exercises of charity, the particular which we are occasioned to speak of here, is not the cloathing, nor feeding of Christ, but the *housing* of him, The providing Christ a house, a dwelling; whether this were the very place, where *Solomons Temple* was after built, is perplexedly, and perchance, impertinently controverted by many; but howsoever, here was the house of *God*, and here was the gate of Heaven. It is true, God may be devoutly worshipped any where; *In omni loco dominationis ejus benedic anima mea Domino*; In all places of his dominion, my Soule shall praise the Lord, sayes *David*. It is not only a concurring of men, a meeting of so many bodies that makes a *church*; If thy soule, and body be met together, an humble preparation of the mind, and a reverent disposition of the body, if thy knees be bent to the earth, thy hands and eyes lifted up to heaven, if thy tongue pray, and praise, and thine ears hearken to his answer, if all thy senses, and powers, and faculties, be met with one unanime purpose to worship thy *God*, thou art, to this intendment, a Church, thou art a Congregation, here are *two or three met together in his name*, and he is in the midst of them, though thou be alone in thy chamber. The Church of God should be built upon a Rock, and yet *Job* had his Church upon a Dunghill; The bed is a scene, and an embleme of wantonnesse, and yet *Hezekiah* had his Church in his Bed; The Church is to be placed upon the top of a Hill, and yet the Prophet *Jeremy* had his Church *in Luto*, in a miry Dungeon; Constancy, and setlednesse belongs to the Church, and yet *Jonah* had his Church in the Whales belly; The Lyon that roares, and

d. Lam. 3:12.

seeks whom he may devour, is an enemy to this Church, and yet *Daniel* had his Church in the Lions den; *Aquae quietudinum*, the waters of rest in the Psalme, were a figure of the Church, and yet the three children had their Church in the fiery furnace; Liberty and life appertaine to the Church, and yet *Peter*, and *Paul* had their Church in prison, and the thiefe had his Church upon the Crosse. Every particular man is himselfe *Templum Spiritus sancti*, a Temple of the holy Ghost;[8] yea, [e]*Solvite templum hoc*, destroy this body by death, and corruption in the grave, yet there shall be *Festum encaeniorum*, a renuing, a reedifying of all those Temples, in the generall Resurrection: when we shall rise againe, not onely as so many Christians, but as so many *Christian Churches*, to glorifie the Apostle, and High-priest of our profession, Christ Jesus, in that eternall Sabbath. [f]*In omni loco dominationis ejus*, Every person, every place is fit to glorifie God in. (*1619*) 2:216–17

6. Man's Spirit: Middle Nature between Soul and Body (Rom. 13:11)

And so the Apostles words are directed to all Christians, and not only to the new convertits of that nation; and so these three terms, salvation, nearness, and believing, (which we proposed to be considered in all the three acceptations of the words) will have this signification. Salvation is the inward means of salvation, the working of the spirit, that sets a seal to the eternal means: the *prope*, the nearness lies in this, that this grace which is this salvation in this sense, grows out of that which is in you already; not out of any thing which is in you naturally, but Gods first graces that are in you, grows into more and more grace. Grace does not grow out of nature; for nature in the highest exaltation and rectifying thereof cannot produce grace. Corn does not grow out of the earth, it must be sowd; but corn grows only in the earth; nature, and naturall reason do not produce grace, but yet grace can take root in no other thing but in the nature and reason of man; whether we consider Gods subsequent graces, which grow out of his first grace, formerly given to us, and well employed by us, or his first grace, which works upon our natural faculties, and grows there; still this salvation, that is, this grace is near us, for it is within us; and then the third term believing, is either, *quando credidistis primum*, when you began to believe, either in an imputative belief of

8. In describing the location of the Church, Donne alludes to a number of scriptural passages. See Matt. 18:20, Job 2:8, 2 Kings 20:1–3, Jer. 38:6, Jonah 2, Ps. 23:2, Acts 12 and 16, and 1 Cor. 6:19.

e. John 2:19.
f. Heb. 3:1.

others in your baptism, or a faint belief, upon your first Catechisings and Instructions; or *quando credidistis tantum*, when you only professed a belief, or faith, and did nothing in declaration of that faith, to the edification of others.

First then, salvation in this second sense is the internal operation of the holy Ghost, in infusing grace: for therefore doth St. *Basil* call the holy Ghost *verbum Dei*, the word of God, (which is the name properly peculiar to the Son) *quia interpres filii, sicut filius patris*; that as the Father had revealed his will in the Prophets, and then the Son comes and interprets all that actually, this prophecy is meant of my coming, this of my dying; and so makes a real comment, and an actual interpretation of all the prophecies, for he does come, and he does die accordingly; so the holy Ghost comes, and comments upon this comment, interprets this interpretation, and tels thy soul that all this that the Father had promised, and the Son had performed, was intended by them, and by the working of their spirit, is now appropriated to thy particular soul. In the constitution and making of a natural man, the body is not the man, nor the soul is not the man, but the union of these two makes up the man; the spirits in a man which are the thin and active part of the blood, and so are of a kind of middle nature, between soul and body, those spirits are able to doe, and they doe the office, to unite and apply the faculties of the soul to the organs of the body, and so there is a man: so in a regenerate man, a Christian man, his being born of Christian Parents, that gives him a body, that makes him of the body of the Covenant, it gives him a title, an interest in the Covenant, which is *jus ad rem*; thereby he may make his claim to the seal of the Covenant, to baptism, and it cannot be denied him: and then in his baptism, that Sacrament gives him a soul, a spiritual seal, *jus in re*, an actual possession of Grace; but yet, as there are spirits in us, which unite body and soul, so there must be subsequent acts, and works of the blessed spirit, that must unite and confirm all, and make up this spiritual man in the wayes of sanctification; for without that his body, that is, his being born within the Covenant, and his soul, that is, his having received Grace in baptism, do not make him up. This Grace is this Salvation; and when this Grace works powerfully in thee, in the ways of sanctification, then is this Salvation neer thee; which is our second term in this second acceptation, *prope*, near.

This neerness, which is the effectuall working of Grace, the Apostle expresses fully, That it [g]*pierceth to the dividing asunder of soul and spirit*; for, though properly the soul and spirit of a man be all one, yet divers faculties and operations give them somtimes divers names in

g. Heb. 4:12.

the Scriptures; *Anima quia animat,* sayes St. *Ambrose,* and *spiritus quia spirat:* The quickning of the body, is the soul; but the quickning of the soul, is the spirit. If this Salvation be brought to this neerness, that is, this grace to this powerfulness, thou shalt find it *in anima,* in thy soul, in those organs wherein thy soul uses thy body, in thy senses, and in the sensible things ordained by God in his Church, Sacraments and Ceremonies; and thou shalt find it neerer, *in spiritu,* as the spirit of God hath sealed it to thy spirit invisibly, inexpressibly: It shall be neer to thee, so as that thy reason shall apprehend it; and neerer then that, thy faith shall establish it; and neerer then all this, it shall create in thee a modest and sober, but yet an infallible assurance, that thy salvation shall never depart from thee: *Magnificabit anima tua Dominum,* as the B. Virgin speaks, *Thy soul shall magnifie the Lord*; all thy natural faculties shall be employed upon an assent to the Gospel, thou shalt be able to prove it to thy self, and to prove it to others, to be the Gospel of Salvation: And then *Exultabit spiritus,* Thy spirit shall rejoyce in God thy Saviour, because by the farther seal of sanctification, thy spirit shall receive testimony from the spirit; that as Christ is *Idem homo cum te,* the same man that thou art, so thou art *Idem spiritus cum Domino,* the same spirit that he is; so far, as that as a spirit cannot be separated in it self, so neither canst thou be separated from God in Christ; And this, this exaltation of Grace, when it thus growes up to this height of sanctification, is that neerness, which brings Salvation farther than our believing does: and that's the last term in this part; Believing. (*1619*) 2:260–63

7. Soul and Spirit (Ps. 6:2, 3)

Thus far then first *David* needed this sanation, this health that he prayes for, that his best actions were corrupt; But the corruption went farther, to the very roote and fountaine of those actions, *Ad ipsam animam,* His very *soule* was *sore vexed.* It is true, that as this word *Anima, the soule,* is sometimes taken in the Scriptures, this may seeme to goe no farther then the former, no more that his soule was vexed, then that his bones were so: for, *Anima,* in many places, is but *Animalis Homo,* The soule signifies but the naturall man: And so *opponitur spiritui,* The *soule* is not onely said to be a diverse thing, but a contrary thing to the *Spirit.* When the Apostle sayes to the Thessalonians, [h]*Now the very God of peace sanctifie you throughout, that your whole spirit, and soule, and body, may be kept blamelesse unto the comming of our Lord Jesus Christ;* And where the same Apostle sayes to the Hebrews, [i]*The word of God divideth asunder the soule and the spirit;*

h. 1. Thes. *ult.* [5:]23.

i. Heb. 4:12.

here is a difference put between corrupt nature, and the working of the Spirit of God, the Holy Ghost in man: for here, the *soule* is taken for *Animalis homo*, The naturall man, and the *Spirit* is taken for the Spirit of God. But besides this, these two words, *Soule* and *Spirit*, are sometimes used by the Fathers, in a sense diverse from one another, and as different things, and yet still as parts of one and the same man; Man is said by them, not onely to have a body, and a soule, but to have a soule, and a spirit; not as Spirit is the Spirit of God, and so an extrinsecall thing, but as Spirit is a constitutive part of the naturall man. So, in particular, amongst many, [j] *Gregory Nyssen* takes the Body to be spoken *De nutribili*, The flesh and bloud of man, And the soule *De sensibili*, The operation of the senses, And the Spirit *De Intellectuali*, The Intellectuall, the reasonable faculties of man; That in the body, Man is conformed to Plants that have no sense, In the soule, to Beasts, that have no reason, In the spirit, to Angels. But so, The Spirit is but the same thing with that, which now we doe ordinarily account the soule to be; for we make account, that the Image of God is imprinted in the soule, and that gives him his conformity to Angels: But divers others of the Ancients have taken *Soule* and *Spirit*, for different things, even in the Intellectuall part of man, somewhat obscurely, I confesse, and, as some venture to say, unnecessarily, if not dangerously. It troubled S. *Hierome* sometimes, how to understand the word *Spirit* in man: but he takes the easiest way, he dispatches himselfe of it, as fast as he could, that is, to speake of it onely as it was used in the Scriptures: [k] *Famosa quaestio*, sayes he, *sed brevi sermone tractanda*; It is a question often disputed, but may be shortly determined, *Idem spiritus hic, ac in iis verbis, Nolite extinguere spiritum*; When we heare of the Spirit in a Man, in Scriptures, we must understand it of the gifts of the Spirit; for so, fully to the same purpose, sayes S. *Chrysostome*, *Spiritus est charisma spiritus*, The Spirit is the working of the Spirit, The gifts of the Spirit: and so when we heare, *The Spirit was vexed, The Spirit was quenched*, still it is to be understood, The gifts of the Spirit. And so, as they restraine the signification of *Spirit*, to those gifts onely, (though the word do indeed, in many places, require a larger extension) so do many restraine this word in our text, *The Soule*, onely *Ad sensum*; to the sensitive faculties of the soule, that is, onely to the paine and anguish that his body suffered; But so far, at least, *David* had gone, in that which he said before, *My bones are vexed*.

. . . .

Corpus instrumentum, anima ars ipsa, sayes S. *Basil*: The body, and the senses are but the tooles, and instruments, that the soule works

j. Ad Hedibiam, q.12.

k. Epist. 150.

with; But the soule is the art, the science that directs those Instruments. The faculties of the soule are the boughs that produce the fruits; and the operations, and particular acts of those faculties are the fruits; but the soule is the roote of all. And *David* sees, that this art, this science, this soule can direct him, or establish him in no good way; That not onely the fruits, his particular acts, nor onely the boughs, and armes, his severall faculties, but the roote it selfe, the soule it selfe, was infected. His bones are shaken, he dares not stand upon the good he hath done, his soule is so too, he cannot hope for any good he shall do: He hath no merit for the past, he hath no free-will for the future; that is his case. (*1623?*) 5:354–56

D. Salvation and the Natural Faculties

1. The Robe of Restored Faculties (Isa. 52:3)

In this redemption then God pursues the devil, in all those steps, by which he had made his profit, of a prodigality; for, first, as we gave away our selves, so he restores us to our selves again. [l]It is well expressed in the parable of the prodigall; and his case is ours. The portion which he asked of his father, was the use of his free-will. God gave it him; *Adams* first Immortality was, *posse non mori* he needed not to have died: It was in his own power whether he would keep a free-will, or no, and he spent that stock, he lost that free-will. He spent not his free-will so as *Bellarmin* understands this spending, that that man may be sayd to spend his life ill, that misimployes it, but yet he hath this life in him still: But the prodigall, *Adam*, spent his utterly: he spent it so, that he and we have no freewill at all left. But yet; even the prodigall sayd, that he would return to his father, and he came; He had not only some sudden thoughts of Repentance, but he put himself actually in the way: *cum longe abesset*, says that parable, when he was a great way off, yet because he was in the way, his father met him and kissed him, and put that Robe upon him, which was not onely *Dignitas, quam perdidit Adam*, as S. *Austin* qualifies it, a restitution to the same integrity, which *Adam* had and had lost, but that was *Amictus sapientiae*; (so S. *Ambrose* calls it) it was an ability to preserve himself in that integrity, to which he was restored. It was a Robe that was put upon him; it was none of his own; but when it was put upon him, it rectified and restored those faculties, which were his own: as the eye sees in a man restored to life, though the soul enable the eye and not the eye it self, so the faculty of free-will works in us as well as it did in *Adam* though onely the grace of God enable that faculty.

l. Luc. 15.

When God hath wrought that first cure (which he does by incorporating us, in the Church by baptisme) that we are our selves again, then (as in the case of prodigals in the law) as they had Tutors, and Curators appointed them, so he sends the Holy Ghost, to be our Guardian our Curator: and as the office of that person, in that law, was double, first to reverse all contracts and bargains, which that prodigal person, in that state, had made, and secondly to inhibit, and hinder him, from making new contracts, so this blessed Spirit of consolation, by his sanctification, seals to our consciences a *Quietus est*, a discharge of all former spiritual debts, he cancells all them, he nails them to the cross of Christ, and then he strengthens us against relapses into the same sins again. (*1615*) 1:162–63

2. Sacrifice the Blood of Will (Col. 1:19, 20)

Before, under the Law, it was *in sanguine hircorum, et vitulorum*; In the bloud of Goats, and Bullocks; here it is *in sanguine ejus*, in his bloud. [m] Not his, as he claims all the beasts of the forrest, all the cattle upon a thousand hils, and all the fowles of the mountaines to be his; not his, as he sayes of Gold and Silver, The Silver is mine, and the Gold is mine; not his, as he is Lord, and proprietary of all, by Creation; so all bloud is his; no nor his, as the bloud of all the Martyrs was his bloud, (which is a neare relation and consanguinity) but his so, as it was the precious bloud of his body, the seat of his soule, the matter of his spirits, the knot of his life. This bloud he shed for me; and I have bloud to shed for him too, though he call me not to the tryall, nor to the glory of Martyrdome. [n] *Sanguis animae meae voluntas mea*, The bloud of my soule is my will; *Scindatur vena ferro compunctionis*, open a veine with that knife, remorce, compunction, *ut si non sensus, certe consensus peccati effluat*, That though thou canst not bleed out all motions to sinne, thou maist all consent thereunto. *Noli esse nimium justus; noli sapere plus quam oportet;* St. *Bernard* makes this use of those Counsels, [o] *Be not righteous overmuch, nor be not overwise, Cui putas venae parcendum, si justitia et sapientia egent minutione*, what veine maist thou spare, if thou must open those two veines, righteousnesse, and wisedome? If they may be superfluously abundant, if thou must bleed out some of thy Righteousnesse, and some of thy wisedome, [p] *cui venae parcendum*, at what veine must thou not bleed?[9] Now in all sacrifices, where bloud was to be offerd, the fat was to be

9. The reference is to Tostatus ("Abulensis," c.1400–1455), bishop of Avila, 1449, and to his commentary on Leviticus. See the complete edition of his works (Venice, 1615).

m. Ps. 50:10. Hag. 2:8.
n. Bern.
o. Eccles. 7:16.
p. Tostat[us]. in Levit. fo.61.D.

offerd to. If thou wilt sacrifice the bloud of thy soule, (as St. *Bernard* cals the will) sacrifice the fat too; If thou give over thy purpose of continuing in thy sin, give over the memory of it, and give over all that thou possessest unjustly, and corruptly got by that sinne; else thou keepest the fat from God, though thou give him the bloud. If God had given over at his second daies work, we had had no sunne, no seasons; If at his fift, we had had no beeing; If at the sixt, no Sabbath; but by proceeding to the seventh, we are all, and we have all. [q]*Naaman*, who was out of the covenant, yet, by washing in Jordan seven times, was cured of his leprosie; seaven times did it even in him, but lesse did not. [r]The Priest in the Law used a seven-fold sprinkling of bloud upon the Altar; and we observe a seven-fold shedding of bloud in Christ; In his Circumcision, and in his Agony, in his fulfilling of that Prophesie, [s]*genas vellicantibus*, I gave my cheeks to them, that plucked off the haire, and in his scourging; in his crowning, and in his nayling, and lastly, in the piercing of his side. These seven channels hath the bloud of thy Saviour found. Poure out the bloud of thy soule, sacrifice thy stubborne and rebellious will seaven times too; seaven times, that is, every day; and seaven times every day; [t]for so often a just man falleth; And then, how low must that man lie at last, if he fall so often, and never rise upon any fall? and therefore raise thy self as often, and as soone as thou fallest. [u]*Jericho* would not fall, but by being compassed seaven dayes, and seaven times in one day. Compasse thy selfe, comprehend thy selfe, seaven times, many times, and thou shalt have thy losse of bloud supplied with better bloud, with a true sense of that peace, which he hath already made, and made by bloud, and by his owne bloud, and *by the bloud of his Crosse*. (*1622*) 4:294–95

3. Enosh: *Faculty of Seeing (Job 36:25)*

We have past through our first part, and the three branches of that; The *object*, *God* in his *works*, and the *faculty* that apprehends, *seeing*, that is *knowing*, and the *person* indued with the faculty, *every man*, even *Adam*. In our second part, which is a tacite answer to a likely objection, (Is not God in the highest heaven, *afar off?* yes; but *man may see afar off*) we have the same three branches too, and yet not the same; the same *object*, *God*, but in another manifestation, then in his *worke*, in *glory*; the same *faculty*, *seeing*, but with other manner of eyes, glorified eyes; the same *person*, *man*, but not *man*, as he is *Adam*, a meere *naturall* and earthly man, but man, as he is *Enosh*,

q. 2. Reg. 5:14.
r. Tostat. in Levit. 4.q.16.
s. Esay 50:6.
t. Prov. 24:16.
u. Jos. 6.

who by having tasted Gods corrections, or by having considered the miseries of this world, is prepared for the joy and glory of the next. And in this part we will begin with the person, *man; Man may behold it afar off*.

. . . .

To end this, the person in our Text is *Enosh, man*; but not every man, as before, *Adam*; but that man upon whom Gods hand hath been in the losse of something, that he had before. As the body of man is mellowed in the grave, and made fit for glory in the resurrection, so the minde of man by suffering is suppled; *Adam* is made *Enosh*; and he may see.

The person is the same, and yet changed; *man*, but another kinde of man; The *meanes* of apprehending is the same, and yet changed too, *seeing*, but another kinde of seeing. This man, thus disposed, thus matured, thus mellowed, thus suppled, thus entendred by Gods easie corrections, he whom God hath not left to himself, nor yet put him beyond himself, not fulfilled all, but yet not frustrated all his desires neither, laid his hand upon him, so as to keep him downe from swelling up against him, but yet so too, as to keep him up, from sinking, or falling from him, that man, that *Enosh* may see the hand of God, and take God by the hand, and bid him *welcome*, and finde a rich, and a sweet advantage in that correction; it is a *seeing of God*, not as before, in his *works* abroad, but in his *working* upon himself, at home. (*1622*) 4:170, 172–73

4. Men Change into the Thing They Love (Ps. 32:9)

The first sin that ever was, was an ascending, a climing too high; when the purest Understandings of all, The Angels, fell by their ascending; when *Lucifer* was tumbled downe, by his [v]*Similis ero Altissimo, I will be like the most High*, then he tried upon them, who were next to him in Dignity, upon Man, how that clambring would worke upon him. He presents to man, the same ladder; He infuses into man the same Ambition, and as he fell with a *Similis ero Altissimo, I will be like the most High*, So he overthrew man, with an *Eritis sicut Dii, Ye shall be as Gods*. It seemes this fall hath broake the neck of Mans ambition, and now we dare not be so like God, as we should be. Ever since this fall, man is so far from affecting higher places, then his nature is capable of, that he is still groveling upon the ground, and participates, and imitates, and expresses more of the nature of the Beast then of his owne. There is no creature but man that degenerates willingly from his naturall Dignity; Those degrees of

v. Esay 14:14.

goodnesse, which God imprinted in them at first, they preserve still; As God saw they were good then, so he may see they are good still; They have kept their Talent; They have not bought nor sold; They have not gained nor lost; They are not departed from their native and naturall dignity, by any thing that they have done. But of Man, it seemes, God was distrustfull from the beginning; He did not pronounce upon Mans Creation, (as he did upon the other Creatures) that *He was good*; because his goodnesse was a contingent thing, and consisted in the future use of his free will. For that faculty and power of the will, is [w]*Virtus transformativa*; by it we change our selves into that we love most, and we are come to love those things most, which are below us. As God said to the Earth, (and it was enough to say so) [x]*Germinet terra juxta genus suum, Let the Earth bring forth according to her kinde*; So, *Vive juxta genus tuum*, sayes S. *Ambrose* to Man, Live according to thy kinde; *Non adulteres genus tuum*, doe not abase, doe not allay, doe not betray, do not abastardise that noble kinde, that noble nature, which God hath imparted to thee, imprinted in thee. (*winter 1624–1625?*) 9:372–73

5. Abilities and Limitations of Mankind (Matt. 28:6)

Our first consideration is upon the persons; and those we finde to be Angelicall women, and Evangelicall Angels: Angels made Evangelists, to preach the Gospell of the Resurrection, and Women made Angels, ([y]*so as John Baptist* is called an *Angel*, and so as the seven Bishops are called *Angels*) that is, Instructers of the Church; And to recompence that observation, that never good Angel appeared in the likenesse of woman, here are good women made Angels, that is, Messengers, publishers of the greatest mysteries of our Religion. For, howsoever some men out of a petulancy and wantonnesse of wit, and out of the extravagancy of Paradoxes, and such singularities, have called the faculties, and abilities of women in question, even in the roote thereof, in the reasonable and immortall soul, yet that one thing alone hath been enough to create a doubt, (almost an assurance in the negative) whether S. *Ambroses* Commentaries upon the Epistles of S. *Paul*, be truly his or no, that in that book there is a doubt made, whether the woman were created according to Gods Image; Therefore, because that doubt is made in that book, the book it self is suspected not to have had so great, so grave, so constant an author as S. *Ambrose* was; No author of gravity, of piety, of conversation in the

w. Dionys.
x. Gen. 1.
y. Mal. 3:1. Apoc. 1:20.

Scriptures could admit that doubt, whether woman were created in the Image of God, that is, in possession of a reasonable and an immortall soul. (*1630*)

* * *

(John 10:10)

What eye can fixe it self upon East and West at once? And he must see more then East and West, that sees God, for God spreads infinitely beyond both: God alone is all; not onely all that is, but all that is not, all that might be, if he would have it be. God is too large, too immense, and then man is too narrow, too little to be considered; for, who can fixe his eye upon an Atome? and he must see a lesse thing then an Atome, that sees man, for man is nothing. First, for the incomprehensiblenesse of God, the understanding of man, hath a limited, a determined latitude; it is an intelligence able to move that Spheare which it is fixed to, but could not move a greater: I can comprehend *naturam naturatam*, created nature, but for that *natura naturans*, God himselfe, the understanding of man cannot comprehend. I can see the Sun in a looking-glasse, but the nature, and the whole working of the Sun I cannot see in that glasse. I can see God in the creature, but the nature, the essence, the secret purposes of God, I cannot see there. There is *defatigatio in intellectualibus*, sayes [z] the saddest and soundest of the Hebrew Rabbins, the soule may be tired, as well as the body, and the understanding dazeled, as well as the eye. It is a good note of the same Rabbi, upon those words of *Solomon*, [a] *fill not thy selfe with hony, lest thou vomit it*, that it is not said, that if thou beest cloyd with it, thou maist be distasted, disaffected towards it after, but thou maist vomit it, and a vomit works so, as that it does not onely bring up that which was then, but that also which was formerly taken. Curious men busie themselves so much upon speculative subtilties, as that they desert, and abandon the solid foundations of Religion, and that is a dangerous vomit; To search so farre into the nature, and unrevealed purposes of God, as to forget the nature, and duties of man, this is a shrewd surfet, though of hony, and a dangerous vomit. [b] It is not needfull for thee, to see the things that are in secret, sayes the wise man; *non indiges*, thou needest not that knowledge: Thou maist doe well enough in this world, and bee Gods good servant, and doe well enough in the next world, and bee a glorious Saint, and yet never search into Gods secrets. [c] *Te decet Hymnus*, (so the

z. R. Moses.
a. Prov. 25:16.
b. Ecclus. 3:23.
c. Psal. 65:1.

vulgar reades that place) To thee, O Lord, belong our Hymnes, our Psalmes, our Prayses, our cheerefull acclamations; and conformably to that, we translate it, *Praise waiteth for thee, O God in Sion:* But if we will take it according to the Originall, it must be, *Tibi silentium laus est,* Thy praise, O Lord, consists in silence: That that man praises God best, that sayes least of him; of him, that is of his nature, of his essence, of his unrevealed will, and secret purposes. *O that men would praise the Lord,* is *Davids* provocation to us all, but how? *O that men would praise the Lord, and declare his wondrous works to the sons of men!* but not to goe about to declare his unrevealed Decrees, or secret purposes, is as good a way of praising him, as the other. And therefore, O that men would praise the Lord, so, forbeare his Majesty, when he is retired into himselfe, in his Decrees, and magnifie his Majesty, as he manifests himselfe to us, in the execution of those Decrees; of which, this in our Text is a great one, that he that is infinitely more then all, descended to him, that is infinitely lesse then nothing; which is the other person whom we are to consider in this part, *ille illis,* I to them, God to us.

The Hebrew Doctors almost every where repeat that adage of theirs, *lex loquitur linguam filiorum hominum,* God speakes mens language, that is, the Holy Ghost in the Scriptures descends to the capacity and understanding of man, and so presents God in the faculties of the minde of man, and in the lineaments of the body of man. But yet, say they, there is never braine, nor liver, nor spleene, nor any other inward part ascribed to God, but onely the heart. God is all heart, and that whole heart, that inexhaustible fountaine of love, is directed wholly upon man. (*1629*) 9:190, 134–35

6. The Crucified Serpent of Wisdom (Gen. 3:14)

In the meane time, (for our comfort in the way) when this Serpent becomes a Lyon, [d]yet there is a Lyon of the Tribe of *Judah,* that is too strong for him. So, if he who is *Serpens serpens humi,* the Serpent condemned to creep upon the ground, doe transforme himselfe into a flying Serpent, and attempt our nobler faculties, there is [e]*Serpens exaltatus,* a Serpent lifted up in the wildernesse to recover all them that are stung, and feel that they are stung with this Serpent, this flying Serpent, that is, these high and continued sinnes. The creeping Serpent, the groveling Serpent, is Craft; the exalted Serpent, the crucified Serpent, is Wisdome. All your worldly cares, all your crafty bargaines, all your subtill matches, all your diggings into other mens es-

d. Apoc. 5:5. *e.* Numb. 21:9.

tates, all your hedgings in of debts, all your planting of children in great allyances; all these diggings, and hedgings and plantings savour of the earth, and of the craft of that Serpent, that creeps upon the earth: But crucifie this craft of yours, bring all your worldly subtilty under the Crosse of Christ Jesus, husband your farmes so, as you may give a good account to him, presse your debts so, as you would be pressed by him, market and bargaine so, as that you would give all, to buy that field, in which his treasure, and his pearle is hid, and then you have changed the Serpent, from the Serpent of perdition creeping upon the earth, to the Serpent of salvation exalted in the wildernesse. Creeping wisedome, that still looks downward, is but craft; Crucified wisedome, that looks upward, is truly wisedome. Between you and that ground Serpent God hath kindled a war; and the nearer you come to a peace with him, the farther ye go from God, and the more ye exasperate the Lord of Hosts, and you whet his sword against your own souls. (*1624?*) 10:188–89

7. Knowledge of the Glory of God (2 Cor. 4:6)

In the Attributes of God, we consider his Knowledge to be *Principium agendi dirigens*, The first proposer, and Director; This should be done: and then his Will to be *Principium imperans*, the first Commander, This shall be done; and then his Power to be *Principium exsequens*, the first Performer, This is done: This should be done, this shall be done, this is done, expresses to us, the Knowledge, the Will, and the Power of God. Now we shall be made partakers of the Divine Nature, and the Knowledge, and the Will, and the Power of God, shall be so far communicated to us there, as that we shall know all that belongs to our happiness, and we shall have a will to doe, and a power to execute, whatsoever conduces to that. And for the knowledge of Angels, that is not in them *per essentiam*, for whosoever knows so, as the Essence of the thing flows from him, knows all things, and that's a knowledge proper to God only: Neither doe the Angels know *per species*, by those resultances and species, which rise from the Object, and pass through the Sense to the Understanding, for that's a deceiveable way, both by the indisposition of the Organ, sometimes, and sometimes by the depravation of the Judgment; and therefore, as the first is too high, this is too low a way for the Angels. Some things the Angels do know by the dignity of their Nature, by their Creation, which we know not; as we know many things which inferior Creatures do not; and such things all the Angels, good and bad know. Some things they know by the Grace of their confirmation, by which they have more given them, then they had by Nature in their Creation; and those things only the Angels that stood, but all they, do know. Some things they know by Revelation, when God is pleased to manifest them unto them; and so some of the Angels know that, which the rest, though confirmed, doe not know. By Creation, they know as his Subjects; by Confirmation, they know as his servants; by Revelation, they know as his Councel. Now, *Erimus sicut Angeli*, says Christ, *There we shall be as the Angels:* The knowledge which I have by Nature, shall have no Clouds; here it hath: that which I have by Grace, shall have no reluctation, no resistance; here it hath: That which I have by Revelation, shall have no suspition, no jealousie; here it hath: sometimes it is hard to distinguish between a respiration from God, and a suggestion from the Devil. There our curiosity shall have this noble satisfaction, we shall know how the Angels know, by knowing as they know. We shall not pass from Author, to Author, as in a Grammar School, nor from Art to Art, as in an University; but, as that General which Knighted his whole Army, God shall Create us all Doctors in a minute. That great Library, those infinite Volumes of the Books of Creatures, shall be taken away, quite away, no more Nature; those reverend Manuscripts, written with Gods own hand, the Scriptures themselves, shall be taken away, quite away; no more preaching, no more reading of Scriptures, and that great School-Mistress, Experience, and Observation shall be removed, no new thing to be done, and in an instant, I shall know more, then they all could reveal unto me. I shall know, not only as I know already, that a Bee-hive, that an Ant-hill is the same Book in *Decimo sexto*,[10] as a Kingdom is in *Folio*, That a Flower that lives but a day, is an abridgment of that King, that lives out his threescore and ten yeers; but I shall know too, that all these Ants, and Bees, and Flowers, and Kings, and Kingdoms, howsoever they may be Examples, and Comparisons to one another, yet they are all as nothing, altogether nothing, less then nothing, infinitely less then nothing, to that which shall then be the subject of my knowledge, for, *it is the knowledge of the glory of God*. (*1622*) 4:127–28

8. God's Method: To Make Men Understand (Ps. 32:8)

Oportet accedentem credere; The Apostle seemes to make that our first step, [f]*Hee that comes to God, must beleeve*. So it is our first step to God, To beleeve, but there is a step towards God, before it come to

10. One of the smallest book formats (16°) and the largest (2°)—depending, of course, on the size of sheet. Properly *sexto-decimo*.

f. Heb. 11:6.

faith, which is, to understand; God works first upon the understanding. God proceeds in our conversion, and regeneration, as he did in our first Creation. There man was nothing; but God breathed not a soule into that nothing; but of a clod of earth he made a body, and into that body infused a soule. Man in his Conversion, is nothing, does nothing. His bodie is not verier dust in the grave, till a Resurrection, then his soule is dust in his body, till a resuscitation by grace. But then this grace does not worke upon this nothingnesse that is in man, upon this meere privation; but Grace finds out mans naturall faculties, and exalts them to a capacity, and a susceptiblenesse of the working thereof, and so by the understanding infuses faith. Therefore God begins his Instruction here at the understanding; and he does not say at first, *Faciam te credere*, I will make thee to beleeve, but *Faciam te intelligere*, I will make thee understand.

That then being Gods Method, To make us understand, certainely those things which belong to our Salvation, are not [g]*In-intelligibilia*, not In-intelligible, un-understandable, un-conceivable things, but the Articles of faith are discernible by Reason. For though Reason cannot apprehend that a Virgin should have a Son, or that God should be made Man and dye, if we put our Reason primarily and immediately upon the Article single, (for so it is the object of faith onely) yet if we pursue Gods Method, and see what our understanding can doe, we shall see, that out of ratiocination and discourse, and probabilities, and very similitudes, at last will arise evident and necessary conclusions; such as these, That as there is a God, that God must be worshiped according to his will, That therefore that will of God must be declared and manifested somewhere, That this is done in some permanent way, in some Scripture, which is the Word of God, That this booke, which we call the Bible, is, by better reasons then any others can pretend, that Scripture; And when our Reason hath carried us so far, as to accept these Scriptures for the Word of God, then all the particular Articles, A Virgins Son, and a mortall God, will follow evidently enough. And then those two Propositions, *Mysteria credenda ut intelligantur*, Mysteries of Religion must be beleeved before they be understood, and *Mysteria intelligenda ut credantur*, Mysteries of Religion must be understood before they can be beleeved, will be all one; For God exalts our naturall facultie of understanding by Grace to apprehend them, and then to that submission and assent, which he by grace produces out of our understanding, by a succeeding and more powerfull Grace he sets to the Seale of Faith. (*winter 1624–1625?*) 9:354–55

g. Tertul.

9. Understanding and Grace (Ps. 32:9)

The *Instruction* then of the whole Psalme, is peace with God, in the merits of Christ, declared in a holy life; which being the summe of all our Christian profession, is farre beyond this *Understanding* in our Text, (*They have no understanding*) but yet upon this Understanding God raises that great building, and therefore wee take this faculty, *The Understanding*, into a more particular consideration. Here is the danger, He that at ripe yeares hath no understanding, hath no grace, A little understanding may have much grace; but he that hath none of the former, can have none of this. God therefore brings us to the consideration, not of the greatest, but of the first thing; not of his superedifications, but of his foundations, our understanding, our reason. For, though [h] *Animalis homo, The naturall man perceiveth not the things that be of the Spirit of God*, yet let him bee what man he will, Naturall or Supernaturall, hee must bee a man, that must *probare spiritum*, prove and discerne the spirit; let him have as much more as you will, it is requisite hee have so much reason, and understanding, as to perceive the maine points of Religion; not that he must necessarily have a naturall explicite reason for every Article of faith, but it were fit he had reason to prove, that those Articles need not reason to prove them. If I beleeve upon the Authority of my Teacher, or of the Church, or of the Scripture, very expedient it were to have reason to prove to my selfe that these Authorities are certaine, and irrefragable. And therefore, *Caeteris animalibus, se ignorare, natura est, homini vitium*, If a Horse or a Mule understand not it selfe, it is never the worse Horse nor Mule, for it is borne with that ignorance; But if man, having opportunities, both in respect of his parts and calling, to be better instructed, either by a negligent and lazy and implicite relying upon the opinion of others, doe but lay himselfe downe as a leafe upon the water, to be carried along with the tide, or by a wilfull drowsinesse, and security in his sins, have given over the debatement, the discussing, the understanding of the maine of his beliefe, and of his life, if either he keepe not his understanding awake, or over-watch it, if he doe nothing with it, or employ it too busily, too fervently, too eagerly upon the world, I would it were true of them, *Facti sicut*, you are like the Horse, and the Mule; but *Utinam essetis*, I would you were so well, as the Horse, and the Mule, who, though they have no understanding, have no forfeiture, no losse, no abuse of understanding to answer for.

First then the Horse, The proud man, hath no understanding; He

h. 1. Cor. 2:14.

hath forgot his letters, his Alphabet; how he was spelled and put together, and made of body and soule. You may as well call him an Anatomist, that knowes how to pare a naile, or cut a corne, or him a Surgeon, that knowes how to cut, and curle haire, as allow him understanding, that knowes how to gather riches, or how to buy an Office, or how to hurt, and oppresse others, when he hath those meanes. That absurdity, that height of strange ignorance, that the Prophet observes in an Idolatrous Image-maker, is in this proud man; [i]*He burnes halfe in the fire, and the residue he makes a god.* He hath seene as great estates as his, burne to ashes, as great persons as himselfe ruined and destroyed, burne out, and vanish into sparks, and stinking smoake; He hath seene halfe his owne time burnt out and wasted, and yet hee dreames of an eternity in himselfe; He sayes, I am, and none else; hee will not say so to me in expresse words, but does hee not say so to the whole world, in his manifest actions?

The Horse then, The proud man, hath no understanding, and the Mule, the licentious man, as little. The Ancients had a purpose to expresse that, when they placed by their Goddesse of Licentiousnesse, *Venus*, A Tortoyse, A Creature that had no heart; capable of no understanding. [j]And it is better expressed in those licentious persons, who pursued *Lots* guests. Their blindnesse brought them to an impossibility of finding the doore, (*They were weary in seeking the doore*) And if they had found it, they had found it shut. A man that hath wallowed long in that sin, when he seekes a doore to repentance, he will quickly be weary, for there lie hard conditions upon him; and he is in danger of finding the doore so shut, as his understanding (and that is all his key) cannot open; Hee will make shift for reasons, why he should continue in that sin, and he will call it ill nature, or falshood, or breach of promise, and inconstancy, to depart from the Conversation that nourishes that sin. The doore will be shut, and his Reason cannot, nay his Reason would not open it, but rather plead in the sins behalfe.

Thus far our first reason hath carried us, Doe it not, least you loose your understanding, The field of that blessed seed, The tree of that fruitfull graft, The materials for that glorious building, Faith; For, the understanding is the receptacle of Faith: But doe it not, the rather, because if ye do it, God will be brought to a necessity, *In chamo et fraeno maxillas constringere,* to hold in your mouths with *bit* and *bridle*, to come to hard usage, when as he would faine have you reduced by faire and gentle meanes. (*winter 1624–1625?*) 9:384–86

i. Esay 44:16.

j. Gen. 19.

10. The Crown of Glory (Job 19:26)

Ego, I, I the same body, and the same soul, shall be recompact again, and be identically, numerically, individually the same man. The same integrity of body, and soul, and the same integrity in the Organs of my body, and in the faculties of my soul too; I shall be all there, my body, and my soul, and all my body, and all my soul. I am not all here, I am here now preaching upon this text, and I am at home in my Library considering whether *S. Gregory*, or *S. Hierome*, have said best of this text, before. I am here speaking to you, and yet I consider by the way, in the same instant, what it is likely you will say to one another, when I have done. You are not all here neither; you are here now, hearing me, and yet you are thinking that you have heard a better Sermon somewhere else, of this text before; you are here, and yet you think you could have heard some other doctrine of downright *Predestination*, and *Reprobation*[11] roundly delivered somewhere else with more edification to you; you are here, and you remember your selves that now yee think of it, this had been the fittest time, now, when every body else is at Church, to have made such and such a private visit; and because you would bee there, you are there. I cannot say, you cannot say so perfectly, so entirely now, as at the Resurrection, *Ego*, I am here; I, body and soul; I, soul and faculties; as Christ sayd to *Peter, Noli timere, Ego sum, Fear nothing, it is I*; so I say to my selfe, *Noli timere*; My soul, why art thou so sad, my body, why dost thou languish? *Ego*, I, body and soul, soul and faculties, shall say to Christ Jesus, *Ego sum*, Lord, it is I, and hee shall not say, *Nescio te, I know thee not*, but avow me, and place me at his right hand. [k]*Ego sum, I am the man that hath seen affliction, by the rod of his wrath; Ego sum*, and I the same man, shall receive the crown of glory which shall not fade. (*1620?*) 3:109–10

11. The doctrine that certain persons are guided to eternal salvation while others are forever damned.

k. Lam. 3:1. 1. Pet. 5:4.

7 Names and Typology

Introduction

In the Renaissance, the tradition of identifying the name with the thing or person being named remained still current. So in his hymn "To the Name above Every Name, the Name of Jesus" (1648), Richard Crashaw celebrates the *Name* as if it were Jesus Himself, capable of the same passion and love, as Christians still speak of "the blood of Christ." The name is the emblem of the divine, the living sign of God, not an extrinsic or fortuitous label without any special character in itself. Here, then, is one idea fundamental to what Donne says throughout this chapter: the name expresses the very life of whatever is being named, and so we see that the names of God not only describe Him but "become" Him.

A second basic principle of the chapter is embodied in *types* (τύποι). Typology associates the records and characters of the Old Testament with the events and persons of the New Testament, seeing in the former prophetical adumbrations of the latter. Typology thus becomes a means of allegorizing or of seeing spiritual or mystical significance in names, words, and acts. For Donne, typology is a "grammar of understanding," a kind of poetic association of names with forces and ideas. The foreshadowings of the Christian dispensation in the events and persons of the Old Testament are but one kind of typological form: so the Israelites' crossing of the Red Sea is the "type" of baptism (1 Cor. 10:1–6); Adam, Abraham, Moses, and David are all "types" of Christ; but later figures associated with the earthly life of Christ, such as John the Baptist and Paul himself, also have a special typological significance of a kind we might style "symbolic."

The chapter begins with the "name" of God. In order that we may have a more immediate and "presentiall knowledge" of God, He expresses Himself through many names or qualities by which we may call upon Him—Creator, Redeemer, Benefactor. God called Himself *I am*, "his bosome name, his viscerall name"—that is, the name that touches most sensitively our deepest feelings. This name is important to Donne's thinking about God as Essence itself, and as a God that we may know closely. Donne refers to the three scriptural names of

God—*Elohim, Adonai,* and *Jehovah*—and, guided by both tradition and temperament, he discovers great significance in the meanings of each of these names. *Elohim* is a plural name that anticipates the New Testament concept of the triune God. *Adonai,* or *Dominus* in Latin, *Lord* in English, suggests the foundation and the power of God. But Jehovah is His name of Essence, Being, and Subsistence, and it is in this radiant circumference that "we live, and move, and have our Being": "*Gods* proper name is *Alwayes Being*" (8 : 75–76). This consideration allows Donne another opportunity—an especially cogent one—of speculating on the nature of God's everlastingness, where man shall discover his own perpetuity, and where time exists in all ages.

The first section of this chapter thus defines and qualifies the names of God, which return to his Essence and express it. Thus He is also called *Germen Jehovae,* the blossom or bud of the Lord, with reference to His offspring; for the Father and the Son are in the same Godhead, and the profession of Jesus is also a profession of God's eternity. *Elohim* conveys His power and strength, "that name, which goes thorow all Gods whole work of the Creation" (1 : 234–35), and signifies His judgment, order, providence, dispensation, and government. The God of power—of *all* power, to give His name in the plural—descends to man in many ways, but never in fear; for fear tells of man's impotency when he tries to separate himself from God. Finally, we learn more about *Adonai*; where *Jehovah* is "essence," *Adonai* is "foundation": "an openinge of our desires and groanings . . . of our consciences to God . . . the corner-stone, and the piller of our buildinge . . . the Church" (2 : 159–60).

Now we pause briefly between the major sections of the chapter, with its study of names, on the one hand, and types, on the other, to consider God in His glory as the perfect type of the monarch, in whom is the idea and preconception of sovereignty. Donne is implicitly touching upon the medieval and Renaissance distinction between God as ruler of Heaven and as governor of man. Since Christ has power both as God and as man, our adoption of His name through baptism means a giving up of any other name that might rival His. So God's power is complete through Christ's authority over the "matriculation" of the members of His Church: monarchy is the type and Christ (Christian) is the name.

Donne's theory of names, as we have seen, other than the Name of God (which is Essence), is closely connected with his thinking about typology. "Is not thy name *Simon Magus,* if thou buy and sell spirituall things thy selfe?" (6 : 219–20). "Postdate the whole Bible," Donne urges, "and whatsoever thou hearest spoken of such, as thou art, before, beleeve all that to be spoken but now, and spoken to thee." Adam, David, and Christ "concern *Mankind collectively*, and so *you*, and *I*, and all have our portion in these calamities" (2:75).

Donne has some favorite types (or names) that represent different spiritual conditions. Jacob is the type of true prayer because of his disclaiming of merit (Gen. 32:10). Having declared this, Donne turns the idea into a suitable and extended consideration of humility, ending at last in a "mysterious" and "significative" figure of God's "overflowing goodness, ever to succor the infirmity of Man" (1:283). The name of Abraham suggests the seed of God, for it shares an *h* with *Jehovah* (or Essence). The notion is a witty play on the making up of names from common letters, where again something new grows out of the old, or is prefigured by it: new names, new promises, new seals, new obligations of the Spirit, and the assurance that the "essential" and "accidental" joys of Heaven shall reign. The scholastic terminology is a reminder of Donne's habit of thought that sees diversity in unity, the principle contained by its expression, and the creator by the created. But David is the name-type whose condition Donne finds most universal; David's Psalms, indeed, are made "not onely to vent *Davids* present holy passion, but to serve the Church of God, to the worlds end" (2:55). "Extend this *Man*, to all *Mankind*," Donne says; "carry *Davids* History up to *Adams* History," for in that place will we find ourselves. Thus Donne extends the historical figure backward in time, but forward, too, so that David embraces the whole and perfected condition of mankind.

Further selections show Donne elaborating other types, generally toward a similarly wide application. Hezekias (Josias), another type of Christ, particularly shows forth spiritual liberality; Jeremiah points to death and eternity, preaching only "the messages of God" (p. 207), though soberly, contentiously, and "satyrically"; Ezekiel is the prophet and type of the Resurrection. And in the Resurrection, we shall all rise—whether we be called Adam, the name of all men, or Mary, the name of all women. Donne reflects especially upon the importance of Mary, the name and the type, known in the Scriptures for comprehensive felicity and wisdom, and often in his own age for regality. He refers in passing to Queen Henrietta Maria, who was often one of his auditors, "that that blessing which God gave to these *Maries* [of the Resurrection] . . . he will also be pleased to give to the greatest of that name amongst us" (9:193). The topicality and the generality here meet.

In John the Baptist, of course, Donne sees his own type, where prophecy, testimony, history, faith, and action all merge. As John the

Baptist was not the light, not Christ, but one who bore witness of Him, so also Donne the preacher understands how his own role is parallel: "Onely that man, whose *conscience* testifies to himself, and whose *actions* testifie to the world, that he *does* what he *can*, can beleeve himself, or be beleeved by others, that he hath the true light of faith" (3:368). Such is the continuing application of John's mission. But even more than this, Donne finds his own spiritual story of conversion in Paul; the chapter ends fittingly with the typology of the New Covenant that translates the spiritual force of the old prophets into a moral application for contemporary man, with "his investing of Christ, his putting on of Christ, his rising againe by the power of a new inanimation, a new soule breathed into him from Christ" (6:206). These words describe the exaltation of the preacher who must fill all his speech with directions for a new heaven and a new earth.

A. The Name of God

1. God's Name: "Presentiall Knowledge" (Ps. 6:1)

There is no recourse but to God, no reliefe but in God; and therefore *David* applied himselfe to the right method, to make his first accesse to God.

It is to God onely, and to God by name, and not in generall notions; for it implies a nearer, a more familiar, and more presentiall knowledge of God, a more cheerfull acquaintance, and a more assiduous conversation with God, when we know how to call God by a Name, a Creator, a Redeemer, a Comforter, then when we consider him onely as a diffused power, that spreads itselfe over all creatures; when we come to him in Affirmatives, and Confessions, This thou hast done for me, then when we come to him onely in Negatives, and say, That that is God, which is nothing els. God is come nearer to us then to others, when we know his Name. For though it be truly said in the Schoole, that no name can be given to God, *Ejus essentiam adaequate repraesentans*, No one name can reach to the expressing of all that God is; and though *Trismegistus* doe humbly, and modestly, and reverently say, *Non spero*, it never fell into my thought, nor into my hope, that the maker and founder of all Majesty, could be circumscribed, or imprisoned by any one name, though a name compounded and complicated of many names, as the Rabbins have made one name of God, of all his names in the Scriptures; [a]Though *Jacob* seeme to have been rebuked *for asking Gods name*, when he wrastled with him; [b]And so

a. Gen. 32:29. *b.* Judg. 13:18.

also the Angel which was to doe a miraculous worke, a worke appertaining onely to God, to give a Childe to the barren, because he represented God, and had the person of God upon him, would not permit *Manoah* to enquire after his name, *Because*, as he sayes there, *that name was secret and wonderfull*; And though God himselfe, to dignifie and authorize that *Angel*, which he made his Commissioner, and the Tutelar and Nationall Guide of his people, sayes of that *Angel*, to that people, [c] *Feare him, provoke him not, for my Name is in him*, and yet did not tell them, what that name was; Yet certainly, we could not so much as say, God cannot be named, except we could name God by some name; we could not say, God hath no name, except God had a name; for that very word, *God*, is his name. God calls upon us often in the Scriptures, *To call upon his Name*; and in the Scriptures, he hath manifested to us divers names by which we may call upon him.

. . . .

Beloved, to know God by name, and to come to him by name, is to consider his particular blessings to thee; to consider him in his power, and how he hath protected thee there; and in his wisedome, and how he hath directed thee there; and in his love, and how he hath affected thee there; and exprest all, in particular mercies. He is but a darke, but a narrow, a shallow, a lazy man in nature, that knows no more, but that there is a heaven, and an earth, and a sea; He that will be of use in this world, comes to know the influences of the heavens, the vertue of the plants, and mines of the earth, the course and divisions of the Sea. To the naturall man, God gives generall notions of himselfe; a God that spreads over all as the heavens; a God that sustaines all as the earth; a God that transports, and communicates all to all as the sea: But to the Christian Church, God applies himselfe in more particular notions; as a Father, as a Son, as a holy Ghost; And to every Christian soule, as a Creator, a Redeemer, a Benefactor. (*1623?*) 5:322–23

2. I AM (Exod. 4:13)

God declares to *Moses*, his bosome name, his viscerall name, his radicall, his fundamentall name, the name of his Essence, *Qui sum, I am; Goe, and tell them, that he whose name is I am, hath sent thee*. It is true, that literally in the Originall, this name is conceived in the future; it is there, *Qui ero, I that shall be*. But this present acceptation, *I am*, that passed through all Translators, and all Commentators, and Fathers, and Councels, and Schooles, and the whole Church of God rests in it. And I know but [d] one, (who is of the Reformation, and of the

c. Exod. 23:20. *d.* Piscator.

most rigid subdivision in the Reformation, and who hath many other singularities besides this)[1] that will needs translate this name, *Qui eram, I was*. Howsoever, all intend, that this is a name that denotes Essence, Beeing: Beeing is the name of God, and of God onely: for, of every other creature, *Plato* saies well, *Ejus nomen est potius non esse*; The name of the Creator is, *I am*, but of every creature rather, I am not, I am nothing. Hee considers it, and concludes it, in the best, and noblest of creatures, Man; for, he, as well as the rest, *plus habet non entis, quam entis*; Man hath more privatives, then positives in him; Man hath but his owne beeing; Man hath not the beeing of an Angel, nor the beeing of a lyon; God hath all in a kind of eminence more excellently then the kinds themselves, onely his name is *I am*. *Plato* pursues this consideration usefully; *Habuit ante aeternum non esse*, Man had an eternall not beeing before; that is, before the creation; for those infinite millions of millions of generations before the Creation, there was a God, whose name was *I am*; but till within these sixe thousand yeares, Man was not, there was no man. And so saies *Plato*, *Haberet aeternum non esse*, As Man had an eternall not beeing before the Creation; so he would have another eternall not-beeing after his dissolution by death, in soule, as well as in body, if God did not preserve that beeing, which he hath imprinted in both, in both. And *jam dum est*, saies he, As man had one eternall not beeing before, and would have another after, so for that beeing which he seemes to have here now, it is a continuall declination into a not being, because he is in continuall change, and mutation, *quae desinit in non esse*, as he saies well; Every change and mutation bends to a not beeing, because in every change, it comes to a not being that which it was before; onely the name of God is *I am*. (*1627*) 8:144–45

3. God: Essence Itself (1 Thess. 4:17)

For whatsoever is any thing, even in that Beeing, and therefore because it is, hath a conformity to God, and an affinity with God, who is Beeing, Essence it self. [e]*In him we have our Beeing*, says the Apostle. But here it is more then so; not only *In illo*, but *Cum illo*, not only *In him*, but *With him*, not only in his Providence, but in his Presence.

The Hypocrite hath a Beeing, and, in God, but it is not with God, [f]*Quia cor longe, With his lips he honours God, but removes his heart far from him*. And God sends him after his heart, that he may keep him at

1. The reference is to Johannes Fischer (1546–1626), German Protestant theologian, controversialist, and translator.

e. Act. 17:28.

f. Esay 29:13.

that distance, (as S. *Gregory* reads and interprets that place of *Esay*) [g]*Redite praevaricatores ad cor,* Return O sinners, follow your own heart, and then I am sure you and I shall never meet. Our Saviour Christ delivers this distance plainly, [h]*Discedite a me, Depart from me, ye cursed, into everlasting fire.* Where the first part of the sentence is incomparably the heaviest, the departing worse then the fire; the intensnesse of that fire, the ayre of that brimstone, the anguish of that worm, the discord of that howling, and gnashing of teeth, is no comparable, no considerable part of the torment, in respect of the privation of the sight of God, the banishment from the presence of God, an absolute hopelesnesse, an utter impossibility of ever comming to that, which sustaines the miserable in this world, that though I see no Sun here, I shall see the Son of God there. The Hypocrite shall not do so; we shall Bee, and *Bee with him,* and *Bee with him for ever;* which is the last thing that doth fall under ours, or can fall under any consideration. (*1622*) 4:86

4. The Three Names of God in Scripture (Ps. 63:7)

The Names of God, which are most frequent in the Scriptures, are these three, *Elohim,* and *Adonai,* and *Jehovah;* and to assure us of his Power to deliver us, two of these three are Names of Power. *Elohim* is *Deus fortis,* The mighty, The powerfull God: And (which deserves a particular consideration) *Elohim* is a plurall Name; It is not *Deus fortis,* but *Dii fortes,* powerfull Gods. God is all kinde of Gods; All kinds, which either Idolaters and Gentils can imagine, (as Riches, or Justice, or Wisdome, or Valour, or such) and all kinds which God himself hath called gods, (as Princes, and Magistrates, and Prelates, and all that assist and helpe one another) God is *Elohim,* All these Gods, and all these in their height and best of their power; for *Elohim,* is *Dii fortes,* Gods in the plurall, and those plurall gods in their exaltation.

The second Name of God, is a Name of power too, *Adonai.* For, *Adonai* is *Dominus* The Lord, such a Lord, as is Lord and Proprietary of all his creatures, and all creatures are his creatures; And then, *Dominium est potestas tum utendi, tum abutendi,* sayes the law; To be absolute Lord of any thing, gives that Lord a power to doe what he will with that thing. God, as he is *Adonai, The Lord,* may give and take, quicken and kill, build and throw downe, where and whom he will. So then two of Gods three Names are Names of absolute power, to imprint, and re-imprint an assurance in us, that hee can absolutely deliver us, and fully revenge us, if he will. But then, his third Name,

g. Esay 46:8. *h.* Matt. 25:41.

and that Name which hee chooses to himselfe, and in the signification of which Name, hee employes *Moses*, for the reliefe of his people under Pharaoh, that Name *Jehovah*, is not a Name of Power, but onely of Essence, of Being, of Subsistence, and yet in the vertue of that Name, God relieved his people. And if, in my afflictions, God vouchsafe to visit mee in that Name, to preserve me in my being, in my subsistence in him, that I be not shaked out of him, disinherited in him, excommunicate from him, devested of him, annihilated towards him, let him, at his good pleasure, reserve his *Elohim*, and his *Adonai*, the exercises and declarations of his mighty Power, to those great publike causes, that more concerne his Glory, then any thing that can befall me; But if he impart his *Jehovah*, enlarge himselfe so far towards me, as that I may live, and move, and have my beeing in him, though I be not instantly delivered, nor mine enemies absolutely destroyed, yet this is as much as I should promise my selfe, this is as much as the Holy Ghost intends in this Metaphor, *Sub umbra alarum, Under the shadow of thy wings*, that is a Refreshing, a Respiration, a Conservation, a Consolation in all afflictions that are inflicted upon me. (*1626*) 7:66–67

5. Jehovah: Being (Ps. 6:1)

And in the first of these, the Person, we shall make these three steps; first that he [David] makes his first accesse to God onely, *O Lord rebuke me not*; doe not thou, and though I will not say, I care not, yet I care the lesse who doe. And secondly, that it is to God by Name, not to any universall God, in generall notions; so naturall men come to God; but to God whom he considers in a particular name, in particular notions, and attributes, and manifestations of himselfe; a God whom he knowes, by his former workes done upon him. And then, that name in which hee comes to him here, is the name of *Jehovah*; his radicall, his fundamentall, his primarie, his essentiall name, the name of *being, Jehovah*. For, he that deliberately, and considerately beleeves himselfe to have his very being from God, beleeves certainely that he hath his well being from him too; He that acknowledges, that it is by Gods providence that he breathes, beleeves that it is by his providence that he eates too. So his accesse is to God, and to God by name, that is by particular considerations, and then, to God in the name of *Jehovah*, to that God that hath done all, from his first beginning, from his Being.

. . . .

Every thing in the world, sayes he, can say, *Creator meus es tu*, Lord thou hast made me; All things that have life, and growth, can say, *Pastor meus es tu*, Lord thou hast fed me, increast me; All men can say, *Redemptor meus es tu*, Lord I was sold to death through originall sin, by one *Adam*, and thou hast redeemed me by another; All that have falne by infirmity, and risen againe by grace, can say, *Susceptor meus es tu*, Lord I was falne, but thou hast undertaken me, and dost sustaine me; But he that comes to God in the name of *Jehovah*, he meanes all this, and all other things, in this one Petition, Let me have a Being, and then I am safe, for *In him we live, and move, and have our Being*. If we solicite God as the Lord of Hosts, that he would deliver us from our enemies, perchance he may see it fitter for us to be delivered to our enemies: If we solicite him as Proprietarie of all the world, as the beasts upon a thousand mountaines are his, as all the gold and silver in the earth is his, perchance he sees that poverty is fitter for us: If we solicite him for health, or long life, he gives life, but he kills too, he heales, but he wounds too; and we may be ignorant which of these, life or death, sicknesse or health, is for our advantage. But solicite him as *Jehovah*, for a Being, that Being which flowes from his purpose, that Being which he knowes fittest for us, and then we follow his owne Instructions, *Fiat voluntas tua*, thy will be done upon us, and we are safe.

Now that which *Jehovah* was to *David*, *Jesus* is to us. Man in generall hath relation to God, as he is *Jehovah*, Being; We have relation to Christ, as he is *Jesus*, our Salvation; Salvation is our Being, *Jesus* is our *Jehovah*. And therfore as *David* delights himself with that name *Jehovah*, for he repeats it eight or nine times in this one short Psalm, and though he asks things of a diverse nature at Gods hands, though he suffer afflictions, of a diverse nature, from Gods hands, yet still he retains that one name, he speaks to God in no other name in all this Psalm but in the name of *Jehovah*: So in the New Testament, he which may be compared with *David*, because he was under great sins, and yet in great favour with God, S. *Paul*, he delights himself with that name of *Jesus* so much, as that S. *Jerome* says, *Quem superflue diligebat, extraordinarie nominavit*, As he loved him excessively, so he named him superabundantly. It is the name that cost God most, and therefore he loves it best; it cost him his life to be a *Jesus*, a Saviour. The name of Christ, which is Anointed, he had by office; he was anointed as King, as Priest, as Prophet. All those names which he had in *Isaiah*, [i] *The Counsellor, The Wonderfull, The Prince of Peace*, and the name of *Jehovah* it self, which the Jews deny ever to be given to him and is evidently given to him in that place, Christ had by nature; But his name of *Jesus*, a Saviour, he had by purchase, and that purchase cost him his bloud. [j] And therefore, as *Jacob* preferred his name of *Israel*, before his former name of *Jacob*, because he had that name upon

i. Esay 9.

j. Gen. 32:28.

his wrastling with God, and it cost him a lamenesse; so is the name of *Jesus* so precious to him who bought it so dearly, that not only every knee bows at the name of *Jesus* here, but Jesus himself, and the whole Trinity, bow down towards us, to give us all those things which we ask in that name. For even of a devout use of that very name, do some of the Fathers interpret that, *Oleum effusum Nomen tuum,* That the name of *Jesus* should be spread as an ointment, breathed as perfume, diffused as a soul over all the petitions of our prayers; As the Church concludes for the most part, all her Collects so, *Grant this O Lord, for our Lord and Saviour Christ Jesus sake.* And so much does S. *Paul* abound in the use of this name, as that he repeats it thrice, in the superscription of one of his Letters, the title of one of his Epistles, his first to *Timothy*. And with the same devotion, S. *Augustine* sayes, even of the name, *Melius est mihi non esse, quam sine Jesu esse,* I were better have no being, then be without Jesus; *Melius est non vivere, quam vivere sine vita,* I were better have no life, then any life without him. For as *David* could finde no beeing without *Jehovah,* a Christian findes no life without *Jesus*. Both these names imply that which is in this Text, in our Translation, *The Lord, Dominus*; to whom only, and intirely we appertaine; his we are. And therefore whether we take *Dominus,* to be *Do minas,* to threaten, to afflict us, or to be *Do manus,* to succour, and relieve us, (as some have pleased themselves with those obvious derivations) as *David* did still, we must make our recourse to him, from whom, as he is *Jehovah,* Beeing, our being, our wel-beeing, our eternall beeing, our Creation, Preservation, and Salvation is derived; all is from him. (*1623?*) 5:320, 326–27

6. God's Proper Name: Always Being (2 Pet. 3:13)

As God hath provided us an *Endlesnesse,* in the world to come, so, to give us an Inchoation, a Representation of the next world, in this, *God* hath instituted an *endlesnesse* in this world too; *God* hath imprinted in every *naturall man,* and doth exalt in the *super-naturall,* and *regenerate* man, an endlesse, and Undeterminable desire of more, then this life can minister unto him. Still *God* leaves man in *expectation*. And truly, that man can scarce prove the *immortality* of the *soule* to himselfe, that feeles not a desire in his *soule,* of something beyond this life. Creatures of an inferiour nature are possest with the *present*; *Man* is a *future Creature*. In a holy and usefull sense, wee may say, that *God is a future God*; to man especially hee is so; Mans consideration of *God* is specially for the *future*. It is plaine, it is evident, that that *name* which *God* hath taken in [k]*Exodus,* signifies, *Essence, Being.*

k. 3:14. Ambros.

Verum nomen Dei, Semper esse, Gods proper name is *Alwayes Being.* That can bee said of no creature, that it *alwayes was*; That which the *Arrians* said blasphemously, of Christ, *Erat, quando non erat,* is true of all creatures, There was a time, when *that thing,* was nothing. But of *God,* more than this may bee said; so much more, as that when we have said all that wee can, more then so much more remaines unsaid. For, [l]*Totum Deum, nemo uno nomine, exprimit, sicut nec totum aerem haurit*; A man may as well draw in, all the aire, at one breath, as expresse *all God, God* entirely, in one name. But the name that reaches farthest towards him, is that name, which he hath taken in *Exodus.* [m]*Deo si conjungimur sumus*; In being derived from *God,* we have a *Being,* we are *something*; *In him we live and move and have our Being*; But *Deo si comparemur, nec sumus*; If we bee compared with *God,* our *Being* with his *Being,* we have no *Being* at all, wee are *Nothing.* For *Being* is the *peculiar* and *proper* name of *God.* But though it be so cleere, that that *Name* of *God* in *Exodus* is *Being,* yet it is not so cleere, whether it be a *present* or a *future Being.* For, though most of the *Fathers* expressed, and our *Translators* rendered in the *present, Sum qui sum, I am that I am,* and, *Goe, and tell Pharaoh that he whose name is I am, hath sent thee*; yet in the *Originall,* it is plaine, and plaine in the *Chalde Paraphrase,*[2] that that name is delivered in the *future, Ero qui ero, I shall bee that I shall be,* and, *Goe, and tell Pharaoh that he whose name is I shall bee, hath sent thee. God* cals upon man, even in the consideration of the name of *God,* to consider his *future state.* For, if we consider *God* in the *present,* to day, now, *God* hath had as long a *forenoone,* as he shall have an *afternoone*; *God* hath beene *God,* as many millions of millions of generations, already, as hee shall be hereafter; but if we consider *man* in the *present,* to day, now, how short a *forenoone* hath any man had; if 60. if 80. yeeres, yet, *few and evill have his daies beene.* Nay, if we take man *collectively, entirely, altogether,* all mankind, how short a *forenoone* hath man had? It is not yet 6000 yeeres, since man had his first *being.* But if we consider him in his *Afternoone,* in his *future state,* in his *life* after *death,* if every minute of his 6000. yeeres, were multiplied by so many millions of *Ages,* all would amount to nothing, meerely nothing, in respect of that *Eternity,* which hee is to dwell in. We can expresse mans *Afternoone,* his future Perpetuity, his Everlastingnesse, but one way; But it is a faire way, a noble way; This; That how late a *Beginning* soever *God* gave Man, Man shall no more see an *end,* no more die, then *God* himselfe, that gave him life. (*1627*)   8:75–76

2. See note 3 to Chap. 1.

l. Nazian[zen].   *m.* Greg.

7. Germen Jehovae *(1 Cor. 12:3)*

There is first an open profession of the tongue required; And therefore the Holy Ghost descended in fiery tongues, *Et lingua propria Spiritui Sancto*, sayes S. *Gregory*, The tongue is the fittest Instrument for the Holy Ghost to worke upon, and to worke by, *Qui magnam habet cognationem cum Verbo*, sayes he, The Son of God is the Word, and the Holy Ghost proceeds from him, And because that faith that unites us to God, is expressed in the tongue, howsoever the heart be the center in which the Holy Ghost rests, the tongue is the Spheare, in which he moves: And therefore, sayes S. *Cyril*, as God set the Cherubim with a fiery sword, to keep us out of Paradise, so he hath set the Holy Ghost in fiery tongues to let us in againe. As long as *John Baptist* was unborne, *Zachary* was dumbe; when hee was borne, *Zachary* spoke; Christ is not borne in us, we are not regenerate in him, if we delight not to speake of his wondrous mercyes, and infinite goodnesse to the sons of men; as soone as he is borne in us, his Spirit speakes in us, and by us; in which, our first profession is *Jesum esse*, That Jesus is, That there is a Jesus.

This is to professe with *Esay*, [n]That he is *Germen Jehovae*, The Bud of the Lord, The Blossome of God himselfe; for this Profession is a two-edged sword; for it wounds the Arians on one side, That Jesus is Jehovah, (because that is the name that signifies the very essence of God) and then it wounds the Jews on the other side, because if Jesus be *Germen Jehovae*, The Bud, the Blossome, the Off-spring of God, then there is a plurality of Persons, Father and Son in the God-head. So that it is a Compendiary and Summary Abridgement, and Catechisme of all our Religion, to professe that Jesus is, for that is a profession of his everlasting Essence, that is, his God-head. It hath been denyed that he was such as he was pretended to be, that is, borne of a Virgin; for the first Heretiques of all, *Cerinthus*, and *Ebion*,[3] who occasioned S. *Johns* Gospel, affirmed him to be a meere man, made by ordinary generation, between *Joseph* and *Mary*. It hath been denyed, that he was such a man, as those Heretiques allowed him to bee, for *Apelles* his Heresie was, That he made himselfe a Body out of the Elements, as hee came downe from Heaven, through them. It hath been

3. Gnostic heretics. Cerinthus (fl.c. 100), along with the Ebionites of the first century, taught that the divine power descended upon Jesus at His baptism, only to depart from Him before the Crucifixion. Also discussed in this selection are Apelles, Cerdo[n], Marcion, and Basilides (all of the second century), who emphasized an extreme dualism of God and Christ.

n. Esay 4:2.

denyed, that he had any Body at all; *Cerdon* and *Marcion* said, That he lived and dyed, but *in Phantasmate*, in apparance, and onely in a forme and shape of a Body assumed; but, in truth, no Body, that did live or dye, but did onely appeare, and vanish. It hath beene denyed that that Body which hee had, though a true and a naturall Body did suffer, for *Basilides* said, That when he was led to Execution, and that on the way, the Crosse was laid upon *Simon* of *Cyren*, Christ cast a mist before their eyes, by which they tooke *Simon* for him, and crucified *Simon*, Christ having withdrawne himselfe invisibly from them, as at other times he had done. It hath been denyed, (though he had a true Body, and suffered truly therein) that he hath any Body now in Heaven, or shall returne with any, for hee that said hee made his Body of the Elements as hee came downe from Heaven, sayes also that hee resolved that Body into those Elements againe, at his returne. It hath beene denyed, That hee was, That he is, That he shall be; but this Profession, that Jesus is, includes all, for, He of whom that is alwayes true, *Est*, He is, He is Eternall, and He that is Eternall, is God: This is therefore a Profession of the God-head of Christ Jesus.

Now, in the next, as we professe him to be *Dominus, A Lord*, we professe him to be God and man, we behold him as he is a mixt person, and so made fit to be the Messias, the Anointed high Priest, King of that Church, which he hath purchased with his blood, And the anointed King of that Kingdome which he hath conquered with his Crosse. As he is *Germen Jehovae*, The off-spring of Jehovah, so he must necessarily be Jehovah; and that is the name, which is evermore translated The Lord; So also as he is Jehovah, which is the fountaine of all Essence and of all Beeing, so he is Lord, by his interest, and his concurrence, in our Creation; It is a devoute exercise of the soule, to consider, how absolute a Lord he is, by this Title of Creation; If the King give a man a Creation by a new Title, the King found before in that man, some vertuous and fit disposition, some preparation, some object, some subject of his favour. The King gives Creations to men, whom the Universities, or other Societies had prepared; They Created persons whom other lower Schooles had prepared; At lowest, he that deales upon him first, finds a man, begotten and prepared by Parents, upon whom he may worke. But remember thy Creator, that called thee, when thou wast not, as though thou hadst beene, and brought thee out of nothing; which is a condition (if we may call it a condition, to be nothing, not to be) farther removed from Heaven, then hell it selfe: Who is the Lord of life, and breathed this life into thee, and sweares by that eternall life, which he is, that he would have this life of thine immortall, *As I live, saith the Lord, I would not the death of a sinner*. (*1624?*) 6:122–24

8. Elohim: *Power and Government (Ps. 55:19)*

As he will be feared, so he will be feared, no otherwise, then as he is God: *Non timuerunt Deum*, is the increpation of the Text, *They feared not God*. It is *timor Dei* and not *timor Jehovae*: God is not here expressed by the name of *Jehovah*, that unexpressible and unutterable, that incomprehensible and unimaginable name of Jehovah. God calls not upon us, to be considered as God in himself, but as God towards us; not as he is in heaven, but as he works upon earth: And here, not in the School, but in the Pulpit; not in Disputation, but in Application. It is not *timor Jehovae*, nor it is not *timor Adonai*: God does not call himself in this place, *The Lord*: for, to be Lord, to be proprietary of all, this is *potestas tam utendi quam abutendi*, It gives the Lord of that thing power, to do, absolutely, what he will with that which is his: And so, God, as absolute Lord, may damn without respect of sin, if he will; and save without respect of faith, if he will. But God is pleased to proceed with us, according to that Contract which he hath made with us, and that Law which he hath given to us, in those two Tables, *Tantummodo crede, Onely believe, and thy faith shall save thee*; and, *Fac hoc et vives, Live well, and thy good works shall make sure thy salvation*. Lastly, God does not call himself here *Dominum exercituum, The Lord of hosts*; God would not onely be considered, and served by us, when he afflicts us with any of his swords, Famine, War, Pestilence, Malice, or the like; but the fear required here, is to fear him as God, and as God presented in this name, *Elohim*; which, though it be a name primarily rooted in power and strength, (for *El* is *Deus fortis*, The powerful God; and as there is no love without fear, so there is no fear without power) yet properly it signifies his Judgment, and Order, and Providence, and Dispensation, and Government of his creatures. It is that name, which goes thorow all Gods whole work of the Creation, and disposition of all creatures, in the first of *Genesis*: in all that, he is called by no other name then this, the name *God*; not by *Jehovah*, to present an infinite Majestie; nor by *Adonai*, to present an absolute power; nor by *Tzebaoth*, to present a Force, or Conquest: but onely in the name of *God*, his name of Government. All ends in this; To fear God, is to adhere to him, in his way, as he hath dispensed and notified himself to us; that is, as God is manifested in Christ, in the Scriptures, and applied to us out of those Scriptures, by the Church: not to rest in Nature without God, nor in God without Christ, nor in Christ without the Scriptures, nor in our private interpretation of Scripture, without the Church. (*1617*) 1:234–35

9. Elohim: *Plural Power Opposes Fear (Ps. 34:11)*

There is nothing so contrary to God, as false fear; neither in his own nature, nor in his love to *us*. Therefore Gods first Name in the Bible, and the Name which he sticks to, in all the worke of the Creation, is his Name of Power, *Elohim*; *El*, is *fortis Deus*, The God of Power; and it is that Name in the plurall, multiplied power, All Power; And what can he feare? God descends to many other humane affections; you shall read that God was Angry, and sory, and weary; But *non timuit Deus*, God was never afraid. Neither would God that man should be. So his first blessing upon man, was to fill the earth, and to *subdue the creatures*, and to *rule over them*, and to eat what he would upon the earth; All Acts of Power, and of Confidence. As soon as hee had offended God, the first impotency that he found in himself, was *fear*: [o]*I heard thy voice, and I was afraid*, says he. He had heard the voice of Lions, and was not afraid. There is not a greater commination of a curse, then that, [p]*They shall be in a great fear, where no fear is*; Which is more vehemently expressed in another place, [q]*I will set my face against you, and you shall flye, when none pursues you; I will send a faintnesse into their hearts, and the sound of a shaken leafe, shall chase them, as a sword*. False feare is a fearfull curse. To feare that all favours, and all preferments, will goe the wrong way, and that therefore I must clap on a byasse, and goe that way too, this inordinate fear is the curse of God. *Davids* last counsail to *Solomon*, (but reflecting upon us all) was, [r]*Be thou strong therefore, and show thy selfe a man. E Culmine corruens, ad gyrum laboris venit*, The Devill fell from his place in heaven, and now is put to *compasse* the earth. The fearfull man that fals from his morall and his Christian constancy, from the fundamentall rules of his religion, fals into labyrinths, of incertitudes, and impertinencies, and ambiguities, and anxieties, and irresolutions. [s]*Militia, vita*; our whole life is a warfare; God would not chuse *Cowards*; hee had rather we were valiant in the fighting of his battels; for battels, and exercise of valour, we are sure to have. (*1624*) 6:107–8

10. Adonai: *Foundation (Ps. 38:9)*

Nowe there are two names of God which are ordinarily in the Scriptures translated by this word Dominus, the Lord. One name is *Jehovah*, and the other is *Adonai*. And *Jehovah* signifies essence, beinge, *Adonai* signifies properly basis, *fundamentum*, that upon

o. Gen. 3:10.
p. Ps. 53:5.
q. Lev. 26:17, 36.
r. 1. Reg. 2:2. Gregor.
s. Job 7:1.

which some buildinge rests, and in this place thats the word, *Adonai*. Soe that this is an openinge of our desires and groanings, of the wounds and scruples of our consciences to God, as God is the Lord, and such a Lord as is the basis and foundation, the corner-stone, and the piller of our buildinge, and that buildinge is the Church. All power of remission of sinnes is in the Lord, but in the Lord in his Church. And therefore since that Church in which God hath sealed thee to him in both sacraments, accordinge to the direction of the Holy Ghost, hath ordayned that sick persons shall make a speciall confession, yf they feele their consciences troubled with any weighty matter, and that after that confession, the priest shall absolve them, let noe man thinke himself wiser then the Church, and for the abuse of a thinge in a corrupt Church, goe forward in an ignorance of what the true Church holds in that point, or defraude himselfe of nourishment out of a false feare of poysons and fumes, when there are none. Let noe man thinke himselfe out of the presence of God, by puttinge himselfe into the presence of his minister, nor doubt but that, that confession is *ante Dominum*, and that absolution is *a Domino*, and from that Lord who is presented heere not as *Jehovah* the Lord of essence and beinge, and so in his generall providence and sustayninge of all creatures, but as *Adonai*, a Lord that is the basis and foundation of his Church. (*1618*) 2:159–60

B. Typology

1. God: Type of Monarchy (Lam. 4:20)

Of all things that are, there *was* an *Idea* in God; there was a modell, a platform, an examplar of every thing, which God produced and created in Time, in the mind and purpose of God before: Of all things God *had* an *Idea*, a preconception; but of Monarchy, of Kingdome, God, who is but one, *is* the *Idea*; God himselfe, in his Unity, *is* the Modell, He *is* the Type of *Monarchy*. He made but one World; for, this, and the next, are not *two Worlds*; This is but the *Morning*, and that the *everlasting Noon*, of one and the same Day, which shall have no Night: They are not *two Houses*; This is the *Gallery*, and that the *Bed-chamber* of one, and the same Palace, which shall feel no ruine. He made this one World, but *one Eye, The Sunne*; The *Moone* is not another Eye, but a Glasse, upon which, the Sunne reflects. He made this one World, but *one Eare, The Church*; He tells not us, that he heares by a left Eare, by Saints, but by that right Eare, the Church he doth. There is *One God, One Faith, One Baptisme*, and these lead us to the love of one

Soveraign, of Monarchy, of Kingdome. In that Name, God hath convayed to us the state of *Grace*, and the state of *Glory* too; and he hath promised both, in injoining that Petition, *Adveniat Regnum, Thy Kingdome Come*, Thy Kingdome of *Grace* here, Thy Kingdome of *Glory* hereafter. All forms of Government have one and the same *Soul*, that is, *Soveraignty*; That resides somewhere in every form; and this Soveraignty is in them all, from one and the same *Root*, from the *Lord of Lords*, from *God* himself, for *all Power is of God*: But yet this form of a *Monarchy*, of a *Kingdome*, is a more lively, and a more *masculin Organe*, and Instrument of this Soul of Soveraigntie, then the other forms are: Wee are sure *Women* have Soules as well as *Men*, but yet it is not so expressed, *that God breathed a Soule into Woman*, as hee did into Man; All formes of Governement have this Soule, but yet God infuseth it more manifestly, and more effectually, in that forme, in a *Kingdome*: All places are alike neare to Heaven, yet Christ would take a *Hill*, for his Ascension; All governments may justly represent God to mee, who is the God of Order, and fountaine of all government, but yet I am more eased, and more accustomed to the contemplation of *Heaven*, in that *notion*, as *Heaven is a kingdome*, by having been borne, and bred in a Monarchy: God is a Type of that, and that is a Type of Heaven. (*1622*) 4:240–41

2. Into the Name of Christ (Gal. 3:27)

To men who were of years, and well known in the world already by their name, if they were converted to the Christian faith, the Church did not use to give *new names* at their baptisme: neither to Children alwayes; but sometimes as an indifferent thing, they left them to the custome of that country, or of that family, from which they were derived. When *Saint Augustine* sayes, that he came to Milan, to S. *Ambrose*, at that time, *quo dari nomina oportuit*, when Names were to be given, it is true, that he speaks of a time, when *Baptisme* was to be administred, but that phrase of *Giving of Names*, was not a receiving of Names at Baptisme, (for neither *Ambrose*, nor *Augustine*, received any new name at their Baptisme) but it was a giving up of their Names, a Registring, a Matriculating of their Names in the book of the profession of the Christian Religion, and a publique declaration of that profession.

To be baptized therefore *into the name* of Christ, is to be translated into his *Family*, by this spirituall adoption, in which adoption (when it was *legall*) as they that were adopted, had also the name of the family into which they were adopted, as of *Octavius Octavianus*, and the rest, so are we so baptized, into *his name*, that we are of *Christus*

Christiani; and therefore to become truly *Christians*, to live Christianly, this is truly to be baptized into *his name*. (*1624?*) 5:164

C. The Postdated Bible

1. Names and Types (Acts 9:4)

This is an impropriation without sacriledge, and an enclosure of a Common[4] without damage, to make God mine owne, to finde that all that God sayes is spoken to me, and all that Christ suffered was suffered for me. And as *Saul* found this voyce at first, to be directed to him, so ever after he bends his eye the same way, and observes the working of God especially upon himselfe; As at the beginning, so in the way too; particularly there, [t]*By the grace of God I am that I am*; and then, *His grace was bestowed on me, And not in vaine*; and againe, *I have laboured more abundantly then all*; And after all, still he considers himselfe, and findes himselfe to be the greatest sinner, *Quorum ego maximus*. It is called a greatnesse of spirit, or constancy, but it is indeed an incorrigible height of pride, when a man will not beleeve that he is meant in a libel, if he be not named in that libel. It is a fearfull obduration, to be Sermon-proofe, or not to take knowledge, that a judgement is denounced against him, because he is not named in the denouncing of that judgement. Is not thy name *Simon Magus*, if thou buy and sell spirituall things thy selfe? and is not thy servants name *Gehazi*, if he exact after? Is not thy name *Cain*, if thou rise up against thy brother? And is not thy name *Zacheus*, if thou multiply thy wealth by oppression? Is not thy name *Dinah*, if thou gad abroad, to see who will solicite thee? And is not the name of *Putiphars* Wife upon thee, if thou stay at home and solicite thy servants? Postdate the whole Bible, and whatsoever thou hearest spoken of such, as thou art, before, beleeve all that to be spoken but now, and spoken to thee. This was one happinesse here, that *Saul* found this voyce to be directed to him; And another (which is our last Consideration) is what this voyce said; it said, *Saul, Saul, why persecutest thou me?* (*1625*) 6:219–20

2. Adam—David—Christ (Ps. 38:3)

There is no soundnesse in my flesh, because of thine anger, neither is there any rest in my bones, because of my sinne.

Which words we shall first consider, as they are our present object,

4. Referring to the act of enclosing, surrounding, or appropriating commonly held land.

t. 1. Cor. 15.

as they are historically, and literally to be understood of *David*; And secondly, in their *retrospect*, as they look back upon the first *Adam*, and so concern *Mankind collectively*, and so *you*, and *I*, and all have our portion in these calamities; And thirdly, we shall consider them in their *prospect*, in their future relation to the *second Adam*, in *Christ Jesus*, in whom also all mankinde was collected, and the calamities of all men had their *Ocean* and their confluence, and the cause of them, the anger of God was more declared, and the cause of that anger, that is sin, did more abound, for the sins of all the world were *his*, by imputation; for this Psalm, some of our Expositors take to be a *historicall*, and *personall* Psalm, determined in *David*; some, a *Catholique*, and *universall* Psalm, extended to the whole condition of *man*; and some a *Propheticall*, and *Evangelicall* Psalm, directed upon *Christ*. None of them inconveniently; for we receive help and health, from every one of these acceptations; first, *Adam* was the *Patient*, and so, his promise, the promise that he received of a *Messiah*, is our *physick*; And then *David* was the *Patient*, and there, his *Example* is our *physick*; And lastly, *Christ Jesus* was the *Patient*, and so, his *blood* is our physick. In *Adam* we shall finde the *Scriptum est*, the medicine is in our books, an assurance of a Messiah there is; In *David* we shall find the *Probatum est*, that this medicine wrought upon *David*; and in *Christ* we finde the receit it self; Thus you may take this physick, thus you may apply it to your selves. In every acceptation, as we consider it in *David*, in *our selves*, in *Christ*, we shall consider first, That specification of humane misery and calamity, expressed here, *sicknesse*, and an *universall sicknesse*; *No soundnesse in the flesh*: And more then that, *trouble*, and an *universall trouble*; *No peace, no rest, not in the bones*.

. . . .

All these particulars will best arise to us in our second consideration, when wee consider, *Humanitatem*, not *Hominem*, our humane condition, as we are all kneaded up in *Adam*, and not this one person *David*. But because we are in the consideration of *health*, and consequently of *physick*, (for the true and proper use of physick, is to *preserve* health, and, but by accident to restore it) we embrace that Rule, [u]*Medicorum theoria experientia est, Practise is a Physicians study*; and he concludes out of events: for, says he, He that professes himself a Physician, without experience, *Chronica de futuro scribit*, He undertakes to write a Chronicle of things before they are done, which is an irregular, and a perverse way. Therefore, in this spirituall physick of

u. Paracels.

the soul, we will deal upon *Experience* too, and see first, how this wrought upon this *particular person*, upon *David*.

. . . .

In this second part, first we contemplate *man*, as the Receptacle, the Ocean of all misery. Fire and Aire, Water and Earth, are not the Elements of man; Inward decay, and outward violence, bodily pain, and sorrow of heart may be rather styled his Elements; And though he be destroyed by these, yet he consists of nothing but these. As the good qualities of all creatures are not for their own use, (for the *Sun* sees not his own glory, nor the *Rose* smells not her own breath: but all their good is for *man*) so the ill conditions of the creature, are not directed upon themselves, (the Toad poisons not it selfe, nor does the Viper bite it self) but all their ill powrs down upon *man*. As though man could be a *Microcosm*, a world in himself, no other way, except all the misery of the world fell upon him. *Adam* was able to decypher the nature of every Creature in the *name* thereof, and the Holy Ghost hath decyphered his in his *name* too; In all those names that the Holy Ghost hath given man, he hath declared him miserable, for, [v]*Adam*, (by which name God calls him, and *Eve* too) signifies but *Redness*, but a *Blushing*: and whether we consider their low materials, as it was but *earth*, or the *redness* of that earth, as they stained it with their own blood, and the blood of all their posterity, and as they drew another more precious blood, the blood of the Messias upon it, every way *both* may be *Adam*, both may *blush*. So God called that pair, our first Parents, man in that root, *Adam*: But the first name, by which God called man in generall, *mankinde*, is *Ish*, [w]*Therefore shall a man leave his Father, etc*. And *Ish*, is but *a sonitu, a rugitu*: Man hath his name from *crying*, and the occasion of *crying, misery*, testified in his entrance into the world, for he is *born crying*; and our very Laws presume, that if he be alive, he will cry, and if he be not heard cry, conclude him to be born dead. And where man is called *Gheber*, (as he is often) which is derived from *Greatness*, man is but great so, as that word signifies; It signifies a Giant, an *oppressour*, Great in power, and in a delight to doe great mischiefs upon others, or *Great*, as he is a *Great mark*, and easily hit by others. But man hath a fourth name too in Scripture, *Enosh*, and that signifies nothing but *misery*. When *David* says, [x]*Put them in fear O Lord, that the Nations may know they are but men*; there's that name *Enosh*, that they are but miserable things. *Adam* is *Blushing*, *Ish* is *lamenting*, *Geber* is *oppressing*, *Enosh* is *all* that; but especially that, which is essentially notified for the

v. Gen. 5:2.
w. Gen. 2:24.
x. Ps. 9:20.

misery in our Text, *Enosh* is *Homo aeger*, a man miserable, in particular, by the misery of *sicknesse*, which is our next step, *Non sanitas, There is no soundnesse, no health in me.* (*1618*) 2:75–79 [see Chap. 2, section A.1]

3. Jacob and True Prayer: Disclaiming Merit (Gen. 32:10)

This text is in the midst of *Jacobs* prayer; and this prayer is in the midst of *Jacobs* preparation in the time of danger.

. . . .

First then this part of the prayer, hath in it, that which is the Center and Basis, and establish-ment of all true prayers, A disclaiming of Merit; for when a man pretends Merit, it is so far from a prayer, as that it is rather a chalenge, an increpation, an exprobation of his slacknes to whom we speak, that he gives us not without asking: I am not worthy sayes *Jacob*. But yet though *Jacob* confess humblie this unworthyness in himselfe, yet he does not say that he is, or was Nothing at all, in respect of these benefits. It is not *Nihil sum, but katon, parvus sum, Impar sum*; Man is no such thing as can invite God to work upon him, but he is such a thing, as nothing else is capable of his working but man. It is not much that he is; but something he is: But *parvus sum, prae omnibus, prae singulis*; whether I take my self altogether, thus grown up in honour, in office, in estate, or whether I take my self in pieces, and consider every step, that thy mighty hand hath led me; I am not worthy of all these, nor of any of these degrees; not of the least of these. Not whether I consider thy mercies, which are the promises that God makes to us at first, out of his meer gracious goodness, or whether I consider thy truth, the assuredness of those promises, to which he hath been pleased to bind himself; *non sum dignus*, not whether we consider this Truth, and fidelity of God *in Spe*, in our own hope, and confident, and patient expectation, that they shall be performed unto us, or whether we consider them *in Re*, in our thankfulness, and experience, as truths already performed unto us; the truth which thou hast shewed, for all these mercies, and all these truths, all these promises, and all these performances, as they found no title at all in me to them at first, so they imprint no other title in me by being come, but to make me his servant, to use them to his glory.

. . . .

Now this littleness, how poor, and small a thing Man is, appears to him, whether he consider himself *in omnibus*, or *in singulis*, as the word imports here, as he is altogether, or as he is taken a sunder.

. . . .

But we may better discern our selves *in singulis*, then *in omnibus*; better by taking ourselves in pieces, then altogether, we understand the frame of mans body, better when we see him naked, than apparrelled, howsoever; and better by seeing him cut up, than by seeing him do any exercise alive; one desection, one Anatomy teaches more of that, than the marching, or drilling of a whole army of living men. Let every one of us therefore dissect and cut up himself, and consider what he was before God raised him friends to bring those abilities, and good parts, which he had, into knowledge, and into use, and into employment; what he was before he had by education, and study, and industry, imprinted those abilities in his soul; what he was before that soul was infused into him, capable of such education; what he was, when he was but in the list, and catalogue of creatures, and might have been left in the state of a worm, or a plant, or a stone; what he was, when he was not so far, but onely in the vast and unexpressible, and unimaginable depth, of nothing at all. But especially let him consider, what he was when he lay smothered up in *massa damnata*, in that leavened lump of *Adam*, where he was wrapped up in damnation. And then let him consider forward again, that God in his decree severed him out, in that lump, and ordained him to a particular salvation; that he provided him parents, that were within the Covenant, that should prepare, and pour out a body for him; that he himself created, and infused an immortal soul into him; that then he put a care in his parents, perchance in strangers, to breed him to a capableness of some course. That then God took him by the hand, and led him into the Court; that there he held him by the hand, and defended him against envy, and practise; that he hath clothed him with the opinions of good men; that he hath adorned him with riches, and with titles; let a man stand thus, and ruminate, and spell over Gods several blessings to him, sylable by sylable, and he shall not onely say, *parvus sum*, when he considers himself at his growth and altogether, but *parvus eram* I was too mean a subject for thee to look or work upon in the least of these expressings of thy goodness.

. . . .

Jacobs happiness appears first now, *quando revertitur*; and now, *quando jubente Domino*, now, when he returned, and now when he returned upon Gods bidding, God had said unto him, [y] turn again into the land of thy fathers, and I will be with thee. Think no step to be directly made towards preferment, if thou have not heard Gods voice directing the way. *Stare in usque*; stand upon the ways, and inquire

y. Gen. 31:3.

not of thy fathers, but of the God of thy fathers, which way thou shalt go: for Gods voice may be heard in every action, if we will stand still a little, and hearken to it. Remember ever more, that *Applica Ephod*; where *David* comes to ask counsell of the Lord, he said to *Abiather*, [z]*Applica Ephod*; bring the *Ephod*; and there *David* askes, *Shall I follow this company, shall I overtake them?* when thou doubtest of any thing, *Applica Ephod*, take this book of God: if, to thine understanding, that reach not home punctually to thy particular case, thou hast an *Ephod* in thy self; God is not departed from thee; thou knowest by thy self, it is a vain complaint that *Plutarch* makes, *defectu oraculorum*, that oracles are ceased; there is no defect of oracles in thine own bosome; as soon as thou askest thy self, how may I corrupt the integrity of such a Judge, undermine the strength of such a great person, shake the chastity of such a woman, thou hast an answer quickly it must be done by bribing, it must be done by swearing, it must be done by calumniating. Here is no *defectus Oraculorum* no ceasing of Oracles, there is a present answer from the Devil. There is no defect of the *Urim*, and *Thummim* of God neither, If thou wilt look into it, for as it is well said of the Morall Man, *Sua cuique providentia Deus* Every mans Diligence, and discretion is a God to himselfe, so it is well said, of the Christian Father *Augustin*, *Recta ratio Verbum Dei* a rectified Conscience is the word of God. *Applica Ephod*, bring thine Actions to the question of the *Ephod*, to the debatment of thy conscience rectified, and [thou] still shalt hear, *Jubentem Dominum* or *Dominum Revocantem*, God will bid thee stop, or God will bid thee go forwards in that way.

But herein had *Jacob* another degree of happiness, That the Commandement of God, was persued with the Testimony of Angells. Not that the voyce of God needs strength; *Teste me ipso* witness my selfe, was always witness enough; and *Quia os Domini Locutum*, the Mouth of the Lord hath spoken it, was always seal enough. But that hath been Gods abundant and overflowing goodness, ever to succor the infirmity of Man, with sensible and visible things; with the pillars in the Wilderness; with the Tabarnacle after; and with the Temple and all the mysterious, and significative furniture thereof after all. So God leaves not *Jacob* to the general knowledge, that the Angels of God protect Gods Children, but he manifested those Angels unto him, *Occurrerunt ei*, the Angels of God met him. The word of God is an infalible guide to thee, But God hath provided thee also visible, and manifest assistants, the Pillar his Church, and the Angels his Ministers in the

z. 1. Sam. 30:7.

Church. The Scripture is thine onely *Ephod*, but *Applica Ephod*, apply it to thee by his Church, and by his visible Angels, and not by thine own private interpretation. (*1618*) 1:268–70, 272–74, 282–83

4. Abraham (Gen. 17:24)

First, he gives him a *new Name*; in which change of his Name, from *Abram*, to *Abraham*, (besides that he was changed from *Pater Magnus*, to *Pater Multitudinis*, from the Father of a *great possession* and *family*, to the Father of *a great succession* and *posterity*, for that diminishes any Greatnesse, to have no posterity to leave that to) this also arises to be noted, that *Gods* Name *Jehovah*, having in that two Letters of one kind, two *HH*, *God* divides with his Servant, *God* affords one of those letters to the dignifying of *Abrahams* name, he adds an *H* of his owne Name to his: *Jehovah* is his *essentiall name*; and in communicating any beame of that Essence, any letter of that Name, we become *semen Dei*, the seed of God; and *filii Dei*, the Sonnes of God; and *participes divinae naturae*, Partakers of the Divine nature; and *idem spiritus cum Domino*, the same spirit with the Lord; and Hearers of that voice; *Ego dixi Dii estis*, I have said you are Gods: If we were carefull to answer our old name, the name of *Christians*, in our conformity to Christ, and performance of Christianly duties, that were well, and other Names needed not, as remembrancers unto us: But God does give us *new Names* and *additions* of *Offices*, and *Titles* in *Schoole*, or *Court*, or *Common-wealth*, as new testimonies of his love, and *rebukes* of our former negligences, and *Remembrancers* of our present Duties in those places, and Encouragers to a more carefull proceeding in them. Secondly, God gave *Abraham* a *new Wife*: in which, the blessing was, that he tooke not from him that virtuous and obedient Wife which he had before, *Sara*, but now he made her a *Wife* unto him, and he supplied *that* onely defect which was in her, *Barrennesse*, and so made her fully a Wife, *a Mother*. Thirdly, he gave him a *new Sonne*; for, God who purposed to blesse all Nations in *Abraham's* seed, would not onely repaire and furnish his *old house*, (that is, blesse *Ismael* with temporall blessings) but he would build him a *new house*, raise him up a new Sonne, *Isaac*: He would not onely fulfill that petition of *Abrahams*, *Oh that Ismael might live in thy sight!* not onely preserve *Ismael*, which signifies, *Exauditionem Domini*, that the Lord had heard that prayer, in the behalf of *Ismael*; but he would give him an *Isaac*, which signifies, *Risum*, *laetitiam*, that is, he would give him a new, and true occasion of *joy*. Fourthly, he gave him a *new promise*; that as in *Adam* he had promised a *Messias*, *in semine mulieris*, *in the seed of the Woman*; now he contracts that promise to

Abraham, in semine tuo, in thy seed shall all Nations be blessed; and so makes *Abraham*, not onely a *Partner* with his other Children, in the Salvation of that *Messias*, but he makes *Abraham a meanes* to derive that Salvation upon others also, *In semine tuo, thou* shalt not onely be blessed *in the Seed of the Woman*, but all Nations shall be blessed in *thy seed*. And lastly, he gives him a *new seale*; not onely *that* seale, under which he was wont to deale with him, not onely an *inward* seale in his *heart*, but he gives him a new seale, a *visible* seale, the seale of *Circumcision*. This being then the Dignity of Gods precepts, that they require a present, and an exact obedience, without any counter-disputing; this being the infirmity of mans nature, that he is ever ready to object and oppose reasons, according to flesh and blood, against Gods precepts; this being the overflowing measure of Gods mercy to his Children, to give them the issue with the tentation; Reason above that Reason, victory at last, and alacrity in the performance of that precept; and this being his infinite bounty, to give us such rewards and retributions for those victories, of which, onely his goodnesse, and his strength, was the Author in us, when we doe performe those duties, (all which we have seen in *Abrahams* obedience to a fleshly Circumcision) *that* Circumcision being come to an end in the Circumcision of *Christ*, performed this day: Let us come to *this* Circumcision, of which, that was but a *Figure*, a *Spirituall Circumcision*, the *Circumcision of the heart*, and God shall give us *new Names* (new Demonstrations, that our names are written in the Booke of life) and *new Marriages* (refresh his promise in the Prophet, that *he will marry himselfe to us for ever*) and *new Sonnes*, new *Isaacks* (assurance of *new Joyes, Essentiall* and *Accidentall*,[5] in the Kingdome of Heaven, and *inchoative* here in the way) and *new promises*, and *new seales* (new obligations of his Blessed Spirit) that that *Infallibility* of salvation which we have conceived, is well grounded. (*1625*) 6:194–95

5. David's Prophecy (Ps. 38:4)

First then, personally in himselfe, prophetically in us, *David* laments our state, *quia peccata*, because we are under sin, sin which is a depravation of man in himself, and a deprivation of God from man. And then our next cause of lamentation is, the *propriety in sin*, that they are *nostra, our own, iniquitates meae*, says *David, My sins, Mine iniquities* are gone over my head.

We are not all *Davids, amabiles*, lovely and beloved in that measure

5. Donne adopts these two terms, usually applied to eucharistic theology, to express the idea that both form and essence are become one.

that *David* was, *men according to Gods heart*: But we are all *Adams, terrestres*, and *lutosi*, earth, and durty earth, red, and bloudy earth, and therefore in our selves, as derived from him, let us finde, and lament all these *numbers*, and all these *weights* of sin. Here we are all born to a patrimony, to an inheritance; an inheritance, a patrimony of sin; and we are all good husbands, and thrive too fast upon that stock, upon the encrease of sin, even to the treasuring up of sin, and the wrath of God for sin. How naked soever we came out of our mothers wombe, otherwise, thus we came all apparelled, apparelled and invested in sin; And we multiply this wardrobe, with new *habits*, habits of customary sins, every day. Every man hath an answer to that question of the Apostle, *What hast thou, that thou hast not received from God?* Every man must say, I have pride in my heart, wantonnesse in mine eyes, oppression in my hands; and that I never received from God. Our sins are our *own*; and we have a covetousnesse of more; a way, to make other mens sins ours too, by drawing them to a fellowship in our sins. (*1618*) 2:101

6. David—Mankind (Ps. 38:2)

[a] *He sent out his Arrows, and scattered them*, sayes *David*; magnifying Gods goodness in his behalf, against his enemies. And so again, [b] *God will ordaine his Arrowes for them that persecute me*. [c] *Complebo sagittas*, says God, *I will heap mischiefs upon them, and I will spend mine arrows upon them*: yea, [d] *Inebriabo sanguine, I will make mine Arrows drunk in their bloud*. It is *Idiotismus Spiritus sancti*, a peculiar character of the holy Ghosts expressing Gods anger, in that Metaphore of shooting *Arrows*. In this place, some understand by these Arrows, foul and infectious *diseases*, in his body, derived by his *incontinence*. Others, the sting of *Conscience*, and that fearfull choice, which the Prophet offered him, *war, famine*, and *pestilence*. Others, his passionate *sorrow* in the *death* of *Bethsheba's first childe*; or in the *Incest* of *Amnon* upon his sister, or in the *murder* upon *Amnon* by *Absolon*; or in the *death* of *Absolon* by *Joab*; or in many other occasions of sorrow, that surrounded *David* and his family, more, perchance, then any such family in the body of story. But these *Psalmes* were made, not onely to vent *Davids* present holy passion, but to serve the Church of God, to the worlds end. And therefore, change the person, and wee shall finde a whole quiver of arrows. Extend this *Man*, to all *Mankind*; carry *David's* History up to *Adams* History, and consider us in that state, which wee inherit from *him*, and we shall see *arrows* fly

a. Ps. 18:14.
b. Ps. 7:13.
c. Deut. 32:23.
d. v.42.

about our ears, *A Deo prosequente*, the anger of God hanging over our heads, in a cloud of arrows; and *a conscientia remordente*, our own consciences shooting *poisoned arrows* of desperation into our souls; and *ab Homine Contemnente*, Men multiplying arrows of *Detraction*, and *Calumny*, and *Contumely* upon our good name, and estimation. Briefly, in that wound, as wee were all shot in *Adam*, we bled out *Impassibilitatem*, and we sucked in *Impossibilitatem*; There we lost our *Immortality*, our *Impassability*, our assurance of Paradise, and then we lost *Possibilitatem boni*, says S. *Augustine*: all possibility of recovering any of this by our selves. So that these arrows which are lamented here, are all those miseries, which sinne hath cast upon us. (*1618*) 2:55

7. Hezekias: Liberality (Isa. 32:8)

This is *Esays* Prophecie of the times of an *Hezekias*, of a *Josias*, the blessing of this civill and morall Liberality, in all these persons. And it is time to passe to our other generall part, from the civill, to the spirituall, and from applying these words, to the good times of a good King, to that, (which is evidently the principall purpose of the Holy Ghost) That in the time of Christ Jesus, and the reigne of his Gospel, this, and all other vertues, should bee in a higher exaltation, then any civill, or morall respect can carry them to.

As an *Hezekias*, a *Josias* is a Type of Christ, but yet but a Type of Christ; so this civill Liberality, which we have hitherto spoken of, is a Type, but yet but a Type of our spirituall Liberality. For, here we doe not onely change termes, the temporall, to spirituall, and to call that, which we called Liberality in the former part, Charity in this part; nor do we onely make the difference in the proportion and measure, that that which was a Benefit in the other part, should be an Almes in this. But we invest the whole consideration in a meere spirituall nature; and so that Liberality, which was, in the former acceptation, but a relieving, but a refreshing, but a repairing of defects, and dilapidations in the body or fortune, is now, in this second part, in this spirituall acceptation, the raising of a dejected spirit, the redintegration of a broken heart, the resuscitation of a buried soule, the re-consolidation of a scattered conscience, not with the glues, and cements of this world, mirth, and musique, and comedies, and conversation, and wine, and women, (miserable comforters are they all) nor with that Meteor, that hangs betweene two worlds, that is, Philosophy, and morall constancy, (which is somewhat above the carnall man, but yet far below the man truly Christian and religious) But this is the Liberality, of which the Holy Ghost himselfe is content to be the

Steward, of the holy, blessed, and glorious Trinity, and to be notified, and qualified by that distinctive notion, and specification, *The Comforter*. (*1628*) 8:245–46

8. Jeremiah: An Emblem of Death (1 Cor. 15:26)

[e] *Surge et descende in domum figuli*, sayes the Prophet *Jeremy*, that is, say the Expositors, to the consideration of thy Mortality. It is *Surge, descende, Arise and go down*: A descent with an ascension: Our grave is upward, and our heart is upon *Jacobs* Ladder, in the way, and nearer to heaven. Our daily Funerals are some Emblemes of that; for though we be laid down in the earth after, yet we are lifted up upon mens shoulders before. We rise in the descent to death, and so we do in the descent to the contemplation of it. In all the Potters house, is there one vessell made of better stuffe then clay? There is his matter. And of all formes, a Circle is the perfectest, and art thou loath to make up that Circle, with returning to the earth again?

Thou must, though thou be loath. *Fortasse*, sayes S. *Augustine*, That word of contingency, of casualty, Perchance, *In omnibus ferme rebus, praeterquam in morte locum habet*: It hath roome in all humane actions excepting death. He makes his example thus: such a man is married; where he would, or at least where he must, where his parents, or his Gardian will have him; shall he have Children? *Fortasse*, sayes he, They are a yong couple, perchance they shall: And shall those Children be sons? *Fortasse*, they are of a strong constitution, perchance they shall: And shall those sons live to be men? *Fortasse*, they are from healthy parents, perchance they shall: And when they have lived to be men, shall they be good men? Such as good men may be glad they may live? *Fortasse*, still; They are of vertuous parents, it may be they shall: But when they are come to that *Morientur*, shall those good men die? here, sayes that Father, the *Fortasse* vanishes; here it is *omnino, certe, sine dubitatione*; infallibly, inevitably, irrecoverably they must die. Doth not man die even in his birth? The breaking of prison is death, and what is our birth, but a breaking of prison? Assoon as we were clothed by God, our very apparell was an Embleme of death. In the skins of dead beasts, he covered the skins of dying men. Assoon as God set us on work, our very occupation was an Embleme of death; It was to digge the earth; not to digge pitfals for other men, but graves for our selves. Hath any man here forgot to day, that yesterday is dead? And the Bell tolls for to day, and will ring out anon; and for as much of every one of us, as appertaines to this

e. Jer. 18:2.

day. *Quotidie morimur, et tamen nos esse aeternos putamus*, sayes S. *Hierome*; We die every day, and we die all the day long; and because we are not absolutely dead, we call that an eternity, an eternity of dying: And is there comfort in that state? why, that is the state of hell it self, Eternall dying, and not dead. (*1622*) 4:51–52

9. Jeremiah: Satyrical Preacher (Ps. 38:2)

Jonas was angry because his Prophesie was not performed; because God would not second his Prophesie in the destruction of Nineveh. *Jeremy* was angry because his Prophesie was like to be performed; he preached heavy Doctrin, and therfore his Auditory hated him; *Woe is me, my Mother*, says he, *that thou hast born me a man of strife, and a man of contention to the whole earth!* I preach but the messages of God; (and *vae mihi si non*, wo be unto me if I preach not them) I preach but the sense of Gods indignation upon mine own soul, in a conscience of mine own sins, I impute nothing to another, that I confesse not of my selfe, I call none of you to confession to me, I doe but confesse my self to God, and you, I rack no mans memory, what he did last year, last week, last night, I onely gather into my memory, and powr out in the presence of my God, and his Church, the sinfull history of mine own *youth*, and yet I am a *contentious man*, says *Jeremy*, a worm, and a burthen to every tender conscience, says he, *and I strive with the whole earth*, I am a bitter, and satyricall preacher; This is that that wearies mee, says hee, *I have neither lent on usury*, nor *men have lent me on usury*, yet, as though I were an oppressing lender, or a fraudulent borrower, *every one of them doth curse me*. (*1618*) 2:52–53

10. Ezekiel and the Prophecy of Resurrection (1 Cor. 15:26)

In that famous, and most considerable propheticall vision which God exhibited to *Ezekiel*, where God set the Prophet in a valley of very many, and very dry bones, and invites the severall joynts to knit again, tyes them with their old sinews, and ligaments, clothes them in their old flesh, wraps them in their old skin, and cals life into them again, Gods principall intention in that vision was thereby to give them an assurance of a Resurrection from their present calamity, not but that there is also good evidence of the last Resurrection in that vision too; Thus far God argues with them *a re nota*; from that which they knew before, the finall Resurrection, he assures them that which they knew not till then, a present Resurrection from those pressures: Remember by this vision that which you all know already, that at last I shall re-unite the dead, and dry bones of all men in a generall Resurrection: And then if you remember, if you consider, if you look upon that, can you doubt, but that I who can do that, can also recollect you, from your present dispersion, and give you a Resurrection to your former temporall happinesse? And this truly arises pregnantly, necessarily out of the Prophets answer; God asks him there, *Son of man, can these bones live?* And he answers, *Domine tu nosti, O Lord God thou knowest*. The Prophet answers according to Gods intention in the question. If that had been for their living in the last Resurrection, *Ezekiel* would have answered God as *Martha* answered Christ, when he said, [f]*Thy brother Lazarus shall rise again, I know that he shall rise again at the Resurrection at the last day*; but when the question was, whether men so macerated, so scattered in this world, could have a Resurrection to their former temporall happinesse here, that puts the Prophet to his *Domine tu nosti*, It is in thy breast to propose it, it is in thy hand to execute it, whether thou do it, or do it not, thy name be glorified; It fals not within our conjecture, which way it shall please thee to take for this Resurrection, *Domine tu nosti*, Thou Lord, and thou only knowest; Which is also the sense of those words, [g]*Others were tortured, and accepted not a deliverance, that they might obtain a better Resurrection*: A present deliverance had been a Resurrection, but to be the more sure of a better hereafter, they lesse respected that; According to that of our Saviour, [h]*He that findes his life, shall lose it*; He that fixeth himself too earnestly upon this Resurrection, shall lose a better.

This is then the propheticall Resurrection for the future, but a future in this world; That if Rulers take counsell against the Lord, the Lord shall have their counsell in derision; [i]If they take armes against the Lord, the Lord shall break their Bows, and cut their Speares in sunder; [j]If they hisse, and gnash their teeth, and say, we have swallowed him up; If we be made their by-word, their parable, their proverb, their libell, the theame and burden of their songs, as *Job* complaines, yet whatsoever fall upon me, damage, distresse, scorn, or *Hostis ultimus*, death it self, that death which we consider here, death of possessions, death of estimation, death of health, death of contentment, yet *Abolebitur*, it shall be destroyed in a Resurrection, in the return of the light of Gods countenance upon me even in this world. And this is the first Resurrection.

But this first Resurrection, which is but from temporall calamities,

f. John 11:24.
g. Heb. 11:35.
h. Mat. 10:39.
i. Ps. 2:4.
j. Ps. 46:9.

doth so little concerne a true and established Christian, whether it come or no, (for still *Jobs* Basis is his Basis, and his Centre, *Etiamsi occiderit*, though he kill me, kill me, kill me, in all these severall deaths, and give me no Resurrection in this world, yet I will trust in him) as that, as though this first resurrection were no resurrection, not to be numbred among the resurrections, S. *John* calls that which we call the second, which is from sin, the first resurrection: [k] *Blessed and holy is he, who hath part in the first resurrection*: And this resurrection, Christ implies, when he saies, [l] *Verely, verely, I say unto you, the houre is comming, and now is when the dead shall heare the voyce of the Son of God; and they that heare it shall live:* That is, by the voyce of the word of life, the Gospell of repentance, they shall have a spirituall resurrection to a new life. (*1622*) 4:57–59

11. Mary: Woman (Matt. 28:6)

Woman, as well as man, was made after the Image of God, in the Creation; and in the Resurrection, when we shall rise such as we were here, her sexe shall not diminish her glory: Of which, she receives one faire beame, and inchoation in this Text, that the purpose of God is, even by the ministery of Angels, communicated to women. But what women? for, their preparation, their disposition is in this Text too; such women, as were not only devout, but sedulous, diligent, constant, perseverant in their devotion; To such women God communicated himself; which is another Consideration in these persons.

As our Saviour Christ was pleased, that one of these women should be celebrated by name, for another act upon him, *Mary Magdalen*, and that wheresoever his Gospell was preached, her act should be remembred, so the rest, with her, are worthy to be known and celebrated by their names; Therfore we consider, *Quae*, and *quales*; first who they were, and then what they were; their names first, and then their conditions. [m] There is an Historicall relation, and observation, That though there be divers Kingdomes in Europe, in which the Crowns may fall upon women, yet, for some ages, they did not, and when they did, it was much at one time, and all upon women of one name, *Mary*. It was so with us in *England*, and in *Scotland* it was so; so in *Denmark*, and in *Hungary* it was so too; all foure, *Maries*.[6] Though regularly women

6. The four Maries are Queen Mary Tudor I of England (1553–1558); Mary Stuart Queen of Scots (d. 1587); Mary of Hungary (1505–1558), sister of Charles V; and Mary,

k. Apoc. 20:6.
l. John 5:25.
m. Bodin de repub. l.6.c.4.

should not preach, yet when these *Legati a latere*, these Angels from heaven did give Orders to women, and made them Apostles to the Apostles, the Commission was to women of that name, *Mary*; for, though our Expositors dispute whether the Blessed Virgin *Mary* were there then, when this passed at the Sepulchre, yet of *Mary Magdalen*, and *Mary* the Mother of *James*, there can be no doubt. Indeed it is a Noble, and a Comprehensive name, *Mary*. It is the name of woman, in generall; For, when *Adam* sayes of *Eve*, [n]*She shall be called Woman*, in the Arabique Translation, there is this name, *She shall be called Mary*; and the Arabique is, perchance, a dialect of the Hebrew. But in pure, and Originall Hebrew, the word signifies *Exaltation*, and whatsoever is best in the kinde thereof. [o]This is the name of that sister of *Aaron*, and *Moses*, that with her Quire of women assisted at that Eucharisticall sacrifice, that Triumphant song of Thanksgiving, upon the destruction, the subversion, the submersion of Aegypt, in the Red Sea. Her name was *Miriam*; and *Miriam* and *Mary* is the same name in women, as *Josuah* and *Jesus* is the same name to men. The word denotes *Greatnesse*, not only in Power, but in Wisdome, and Learning too; and so signifies often Prophets, and Doctors; and so falls fitliest upon these blessed women, who, in that sense, were all made *Maries*, Messengers, Apostles to the Apostles; in which sense, even those women were made *Maries*, (that is, Messengers of the Resurrection) who, no doubt, had other names of their own. [p]There was amongst them, the wife of *Chusa*, a great man in *Herods* Court, his Steward; and her name was *Joanna*, *Joane*. So that here was truly a Pope *Joane*, a woman of that name, above the greatest men in the Church. For the dignity of the Papacy, they venture to say, that whosoever was S. *Peters* Successor in the Bishoprick of Rome, was above any of the Apostles, that over-lived *Peter*; as S. *John* did; Here was a woman, a Pope *Joane*, Superiour to S. *Peter* himself, and able to teach him. But though we found just reason to celebrate these women by name, we meant not to stay upon that circumstance; we shut it up with this

Queen of Norway, Sweden, and Denmark (1353–1412). Bodin (in note *m*) means to show that women are unfit to rule by citing the example of these variously unfortunate queens. But Donne is impressed by the coincidence of names, not fortunes. His elaborate playfulness includes also Joanna, Chusa's wife, who is associated with Mary Magdalene and Mary the mother of James as a messenger of the Resurrection (Luke 8:3 and 24:10); Joanna (Joan) reminds Donne of Pope Joan, the legendary female Pope (of about 1100). Donne even manages an oblique reference to Queen Henrietta *Maria*.

n. Gen. 2:23.
o. Exod. 15:20.
p. Luke 8:3 and 24:10.

prayer, That that blessing which God gave to these *Maries*, which was, to know more of Christ, then their former teachers knew, he will also be pleased to give to the greatest of that name amongst us, That she may know more of Christ, then her first teachers knew. (*1630*) 9:192–93

12. Simeon (Luke 2:29, 30)

Having thus seene *Simeon* in these his Dimensions, with these holy impressions, these blessed characters upon him; first, [1]A man in a reverend age, and then, [2]In a holy function and calling, and with that, [3]Righteous in the eyes of men, and withall, [4]Devout in the eyes of God, [5]And made a Prophet upon himselfe by the holy Ghost, [6]still wayting Gods time, and his leasure, [7]And in that, desiring that his joy might be spread upon the whole Israel of God, [8]Frequenting holy places, the Temple, [9]And that upon holy motions, and there, [10]seeing the salvation of the Lord, that is, Discerning the application of salvation in the Ordinances of the Church, [11]And lastly, contenting himselfe with so much therein, as was according to his word, and not inquiring farther then God had beene pleased to reveale; and having reflected all these severall beames upon every worthy Receiver of the Sacrament, the whole Quire of such worthy receivers may joyne with *Simeon* in this Antiphon, *Nunc Dimittis, Lord now lettest thou thy servant depart in peace, etc.* S. *Ambrose* reades not this place as we doe, *Nunc dimittis*, but *Nunc dimitte*; not, Lord thou doest so, but, Lord doe so; and so he gives it the forme of a prayer; and implyes not only a patience, and a contentednesse, but a desire, and an ambition that he might die; at least such an indifferency, and equanimity as *Israel* had, when he had seen *Joseph*, [q]Now let me die, since I have seen thy face; after he had seen his face, the next face that he desired to see, was the face of God. For, howsoever there may bee some disorder, some irregularity, in S. *Pauls Anathema pro fratribus*, that he desired to be separated from Christ, rather then his brethren should, (that may scarce be drawen into consequence, or made a wish for us to imitate) yet to S. *Pauls Cupio dissolvi*, to an expresse, and to a deliberate desire, to be dissolved here, and to be united to Christ in heaven, (still with a primary relation to the glory of God, and a reservation of the will of God) a godly, a rectified and a well-disposed man may safely come. And so, (I know not upon what grounds) *Nicephorus* sayes, *Simeon* did wish, and had his wish; he prayed that he might die, and actually he did die

q. Gen. 46:30.

then. Neither can a man at any time be fitter to make and obtain this wish, then when his eyes have seen his salvation in the Sacrament. (*1626*) 7:296–97

13. John Baptist: Testimony (John 1:8)

Of *him*, who was this light, which *John Baptist* is here denyed to be, I spoke out of these words, and out of this place, the first time that I ascended to it, upon the *great Epiphany*, (as the first Church used to call it) the manifestation of *Christ Jesus* in the flesh, *Christmas day*; I reserved the rest of the Text, which concernes *John Baptist* himself, and his *office*, for *this* day, in which the Church celebrates *his memory*, who, though *he were not that light*, was *sent to beare witnesse of that light*.

We shall make our parts but two, *Testem*, and *Testimonium*, the *person*, and the *Office*; first, *who* the witnesse is, and then *what* he witnesses. In the first, we shall consider first, the *dignity*, the *fitnesse* of the person, implyed in the first word of this part of our Text, *but; he was not that light*; that is true, but yet he was something towards it; he was *nothing* considered with *Christ*, but he was *much* considered with any *other* man. And then we shall see his *title* to his office, *Missus est*, as he was fit in himself, so he was *sent* by him that had power to give Commission; and from these two, in which we shall determine our first part, the consideration of his *person*, we shall descend to the other, his *office*; and therein stop but upon two steps neither; first, *why any* testimony was required to so cleare a thing as *light*, and *such* a light, *that light*; and then, *what kinde* of testimony *John Baptist* did give to that light. (*1622*) 4:145–46

14. John Baptist's Mission (John 1:8)

If he think it enough to be excrementall *nayles*, to scratch and gripe others by his lazy usury, and extortion, or excrementall *hayre*, made onely for ornament, or delight of others, by his *wit*, or *mirth*, or delightfull conversation, these men have not yet felt this third citation, by which they are called to glorifie God, and so to *witnesse* for him, in such publique actions, as Gods cause for the present requires, and comports with their calling.

And then *John Baptist* had a fourth citation to bear witnesse for Christ, by laying down his life for the Truth; and this was that that made him a witnesse, in the highest sense, a *Martyr*. God hath not served this citation upon us, nor doth he threaten us, with any approches towards it, in the feare of *persecution* for religion. But remember that *John Baptists* Martyrdome, was not for the *fundamentall rock*, the body of the *Christian religion*, but for a *morall truth*, for matter of *manners*. A man may be bound to suffer much, for a lesse matter then the utter overthrow, of the whole frame and body of religion. But leaving this consideration, for what causes a man is bound to lay downe his life, consider we now, but this, that a man lays downe his life for Christ, and beares witnesse of him, even in death, when he prefers Christ before this world, when he *desires to be dissolved, and be with him*, and obeyes cheerefully that citation, by the hand of death, whensoever it comes; and that citation must certainly be served upon you all; whether this night in your beds, or this houre, at the doore, no man knowes. You who were cited *hither*, to *heare*, and cited *here*, to *consider*, and cited *hence*, to *worke* in a *calling* in the world, must be cited *from thence* too, from the face to the bosome of the earth, from treading upon other mens, to a lying downe in your owne graves. And yet that is not your last citation, there is a fifth.

In the grave, *John Baptist* does, and we must attend a *fifth citation*, from the grave to a *Judgement*. (*1622*) 4:160–61

15. John Baptist: Prophecy and History (John 1:8)

I am commanded *scrutari Scripturas, to search the scriptures*; now, that is not to be able to *repeat* any history of the Bible without booke, it is not to *ruffle* a Bible, and upon any word to turne to the Chapter, and to the verse; but this is *exquisita scrutatio*, the true searching of the Scriptures, to finde all the *histories* to be *examples* to me, all the *prophecies* to induce a Saviour for *me*, all the *Gospell* to apply Christ Jesus to *me*. Turne over all the folds, and plaits of thine owne heart, and finde there the infirmities, and waverings of thine *owne faith*, and an ability to say, *Lord, I beleeve, help mine unbeleefe*, and then, though thou have no Bible in thy hand, or though thou stand in a dark corner, nay though thou canst not reade a letter, thou hast searched that Scripture, thou hast turned to *Marke* 9. *ver*. 24. Turne thine eare to God, and heare him turning to thee, and saying to thy soule, *I will marry thee to my selfe for ever*; and thou hast searched that Scripture, and turned to *Hos*. 2. *ver*.19. Turne to thine owne *history*, thine *owne life*, and if thou canst reade there, that thou hast endeavoured to turne thine *ignorance* into *knowledge*, and thy knowledge into *Practice*, if thou finde thy selfe to be an example of that rule of Christs, *If you know these things, blessed are you, if you do them*, then thou hast searched that Scripture, and turned to *Jo*. 13. *ver*.17. This is *Scrutari Scripturas, to search the Scriptures*, not as though thou wouldest make a *concordance*, but an *application*; as thou wouldest search a *wardrobe*, not to make an *Inventory* of it, but to finde in it something fit for thy wearing. *John Baptist was not the light*, he was not Christ, *but he bore witnesse of him*. The light of *faith*, in the highest exaltation that can be had, in the *Elect*, here, is not that very *beatificall vision*, which we shall have in heaven, but it beares witnesse of that light. The light of *nature*, in the highest exaltation is not *faith*, but it *beares witnesse* of it. The lights of *faith*, and of *nature*, are subordinate *John Baptists*: *faith* beares me witnesse, that I have *Christ*, and the light of nature, that is, the *exalting of my naturall faculties* towards *religious uses*, beares me witnesse that I have *faith*. Onely that man, whose *conscience* testifies to himself, and whose *actions* testifie to the world, that he *does* what he *can*, can beleeve himself, or be beleeved by others, that he hath the true light of faith. (*1621*) 3:367–68

16. Stephen: Name as Debt (Acts 7:60)

Stephen, Stephanos is a leading, an exemplar name, a Significative, a Propheticall, a Sacramentall, a Catechisticall name; a Name that carries much instruction with it. Our Countryman *Bede* takes it to be an Hebrew name, and it signifies (saith hee) *Normam vestram*, Your Rule, Your Law: To obey the Law, to follow, to embrace the Law is an acceptable service to God, especially the invariable Law, the Law of God himselfe: But wee are sure that this name *Stephen, Stephanos* signifies a Crowne; to obey the Crowne, to follow, to serve the Crowne, is an acceptable service to God, especially the immarcessible Crown, the Crown of Glory. *Nomen Omen*; scarce any man hath a name, but that name is Legal and Historicall to him: His very name remembers him of some rules, and lawes of his actions, so his name is legall; and his name remembers him of some good men of the same name; and so his name is historicall. *Nomina Debita*: In the old formularies of the Civill Law, if a man left so many names to his Executors, they were so many specialties for debts. Our Names are Debts, every man owes the world the signification of his name, and of all his names; every addition of honour, or of office, layes a new Debt, a new Obligation upon him; and his first name, his Christian-Name above all. For, when new names are given to men in the Scriptures, that doth not abolish or extinguish the old: *Jacob* was called *Jacob* after God had called him *Israel*; and *Gedeon Gedeon* after he was called *Jerubaal*, and *Simon* when he was *Peter* too, was called *Simon*. Changes of Office and additions of Honour must not extinguish our Christian Name; The duties of our Christianity, and our Religion must preponderate and weigh down the duties of all other places, and for all together. Saint *Gregory* presents us a good use of this diligence to answere our Names, *Quo quis timet magis, ne quod dicitur non esset, eo plus quam dicitur erit*; The more a man is afraid that hee is not worthy of the name hee beares, whether the name of office or his Christian-Name, the better Officer and the better Christian he will be for that feare, and that solicitude; and therefore it is an usefull and an applyable Prayer for great Persons, which that Father makes in their behalfe, *Praesta, quaesumus Domine, ut quod in ore hominum sumus, in conspectu tuo esse valeamus*: Grant, O Lord, that wee may alwayes be such in thine eyes, as wee are in their tongues that depend upon us, and justifie their acclamations with thy approbations. And so far *Stephens* name, as his name signifies the Law, and as his name signifies the reward of fulfilling the Law, a Crown; hath carried us to the consideration of the duty of answering the signification of our names; But then there are other passages in his History and Actions that carries us farther.

First then we receive Saint *Stephen* to have been Saint *Paul*'s kinsman in the flesh, and to have been his fellow pupill under *Gamaliel*, and to have been equall to him, at least in the foundations, in natural faculties, and in the super-edifications too, in learnings of acquisition and study; And then to have had this great advantage above him, That hee applied himselfe as a Disciple to Christ before Saint *Paul* did; and in that profession became eminent ([r]for all the Sects, the Libertines themselves taking the liberty to dispute against him, they were not able to resist the wisedome and the Spirit by which hee spake) as that his Cosin *Paul*, then but *Saul*, envied him most, and promoved and assisted at his execution: For upon those words but two verses before our Text, That [s]*they that stoned* Stephen, *laid down their clothes at* Saul's *feet*, Saint *Augustine* sayes, *In manu omnium eum lapidavit*, That it was *Saul* that stoned *Stephen*, though by the hands of other executioners. Men of the best extraction and families, Men of the best parts and faculties, Men of the best education and proficiencies, owe themselves to God by most obligations. Him that dyes today God shall not only aske, where is that Soule? Is it as cleane as I made it at first? No stayn of Sin? or is it as clean as I washed it in Baptisme? No sting? No venome of original sinne in it? Or is it as clean as I left it when wee met last at the Sacrament? No guiltinesse of actuall sinne in it? God shall not only aske this, Where is that Soul? Nor only aske where is that Body? Is it come back in that Virginal integrity in which I made it? Or is it no farther departed from that then Marriage, which I made for it, hath made it? Are those *Maritales ineptiae* (that we may put *Luther*'s words into God's mouth) the worst

r. Act. 6:9. *s.* [Acts] 7:58.

that is faln upon that body? God shall not only ask for that Soul and that Body but aske also, Where is that Wit, that Learning, those Arts, those languages which by so good education I afforded thee? Truly when a weake and ignorant man departs into any vicious way, though in that case he doe adhere to the Enemy, and doe serve the Devill against God, yet he carries away but a single Man, and serves but as a common Souldier: But he that hath good parts, and good education, carries a Regiment in his person, and Armies and munition for a thousand in himself. Though then thy kinsmen in the flesh, and thy fellow pupils under *Gamaliel*, men whom thou hast accompanied heretofore in other waies, think thy present fear of God, but a childishness and pusilanimity, and thy present zeal to his service but an infatuation and a melancholy, and thy present application of thy self to God in prayer, but an argument of thy Court-dispaire, and of thy falling from former hopes there; yet come thou early, if it be early yet; and if it be not early, come apace to Christ Jesus: how learned soever thou art, thou art yet to learn thy first letters, if thou know not that Christ Jesus is *Alpha* and *Omega*, he in whom thou must begin and determine every purpose: Thou hast studied thy self but into a dark and damnable ignorance, if thou have labored for much learning only to prove that thou canst not be saved, only to dispute against the person and the Gospel of Christ Jesus. But propose to thine imitation *Stephen*, who though enriched with great parts, and formerly accustomed to the conversation of others of a different perswasion, applied himself early to Christ as a Disciple, and more then in that general application, in a particular function and office as a Deacon, [t] as is expressed in the former Chapter.

. . . .

The name of *Stephen* hath enough in it to serve not only the vehementest affection, but the highest ambition; for there is a Coronation in the Name as we told you before. And therefore in the Ecclesiastical story and Martyrologes of the Church, there are (I think) more Martyrs of this name, *Stephen*, then of any other Name; indeed they have all that Name, for the Name is a Coronation. And therefore the Kingdome of heaven, which is expressed by many precious Metaphors in the Gospel, is never called a Crown, till after *Stephens* death, till our Coronation was begun in his Martyrdome, but after in the Epistles often, and in the *Revelation* very often. For to suffer for God, man to suffer for God, I to suffer for my Maker, for my Redeemer, is such a thing, as no such thing, excepting only Gods sufferings for man can fall into the consideration of man. Gods suffering for man was the

t. [Acts 6:] v.5.

Nadir, the lowest point of Gods humiliation, mans suffering for God is the Zenith, the highest point of mans exaltation: That as man needed God, and God would suffer for man, so God should need man, and man should suffer for God. (*1628*) 8:180–85

17. Paul's Investing in Christ (Acts 9:4)

[u]*Let us now praise famous Men, and our Fathers that begat us,* (saies the Wiseman) that is, that assisted our second generation, our spirituall Regeneration; Let us praise them, commemorate them. [v]*The Lord hath wrought great glory by them, through his power from the beginning,* saies he there, that is, It hath alwaies beene the Lords way to glorifie himselfe in the conversion of Men, by the ministery of Men. For he adds, [w]*They were leaders of the people by their counsaile, and by their knowledge and learning meet for the people, wise and eloquent men in their instructions*; and that is, That God who gives these gifts for this purpose, looks for the employment of these gifts, to the edification of others, to his glory. [x]*There be of them, that have left a name behinde them,* (as it is also added in that place) that is, That though God can amply reward his servants in the next world, yet he does it sometimes in this world; and, though not with temporall happinesses, in their life, yet with honor, and commemorations, and celebrations of them, after they are gone out of this life, they leave a name behind them. And amongst them, in a high place, shines our blessed and glorious Apostle S. *Paul,* whose Conversion the Church celebrates now, and for the celebration thereof, hath appointed this part of Scripture from whence this text arises, to be the Epistle of the Day, *And he fell to the earth, and heard a voyce, saying, Saul, Saul, why persecutest thou me?*

There are words in the text, that will reach to all the Story of S. *Pauls* Conversion, embrace all, involve and enwrap all; we must contract them; into lesse then three parts, we cannot well; those will be these; first, The Person, *Saul,* He, *He fell to the earth*; and then, his humiliation, his exinanition of himselfe, his devesting, putting off of himselfe, *He fell to the earth*; and lastly, his investing of Christ, his putting on of Christ, his rising againe by the power of a new inanimation, a new soule breathed into him from Christ, *He heard a voyce, saying, Saul, Saul, why persecutest thou me?* (*1625*) 6:205–6

u. Ecclus. 44:1.
v. Ver.2.
w. Ver.4.
x. Ver.8.

8 *Image, Idol, Example, and Imitation*

Introduction

In this chapter we see Donne in his most characteristic Anglican manner; he maintains the so-called "middle way" between the Roman use of images and the Puritan abolition of them. Donne believes that the best, and perhaps only, image of God is in man, imprinted by two seals, "his *Image* in our soules, at our *making*, his *Image*, that is his *Sonne*, upon our bodies and soules, in his *incarnation*" (6:160). God's image is described in a variety of figurative terms, but one particularly expressive image depends upon direction. The east is where we must begin; "we must look to this East, the confession of the Trinity" (9:49). The west symbolizes our mortality; as heirs of Adam, we are "but red earth, earth dyed red in bloud, in Soul-bloud, the bloud of our own soules." In the north, whence the wind blows, is the "dissipation of that darknesse . . . that we are not all earth," and in the south is a knowledge that we cannot die. The compass holds these four quarters as we voyage in this life; but Donne aims to take us beyond these directions, away from this compass, "to see that God essentially, and face to face, after whose Image, and likenesse we were made before." Donne returns to these terms later in the chapter (see especially pp. 259–60), and to the circle (or compass) that contains the lines of direction (see sections D and E, on Emblems and Images), for they so aptly describe his typical attitudes.

Like man, the Church also bears God's seal in its liturgy, or public rites and offices. Donne, of course, is referring to the Church of England, "in which God hath given us our station" (6:284–85), neither "a *painted Church*" (that is, Roman) nor "*a naked Church*" (that is, Reformed, especially according to Calvin). In this simplified view of Anglicanism, which supposedly provides a way between "extremes," Donne is reflecting popular belief. The English Church offers not so much a compromise or *via media* (notions formulated much later, especially in the nineteenth century by Newman and the Tractarians), but an ideal church polity, through which "the whole Congregation sees God face to face."

Later generations have often regarded the Church of England as peculiarly national, supported by the conditions of a local culture. But this is not the way in which Donne regarded his Church; while he saw it as possessed of boundaries, he also celebrated its universal appeal and superiority:

> And though to all my thanksgivings to God, I ever humbly acknowledg, as one of his greatest Mercies to me, that he gave me my Pasture in this Park, and my milk from the brests of this Church, yet out of a fervent, and (I hope) not inordinate affection, even to such an Unity, I do zealously wish, that the whole catholick Church, were reduced to such Unity and agreement, in the form and profession Established, in any one of these Churches [Roman or Reformed] (though ours were principally to be wished) which have not by any additions destroyed the foundation and possibility of salvation in Christ Jesus. (*Essays in Divinity*, ed. Evelyn M. Simpson, Oxford, 1952, pp. 51–52)

Modern and recent gestures toward compromise and ecumenicism may be slightly foreshadowed here, but not relativism, where one belief is held to have no more inherent value than another. Donne has in mind the Church of England when he says, "The Church of God, by his Ordinance, hath set his stampe, upon a Liturgie and Service, for his house" (4:310). The best liturgy is one that is "fixed and stationary," not "occasionall and transitory," and one that expresses, in exemplary English, the historical continuity of the Apostolic church and avoids "extemporall effusions of irkesome and indigested Prayers" (the words are John Cosin's, from *A Collection of Private Devotions*, 1627). Yet Donne's desire is finally for a Church "discharged of disputations, and misapprehensions, and this defensive warr, [which] might contemplate Christ clearly and uniformely" (*Essays in Divinity*, p. 52).

Donne's repeated warnings about the "idolatrous love of the Creature" (1:199–200) have their origin in Reformation thought, and as well the process or change implicit in his reminder that "all love which is placed upon lower things, admits satiety; but this love of this pureness, always grows, always proceeds." Nevertheless, by contrasting the "abuse" made of images and ceremonies in the Roman Church with the "good use" to which they are put in the English Church, Donne reveals the extent to which he was also affected by the *Uti-Frui* (Use and Enjoyment) thesis espoused by St. Augustine in his *De Doctrina Christiana* (397–426): premature enjoyment is the abuse of an image. He writes in the same spirit as the author of the appendix to the first Book of Common Prayer (1549), "Of Ceremonies, Why Some Be Abolished and Some Retained," where Augustine is invoked in support of "those ceremonies which do serve to a decent order and godly discipline" because they encourage purity of devotion, and do not obscure reverent worship with "superstitious blindness." Thus Donne would have us "by preaching, and all convenient wayes of instruction, to deliver people out of that ignorance" such as possesses those who adhere to the "Roman captivity" (8 : 331). "It is a perverse way," Donne says, echoing the Prayer Book (and Augustine), "rather to abolish Things and Names . . . because they have been abused, then to reduce them to their right use" (7 : 325).

Donne insists that images are important as examples; then "Rule and Example together, direct us fully" (4 : 98–99). Christ is Himself a first example, and by His example, from which rules come, we may learn good patterns and become fit patterns for others: "God, we see, was the first, that made Images; and he was the first, that forbad them. He made them for imitation; he forbad them in danger of adoration" (9 : 75). Since God never acts without "an eternall pre-conception, an eternall Idea" (7 : 60), man cannot afford to live outside of this plan according to his own instruments. "What greater injustice, then to propose no Image, no pattern to thy selfe to imitate; and yet propose thy selfe for a pattern, for an Image to be adored?" (9 : 75). Singularity of opinion is the sad result of this injustice, and the end of the unpatterned life is "extemporall prayer [that is, hastily made for the occasion], and extemporall preaching . . . extemporall faith, and extemporall religion . . . [and] an extemporall Heaven" (7 : 61). The "Catholique Church," by which Donne means an historically continuous Church in England, does not lie in the direction of such extemporaneity, but in the place of formerly and still held ideas, examples, patterns, and beliefs.

Much of what Donne says in the section on "Emblems, Characters, and Signs," and in the one following on particular images, is important to his poetry and to the poetry of his time. The emblems of evening, of the circle, the compass, the centre: all of these occur in Donne's poetry, but they have the richness not only of prior association but also of expansive meditation. Furthermore, Donne also explicates images that are uniquely biblical, such as the red earth of man's creation, the waters of tribulation, the wings of mercy, the spiritual kinds of armor. Through this range of symbols and images, Donne well demonstrates the ease with which he thinks in terms of metaphor and sees the natural world as a sign for the transcendent and invisible one of glory: "God does give signes . . . he gives also irradiations, illustrations of the understanding, that they may be discerned to be his signes" (6 : 177).

Donne's imagination lingers especially on the location of the *Ubi*, the dwelling *Place* of God. On the one hand, He is in the Church and in the sacrament; Donne argues that God "returnes to us here, as in his *Ubi*, as in his own place. . . . He returnes to us in this place, as often as he maketh us partakers of his flesh, and his bloud" (5:368). On the other hand, Donne reminds us what the Maries learned at the sepulcher: "*Non hic . . . He is risen.*" But sacred place for Donne is preeminently internal, where spiritual comfort may be found: "Live Christianly, or thou art as far from Christ in the Sepulchre, and from all benefit of his Resurrection, as they that were hired to watch the Sepulchre, and to seale the Sepulchre to prevent the Resurrection, or as if he that lay in the Sepulchre had never dyed" (9:211–12). So God has really entered into us; though He is risen, we are risen in Him, and there is then "no Transubstantiation, no Ubiquitisme." Once more Donne resolves the problems of mortality and the circumscriptions of space by exalting the language of devotion.

A. Image: The Sight of God in Man

1. Image in Self

i. The Sight of God Here (1 Cor. 13:12)

That therefore you may the better know him, when you come *to see him face to face, then*, by having *seen him in a glasse now*, and that your seeing him now in his Ordinance, may prepare you to see him then in his Essence, proceed we thus in the handling of these words. First, That there is nothing brought into comparison, into consideration, nothing put into the balance, but the sight of God, the knowledge of God; It is not called a better sight, nor a better knowledge, but there is no other sight, no other knowledge proposed, or mentioned, or intimated, or imagined but this; All other sight is blindnesse, all other knowledge is ignorance; And then we shall see how there is a twofold sight of God, and a twofold knowledge of God proposed to us here; A sight, and a knowledge here in this life, and another manner of sight, and another manner of knowledge in the life to come: For, here we see God *In speculo, in a glasse*, that is, by reflexion, And here we know God *in aenigmate*, sayes our Text, *Darkly*, (so we translate it) that is, by obscure representations, and therefore it is called a *Knowledge but in part*; But in heaven, our sight is *face to face*, And our knowledge is *to know, as we are knowne*.

For our sight of God here, our Theatre, the place where we sit and see him, is the whole world, the whole house and frame of nature, and our *medium*, our *glasse*, is the Booke of Creatures, and our light, by which we see him, is the light of Naturall Reason.[1] And then, for our knowledge of God here, our Place, our Academy, our University is the Church, our *medium*, is the Ordinance of God in his Church, Preaching, and Sacraments; and our light is the light of faith. Thus we shall finde it to be, for our sight, and for our knowledge of God here. But for our sight of God in heaven, our place, our Spheare is heaven it selfe, our *medium* is the Patefaction, the Manifestation, the Revelation of God himselfe, and our light is the light of Glory. And then, for our knowledge of God there, God himself is All; God himself is the place, we see Him, in Him; God is our *medium*, we see Him, by him; God is our light; not a light which is His, but a light which is He; not a light which flowes from him, no, nor a light which is in him, but that light which is He himself. *Lighten our darknesse, we beseech thee, O Lord, O Father of lights, that in thy light we may see light*, that now we see this through this thy *glasse*, thine Ordinance, and, by the good of this, hereafter *face to face*. (*1628*) 8:220–21

ii. The Sealed Image (Apoc. 7:9)

This seale seales the contract betweene God and Man: And then consider how generall this seale is: First, God sealed us, in imprinting his *Image* in our soules, and in the powers thereof, at our *creation*; and so, every man hath this seale, and he hath it, as soone as he hath a soule: The *wax*, the *matter*, is in his *conception*; the *seale*, the forme, is in his quickning, in his *inanimation*; as, in *Adam*, the waxe was that *red earth*, which he was made of, the *seale* was that *soule*, that *breath* of *life*, which God breathed into him. Where the Organs of the body are so indisposed, as that this soule cannot exercise her faculties, in that man, (as in *naturall Idiots*, or otherwise) there, there is a *curtaine* drawn over this Image, but yet there this Image is, the Image of God, is in the most *naturall Idiot*, as well as in the wisest of men: worldly men draw *other pictures* over this picture, other images over this image: The *wanton* man may paint *beauty*, the *ambitious* may paint

1. Compare to Richard Hooker's statement (of 1593): "Whatsoever either men on earth, or the Angels of heaven do know, it is as a drop of that unemptiable fountaine of wisdom, which wisdom hath diversly imparted her treasures unto the world. As her waies are of sundry kinds, so her maner of teaching is not meerely one and the same. Some things she openeth by the sacred bookes of Scripture; some things by the glorious works of nature: with some things she inspireth them from above by spirituall influence, in some thinges she leadeth and trayneth them onely by worldly experience and practise. We may not so in any one speciall kind admire her that we disgrace her in any other, but let all her wayes be according unto their place and degree adored" (*Of the Laws of Ecclesiastical Polity*, ed. Georges Edelen, Cambridge, Mass., 1977, book 2, 1.4, in the Folger Library Edition of the *Works*, 1:147–48).

honour, the *covetous wealth*, and so deface this image, but yet there this image is, and even *in hell* it selfe it will be, in him that goes down into hell: *uri potest in gehenna, non exuri*, sayes St. *Bernard*, The Image of God may burne in hell, but as long as the soule remaines, that image remaines there too; And then, thou who wouldest not burne their picture, that loved thee, wilt thou betray the picture of thy Maker, thy Saviour, thy Sanctifier, to the torments of hell? Amongst the manifold and perpetuall interpretations of that article, *He descended into hell*, this is a new one, that thou sentest him to hell in thy soule: Christ had his *Consummatum est*, from the *Jewes*; he was able to say at last, *All is finished*, concerning *them*; shall he never have a *Consummatum est* from thee; never be at an end with thee? Never, if his Image must burne eternally in thy soule, when thou art dead, for everlasting generations.

Thus then we were *sealed*; all sealed; all had his *image* in our *creation*, in the faculties of our soules: But then we were all sealed againe, sealed in our *very flesh*, our mortall flesh, when the image of the invisible God, *Christ Jesus*, the onely Sonne of God, tooke our nature: for, as the *Tyrant* wished, that all mankinde were but one body, that he might behead all mankinde at a blow, so God tooke into his mercie, all mankinde in one person: As intirely, as all mankinde was in *Adam*, all mankinde was in *Christ*; and as the *seale of the Serpent* is in all, by *originall sinne*, so the *seale* of God, *Christ Jesus*, is on us *all*, by his assuming our *nature*. Christ Jesus tooke our souls, and our bodies, our whole nature; and as no Leper, no person, how infectiously soever he be diseased in his body, can say, surely Christ never tooke this body, this Leprosie, this pestilence, this rottennesse, so no Leprous soule must say, Christ never tooke this pride, this adultery, this murder upon himself; he sealed us all in *soule* and *body*, when he tooke *both*, and though both dye, the *soule in sin* daily, the *body in sicknesse*, perchance this day, yet he shall afford a resurrection to both, to the *soule* here, to the *body* hereafter, for his seale is upon both.

These two seales then hath God set upon us all, his *Image* in our soules, at our *making*, his *Image*, that is his *Sonne*, upon our bodies and soules, in his *incarnation*; And both these seales he hath set upon us, then when neither we our selves, nor any body else knew of it: He sets another seale upon us, when, though *we* know not of it, yet the *world*, the *congregation* does, in the Sacrament of *Baptisme*, when the seale of his *Crosse*, is a testimony, not that Christ was *borne*, (as the former seale was) but that also he *dyed* for us; there we receive that seale upon the *forehead*, that we should conforme our selves to him, who is so sealed to us. And after all these seales, he offers us another, and another seale, [a]*Set me as a seale upon thy heart, and as a seale upon thine arme,* says Christ to all us, in the person of the spouse; in the *Heart*, by a constant *faith*, in the *Arme*, by *declaratory works*; for then are we sealed, and *delivered*, and *witnessed*; that's our full evidence, then have we *made sure our salvation*, when the works of a holy life, doe daily refresh the contract made with God there, at our *Baptisme*, and testifie to the Church, that we doe carefully remember, what the *Church* promised in our behalfe, at that time: for, otherwise, beloved, without this *seale upon the arme*, that is, a stedfast proceeding in the *works* of a holy life, we may have received many of the other seales, and yet deface them all. 6:158–60

iii. God Looks at His Image in Men (Ps. 6:4,5)

If the King come to thy house, thou wilt professe to take it for an honour, and thou wilt entertaine him; and yet his comming cannot be without removes, and troubles, and charges to thee. So when God comes to thee, in his word, or in his actions, in a Sermon, or in a sicknesse, though his comming dislodge thee, remove thee, put thee to some inconvenience, in leaving thy bed of sinne, where thou didst sleepe securely before, yet here is the progresse of the Holy Ghost, intended to thy soule, that first he comes thus to thee, and then if thou turne to him, he returnes to thee, and settles himselfe, and dwels in thee.

This is too lovely a Prospect, to depart so soone from; therefore looke we by S. *Augustines* glasse, upon Gods comming and returning to man. God hath imprinted his Image in our soules; and God comes, sayes that Father, *Ut videat imaginem*; Where I have given my Picture, I would see how it is respected: God comes to see in what case his Image is in us; If we shut doores, if we draw Curtaines between him and his Image, that is, cover our soules, and disguise and palliate our sinnes, he goes away, and returnes in none of those former senses. But if we lay them open, by our free confessions, he returnes againe; that so, in how ill case soever he finde his Image, he may wash it over with our teares, and renew it with his own bloud, and, *Ut resculpat imaginem*, that he may refresh and re-engrave his Image in us againe, and put it in a richer and safer Tablet. And as the Angel which came to *Abraham* at the promise and conception of *Isaac*, gave *Abraham* a farther assurance of his Returne at *Isaacs* birth, [b]*I will certainly returne unto thee, and thy wife shall have a Sonne*; So the Lord, which was with thee in the first conception of any good purpose, Returnes to thee againe, to give thee a quickning of that blessed childe of his, and

a. Cant. 8:6. *b.* Gen. 18:10.

againe, and againe, to bring it forth, and to bring it up, to accomplish and perfect those good intentions, which his Spirit, by over-shadowing thy soule, hath formerly begotten in it. So then, he comes in Nature, and he returnes in Grace;[2] He comes in preventing, and returnes in subsequent graces; He comes in thine understanding, and returnes in thy will; He comes in rectifying thine actions, and returns in establishing habits; He comes to thee in zeale, and returnes in discretion; He comes to thee in fervour, and returnes in perseverance; He comes to thee in thy peregrination, all the way, and he returns in thy transmigration, at thy last gaspe. So God comes, and so God returnes. (*1623?*) 5:371–72

iv. The Image New-Minted in Christ (Col. 1:19, 20)

Not disputing therefore, what other wayes God might have taken for our redemption, but giving him all possible thanks for that way which his goodnesse hath chosen, by the way of satisfying his justice, (for, howsoever I would be glad to be discharged of my debts any way, yet certainly, I should think my selfe more beholden to that man, who would be content to pay my debt for me, then to him that should entreat my creditor to forgive me my debt) for this work, to make Christ able to pay this debt, there was something to be added to him. First, he must pay it in such money as was lent; in the nature and flesh of man; for man had sinned, and man must pay. And then it was lent in such money as was coyned even with the Image of God; man was made according to his Image: That Image being defaced, in a new Mint, in the wombe of the Blessed Virgin, there was new money coyned; The Image of the invisible God, the second person in the Trinity, was imprinted into the humane nature. And then, that there might bee *omnis plenitudo*, all fulnesse, as God, for the paiment of this debt, sent downe the Bullion, and the stamp, that is, God to be conceived in man, and as he provided the Mint, the womb of the Blessed Virgin, so hath he provided an Exchequer, where this mony is issued; that is his Church, where his merits should be applied to the discharge of particular consciences. (*1622*) 4:288

v. The Seal of God in Human Nature (2 Cor. 4:6)

All knowledge is ignorance, except it conduce to the knowledge of the Scriptures, and all the Scriptures lead us to Christ. [c]*He is the*

2. *Nature* signifies that sense inherent in rational creatures for the reasonable ordering of moral conduct, a characteristic implanted in mankind by the Creator; *Grace* describes the supernatural assistance of God bestowed upon these rational beings that will sanctify them.

c. Heb. 1:3. Sap. 7:26.

brightness of his Fathers glory, and the express image of his person. The brightness of the everlasting light, and the image of his goodness. And, to insist upon a word of the fittest signification, [d]*Him hath God the Father sealed*. Now, *Sigillum imprimitur in Materia diversa*: A Seal graven in gold or stone, does not print in stone or gold: in Wax it will, and it will in Clay; for this Seal in which God hath manifested himself, we consider it not, as it is printed in the same metal, in the eternal Son of God: but as God hath sealed himself in Clay, in the humane Nature; but yet in Wax too, in a person ductile, pliant, obedient to his will. And there, [e]*Signatum super nos Lumen vultus tui*, says *David, The light of thy countenance*, that is, the image of thy self, *is sealed*; that is, derived, imprinted, upon us, that is, upon our nature, our flesh. [f]*Signatum est, id est, significatum est*: God hath signified this presence, manifested, revealed himself in the face of *Jesus Christ*. For that is the Office, and service, that Christ avows himself to have done; *O Father, I have manifested thy Name*: that is, thy Name of Father, as thou art a Father: for, [g]*Qui solum Deum novit Creatorem, Judaicae mensuram prudentiae non excedit*. Knowest thou that there is a God, and that that God created the world? What great knowledge is this? The Jews know it too. [h]*Non est Idem, nosse Deum opificem esse, et habere filium*. It is another Religion, another point of Faith, to know that God had a Son of eternal begetting, and to have a world of late making. God therefore hath shined in no mans heart, till he know the glory of GOD in the face of Jesus Christ, till he come to the manifestation of God, in the Gospel. So that, that man comes short of this light, that believes in God, in a general, in an incomprehensible power, but not in Christ; and that man goes beyond this light, who will know more of God, then is manifested in the Gospel, which is the face of Christ Jesus: the one comes not to the light, the other goes beyond, and both are in blindness. Christ is the Image of God, and the Gospel is the face of Christ: and now, I rest not in Gods picture, as I find it in every Creature; though there be in every Creature an Image of God; I have a livelier Image of God, Christ. (*1622*) 4:124

vi. The Inner and Outer Garment (Gal. 3:27)

There is a degree of vanity, and pride, whereby some Men delight to weare their richest clothes innermost, and most out of sight; But in this double garment of a Christian, it is necessarily so; for *faith* is the richest, and most precious part of this garment; and this, which is our

d. Jo. 6:27. Hilary.
e. Ps. 4:6.
f. Tertul.
g. Cyrill.
h. Chrysost.

Holy-day garment, is worne innermost; for that (our faith) is onely seen by God; but our outward garment, of *workes*, which is our *worky-day garment*, that is our *sanctification*, is seen of all the world. And that also must be put on, or else we have not put on *Christ*: and it must cover us *all over*; that is, our sanctification must goe through our *whole life* in a constant, and an even perseverance; we must not onely be *Hospitales*, and feed the poore at Christmas, be sober, and abstinent, the day that we *receive*, repent, and thinke of amendment of life, in the day of visitation, and *sicknesse*; but, as the garment, which Christ wore, was *seamlesse*, and intire, so this garment, which is *Christ Jesus*, that is, our sanctification, should be intire, and uninterrupted, in the whole course of our lives; we must remember, that at the Mariage which figured the kingdome of heaven, the master of the feast reprehended, and punished him, that was come in, not expresly because he had not a *wedding garment*, but [i]*Quomodo intrasti*, says he, *how camest thou in, not having on thy wedding garment?* So that (if it could be possible) though we had put on the inside of this garment, which is *Christ*, that is, if we had *faith*, yet if we have not the outside too, that is *sanctification*, we have not put on Christ, as we should; for this is *Indui virtute ex alto*; to have both inside, *faith*, and outside, *sanctification*: and to put it on so, that it may cover us all over, that is, all our life; because it is not in our power, if we put it off, by *new sinnes*, to put it on againe, when we will. [j]*I have put off my coate, how shall I put it on?* was the doubt of the spouse, in the Canticles, even when Christ had called her: So hard a thing is it, if we devest the righteousnesse of Christ, after we have put it on, to cloth our selves againe in that garment. (*1624?*) 5:156

vii. Image of God and Devil at Once (Ps. 38:2)

In the first minute that my soul is infused, the Image of God is imprinted in my soul; so forward is God in my behalf, and so early does he visit me. But yet *Originall sin* is there, as soon as that Image of God is there. My soul is capable of *God*, as soon as it is capable of *sin*; and though sin doe not get the start of God, God does not get the start of sin neither. Powers, that dwell so far asunder, as *Heaven*, and *Hell*, *God* and the *Devill*, meet in an instant in my soul, in the minute of my quickning, and the Image of *God*, and the Image of *Adam*, Originall sin, enter into me at once, in one, and the same act. So swift is this arrow, *Originall sin*, from which, all arrows of subsequent tentations, are shot, as that God, who comes to my first minute of life, cannot come before death. (*1618*) 2:59

i. Mat. 22. *j.* 5:3.

viii. The Picture of Death (Acts 7:60)

Many have wondred at that note of Saint *Chrysostom's*, That till Christ's time death was called death, plainly, literally death, but after Christ, death was called but sleepe; for, indeede, in the old-Testament before Christ, I thinke there is no one metaphor so often used, as Sleepe for Death, and that the Dead are said to Sleepe: Therefore wee wonder sometimes, that Saint *Chrysostome* should say so: But this may be that which that holy Father intended in that Note, that they in the old-Testament, who are said to have slept in Death, are such as then, by Faith, did apprehend, and were fixed upon Christ; such as were all the good men of the old-Testament, and so there will not bee many instances against Saint *Chrysostome*'s note, That to those that die in Christ, Death is but a Sleepe; to all others, Death is Death, literally Death. Now of this dying Man, that dies in Christ, that dies the Death of the Righteous, that embraces Death as a Sleepe, must wee give you a Picture too.

There is not a minute left to do it; not a minutes sand; Is there a minutes patience? Bee pleased to remember that those Pictures which are delivered in a minute, from a print upon a paper, had many dayes, weeks, Moneths time for the graving of those Pictures in the Copper; So this Picture of that dying Man, that dies in Christ, that dies the death of the Righteous, that embraces Death as a Sleepe, was graving all his life; All his publique actions were the lights, and all his private the shadowes of this Picture. And when this Picture comes to the Presse, this Man to the streights and agonies of Death, thus he lies, thus he looks, this he is. His understanding and his will is all one faculty; He understands Gods purpose upon him, and he would not have God's purpose turned any other way; hee sees God will dissolve him, and he would faine be dissolved, to be with Christ; His understanding and his will is all one faculty; His memory and his fore-sight are fixt, and concentred upon one object, upon goodnesse; Hee remembers that hee hath proceeded in the sinceritie of a good Conscience in all the wayes of his calling, and he foresees that his good name shall have the Testimony, and his Posterity the support of the good men of this world; His sicknesse shall be but a fomentation to supple and open his Body for the issuing of his Soule; and his Soule shall goe forth, not as one that gave over his house, but as one that travelled to see and learne better Architecture, and meant to returne and re-edifie that house, according to those better Rules: And as those thoughts which possesse us most awake, meete us againe when we are asleepe; So his holy thoughts, having been alwaies conversant upon the directing of his family, the education of his Children, the discharge of his place, the safety of the State, the happinesse of the King all his life; when he is faln a sleepe in Death, all his Dreames in that blessed Sleepe, all his devotions in heaven shall be upon the same Subjects, and he shal solicite him that sits upon the Throne, and the Lamb, God for Christ Jesus sake, to blesse all these with his particular blessings: for, so God giveth his beloved sleep, so as that they enjoy the next world and assist this. (*1628*) 8:189–90

ix. The Image of God Shall Never Burn Out (Eccles. 12:1)

He created thee, *ex nihilo*, he gave thee a being, there's matter of exaltation, and yet all this from nothing; thou wast worse then a worm, there's matter of humiliation; but he did not create thee *ad nihilum*, to return to nothing again, and there's matter for thy consideration, and study, how to make thine immortality profitable unto thee; for it is a deadly immortality, if thy immortality must serve thee for nothing but to hold thee in immortal torment. To end all, that being which we have from God shall not return to nothing, nor the being which we have from men neither. As St. *Bernard* sayes of the Image of God in mans soul, *uri potest in gehenna, non exuri*, That soul that descends to hell, carries the Image [of] God in the faculties of that soul thither, but there that Image can never be burnt out, so those Images and those impressions, which we have received from men, from nature, from the world, the image of a Lord, the image of a Counsailor, the image of a Bishop, shall all burn in Hell, and never burn out; not only these men, but these offices are not to return to nothing; but as their being from God, so their being from man, shal have an everlasting being, to the aggravating of their condemnation. (*1619*) 2:247

x. The Geography of Image (Gen. 1:26)

We shall pursue our great examples; God in doing, *Moses* in saying; and so make hast in applying the parts. But first receive them. And since we have the whole world in contemplation, consider in these words, the foure quarters of the world, by application, by fair, and just accommodation of the words. First, in the first word, that God speaks here, *Faciamus*, Let us, us in the plurall, (a denotation of divers Persons in one Godhead) we consider our East where we must beginne, at the knowledge and confession of the Trinity. For, though in the way to heaven, we be travelled beyond the Gentiles, when we come to confess but one God, (The Gentiles could not do that) yet we are still among the *Jews*, if we thinke that one God to be but one Person. [k]Christs name is *Oriens*, the *East*; if we will be named by him, (called Christians) we must look to this East, the confession of the Trinity. There's then our East, in the *Faciamus*; Let us, us make man: And then our West is in the next word, *Faciamus Hominem*. Though we be thus made, made by the counsell, made by the concurrence, made by the hand of the whole Trinity; yet we are made but men: And man, but in the appellation, in this text: and man there, is but *Adam*: and *Adam* is but earth, but red earth, earth dyed red in bloud, in Soul-bloud, the bloud of our own soules. To that west we must all come, to the earth. [l]*The Sunne knoweth his going down*: Even the Sun for all his glory, and heighth, hath a going down, and he knowes it. The highest cannot devest mortality, nor the discomfort of mortality. [m]*When you see a cloud rise out of the west, straightway you say there commeth a storm*, says Christ. When out of the region of your west, that is, your later days, there comes a cloud, a sicknesse, you feele a storme, even the best morall constancy is shaked. But this cloud, and this storme, and this west there must be; And that's our second consideration. But then the next words designe a North, a strong, and powerfull North, to scatter, and dissipate these clouds: *Ad imaginem, et similitudinem*; That we are made according to a pattern, to an image, to a likenesse, which God proposed to himselfe for the making of man. This consideration, that God did not rest in that praeexistent matter, out of which he made all other creatures, and produced their formes, out of their matter, for the making of man; but took a forme, a patterne, a modell for that work: [n]This is the North winde, that is called upon to carry out the perfumes of the garden, to spread the goodnesse of God abroad. This is that which is intended in *Job*; [o]*Fair weather commeth out of the North*. Our West, our declination is in this, that we are but earth; our North, our dissipation of that darknesse, is in this, that we are not all earth: though we be of that matter, we have another forme, another image, another likenesse. And then, whose image and likenesse it is, is our Meridionall height, our noon, our south point, our highest elevation; *In Imagine nostra, Let us make man in our Image*. Though our Sun set at noon, [p]*as the Prophet Amos* speakes; though we die in our youth, or fall in our height: yet even in that Sunset, we shall have a Noon. For this Image of God shall never depart from our soule; no, not when that soule departs from our body. And that's our South, our Meridionall height and glory. And when we have thus seen this East, in the *faciamus*, That I am the workmanship

k. Zech. 6:12.
l. Psal. 104:19.
m. Luke 12:54.
n. Cant. 4:16.
o. 37:22.
p. 8:9.

and care of the whole Trinity; And this West in the *Hominem*, That for all that, my matter, my substance, is but earth: But then a North, a power of overcomming that low and miserable state, *In Imagine*; That though in my matter, the earth, I must die; yet in my forme, in that Image which I am made by, I cannot die: and after all, a South, a knowledge, That this Image is not the Image of Angels, to whom we shall be like, but it is by the same life, by which those Angels themselves were made; the Image of God himselfe. When I am gone over this east, and west, and north, and south, here in this world, I should be as sorry as *Alexander* was, if there were no more worlds. But there is another world, which these considerations will discover, and lead us to, in which our joy, and our glory shall be, to see that God essentially, and face to face, after whose Image, and likenesse we were made before. But as that Pilot which had harbored his ship so farre within land, as that he must have change of Winds, in all the points of the Compasse, to bring her out, cannot hope to bring her out in one day: So being to transport you, by occasion of these words, from this world to the next; and in this world, through all the Compasse, all the foure quarters thereof; I cannot hope to make all this voyage to day. To day we shall consider onely our longitude, our East, and West; and our North and South at another tyde, and another gale. (*1629*) 9:49–50

xi. The Image of God in Rich and Poor (Prov. 14:31)

Again, rich and poor are Images, Pictures of God; but, (as *Clement of Alexandria* says wittily and strongly) The poor is *Nuda Imago*, a naked picture of God, a picture without any drapery, any clothes about it. And it is much a harder thing, and there is much more art showed in making a *naked picture*, then in all the rich attire that can be put upon it. And howsoever the rich man, that is invested in Power, and Greatnesse, may be a better picture of God, of God considered *in himself*, who is all Greatnes, all Power, yet, of God considered in *Christ*, (which is the contemplation that concerns us most) the poor man is the better picture, and most resembles Christ who lived in continual poverty. And so, he that oppresses the poor, reproaches God, God in his *Orphans*, God in his *Picture*.

. . . .

Saint *Chrysostome* carries this consideration farther then this of Saint *Augustine*. That whereas every creature hath *filiationem vestigii*, that because God hath imparted a being, an essence, from himselfe, who is the roote, and the fountaine of all essence, and all being, therefore every creature hath a filiation from God, and is the Sonne of God so, as we read in *Job*, God is *the father of the raine*; and whereas every man hath *filiationem imaginis*, as well *Pagan* as *Christian*, hath the Image of God imprinted in his soule, and so hath a filiation from God, and is the Sonne of God, as he is made in his likenesse; and whereas every Christian hath *filiationem Pacti*, by being taken into the Covenant made by God, with the Elect, and with their seed, he hath a filiation from God, and is the Sonne of God, as he is incorporated into his Sonne Christ Jesus, by the *Seals of the Christian Church*; besides these filiations, of being in all creatures, of the Image in all men, of the Covenant in all Christians, The poore, sayes that Father, are not onely *filii*, but *Haeredes*, and *Primogeniti*, Sonnes and eldest Sonnes, Sonnes, and Sonnes and Heires. And to that purpose he makes use of those words in St. *James*, *Hearken, my beloved brethren, hath not God chosen the poore of this world, rich in faith, and Heirs of that Kingdome?* Heirs, for, *Ipsorum est*, sayes Christ himself, [q] *Theirs is the Kingdome of heaven*; And upon those words of Christ, Saint *Chrysostome* comments thus, *Divites ejus regni tantum habent, quantum a pauperibus, eleemosynis coemerunt*, The rich have no more of that Kingdome of heaven, then they have purchased of the poore, by their almes, and other erogations to pious uses. And so he that oppresses the poore reproaches God, God in his *Orphans*, God in his *Image*, God in the *Members* of his own Body, God in his Sonnes, and Heires of his Kingdome. (*1628*) 8:285–86

2. *Image in the Church*

i. Image: The Vision of the Church (Cant. 3:11)

And therefore you daughters of Sion, holy and religious souls, (for to them onely this indulgent mother speaks here) hearken ever to her voice; quarrell not your mothers honor, nor her discretion: Despise not her person, nor her apparell; Doe not say, *she is not the same woman, she was heretofore, nor that she is not so well dressed, as she was then*; Dispute not her *Doctrine*, Despise not her *Discipline*; that as you *sucked her breasts* in your *Baptism*, and in the *other Sacrament*, when you entred, and whilst you stayd in this life, so you may *lie in her bosome*, when you goe out of it. *Hear her*; and a good part of that, which you are to hear from her, is envolved and inwrapped in that which we have proposed to you, for our third part, *Goe forth, and behold Solomon, etc.*

Here are two duties enjoyned; at least two steps, two degrees; *Egredimini, Go forth*, and then, *Videte, Behold*, contemplate; And,

q. Mat. 5:3.

after the duty, or wrapped in the duty, we have *the Object*, which we are to look upon, and in that, divers things to be considered; as we shall see in their order. First, when we are bid to *Go forth*, it is not to go so far, as *out* of that Church, in which God hath given us our station; for, as *Moses* says, That *the word of God is not beyond Sea*; so the Church of God, is not so *beyond Sea*, as that we must needs seek it *there*, either in a *painted Church*, on one side, or in *a naked Church*, on another; a Church in a *Dropsie*, overflowne with *Ceremonies*, or a Church in a *Consumption*,[3] for want of such Ceremonies, as the primitive Church found usefull, and beneficiall for the advancing of the glory of God, and the devotion of the Congregation. That which Christ says to the Church it selfe, the Church says to every soule in the Church: [r]*Goe thy way forth, by the footsteps of the flocke*; Associate thy selfe to the true shepheard, and true sheep of Christ Jesus, and stray not towards *Idolatrous Chappels*, nor towards *schismaticall Conventicles*,[4] *but goe by the footsteps of the flock*; there must be *footsteps*, some must have gone that way before, take heed of *Opinions*, that begin in thy selfe; and the whole flock must have gone that way, take heed of opinions vented by a *few new men*, which have not had the establishment of a Church. And truly the best way to discerne footsteps, is *Daniels way*, *Daniels* way was to *straw ashes*, and so their footsteps that had been there, were easily discerned: Walke in thine own *ashes*, in the meditation of thine own death, or in the *ashes of Gods Saints*, who are dead before thee, in the contemplation of their example, and thou wilt see some *footsteps of the flock*, some impressions, some directions, how they went, and how thou art to follow, to the heavenly Jerusalem. (*1625*) 6:284–85

ii. God's Face: His Ordinance (Ps. 32:8)

This guiding then with the eye, we consider to be his particular care, and his personall providence upon us, in his Church; For, a man may be in the Kings presence, and yet not in his eye; and so he may in Gods. [s]Gods whole Ordinance in his Church, is Gods face; For, that is the face of God, by which God is manifested to us; But then, that eye in that face, by which he promises to guide us, in this Text, is that blessed Spirit of his, by whose operation he makes that grace, which

3. Dropsy and consumption were morbid conditions associated respectively with an accumulation of fluid in the body and with a wasting away of the body by disease.

4. Donne makes his point through an exaggerated condemnation of nonconforming Protestants on one side and dissenters on the other, all of them, in his view, having questionable theological opinions. Cf. pp. 272–73.

r. Cant. 1:8. *s.* August.

does evermore accompany his Ordinances, effectuall upon us; The whole Congregation sees God face to face, in the Service, in the Sermon, in the Sacrament; but there is an eye in that face, an eye in that Service, an eye in that Sermon, an eye in that Sacrament, a piercing and an operating Spirit, that lookes upon that soule, and foments and cherishes that soule, who by a good use of Gods former grace, is become fitter for his present.

And this guiding us with his eye, manifests it selfe in these two great effects; conversion to him, and union with him. First, his eye works upon ours; His eye turnes ours to looke upon him. Still it is so expressed with an [t]*Ecce; Behold, the eye of the Lord is upon all them that feare him*; His eye cals ours to behold that; And then our eye cals upon his, to observe our cheerefull readinesse, [u]*Behold, as the eye of a servant looks to the hand of his Master, so our eyes waite upon the Lord our God, till he have mercy upon us*. Where the *Donec, Untill*, is an everlasting *Donec*, as the blessed Virgins was; A Virgin *Donec, till she brought forth her first Son*, and a Virgin ever after; So our eyes waite upon God, *till hee have mercy*, that is, while he hath it, and that he may continue his mercy; for it was his mercifull eye that turned ours to him, and it is the same mercy, that we waite upon him. And then, when, as a well made Picture doth alwaies looke upon him, that lookes upon it, this Image of God in our soule, is turned to him, by his turning to it, it is impossible we should doe any foule, any uncomely thing in his presence. (*winter 1624–1625?*) 9:367–68

iii. Liturgy: The Stamp of Payment (Rom. 13:7)

The Church is the house of prayer, so, as that upon occasion, preaching may be left out, but never a house of preaching, so, as that Prayer may be left out. And for the debt of prayer, God will not be paid, with money of our owne coyning, (with sudden, extemporall, inconsiderate prayer) but with currant money, that beares the Kings Image, and inscription; The Church of God, by his Ordinance, hath set his stampe, upon a Liturgie and Service, for his house. *Audit Deus in corde cogitantis, quod nec ipse audit, qui cogitat*, sayes S. *Bernard*: God heares the very first motions of a mans heart, which, that man, till he proceed to a farther consideration, doth not heare, not feele, not deprehend in himselfe.

That soule, that is accustomed to direct her selfe to God, upon every occasion, that, as a flowre at Sunrising, conceives a sense of God, in every beame of his, and spreads and dilates it selfe towards him, in a

t. Psal. 33:18. *u*. 123:2.

thankfulnesse, in every small blessing that he sheds upon her; that soule, that as a flowre at the Suns declining, contracts and gathers in, and shuts up her selfe, as though she had received a blow, when soever she heares her Saviour wounded by an oath, or blasphemy, or execration; that soule, who, whatsoever string be strucken in her, base or treble, her high or her low estate, is ever tuned toward God, that soule prayes sometimes when it does not know that it prayes. I heare that man name God, and aske him what said you, and perchance he cannot tell; but I remember, that he casts forth some of those *ejaculationes animae*, (as S. *Augustine* calls them) some of those darts of a devout soule, which, though they have not particular delibera-tions, and be not formall prayers, yet they are the *indicia*, pregnant evidences and blessed fruits of a religious custome; much more is it true, which S. *Bernard* saies there, of them, *Deus audit*, God heares that voice of the heart, which the heart it selfe heares not, that is, at first considers not. Those occasionall and transitory prayers, and those fixed and stationary prayers, for which, many times, we binde our selves to private prayer at such a time, are payments of this debt, in such peeces, and in such summes, as God, no doubt, accepts at our hands. But yet the solemne dayes of payment, are the Sabbaths of the Lord, and the place of this payment, is the house of the Lord, where, as *Tertullian* expresses it, *Agmine facto*, we muster our forces together, and besiege God; that is, not taking up every tattered fellow, every sudden ragge or fragment of speech, that rises from our tongue, or our affections, but mustering up those words, which the Church hath levied for that service, in the Confessions, and Absolutions, and Col-lects, and Litanies of the Church, we pay this debt, and we receive our acquittance. (*1623?*) 4:310–11

B. The Danger of Images and Their Idolatrous Worship

1. Idolatrous Love

i. The Idolatrous Love of Creature (Prov. 22:11)

Love, in Divinity, is such an attribute, or such a notion, as designs to us one person in the Trinity; and that person who communicates, and applies to us, the other two persons, that is, *The Holy Ghost*: So that, as there is no *power*, but with relation to the *Father*, nor *wisdom* but with relation to the *Son*, so there should be no *love* but in the *Holy Ghost*, from whom comes this pureness of heart, and consequently the love of it necessarily: For, the love of this pureness is part of this pureness it self, and no man hath it, except he love it. All love which is placed upon lower things, admits satiety; but this love of this pureness, always grows, always proceeds: It does not onely file off the rust of our hearts, in purging us of old habits, but proceeds to a daily polishing of the heart, in an exact watchfulness, and brings us to that brightness, [v] *Ut ipse videas faciem in corde, et alii videant cor in facie,* That thou maist see thy face in thy heart, and the world may see thy heart in thy face; indeed, that to both, both heart and face may be all one: Thou shalt be a Looking-glass to thy self, and to others too.

The highest degree of other love, is the love of woman: Which love, when it is rightly placed upon one woman, it is dignified by the Apostle with the highest comparison, [w] *Husbands love your wives, as Christ loved his Church*: And God himself forbad not that this love should be great enough to change natural affection, [x] *Relinquet patrem,* (for this, a man shall leave his Father) yea, to change nature it self, *caro una,* two shall be one. Accordingly *David* expresses himself so, in commemoration of *Jonathan,* [y] *Thy love to me was wonderful, passing the love of women*: A love above that love, is wonderful. Now, this love between man and woman, doth so much confess a satiety, as that if a woman think to hold a man long, she provides herself some other capacity, some other title, then meerly as she is a woman: Her wit, and her conversation, must continue this love; and she must be a *wife,* a *helper*; else, meerly as a woman, this love must necessarily have intermissions. And therefore St. *Jerome* notes a custom of his time, (perchance prophetically enough of our times too) that to uphold an unlawful love, and make it continue, they used to call one another *Friend,* and *Sister,* and *Cousen, Ut etiam peccatis induant nomina caritatis,* that they might apparel ill affections in good names; and those names of natural and civil love might carry one, and continue a work, which otherwise would sooner have withered. In Parables, and in Mythology, and in the application of Fables, this affection of love, for the often change of subjects, is described to have *wings*; whereas the true nature of a good love (such as the love of this Text) is a constant union. But our love of earthly things is not so good as to be *volatilis,* apt to fly; for it is always groveling upon the earth, and earthly objects: As in spiritual fornications, the Idols are said to have ears and hear not, and eyes and see not; so in this idolatrous love of the Creature, love hath wings, and flies not; it flies not upward, it never ascends to the contemplation of the Creator, in the Creature. The *Poets* afford us but one Man, that in his love flew so high as the Moon; *Endymion* loved the Moon. The sphear of our loves is sublunary, upon things naturally inferior to our selves. (*1617*) 1:199–200

v. Augustine.
w. Ephes. 5:25.
x. Gen. 2:24.
y. 2. Sam. 1:26.

ii. Idolatry vs. Sincerity (Judges 5:20)

God hath put *Truth* and *Falshood, Idolatrie* and *Sinceritie* so farre asunder, and infused such an incompatibilitie, and imprinted such an implacabilitie betweene them, as that they cannot flow into one another: And therefore, there, *Maledicti Pacifici*, It is an opposition against God, by any colourable Modifications, to reconcile opinions diametrally contrary to one another, in fundamentall things. *Day* and *Night* may joyne and meet, *In Diluculis* and *in Crepusculis*. The dawning of the day, in the Morning, and the shutting in of the day in the Evening, make day and night so much one, as sometimes you cannot tell which to call them: but *Lux et tenebrae*, light and darknes, *Midnight* and *Noone* never met, never joyned.

. . . .

Every man is a little world, sayes the *Philosopher*; Every man is a little *Church* too; and in every man, there are two sides, two armies: the flesh fights against the Spirit. This is but a *Civill warre*, nay it is but a *Rebellion* indeed; and yet it can never be absolutely quenched. So every Man is also a Souldier in that great and generall warre, betweene *Christ*, and *Beliall*, the Word of *God*, and the will of man. Every man is bound to hearken to a peace, in such things as may admit peace, in differences, where men differ from men; but bound also to shut himselfe up against all overtures of peace, in such things, as are in their Nature irreconcileable, in differences where men differ from *God*. That warre *God* hath kindled, and that warre must bee maintained, and maintained by his way; and his way, and his *Ordinance* in this warre, is Preaching. (*1622*) 4:193–94

2. Use and Abuse

i. Good Use (Acts 28:6)

And then, since man is also naturally apt to stray into a superstitious worship of God, let us be Christianly diligent, to preclude all waies, that may lead us into that tentation, or incline us towards superstition. In which, I doe not intend, that we should decline all such things, as had been superstitiously abused, in a superstitious Church; But, in all such things, as being in their own nature indifferent, are, by a just commandment of lawfull authority, become more then indifferent (necessary) to us, though not *Necessitate medii*, yet *Necessitate praecepti*, (for, though salvation consist not in Ceremonies, Obedience doth, and salvation consists much in Obedience) That in all such things, we alwayes informe our selves, of the right use of those things in their first institution, of their abuse with which they have been depraved in the Roman Church, and of the good use which is made of them in ours. That because pictures have been adored, we do not abhor a picture; Nor sit at the Sacrament, because Idolatry hath been committed in kneeling. That Church, which they call Lutheran, hath retained more of these Ceremonies, then ours hath done; And ours more then that which they call Calvinist; But both the Lutheran, and ours, without danger, because, in both places, we are diligent to preach to the people the right use of these indifferent things. For this is a true way of shutting out superstition, Not alwayes to abolish the thing it selfe, because in the right use thereof, the spirituall profit, and edification may exceed the danger, but by preaching, and all convenient wayes of instruction, to deliver people out of that ignorance, which possesses people in the Roman captivity. (*1629*) 8:331

ii. The Right Use of Ceremonies (Matt. 5:8)

The Church, which is the Daughter of God, and Spouse of Christ, celebrates this day, the Purification of the blessed Virgin, the Mother of God: And she celebrates this day by the name, vulgarly, of *Candlemas day*. It is *dies luminarium*, the day of lights; The Church took the occasion of doing so, from the Gentiles; At this time of the yeare, about the beginning of February, they celebrated the feast of *Februus*, which is their *Pluto*; And, because that was the God of darknesse, they solemnized it, with a multiplicity of Lights. The Church of God, in the outward and ceremoniall part of his worship, did not disdain the ceremonies of the Gentiles; Men who are so severe, as to condemne, and to remove from the Church, whatsoever was in use amongst the Gentiles before, may, before they are aware, become Surveyors, and Controllers upon Christ himself, in the institution of his greatest seales: for Baptisme, which is the Sacrament of purification by washing in water, and the very Sacrament of the Supper it self, religious eating, and drinking in the Temple, were in use amongst the Gentiles too. It is a perverse way, rather to abolish Things and Names, (for vehement zeale will work upon Names as well as Things) because they have been abused, then to reduce them to their right use. (*1627?*) 7:325

iii. Pater, *not* Frater Noster (Ps. 32:6)

Ad Te, To God, because he can heare; And then *Ad te*, to God, because he can give. Certainely it were a strange distemper, a strange singularity, a strange circularity, in a man that dwelt at Windsor, to fetch all his water at London Bridge: So is it in him, that lives in Gods presence, (as he does, that lives religiously in his Church) to goe for all his necessities, by Invocation to Saints. *David* was willing to bee our example for Prayer, but he gives no example of scattering our prayers upon any other then God. Christ Jesus was willing to give us a Rule for Prayer: but if hee had intended that his Rule should have beene deflected and declined to Saints, he would have taught us to say, *Frater noster qui es in Coelis*, and not only *Pater noster*; to pray to our Brethren which are there too, and not onely to our Father which is in Heaven. If any man have tasted at Court, what it is to be ever welcome to the King himselfe, and what it is to speake to another to speake for him, he will blesse that happinesse, of having an immediate accesse to God himselfe in his prayers. They that come so low downe the streame, as wee said before, to London Bridge, they will go lower and lower, to Gravesend too; They that come to Saints, they will come to the Images, and Reliques of Saints too; They come to a brackish water, betweene salt and fresh, and they come at last, to be swallowed up in that sea which hath no limit, no bottome, that is, to direct all their devotions to such Saints, as have no certainty, not onely not in their ability, we know not what those Saints can doe, but not in their history, we know not that such as they pray to, are Saints; nay, we know not whether they ever were at all. (*winter 1624–1625?*) 9:321–22

iv. Idolatry and Sin (Micah 2:10)

Our dignity, and our greatest height, is in our interest in God, and in the world, and in our selves; and we fall from all, either *non utendo*, or *abutendo*; either by neglecting God, or by over-valuing the world; our greatest fall of all is, into *Idolatry*; and yet Idolatry is an ordinary fall; for [z] *tot habemus Deos recentes, quot habemus vitia*, As many habituall sins as we embrace, so many Idols we worship; If all sins could not be called so, Idols, yet for those sins, which possesse us most ordinarily, and most strongly, we have good warrant to call them so; which sins are *Licentiousnesse* in our youth, and *Covetousnesse* in our age, and *voluptuousnesse* in our middle time. For, for *Licentiousnesse*, *Idolatry*, and that, are so often called by one anothers names in the Scriptures, as many times we cannot tell, when the Prophets mean *spirituall Adultery*, and when *Carnall*; when they mean *Idolatry*, and when *Fornication*. For *Covetousnesse*, that is expresly called *Idolatry* by the Apostle: and so is *voluptuousnesse* too, in those men, *whose belly is their God*. We fall then into that desperate precipitation of Idolatry by *lust*, when by fornication, we profane the temple of the Holy Ghost, and make even his temple, our bodies, a Stewes: And we fall into Idolatry by *Covetousnesse*, when we come to

z. Hieron.

be, [a] *tam putidi minutique animi*, of so narrow, and contracted a soule, and of so sick, and dead, and buried, and putrefied a soule, as to lock up our soule, in a Cabinet where we lock up our money, to ty our soul in the corner of a handkerchiefe, where we ty our money, to imprison our soule, in the imprisonment of those things, [b] *Quae te ad gloriam subvecturae*, the dispensation, and distribution whereof, would carry thy soul to eternall glory. And when, by our *voluptuousnesse*, we raise the prices of necessary things, *Et eorum vulnera, qui a Deo flagris caeduntur, adaugemus*; and thereby scourge them with deeper lashes of famine, whom God hath scourged with poverty before, we fall into Idolatry by voluptuousnesse; [c] *Numismatis inscriptiones inspictis, et non Christi in fratre*, thou takest a pleasure, to look upon the figures, and Images of Kings in their severall coyns, and thou despisest thine own Image in thy poore brother, and Gods Image in thy ruinous, and defaced soule, and in his Temple, thy body, demolished by thy Licentiousnesse, and by all these Idolatries. This is the fall, when we fall so farre into those sins, which have naturally a tyranny in them, and that that sinne becomes an Idoll to us; which fall of ours, God intimates unto us, and rebukes us for, by so mild a way, as to bid us rise from it. (*1621 or 1623?*) 5:202–3

C. Pattern and Example

1. Necessity of Idea: Pattern (Ps. 63:7)

First then, from the meanest artificer, through the wisest Philosopher, to God himselfe, all that is well done, or wisely undertaken, is undertaken and done according to pre-conceptions, fore-imaginations, designes, and patterns proposed to our selves beforehand. A Carpenter builds not a house, but that he first sets up a frame in his owne minde, what kinde of house he will build. The little great Philosopher *Epictetus*, would undertake no action, but he would first propose to himselfe, what *Socrates*, or *Plato*, what a wise man would do in that case, and according to that, he would proceed. Of God himselfe, it is safely resolved in the Schoole, that he never did any thing in any part of time, of which he had not an eternall pre-conception, an eternall Idea, in himselfe before. Of which Ideaes, that is, preconceptions, pre-determinations in God, S. *Augustine* pronounces, *Tanta vis in Ideis constituitur*, There is so much truth, and so much power in these Ideaes, as that without acknowledging them, no man

a. Basil.
b. Idem.
c. Idem.

can acknowledge God, for he does not allow God Counsaile, and Wisdome, and deliberation in his Actions, but sets God on worke, before he have thought what he will doe. And therefore he, and others of the Fathers read that place, (which we read otherwise) [d]*Quod factum est, in ipso vita erat*; that is, in all their Expositions, whatsoever is made, in time, was alive in God, before it was made, that is, in that eternall Idea, and patterne which was in him. So also doe divers of those Fathers read those words to the Hebrews, (which we read, [e]*The things that are seene, are not made of things that doe appeare) Ex invisibilibus visibilia facta sunt, Things formerly invisible, were made visible*; that is, we see them not till now, till they are made, but they had an invisible being, in that Idea, in that pre-notion, in that purpose of God before, for ever before. Of all things in Heaven, and earth, but of himselfe, God had an Idea, a patterne in himselfe, before he made it.

And therefore let him be our patterne for that, to worke after patternes; To propose to our selves Rules and Examples for all our actions; and the more, the more immediately, the more directly our actions concerne the service of God. If I aske God, by what Idea he made me, God produces his *Faciamus hominem ad Imaginem nostram*, That there was a concurrence of the whole Trinity, to make me in *Adam*, according to that Image which they were, and according to that Idea, which they had pre-determined. If I pretend to serve God, and he aske me for my Idea, How I meane to serve him, shall I bee able to produce none? If he aske me an Idea of my Religion, and my opinions, shall I not be able to say, It is that which thy word, and thy Catholique Church hath imprinted in me? If he aske me an Idea of my prayers, shall I not be able to say, It is that which my particular necessities, that which the forme prescribed by thy Son, that which the care, and piety of the Church, in conceiving fit prayers, hath imprinted in me? If he aske me an Idea of my Sermons, shall I not be able to say, It is that which the Analogy of Faith, the edification of the Congregation, the zeale of thy worke, the meditations of my heart have imprinted in me? But if I come to pray or to preach without this kind of Idea, if I come to extemporall prayer, and extemporall preaching, I shall come to an extemporall faith, and extemporall religion; and then I must looke for an extemporall Heaven, a Heaven to be made for me; for to that Heaven which belongs to the Catholique Church, I shall never come, except I go by the way of the Catholique Church, by former Idea's, former examples, former patterns, To beleeve according to ancient beliefes, to pray according to ancient

d. Joh. 1:3, 4.

e. Heb. 11:3.

formes, to preach according to former meditations. God does nothing, man does nothing well, without these Idea's, these retrospects, this recourse to pre-conceptions, pre-deliberations. (*1626*) 7:60–61

2. God's Example (2 Cor. 4:6)

God proceeds by example, by pattern: Even in this first great act presented in our Text, in the Creation he did so. God had no external pattern in the Creation, for there was nothing extant; but God had from all Eternity an internal pattern, an *Idaea*, a pre-conception, a form in himself, according to which he produced every Creature. And when God himself proceeds upon pre-conceptions, pre-meditations, shall we adventure to do, or to say any thing in his service unpremeditately, extemporally? It is not Gods way. Now, it is a penurious thing, to have but one Candle in a room: it is too dim a light to work by, to live by, to have but Rule and Precept alone; Rule and Example together, direct us fully. Who shall be our Example? [f] *Idaea novi hominis Christus Jesus*.

. . . .

To be produced by this *Idaea*, built up by this Model, copied by this Original, is truely, is onely to be a new Creature. But that thou mayst put thy self into the way to this, it is usefully said, [g] *Enim vero, certum vitae genus sibi constituere*; Certainly to undertake a certain Profession, a Calling in this world, and to propose to our selves the Example of some good, and godly man in that Calling, whose steps we will walk in, and whom we will make our precedent, *Tanti Momenti esse duco*, says that Father, is a matter of so great importance, as that upon that (says he) lies the building of our whole life. (*1622*) 4:98–99

3. Example: A Seed Sowed (Matt. 5:16)

[h] *Herein is my Father glorified*, (sayes Christ) *that ye beare much fruit*. [i] The seed sowed in good ground, bore some an hundred fold, the least thirty. The seed (in this case) is the example that is before you, of those good men, whose light hath shined out so, that you have seene their good workes. Let this seed, these good examples bring forth hundreds, and sixties, and thirties in you, much fruit; for herein is your Father glorified, that you beare much fruit. Of which plentifull encrease, I am afraid there is one great hinderance that passes through many of you, that is, that when your Will lyes by you, in which some little lamp of this light is set up, something given to God in pious uses, if a Ship miscarry, if a Debtor break, if your state be any way empaired, the first

f. Hierom.
g. Nazianz.
h. John 15:8.
i. Mar. 4:20.

that suffers, the first that is blotted out of the Will, is God and his Legacy; and if your estates encrease, portions encrease, and perchance other legacies, but Gods portion and legacy stands at a stay. Christ left two uses of his passion; application and imitation. [j] *He suffered for us*, sayes the Apostle; for us, that is, that we might make his death ours, apply his death, and (as it follows there) *he left us an example*. So Christ gives us two uses of the Reformation of Religion; first, the doctrine, how to doe good works without relying upon them, as meritorious; and then example, many, very many men (and more by much, in some kindes of charity since the Reformation of Religion, then before) even in this City, whose light hath shined out before you, and you have seen their good works. (*1624?*) 10:101–2

4. Rule and Example (Ps. 32:3, 4)

There can be no example, no patterne to make God by: for, that were to make God a Copy, and the others, by which he were made, the Originall. If thou have a tentation to withdraw thy selfe from the Discipline of that Church, in which God hath given thee thy Baptisme, finde an Example, to satisfie thy Conscience, and Gods people, in what age, in what place, there was any such Church instituted, or any such Discipline practised, as thou hast fancied to thy selfe. Beleeve nothing for which thou hast not a Rule; Doe nothing for which thou hast not an Example; for there is not a more dangerous distemper in either Beliefe or Practise, then singularity; for there onely may we justly call for Miracles, if men will present to us, and binde us to things that were never beleeved, never done before. *David* therefore, in this Psalme, his Psalme of Instruction, (as himselfe calls it) doth both; He lays downe the Rule, he establishes it by Example. (*winter 1624–1625?*) 9:277–78

5. Image for Imitation (Gen. 1:26)

Goe thou then the same way. If God wrought by a pattern, and writ by a copie, and proceeded by a precedent, doe thou so too. Never say, There is no Church without error: therefore I will be bound by none; but frame a Church of mine owne, or be a Church to my selfe. What greater injustice, then to propose no Image, no pattern to thy selfe to imitate; and yet propose thy selfe for a pattern, for an Image to be adored? Thou wilt have singular opinions, and singular ways differing from all other men; and yet all that are not of thy opinion must be heretiques; and all reprobates, that goe not thy wayes. Propose good

j. 1. Pet. 2:21.

patterns to thy selfe; and thereby become a fit pattern for others. God, we see, was the first, that made Images; and he was the first, that forbad them. He made them for imitation; he forbad them in danger of adoration. For, [k]*Qualis dementiae est id colere, quod melius est?* What a drowzinesse, what a lazinesse, what a cowardlinesse of the soule is it, to worship that, which does but represent a better thing then it selfe? Worship belongs to the best, know thou thy distance, and thy period, how far to goe, and where to stop. Dishonor not God by an Image in worshiping it; and yet benefit thy selfe by it, in following it. There is no more danger out of a picture, then out of a history, if thou intend no more in either, then example. Though thou have a West, a darke and a sad condition, that thou art but earth, a man of infirmities, and ill counsailed in thy selfe: yet thou hast herein a North, that scatters and dispells these clouds, that God proposes to thee in his Scriptures, and otherwise, Images, patterns, of good and holy men to goe by. But beyond this North, this assistance of good examples of men, thou hast a South, a Meridionall heighth, by which thou seest thine Image, thy pattern, to be no copy; no other man, but the originall it selfe, God himselfe: *Faciamus ad nostram, Let us make man in our Image, after our likenesse.*

Here we consider first, where this Image is, and then what it does: first, in what part of man God hath imprinted this his Image; And then what this Image confers, and derives upon man; what it works in man. And, as when we seek God in his essence, we are advised to proceed by negatives, God is not mortall, not passible: so when we seek the Image of God in man, we beginne with a negative; This Image is not in his body.

. . . .

But the better to prevent the losse, let us consider the having of this Image: in what respect, in what operation, this Image is in our soule. For, whether this Image, bee in those faculties, which we have in Nature; or in those qualifications, which we may have in Grace; or in those super-illustrations, which the blessed shall have in Glory; hath exercised the contemplation of many. Properly this Image is in Nature; in the naturall reason, and other faculties of the immortall Soule of man. For, thereupon doth Saint *Bernard* say, *Imago Dei uri potest in Gehenna, non exuri*: Till the soule be burnt to ashes, to nothing, (which cannot be done, no not in hell) the Image of God cannot be burnt out of that soule. For it is radically, primarily, in the very soule it selfe. And whether that soule be infused into the Elect, or into the

k. Arnob[ius].

Reprobate, that Image is in that soule, and as far, as he hath a soule by nature, he hath the Image of God by Nature in it. But then the seale is deeper cut, or harder pressed, or better preserved in some, then in others; and in some other considerations, then meerly naturall. Therefore we may consider Man who was made here to the Image of God; and of God, in three Persons, to have been made so, in Gods intendment, three ways: Man had this Image in Nature, and does deface it; he hath it also in Grace here, and so does refresh it; and he shall have it in Glory hereafter, and that shall fix it, establish it. And in every of these three, in this Trinity in man, Nature, Grace, and Glory, man hath not onely the Image of God, but the Image of all the Persons of the Trinity, in every of the three capacities. He hath the Image of the Father, the Image of the Sonne, the Image of the holy Ghost in Nature; and all these also in Grace; and all in Glory too. (*1629*)
9:75–76, 81

6. Exemplary Action (Cant. 5:3)

If you be all *Gods Saints*, you are all *Gods Preists*; and if you be his preists, it is your office to preach too; as we by words, you by your holy works; as we by contemplation, you by conversation; as we by our doctrine, so you by your lives, are appointed by God to preach to one another: and therefore every particular Man, must wash his owne feet, looke that he have *speciosos pedes*, that his example may preach to others, for this is truly *Regale Sacerdotium*, a regall preisthood, not to work upon others by words, but by actions. If we love one another, as Christ loved us, we must *wash one anothers feet*, as he commanded his Apostles; There is a preistly duty lies upon every Man, brotherly to reprehend a brother, whom he sees trampling in foule ways, wallowing in foule sinnes; [l]but I may *preach to others and be my selfe a reprobate*, (as Saint *Paul* speakes with terror to Men of our coate) in his owne person, I may bring others to heaven, and bee shut out my selfe; [m]And thou maist preach that a *Man should not steale, and steale, That a Man should not commit adultery, and commit it*; And in these cases, *Non speciosi pedes*, here are no cleane, no faire feet, and therefore no edifying. Nay if, in either kind, we, or you, *abhor Idols, and yet commit sacriledge*, that is, reprehend a sinne in another, which we are free from our selves, but yet are guilty our selves, of another sinne as great, here's no cleane feet, no profitable preaching; And therefore the onely way to doe God service, is, to wash and to censure the feet, (that is, *particular actions*) but principally, *our owne* feet, that which we doe our selves. (*1619?*) 5:180–81

l. 1. Cor. 9:27. *m.* Rom. 2:21.

D. Emblems, Characters, and Signs

1. Ecce Homo *(Lam. 3:1)*

You remember in the history of the *Passion* of our Lord and Saviour Christ Jesus, there was an *Ecce homo*, a shewing, an exhibiting of that *man*, in whom we are all blessed. *Pilat* presented him to the Jews so, with that [n]*Ecce homo, Behold the man*. That man upon whom the wormwood and the gall of all the ancient Prophecies, and the venome and malignity of all the cruell instruments thereof, was now poured out; That man who was left *as a tender plant, and as a roote out of a dry ground, without forme, or beauty, or comelinesse, that wee should desire to see him*, as the Prophet *Esay* exhibits him; That man who upon the brightnesse of his eternall generation in the bosome of his Father, had now cast a cloud of a temporary and earthly generation in the wombe of his mother, that man, who, as he entred into the wombe of his first mother, the blessed Virgin, by a supernaturall way, by the *overshadowing of the holy Ghost*, so he vouchsafed to enter into the wombe of her, whom he had accepted for his second mother, the *earth*, by an unnaturall way, not by a naturall, but by a violent, and bitter death, that man so torne and mangled, wounded with thornes, oppressed with scornes and contumelies, *Pilate* presents and exhibits so, *Ecce homo, Behold the man*. But in all this depression of his, in all his exinanition, and evacuation, yet he had a *Crown* on, yet he had a *purple garment* on, the emblems, the Characters of majesty were always upon him. (*after 1625?*) 10:192–93

2. Emblems of Purity (Matt. 5:16)

[o]*Christ gave himself for us*, sayes the Apostle, *that he might purifie to himself a peculiar people*. How shall this purification appeare? It follows; *They shall be zealous of good works*; They shall not wrangle about faith and works, but be actually zealous of good works. [p]For, purification was accompanied with an oblation, something was to be given; A Lamb, a Dove, a Turtle; All, emblemes of mildnesse; true purity is milde, meek, humble, and to despise and undervalue others, is an inseparable mark of false purity. The oblation of this dayes purification is light: so the day names it, Candlemas-day, so your custome celebrates it, with many lights. Now, when God received lights into his Tabernacle, hee received none of Tallow, (the Oxe hath hornes) he received none of Waxe, (the Bee hath his sting) but he received

n. Joh. 19:5.
o. Tit. 2:14.
p. Levit. 12:6.

only lampes of oyle. And, though from many fruits and berries they pressed oyle, yet God admitted no oyle into the service of the Church, but only of the Olive; the Olive, the embleme of peace. Our purification is with an oblation, our oblation is light, our light is good works; our peace is rather to exhort you to them, then to institute any solemne, or other then occasionall comparison between faith and them. (*1624?*) 10:84–85

3. Sin and the Emblem of Evening (Ps. 6:6, 7)

And this may be some Embleme, some useful intimation, how hastily Repentance follows sinne; *Davids* sinne is placed, but in the beginning of the night, in the Evening, (*In the evening he rose, and walked upon the Terase, and saw Bathsheba*) and in the next part of time, in the night, he falls a weeping: no more between the sweetnesse of sinne, and the bitternesse of repentance, then between evening, and night; no morning to either of them, till the Sunne of grace arise, and shine out, and proceed to a Meridionall height, and make the repentance upon circumstance, to be a repentance upon the substance, and bring it to be a repentance for the sinne it selfe, which at first was but a repentance upon some calamity, that that sinne induced.

He wept then, and wept in the night; in a time, when he could neither receive rest in himselfe, which all men had, nor receive praise from others, which all men affect. And he wept *Omni nocte*; which is not onely *Omnibus noctibus*, sometime every night, but it is *Tota nocte*, cleane through the night; And he wept in that abundance, as hath put the Holy Ghost to that Hyperbole in *Davids* pen to expresse it, *Liquefecit stratum, natare fecit stratum*, it drowned his bed, surrounded his bed, it dissolved, it macerated, it melted his bed with that brine. Well; [q] *Qui rigat stratum*, he that washes his bed so with repentant teares, *Non potest in cogitationem ejus libidinum pompa subrepere*: Tentations take hold of us sometimes after our teares, after our repentance, but seldome or never in the act of our repentance, and in the very shedding of our teares; At least *Libidinum pompa*, The victory, the triumph of lust breaks not in upon us, in a bed, so dissolved, so surrounded, so macerated with such teares. Thy bed is a figure of thy grave; Such as thy grave receives thee at death, it shall deliver thee up to Judgement at last; Such as thy bed receives thee at night, it shall deliver thee in the morning: If thou sleepe without calling thy selfe to an account, thou wilt wake so, and walke so, and proceed so, without ever calling thy selfe to an account, till Christ Jesus call thee in the Clouds. (*1628*) 8:202–3

q. Hieron.

4. God's Circular Emblems (Isa. 7:14)

One of the most convenient Hieroglyphicks of God, is a Circle; and a Circle is endlesse; whom God loves, hee loves to the end: and not onely to their own end, to their death, but to his end, and his end is, that he might love them still. His hailestones, and his thunder-bolts, and his showres of bloud (emblemes and instruments of his Judgements) fall downe in a direct line, and affect and strike some one person, or place: His Sun, and Moone, and Starres, (Emblemes and Instruments of his Blessings) move circularly, and communicate themselves to all. His Church is his chariot; in that, he moves more gloriously, then in the Sun; as much more, as his begotten Son exceeds his created Sun, and his Son of glory, and of his right hand, the Sun of the firmament; and this Church, his chariot, moves in that communicable motion, circularly; It began in the East, it came to us, and is passing now, shining out now, in the farthest West. As the Sun does not set to any Nation, but withdraw it selfe, and returne againe; God, in the exercise of his mercy, does not set to thy soule, though he benight it with an affliction.

. . . .

Onely he can raise a Tower, whose top shall reach to heaven: The Basis of the highest building is but the Earth; But though thou be but a Tabernacle of Earth, God shall raise thee peece by peece, into a spirituall building; And after one Story of Creation, and another of Vocation, and another of Sanctification, he shall bring thee up, to meet thy selfe, in the bosome of thy God, where thou wast at first, in an eternall election: God is a circle himselfe, and he will make thee one; Goe not thou about to square eyther circle, to bring that which is equall in it selfe, to Angles, and Corners, into dark and sad suspicions of God, or of thy selfe, that God can give, or that thou canst receive no more Mercy, then thou hast had already.

This then is the course of Gods mercy, He proceeds as he begun, which was the first branch of this second part; It is alwayes in motion, and alwayes moving towards *All*, alwayes perpendicular, right over every one of us, and alwayes circular, alwayes communicable to all; And then the particular beame of this Mercy, shed upon *Achaz* here in our Text, is, *Dabit signum, The Lord shall give you a signe*. It is a great Degree of Mercy, that he affords us signes. A naturall man is not made of Reason alone, but of Reason, and Sense: A Regenerate man is not made of Faith alone, but of Faith and Reason; and Signes, externall things, assist us all. (*1624*) 6:173, 175

5. *Sign: God's Call (Isa. 7:14)*

There are signes of another sort, not fixed by Gods Ordinance, but signes which particular men, have sometimes desired at Gods hand, for a farther manifestation of Gods will, in which, it is not, otherwise, already fully manifested, and revealed. For, to seeke such signes, in things which are sufficiently declared by God, or to seeke them, with a resolution, That I will leave a duty undone, except I receive a signe, this is to tempt God, and to seeke a way to excuse my selfe, for not doing that, which I was bound to doe, by the strength of an old commandement, and ought not to look for a new signe. But the greatest fault in this kinde, is, that if God, of his abundant goodnesse, doe give me a signe, for my clearer directions, and I resist that signe, I dispute against that signe, I turne it another way, upon nature, upon fortune, upon mistaking, that so I may goe mine owne way, and not be bound, by beleeving that signe to be from God, to goe that way, to which God by that signe calls me. And this was *Achaz* case; God spoke unto him, and said, [r]*Aske a signe* (that he would deliver him, from the enemy, that besieged Jerusalem) and he said, *I will not aske a signe, nor tempt God*; For, though St. *Augustine*, and some with him, ascribe this refusall of *Achaz*, to a religious modesty, yet St. *Hierome*, and with him, the greatest party, justly impute this, for a fault to *Achaz*: both because the signe was offered him from God, and not sought by himselfe, (which is the case that is most subject to errour) And because the Prophet, who understood Gods minde, and the Kings minde to, takes knowledge of it, as of a great fault, *In this, thou hast contemned, and wearyed, not Man but God*. For, though there be but a few cases, in which we may put God to give a signe, (for Christ calls the Pharisees [s]*an evill, and an adulterous generation*, therefore, because they *sought a signe*) yet God gave *Moses* a signe, of a Rod changed into a Serpent, and a signe of good flesh changed into leprous, and leprous into good, unasked: [t]And after, *Abraham* askes a signe, whereby shall I know, that I shall inherit the land? and God gave him a signe. [u]*So Gideon*, in a modest timorousnesse askes a signe, and presses God to a second signe: First, he would have all the dew upon the fleece, and then, none of the dew upon the fleece. God does give signes, and when he does so, he gives also irradiations, illustrations of the understanding, that they may be discerned to be his signes; and when they are so, it is but a pretended modesty, to say, we will not tempt God to ask a sign, we will not trouble God to tell us whether this be a sign or no, but

r. [Isa. 7:]v.11.
s. Mat. 12:39. Exod. 4.
t. Gen. 15:8.
u. Jud. 6:36.

against all significations from God, goe on, as though all were but naturall accidents.

God gives signes *recte petentibus*, to them that aske them upon due grounds, (so to *Abraham*, so to *Gideon*) And it is too long for this time, to put cases, when a man may or may not put God to a signe; He gives signes also *Non petentibus*, without being asked, to illustrate the case, and to confirme the person, and so he did to *Moses*. Both these are high expressions of his mercy; for what binds God, to begin with man, and give him a signe before he aske; or to waite upon man, and give it him, when he askes? . . .

But *noli inquirere Quomodo*, (saies S. *Basil* still) never come to that question, how it was done, *cum ad hoc nihil sit quod responderi possit*, for God hath given us no faculties to comprehend it, no way to answer it. That's enough, which we have in S. *John, Every spirit, that confesses, that Jesus is come in the flesh, is of God*: for, since it was a comming of Jesus, Jesus was before; so he was God; and since he came in the flesh, hee is now made man; And, that God and Man, are so met, is a signe to mee, that God, and I, shall never bee parted.

This is the signe in generall; That God hath had such a care of all men, is a signe to me, That he hath a care of me. (*1624*) 6:176–77, 179

E. Some Specific Images

1. The Circle

i. God as a Circle (Ps. 63:7)

The key of the psalme, (as S. *Hierome* calls the Titles of the psalmes) tells us, that *David* uttered this psalme, *when he was in the wildernesse of Judah*; There we see the present occasion that moved him; And we see what was passed between God and him before, in the first clause of our Text; (*Because thou hast been my helpe*) And then we see what was to come, by the rest, (*Therefore in the shadow of thy wings will I rejoyce*.) So that we have here the whole compasse of Time, Past, Present, and Future; and these three parts of Time, shall be at this time, the three parts of this Exercise; first, what *Davids* distresse put him upon for the present; and that lyes in the Context; secondly, how *David* built his assurance upon that which was past; (*Because thou hast been my help*) And thirdly, what he established to himselfe for the future, (*Therefore in the shadow of thy wings will I rejoyce*.) First, His distresse in the Wildernesse, his present estate carried him upon the memory of that which God had done for him before, And the Remembrance of that carried him upon that, of which he assured himselfe after. Fixe upon God any where, and you shall finde him a Circle; He is with you now, when you fix upon him; He was with you before, for he brought you to this fixation; and he will be with you hereafter, for [v] *He is yesterday, and to day, and the same for ever.* (*1626*) 7:52

ii. "God is the Center" (Ps. 32:10, 11)

If you carry a Line from the Circumference, to the Circumference againe, as a Diameter, it passes the Center, it flowes from the Center, it looks to the Center both wayes. God is the Center; The Lines above, and the Lines below, still respect and regard the Center; Whether I doe any action honest in the sight of men, or any action acceptable to God, whether I doe things belonging to this life, or to the next, still I must passe all through the Center, and direct all to the glory of God, and keepe my heart right, without variation towards him. (*winter 1624–1625?*) 9:406–7

iii. The Compass as the Word of God (1 Tim. 3:16 [a Lent sermon])

Here is the compass, that the essential Word of God, the Son of God, *Christ Jesus*, went: He was God, *humbled in the flesh*; he was Man, *received into glory*. Here is the compasse that the written Word of God, *went*, the Bible; that begun in *Moses*, in darknesse, in the *Chaos*; and it ends in Saint *John*, in clearnesse, in a Revelation. Here is the compass of all time, as time was distributed in the Creation, *Vespere et mane*; darknesse, and then light: the Evening and the Morning made the Day; Mystery and Manifestation make the Text.

The Doctrine of the present Season, is Mortification, Humiliation; and the experience of the present Place, where we stand now in Court, is that the glory of the persons, in whose presence we stand, occasions Humility in us; the more glorious *they* are, the humbler *we* are; and therefore to consider Christ, as he is *received into glory*, is as much the way of our Humiliation and Mortification, as to consider him in his Passion, in his exinanition: At least, how small account should we make of those things which we suffer for Christ in this world, when we see in this Text, that in the describing the History of Christ from his Incarnation to his Ascension, the Holy Ghost pretermits, never mentions, never seems to consider the Passion of Christ; as though all that he had suffered for man, were nothing in respect of that he would suffer, if the justice of God had required any heavier satisfaction. (*1621*) 3:206–7

v. Heb. 13:8.

iv. "This life is a Circle" (Ps. 89:48)

And this brought in that Custome into the Primitive Church, that they called the Martyrs dayes, wherein they suffered, *Natalitia Martyrum*, their birth dayes; birth, and death is all one.

Their death was a birth to them into another life, into the glory of God; It ended one Circle, and created another; for immortality, and eternity is a Circle too; not a Circle where two points meet, but a Circle made at once; This life is a Circle, made with a Compasse, that passes from point to point; That life is a Circle stamped with a print, an endlesse, and perfect Circle, as soone as it begins. Of this Circle, the Mathematician is our great and good God; The other Circle we make up our selves. (*1619*) 2:200

v. Circle of Nothing (Isa. 32:8)

To have been once nothing, and to be now co-heire with the Son of God, is such a Circle, such a Compasse, as that no revolutions in this world, to rise from the lowest to the highest, or to fall from the highest to the lowest, can be called or thought any Segment, any Arch, any Point in respect of this Circle; To have once been nothing, and now to be co-heires with the Son of God: That Son of God, who if there had been but one soule to have been saved, would have dyed for that; nay, if all soules had been to be saved, but one, and that that onely had sinned, he would not have contented himselfe with all the rest, but would have dyed for that. And there is the goodnesse, the liberality of our King, our God, our Christ, our Jesus. (*1628*) 8:250–51

vi. Circle of Creation (Hosea 2:19)

When I consider Christ to have been from before all beginnings, and to be still the Image of the Father, the same stamp upon the same metall, and my self a peece of rusty copper, in which those lines of the Image of God which were imprinted in me in my Creation are defaced and worn, and washed and burnt, and ground away, by my many, and many, and many sins: When I consider Christ in his Circle, in glory with his Father, before he came into this world, establishing a glorious Church when he was in this world, and glorifying that Church with that glory which himself had before, when he went out of this world; and then consider my self in my circle, I came into this world washed in mine own tears, and either out of compunction for my self or compassion for others, I passe through this world as through a valley of tears, where tears settle and swell, and when I passe out of this world I leave their eyes whose hands close mine, full of tears too. (*1621*) 3:250

vii. Perpetuity and Eternity (Rev. 4:8)

In respect of Eternity (which is necessary in a God) Perpetuity is but *Mobilis Imago* (as *Plato* cals it) a faint and transitory shadow of Eternity; and *Pindarus* makes it lesse; *Idolum Aeternitatis*; Perpetuity is but an Idol compared to eternity; And, *an Idol is nothing*, sayes the Apostle. Our soules have a blessed perpetuity, our soules shall no more see an end, then God, that hath no Beginning; and yet our soules are very far from being eternal. But those gods are so far from being eternall, as that, considered as Gods (that is, celebrated with Divine worship) they are not perpetual. But [w]*God is our God for ever and ever*; ever, without beginning; and ever, without end. [x]*My dayes are like a shadow that fadeth, and I am withered like grasse; but thou O Lord dost remaine for ever, and thy remembrance from generation to generation*; It is a *remaining*, and it is a *remembrance*; which words denote a former being. So that God, our God, and onely he, is eternall. (*1627*) 8:58

2. On the Work and Expression of the Holy Ghost

i. Red and White (Gen. 1:26)

He made us all of earth, and all of red earth. Our earth was red, even when it was in Gods hands: a rednesse that amounts to a shamefastnesse, to a blushing at our own infirmities, is imprinted in us, by Gods hand. For this rednesse, is but a conscience, a guiltinesse of needing a continuall supply, and succession of more, and more grace. And we are all red, red so, even from the beginning, and in our best state. *Adam* had, the Angells had thus much of this infirmity, that though they had a great measure of grace, they needed more. The prodigall child grew poore enough, after he had received his portion: and he may be wicked enough, that trusts upon former, or present grace, and seeks not more. This rednesse, a blushing, that is, an acknowledgement, that we could not subsist, with any measure of faith, except we pray for more faith, nor of grace, except we seek more grace, we have from the hand of God: And another rednesse from his hand too, the bloud of his Sonne, for that bloud was effused by Christ, in the value of the ransome for All, and accepted by God, in the value thereof for All: and this redness is, in the nature thereof, as extensive,

w. Psal. 48:14. *x*. Psal. 102:11.

as the redness derived from *Adam* is; Both reach to all. So we were red earth in the hands of God, as redness denotes our generall infirmities, and as redness denotes the bloud of his Sonne, our Saviour, all have both. But that redness, which we have contracted from bloud shed by our selves, the bloud of our own souls, by sinne, was not upon us, when we were in the hands of God. That redness is not his tincture, not his complexion. No decree of his is writ in any such red inke. Our sinnes are our owne, and our destruction is from our selves. (*1629*) 9:64–65

ii. Water: Frequent Metaphor of the Holy Ghost (Ps. 32:6)

The Holy Ghost who is a direct worker upon the soule and conscience of man, but a Metaphoricall, and Figurative expresser of himselfe, to the reason, and understanding of man, abounds in no Metaphor more, then in calling Tribulations, *Waters*: particularly, [y]*He would bring in waters upon Tyrus*, And, *He would poure out his wrath upon his enemies, like waters*. Neither doth he onely intimate temporall, but spirituall afflictions too, in the name of *Waters*. And as S. *Hierome* understands this whole place of the Church, collectively, so S. *Augustine* understands these *waters*, to be *Variae Doctrinae*, those diverse opinions, that disquiet and trouble the Church. And though the Church of God were built upon a hill, and compassed, and environed, and fenced with the blood of him that built it, and defended and guarded by the vigilancy of the Apostles; yet into this Jerusalem did these waters breake, even in the Apostles time, as we see by those severall, those manifold, those contradictory Heresies, that sprung up then. Christ and his Apostles had carried two Waters about his Church: The water of Baptisme, that is *Limen Ecclesiae*, and *Janua Sacramentorum*, The first Ferry, by which we passe into the Church; and by this Water came three thousand, and five thousand at once to the Church, upon particular Sermons of S. *Peter*. And then Christ gave another Water, by which, they came to another Ablution, to Absolution from actuall sins, the water of contrite teares, and repentance, which he had promised before, [z]*I will poure cleane water upon you, and you shall be cleane*, And by this water came *Peter* himselfe, when his faith had failed, And by this water came *Mary Magdalen*, when her life had been defiled. But yet for all these Waters, other Waters soaked in, and corrupted them earely; for, for Baptisme, the Disciples of *Simon Magus* annulled Christs Baptisme, and baptized in *Simons*

y. Ezek. 26:3. Hosea 5:[10]. *z*. Ezek. 36:25.

name; and his Disciple *Menander* annulled the Baptisme of Christ, and *Simon*, and baptized in his owne name. And then, for the other Water, Repentance, the Heretiques drained up that shrewdly, when they took away all benefit of repentance for sins committed after Baptisme. *David* denies not, nay *David* assures us, that collectively, the whole Church shall be beaten upon with waters. (*winter 1624–1625?*) 9:328–29

iii. The Metaphor of Wings (Ps. 63:7)

[a]The Mercy-seat it selfe was covered with the Cherubims Wings; and who would have more then Mercy? and a Mercy-seat; that is, etablished, resident Mercy, a permanent and perpetuall Mercy; present and familiar Mercy; a Mercy-seat. Our Saviour Christ intends as much as would have served their turne, if they had laid hold upon it, when hee sayes, [b]*That hee would have gathered Jerusalem, as a henne gathers her chickens under her wings*. And though the other Prophets doe (as ye have heard) mingle the signification of Power, and actuall deliverance, in his Metaphor of Wings, yet our Prophet, whom wee have now in especiall consideration, *David*, never doth so; but in every place where hee uses this Metaphor of Wings (which are in five or sixe severall Psalmes) still hee rests and determines in that sense, which is his meaning here; That though God doe not actually deliver us, nor actually destroy our enemies, yet if hee refresh us in the shadow of his Wings, if he maintaine our subsistence (which is a religious Constancy) in him, this should not onely establish our patience, (for that is but halfe the worke) but it should also produce a joy, and rise to an exultation, which is our last circumstance, *Therefore in the shadow of thy wings, I will rejoice*. (*1626*) 7:68

iv. The Symbol of Feet (Ezek. 34:19)

Now, in the Scriptures, when this word, *feet*, doth not signifie that part of mans body which is ordinarily so called, but is transferred to a *Metaphoricall* signification, (as in our text it is) it does most commonly signifie *Affections*, or *Power*. [c]So the *Lord will keep the feet* of his Saints; that is, direct their *desires*, and *affections* in the ways of holinesse. And then for *Power*, (which is the more frequent acceptation of the word) [d]he will not suffer *thy foot* to be moved, that is, thy *Power* to be shaked; And all such places, [e]*qui festinus*, he that hasteth with *his*

a. Exod. 25:20.
b. Matt. 23:37.
c. 1. Sam. 2:9.
d. Psal. 121:3.
e. Prov. 19:2.

feet sinneth, our interpreters expound of a hasty abuse of *Power*; And those, [f]they have not refrained *their feet*, and then, *thy feet* are sunk in the mire, are still interpreted of *Power*, of a wanton abuse of Power, or of a withdrawing this Power from man, *by God*; *feet* signifies Affections, and them corrupted and depraved, and power, and that abused. *David* seems to have joyned them, (as when they are joyned, they must necessarily be the most heavy) in that prayer, [g]Let not *the foot of pride* come against me. The *hand* of pride, nay the *sword* of pride, affects not a tender soule so much, as the *foot* of pride; to be oppressed, and that with *scorne*; not so much in an *anger*, as in a *wantonnesse*. (*1625?*) 10:154–55

v. Images of Armor (Ps. 63:7)

As God hath spangled the firmament with starres, so hath he his Scriptures with names, and Metaphors, and denotations of power. Sometimes he shines out in the name of a *Sword*, and of a *Target*, and of a *Wall*, and of a *Tower*, and of a *Rocke*, and of a *Hill*; And sometimes in that glorious and manifold constellation of all together, *Dominus exercituum, The Lord of Hosts*. God, as God, is never represented to us, with Defensive Armes; He needs them not. When the Poets present their great Heroes, and their Worthies, they alwayes insist upon their Armes, they spend much of their invention upon the description of their Armes; both because the greatest valour and strength needs Armes, (*Goliah* himselfe was armed) and because to expose ones selfe to danger unarmed, is not valour, but rashnesse. But God is invulnerable in himselfe, and is never represented armed; you finde no shirts of mayle, no Helmets, no Cuirasses in Gods Armory. [h]In that one place of *Esay*, where it may seeme to be otherwise, where God is said *to have put on righteousnesse as a breastplate, and a Helmet of Salvation upon his head*; in that prophecy God is Christ, and is therefore in that place, called *the Redeemer*. Christ needed defensive armes, God does not. Gods word does; His Scriptures doe; And therefore S. *Hierome* hath armed them, and set before every booke his *Prologum galeatum*, that prologue that armes and defends every booke from calumny. But though God need not, nor receive not defensive armes for himselfe, yet God is to us a Helmet, a Breastplate, a strong tower, a rocke, every thing that may give us assurance and defence; and as often as he will, he can refresh that Proclamation, [i]*Nolite tangere Christos meos*, Our enemies shall not so much as touch us. (*1626*) 7:65

f. Jer. 14:10; 38:22.
g. Psal. 36:11.
h. Esay 59:17.
i. Psal. 105:15.

vi. The Crown (Cant. 3:11)

The Crown, which we are called to see him crowned with, *his mother* put upon him; The Crown which his *Father gave him*, was that glory, wherewith he was glorifyed, with the Father, *from all eternity*, in his *divine nature*: And the Crown wherewith his Father crowned his *Humane nature*, was the glory given to that, in his *Ascension*. *His Mother* could give him no such Crown: she her selfe had no Crown, but that, which *he* gave her. The Crown that *she* gave him, was that substance, that he received from her, *our flesh*, our *nature*, our *humanity*; and this, *Athanasius*, and this, Saint *Ambrose*, calls the *Crown*, wherewith *his Mother crowned him*, in this text, his infirm, his humane nature. Or, *the Crown wherewith his Mother crowned him*, was that Crown, to which, that infirme nature which he tooke from her, submitted him, which was his *passion*, his *Crown of thornes*; for so *Tertullian*, and divers others take this Crown of his, from her, to be his *Crown of thorns*: [j]*Woe to the Crown of pride, whose beauty is a fading flower*, says the Prophet; But blessed be this Crown of Humiliation, whose flower cannot fade. Then was there truly a *Rose* amongst *Thorns*, when through his Crown of *Thorns*, you might see his title, *Jesus Nazarenus*: for, in that very name *Nazarenus*, is involved the signification of a *flower*; the very word signifies a *flower*. *Esay's* flower in the Crown of pride fades, and is removed; This flower in the Crown of Thornes fades not, nor could be removed; for, for all the importunity of the Jews, *Pilate* would not suffer *that title* to be removed, or to be changed; still *Nazarenus* remained, and still a rose amongst thorns. You know the curse of the earth, [k]*Thorns and thistles shall it bring forth unto thee*; It did so to our *Solomon* here, it brought forth thornes to Christ, and he made a *Crown* of those thorns, not onely for *himself*, but for us too, [l]*Omnes aculei mortis, in Dominici Corporis tolerantia, obtusi sunt*, All the thorns of life and death, are broken, or blunted upon the head of our *Solomon*, and now, even our *thorns* make up *our Crown*, our tribulation in life, our dissolution in death, conduce to our glory: *Behold him crowned with his Mothers Crown*, for even that brought him to his *Fathers Crown*, his humiliation to exaltation, his passion to glory.

Behold your Solomon, your Saviour again, and you shall see another *beam* of Comfort, in your tribulations from his; for even this *Humiliation* of his, is called his *Espousals*, his *marriage*, *Behold him crowned in the day* of *his Espousals*. His Spouse is the *Church*, His marriage is

j. Esa. 28:1.
k. Gen. 3:18.
l. Tertul.

the *uniting* of himselfe to this Spouse, in his becomming *Head of the Church.* [m]The great City, the heavenly Jerusalem, is called *The Bride*, and *The Lambs wife*, in the *Revelation*: And he is the *Head* of this body, the *Bridegroom* of this Bride, the Head of this Church, as he is *The first-borne of the Dead*; Death, that dissolves all ours, made up this marriage. His Death is his Marriage, and upon his Death flowed out from his side, those two *Elements of the Church, water* and *bloud*; The Sacraments of *Baptisme*, and of the *Communion* of himself. Behold then this *Solomon crowned* and *married*; both words of *Exaltation*, and *Exultation*, and both by *Death*; and trust him for working the same effects upon thee; That thou (*though by Death*) shalt be *crowned* with a Crown of Glory, and *married* to him, in whose right and merit thou shalt have that Crown. (*1625*) 6:287–88

3. Sacred Place

i. Church: House and Court (Gen. 28:16, 17)

Now, his most glorious *Creatures* are but *vehicula Dei*; they are but chariots, which convey God, and bring him to our sight; The *Tabernacle* it selfe was but *Mobilis domus*, and *Ecclesia portatilis*, a house without a foundation; a running, a progresse house: but the Church is his standing house; there are his offices fixed: there are his provisions, which fat the Soule of Man, as with marrow and with fatnesse, his precious bloud, and body: there work his seales; there beats his Mint; there is absolution, and pardon for past sinnes, there is grace for prevention of future in his Sacraments. But the Church is not onely *Domus Dei*, but *Basilica*; not onely his house, but his Court: he doth not onely dwell there, but reigne there: which multiplies the joy of his houshold servants: *The Lord reigneth, let all the earth rejoyce, yea let the multitude of the Islands be glad thereof*. That the Church was usually called *Martyrium*, that is, a place of *Confession*, where we open our wounds and receive our remedy, That it was called *Oratorium*, where we might come, and aske necessary things at Gods hands, all these teach us our severall duties in that place, and they adde to their spirituall comfort, who have been Gods instruments, for providing such places, as God may be glorified in, and the godly benefited in all these ways.

But of all Names, which were then usually given to the Church, the name of *Temple* seems to be most large, and significant, as they derive it *a Tuendo*; for *Tueri* signifies both our beholding, and contemplating

m. 21:9.

God in the Church: and it signifies Gods protecting, and defending those that are his, in his Church. (*1619?*) 2:221

ii. Symbols of North, South, East, West (Gen. 1:26)

In this point, the North, we place our first comfort. The North is not always the comfortablest clime: nor is the North always a type of happines in the Scriptures. Many times God threatens stormes from the North. But even in those Northern stormes, we consider that action, that they scatter, they dissipate those clouds, which were gathered, and so induce a serenity: And so, [n]fair weather comes from the North. And that's the use which we have of the North in this place. The consideration of our West, our low estate; that we are but earth, but red earth, dyed red by our selves: and that imaginary white, which appeares so to us, is but a white of leprosie: this West enwraps us in heavy clouds of murmuring, in this life, that we cannot live so freely as beasts doe; and in clouds of desperation for the next life, that we cannot dye so absolutely as beasts do; we dye all our lives, and yet we live after our deaths. These are our clouds; And then the North shakes these clouds. [o]*The North Winde driveth away the rain*, says *Solomon*. There is a North in our text, that drives all those teares from our eyes. [p]Christ calls upon the North, as well as the South, to blow upon his Garden, and to diffuse the perfumes thereof. Adversity, as well as prosperity, opens the bounty of God unto us; and oftentimes better. But that's not the benefit of the North in our present consideration. But this is it, that first our sunne sets in the West. The Eastern dignity, which we received in our first Creation, as we were the worke of the whole Trinity, falls under a Western cloud, that that Trinity made us but earth. And then blowes our North, and scatters this cloud; that this earth hath a nobler forme, then any other part or limbe of the world. For, we are made by a fairer pattern, by a nobler Image, by a higher likenesse. *Faciamus*; Though we make but a man, *Let us make* him, *in our Image, after our likenesse*. (*1629*) 9:70 (see above, A.1.x)

iii. Shubah: *The Return of God to His Place (Ps. 6:4, 5)*

And so, *Shubah, To Returne*, is *Redire ad locum suum*, To returne to that place, to which a thing is naturally affected; So heavy things returne to the Center, and light things returne to the Expansion; [q]*So Mans breath departeth*, sayes *David*, *Et redit in terram suam, He returnes into his Earth*; That earth, which is so much his, as that it is he

n. Job 37:22.
o. Prov. 25:23.
p. Cant. 4:16.
q. Psal. 146:4.

himselfe; Of earth he was, and therefore to earth he returnes. But can God returne in such a sense as this? Can we finde an *Ubi* for God? A place that is his place? Yes; And an Earth which is his earth; [r]*Surely the vineyard of the Lord of Hosts, is the house of Israel, and the men of Judah are his pleasant plant*. So the Church, which is his Vineyard, is his *Ubi*, his place, his Center, to which he is naturally affected. And when he calls us hither, and meets us here, upon his Sabbaths, and sheds the promises of his Gospel upon the Congregation in his Ordinance, he returnes to us here, as in his *Ubi*, as in his own place. And as he hath a place of his owne here, so he hath an Earth of his owne in this place. Our flesh is Earth, and God hath invested our flesh, and in that flesh of ours, which suffered death for us, he returnes to us in this place, as often as he maketh us partakers of his flesh, and his bloud, in the blessed Sacrament. So then, though in my dayes of sinne, God have absented himselfe from me, (for God is absent when I doe not discerne his presence) yet if to day I can heare his voyce, as God is returned to day to this place, as to his *Ubi*, as to his own place; so in his entring into me, in his flesh and bloud, he returnes to me as to his Earth, that Earth which he hath made his by assuming my nature, I am become his *Ubi*, his place; *Delitiae ejus, His delight is to be with the sonnes of men*, and so with me; and so in the Church, in the Sermon, in the Sacrament he returnes to us, in the first signification of this word *Shubah*, as to that place to which he is naturally affected and disposed. (*1623?*) 5:368

iv. Non Hic: *He Is Risen* (Matt. 28:6)

Places of prophane and secular use should not be made equall with holy places; nor should holy actions, and motions, and gestures, and positions of the body in divine service, be submitted to scorne and derision. They have their use; either in a reall exaltation of Devotion, or for a peaceable conservation of uniformity, and decency, or for a reverentiall obedience to lawfull Authority; and any of these is enough, to authorize things in their use, which in themselves and in their owne nature are indifferent. And though the principall purpose of the Angell, in shewing these women the place, were to assure them, that Christ was risen, yet may there also be an intimation of the helpe and assistance that we receive from holy places, in this their *Ecce locus, Come, and see the place*.

But this is farre, very very far from that superstitious fixing of God to the free-hold, which they have induced in the Roman Church, and

r. Esay 5:[7].

upon which, they have super-induced their meritorious Pilgrimages to certaine places.[5]

. . . .

In detestation of this locall and stationary salvation of these meritorious pilgrimages to certaine places, some of the blessed Fathers spoke much, long before they were come to that enormous abuse, in which the later times exceeded. S. *Hierom* had occasion to say much of it, by a solicitation from *Polinus*, and he saies this, [s]*Quanti hodie portant funera sua?* How many men carry Sepulchres to the Sepulchre, when they carry themselves to Jerusalem? *Non Hierosolymis vixisse,* saies he, To have lived well at Jerusalem is praiseworthy, but not to have lived there. *Non audeo concludere,* I dare not shut up that God, whom the Heavens cannot containe, in a corner of the earth; and Jerusalem is but so. *Et de Britannia, et de Hierosolymis aequaliter patet aula coelestis,* Heaven is as neare England, (saies S. *Hierom*) as it is to Jerusalem. And Christ, (saies he) was then in Jerusalem, in that holy place, when he said, [t]*Abeamus hinc, Let us go from hence*; as holy as the place was, he made haste out of it; for, (as that Father adds) it is a place full of mutinous Souldiers, of licentious prostitutes, of Players and Jesters; and these are the elements of the holinesse of that place.

Gregory Nyssen (in the same time with *Hierom*) had a particular occasion to deliver his opinion of these pilgrimages to Jerusalem; for he had beene there himselfe, though not as a Pilgrim. *Sunt aliqui,* There are some that make it a part of Religion, to have beene at Jerusalem, *Sin praeter praeceptum Domini,* But, saies he, if Christ never commanded it, (that is his Rule) I know not what can justifie that man, that makes himselfe the Rule of his Religion. Christ never called that, Blessednesse, saies he, to have beene at Jerusalem, nor ever called this Jerusalem the way to Heaven; why any man should do so, when Christ did not, *Qui mentem habet, consideret,* (saies that Father) Let him that is not distracted, consider.

. . . .

I beleeved that Christ was risen, before I saw the empty Sepulchre; And though (I thank God for it) I lost none of my faith at Jerusalem,

5. Donne takes strong exception to the Roman Catholic doctrine of merit, whereby man is supposed to receive some kind of reward for a work done for God. A pilgrimage to a holy shrine, for example, might produce so much merit, the place itself being no more than a kind of estate, Donne contemptuously says, where God is confined to a "free-hold" dwelling. "Stationary salvation" is thus fixed to a certain and unchanging place or action.

s. Epist. 13. *t.* John 14:31.

yet I encreased it not there. *Si perverse vivas;* live Christianly, or thou art as far from Christ in the Sepulchre, and from all benefit of his Resurrection, as they that were hired to watch the Sepulchre, and to seale the Sepulchre to prevent the Resurrection, or as if he that lay in the Sepulchre had never dyed.

. . . .

You have heard the Angels information to them, *Non hic,* that Christ was not there, and yet comfort in that; God raises comfort out of all things, even out of discomfort it self to the godly. You have heard the reason added, *Quia surrexit, for he is risen;* And if this be a good reason, there is no Transubstantiation, no Ubiquitisme,[6] for then Christ might have been there, though he were risen. *He is risen,* not only raised, and therefore the Son of God; and *risen for our Justification,* therefore we are risen in him. (*1630*) 9:209–12

6. See note 3 in Chap. 4.

9 *Hermeneutics— Interpretation and Revelation*

Introduction

Hermeneutics (from ἑρμηνεύω, "to interpret") is the science that describes methods of right interpretation of Scripture, and leads to the ways in which a reader may find the true meaning of the literal words. It is thus distinguished from exegesis, or the practical application of the theory of interpretation. More generally, hermeneutics is applied to the interpretation of any literary text, not necessarily scriptural. According to this wider sense (though not by this term), Donne and his contemporaries eagerly and frequently practised their interpretive skills. The ancient and traditional method of hermeneutic interpretation that Donne inherited looked for levels of increasingly complex meaning interpenetrating one another, of the kind Spenser supposedly intended in *The Faerie Queene*, or claimed to have devised in his "continued Allegory, or darke conceit"; or Chapman, whose vision of Homer informed him that only he could understand and "translate" the mysteries of Homer's divine poetry, that verse which "Some meere celestiall nature did adorne" ("To the Reader," line 109, *Poems*, ed. P. B. Bartlett, 1941).

The different kinds of meaning are traditionally fourfold, though seldom clearcut: literal, allegorical (or "historical"), tropological (or "moral"), and anagogical (or "spiritual"). Donne recommends that the literal meaning is foremost in all interpretation, and that the other meanings belong to the "figurative" senses. Thus he writes that "the literall sense of every place, is the principall intention of the Holy Ghost, in that place . . . so that in many places of Scripture, a figurative sense is the literall sense" (6:62). While Donne wishes to emphasize the literal sense, he finds the other senses mingled with each other, so trained is he in the system of seeing manifold significance in every literal declaration. On the text from Ps. 38:4, "For mine iniquities are gone over my head, as a heavy burden, they are too heavy for me," Donne summarizes this division: "all these things are *literally* spoken of *David*; By *application*, of us; and by *figure*, of Christ. *Historically*, *David*; *morally*, we; *Typically* [or spiritually, mystically] Christ is the subject of this text" (2:97).

Interpretation depends upon the close study of meaning and its possibilities, which need also to be demonstrated. Donne commends the preacher who can help to unravel ways and straighten paths for a willing auditor; yet pulpit eloquence is merely diverting for the man who only hears the sermon and neglects the word—a message similar to the reservations Donne makes elsewhere about witty and learned preaching (see pp. 343–44). The rule should be to "avoid excesse" and to advance "plaine, and simple, and fundamentall doctrines . . . which are truely necessary to salvation." The discovery of truth is difficult, the testimony in its favor varied and often obscure, the freedom to find it as irrevocable as the charity demanded of all who interpret it. "But what is truth?" Donne asks. "God" is the answer. "And what is God? Charity; Therefore let Charity reconcile . . . differences. . . . Let us use our liberty of reading Scriptures according to the Law of liberty; that is, charitably to leave others to their liberty, if they but differ from us, and not differ from Fundamentall Truths" (9:95). Such liberty of interpretation must have limitations, or else failure is the end of our study. The liberty urged here carries an implicit warning, expressed directly in another place, that we are "not to rest in Nature without God, nor in God without Christ, nor in Christ without the Scriptures, nor in our private interpretation of Scripture, without the Church" (1:235).

From the varieties of interpretation to the dangers inherent in their false or misleading use, we turn to the hope of revelation. Revelation keeps us steadily and reverently on the truest course, where we should not bend, as we have just seen, before the chances of private and uninformed interpretation. Donne reaffirms this principle in a later passage selected from the same sermon: man's infirmity and his inclination toward error is eased through things that are visible, especially the Church, which directs the right knowledge of Scripture. As the text from 2 Cor. 4:6 declares, the light that God made out of darkness shines also in our hearts, where the ministry of the gospel has its beginning. Once more, Donne recalls his own circumstances as a preacher who acts on behalf of the historical Church, and he speaks cautiously and self-consciously about his ambitions. The mysteries of salvation are best related "plainly, sincerely, inelegantly, inartificially"; and he urges his hearers to look "for the Gold, and not for the Fashion; for the Matter, and not for the Form" (4:91). Only revelation through knowledge received from God, "the roote of goodnesse," may be justly "communicated, and transfused, and shed, and spred, and derived, and digested upon others" (p. 26). Christian example depends on an interior radiance and light, and Donne returns again and again to this holy necessity.

While Donne aims to work within the guidance of the Church, he regularly appeals to "the mystery of godliness"; and while he extols plainness in speech, he makes use of all the eloquence in his power. There is no real problem or "tension" in this seeming contrast, no more than in Herbert's *Temple*, where the same issues occur. The tendency to think in unified contraries is habitual to Donne and his age, and he would have been unable to see any inconsistency where none in fact should be apprehended. Donne thrives on paradox, the pun (or more correctly, *paronomasia*), and double vision: hearers and preachers are both doctors; light is faith; "the armor of light is knowledge; an ignorant man is a disarmed man, a naked man" (4:119–21); but Christ has burned his library and "annihilated his wisdom" by shining in our hearts with the knowledge of the gospel.

With an easy transition, we move to the more practical considerations of the chapter, to exegesis and lastly to the actions—the results—of interpretation. The specific explanation of biblical texts, or exegesis, is governed by the principles of hermeneutics, and Donne's description of exegesis acknowledges its detailed concerns: "In the words, and by occasion of them, we consider the Text, the Context, and the Pretext. . . . In a word, In the Text, the Words; in the Context, the Occasion of the words; In the Pretext, the Pretence, the purpose, the disposition of him who gave the occasion" (6:224). As we know, the Scriptures are for Donne inextricably linked with the Church. Although the Spirit of God gives life to them, the Church authorizes and explicates them. Cleverly playing on the formation and extension of the Word in time, Donne aligns voice with echo, what is said with what can afterward be heard: "In the Scriptures you have *Praeceptum*, The thing it self, What; In the Church, you have the *Nunc*, The time, When. The Scriptures are Gods Voyce; The Church is his Eccho; a redoubling, a repeating of some particular syllables, and accents of the same voice" (6:223). Hence, context and pretext show that Scripture is revealed to the Church for certain occasions and times, with the Holy Ghost acting as interpreter and commentator, first conveyed to us in the creation, then again in our regeneration. Wherever there is breath and speech, there also is the voice of the Holy Ghost: "Thou knowest not from whence all this goodnesse comes, but meerly from his goodness" (6:130). Exegesis rests ultimately on a joyful mystery.

Finally, the chapter gathers Donne's statements on the relationships of preaching itself to interpretation and moral behavior, and on the central role of those who listen to the preacher, who, in actively hearing, learn themselves how to "preach," or to be good models to others. Donne has in mind a community of believers who "speake one anothers language, and preach to one anothers conscience" (5:50–

51). Right speech is procured, Donne says, through the "*Grace of lips*"; and thus governed, a man "is bound to enable himself to be useful and profitable to the Publick, in some course, in some vocation" (1:206–7). Social actions are a part of this world, in which man should represent God in his conversation; but not all actions are equally good, or good simply because they are well meant, or because some good effects result. The design of common speech that Donne espouses is complicated by man's fragile and corrupt nature: "no Example of man is sufficient to constitute a certaine and constant rule; All the actions of the holiest man are not holy" (9:158). The solution lies in the Redemption, an act that is past while yet awaiting future application.

A. Methods of Interpretation

1. Importance of the Literal Sense (Apoc. 20:6)

In the first book of the Scriptures, that of Genesis, there is danger in departing from the letter; In this last book, this of the Revelation, there is as much danger in adhering too close to the letter. The literall sense is alwayes to be preserved; but the literall sense is not alwayes to be discerned: for the literall sense is not alwayes that, which the very Letter and Grammer of the place presents, as where it is literally said, *That Christ is a Vine*, and literally, *That his flesh is bread*, and literally, *That the new Jerusalem is thus situated, thus built, thus furnished*: But the literall sense of every place, is the principall intention of the Holy Ghost, in that place: And his principall intention in many places, is to expresse things by allegories, by figures; so that in many places of Scripture, a figurative sense is the literall sense, and more in this book then in any other. As then to depart from the literall sense, that sense which the very letter presents, in the book of Genesis, is dangerous, because if we do so there, we have no history of the Creation of the world in any other place to stick to; so to binde our selves to such a literall sense in this book, will take from us the consolation of many spirituall happinesses, and bury us in the carnall things of this world.

The first error of being too allegoricall in Genesis, transported divers of the ancients beyond the certain evidence of truth, and the second error of being too literall in this book, fixed many, very many, very ancient, very learned, upon an evident falshood; which was, that because here is mention *of a first Resurrection, and of raigning with Christ a thousand years after that first Resurrection*, There should be to all the Saints of God, a state of happinesse in this world, after Christs comming, for a thousand yeares; In which happy state, though some of them have limited themselves in spirituall things, that they should enjoy a kinde of conversation with Christ, and an impeccability, and a quiet serving of God without any reluctations, or concupiscences, or persecutions; yet others have dreamed on, and enlarged their dreames to an enjoying of all these worldly happinesses, which they, being formerly persecuted, did formerly want in this world, and then should have them for a thousand yeares together in recompence. And even this branch of that error, of possessing the things of this world, so long, in this world, did very many, and very good, and very great men, whose names are in honour, and justly in the Church of God, in those first times stray into; and flattered themselves with an imaginary intimation of some such thing, in these words, *Blessed and holy is he, that hath part in the first Resurrection.*

Thus far then the text is literall, That this Resurrection in the text, is different from the generall Resurrection. The first differs from the last: And thus far it is figurative, allegoricall, mysticall, that it is a spirituall Resurrection, that is intended. But wherein spirituall? or of what spirituall Resurrection? In the figurative exposition of those places of Scripture, which require that way oft to be figuratively expounded, that Expositor is not to be blamed, who not destroying the literall sense, proposes such a figurative sense, as may exalt our devotion, and advance our edification; And as no one of those Expositors did ill, in proposing one such sense, so neither do those Expositors ill, who with those limitations, that it destroy not the literall sense, that it violate not the analogy of faith, that it advance devotion, do propose another and another such sense. So doth that preacher well also, who to the same end, and within the same limit, makes his use of both, of all those expositions; because all may stand, and it is not evident in such figurative speeches, which is the literall, that is, the principall intention of the Holy Ghost. (*1624*) 6:62–63

2. Literal, Moral, Typical (Ps. 38:4)

In his *many* sins, we shall touch thus many circumstances: First, they were *peccata*, sins, iniquities; and then *peccata sua*, his sins, his iniquities, which intimates *actuall sins*; for though God inflict miseries for originall sin, (*death*, and that, that induces it, *sicknesse*, and the like) yet those are miseries common to all, because the sin is so too; But these, are his punishments, personall calamities, and the sins are *his own* sins; And then, (which is a third circumstance) they are sins in the *plurall*, God is not thus angry for *one* sin; And again, they are such sins, as have been long in going, and are now got over, *supergressae sunt*, they are gone, gone over; And then lastly, for that first part, *supergressae Caput*, they are gone over my head, In which exaltation, is intimated all this; first, *sicut tectum, sicut fornix*, they are over his head, as a roofe, as a cieling, as an Arch, they have made a wall of separation, betwixt God and us, so they are above our head; And then *sicut clamor*, they are ascended as a noise, they are got up to heaven, and cry to God for vengeance, so they are above our head; And again *sicut aquae*, they are risen and swollen as waters, they compass us, they smother us, they blinde us, they stupefie us, so they are above our head; But lastly and principally, *sicut Dominus*, they are got above us, as a Tyran, and an usurper, for so they are above our head too: And in these we shall determine our first part. When from thence we come to our second part, in which (as in this we shall have done their *number*) we shall consider their *greatnesse*, we finde them first *heavy*, sinne is no light matter; And then, they are *too heavy*, a little weight would but ballast us, this sinkes us; Too heavy for *me*, even for a man equall to *David*; and where is he? when is that man? for, says our text, they are as heavy, as a heavy *Burden*; And the nature, and inconvenience of a Burden is, first to *Crooken*, and bend us downward from our naturall posture, which is erect, for this incurvation implies a declination in the inordinate love of the Creature, *Incurvat*. And then the nature of a burden is, to *Tyre* us; our very sinne becomes fulsome, and wearisome to us, *fatigat*; and it hath this inconvenience too, *ut retardet*, it slackens our pace, in our right course, though we be not tired, yet we cannot goe so fast, as we should in any way towards godliness; and lastly, this is the inconvenience of a burden too, *ut praecipitet*, it makes us still apt and ready to stumble, and to fall under it: It crookens us, it deprives us of our *rectitude*; it tires us, extinguishes our alacrity; It slackens us, enfeebles and intepidates our zeale; It occasions our stumbling, opens and submits us, to every emergent tentation. And these be the dangers, and the mischievous inconveniences, notified to us, in those two Elegancies of the holy Ghost, the *supergressae*, the multiplicity of sinnes, *They are gone over my head*, and the *gravatae, They are a heavy burden, too heavy for me*.

First then, all these things are *literally* spoken of *David*; By *application*, of us; and by *figure*, of Christ. *Historically*, *David*; *morally*, we; *Typically*, Christ is the subject of this text.

. . . .

Though this will be a good rule, for the most part, in all *Davids* confessions and lamentations, that though that be always literally true of himself, for the *sinne*, or for the *punishment*, which he says, *personally*

David did suffer, that which he complains of in the *Psalms*, in a great measure, yet *David* speaks *prophetically*, as well as *personally*, and to us, who exceed him in his sins, the exaltation of those miseries, which we finde so often in this book, are especially intended; That which *David* relates to have been his own case, he foresees will be ours too, in a higher degree. And that's our second, and our principall object of all those circumstances, in the *multiplicity*, and in the *hainousnesse* of sin; And therefore, to that second part, these considerations in our selves, we make thus much hast. (*1618*) 2:96–97, 99

3. Interpretation: A Way Not a Rest (John 1:8)

First, that you *prepare the way of the Lord*. But when we bid you do so, we do not meane, that this preparing or pre-disposing of your selves, is *in your selves*, that you can prevent Gods *preventing grace*, or mellow, or supple, or fit your selves for the entrance of that grace, by any *naturall faculty* in your selves. When we speak of a *co-operation*, a joint working with the grace of God, or of a *post-operation*, an after working upon the virtue of a former grace, this *co-operation*, and this *post-operation* must be mollified with a good concurrent cause with that grace. So there is a good sense of *co-operation*, and *post-operation*, but *praeoperation*, that we should work, *before* God work upon us, can admit no good interpretation. I could as soon beleeve that I had a being before *God* was, as that I had a *will* to good, before God moved it. But then, God having made his way into you, by his *preventing grace, prepare that way,* not *your* way, but *his* way, (sayes our Commission) that is, that way that he hath made in you, prepare that by forbearing and avoiding to cast new hinderances in that way. In *sadnesse* and *dejections* of spirit, seek not your comfort in *drinke*, in *musique*, in *comedies*, in *conversation*; for, this is but a preparing a way of your owne. To prepare the *Lords way*, is to look, and consider, what way the Lord hath taken, in the like cases, in the like distresses with other servants of his, and to prepare that way in thy self, and to assure thy selfe, that God hath but practised upon *others*, that he might be perfect when he comes to *thee*, and that he intends to thee, in these thy tribulations, all that he hath promised to all, all that he hath already performed to any one. Prepare *his way*; apply that way, in which he hath gone *to others*, to thy self.

And then, by our Commission we cry out to you, *to make streight his paths*. In which we do not require, that you should absolutely rectifie all the deformities and crookednesses, which that *Tortuositas Serpentis*, the winding of the old Serpent hath brought you to; for, now the streame of our corrupt nature, is accustomed to that crooked channell, and we cannot divert that, we cannot come to an absolute directnesse, and streightnesse, and profession in this life; and, in this place, the holy Ghost speaks but of *a way*, a path; not of *our rest* in the end, but of our labour in the way. Our Commission then is not to those *sinlesse* men, that think they have nothing for God to *forgive*; But, when we bid you make streight *his paths*, (as before we directed you, to take knowledge what *his* wayes towards *others* had been) so here we intend, that you should observe, which is the Lords path into you, by what way he comes oftnest into you, who are his *Temple*, and do not lock that doore, do not pervert, do not crosse, do not deface that path. The ordinary way, even of the *holy Ghost*, for the conveying of *faith*, and supernaturall graces, is (as the way of worldly knowledge is) by the *senses*: where his way is by the *eare*, by hearing his word *preached*; do not thou crosse that way of his, by an inordinate delight, in hearing the eloquence of the preacher; for, so thou hearest the man, and not *God*, and goest *thy way*, and not *his*. God hath divers wayes into divers men; into some he comes at noone, in the sunshine of prosperity; to some in the *dark* and *heavy* clouds of adversity. Some he affects with the musick of the Church, some with some particular Collect or Prayer; some with some passage in a Sermon, which takes no hold of him, that stands next him. Watch the way of the Spirit of God, into thee; that way which he makes his path, in which he comes oftnest to thee, and by which thou findest thy self most affected, and best disposed towards him, and pervert not that path, foule not that way. *Make streight his paths*, that is, keepe them *streight*; and when thou observest, which is his path in thee, (by what means especially he workes upon thee) meet him in that path, embrace him in those meanes, and alwayes bring a facile, a fusil, a ductile, a tractable soule, to the offers *of his grace*, in his way.

. . . .

Now, this Commission, *John Baptist* was, and we are, to publish *in deserto*, in the Desert, in the wildernesse; that is, as Saint *Hierome* notes, not in *Jerusalem*, in a tumultuary place, a place of distraction, but in the *Desert*, a place of solitude, and retirednesse. And yet this does not imply an abandoning of society, and mutuall offices, and callings in the world, but onely informes us, that every man is to have a *Desert in himself*, a retiring into himself, sometimes of emptying himself of worldly businesses, and that he spend some houres in such solitudes, and lay aside, (as one would lay aside a garment) the *Lawyer*, the *Physician*, the *Merchant*, or whatsoever his profession be, and say, *Domine hic sum*, Lord, I am here, I, he whom thou madest, and such as thou madest him, not such as the world hath made me, *Hic sum*, I am here, not where the affairs of the world scatter me, but *here*, in this retirednesse, Lord, *I am here, command what thou wilt*; in this retirednesse, in this solitude, (but is not a Court, is not an Army, is not a Fair a solitude, in respect of this association, when God and a good soul are met?) but in this home solitude, in this home Desert, are we commanded to publish this Commission, as the fittest time to make impressions of all the parts thereof, *Prepare the way of the Lord, make streight his paths, exalt your vallies, and bring down your mountains*. And this was *John Baptists* Commission, *What* to do; And then he had *Instructions* with his *Commission, how to doe it*; which is another consideration. (*1622*)   4:224–26, 228–29

4. Charity and Liberty in Interpretation (Gen. 1:2)

First then, undertaking the consideration of the literall sense, and after, of the spirituall, we joyne with S. *Augustine*, [a]*Sint castae deliciae meae Scripturae tuae*; Lord I love to be conversant in thy Scriptures, let my conversation with thy Scriptures be a chast conversation; that I discover no nakednesse therein; offer not to touch any thing in thy Scriptures, but that, that thou hast vouchsafed to unmask, and manifest unto me: *Nec fallar in eis, nec fallam ex eis*; Lord, let not me mistake the meaning of thy Scriptures, nor mis-lead others, by imputing a false sense to them. *Non frustra scribuntur*, sayes he; Lord, thou hast writ nothing to no purpose; thou wouldst be understood in all: But not in all, by all men, at all times; *Confiteor tibi quicquid invenero in libris tuis*; Lord, I acknowledge that I receive from thee, whatsoever I understand in thy word; for else I doe not understand it. Thus that blessed Father meditates upon the word of God; he speakes of this beginning of the Book of *Genesis*; and he speaks lamenting, *Scripsit Moses et abiit*, a little *Moses* hath said, and alas he is gone; [b]*Si hic esset, tenerem eum, et per te rogarem*, If *Moses* were here, I would hold him here, and begge of him, for thy sake to tell me thy meaning in his words, of this Creation. But sayes he, since I cannot speake with *Moses, Te, quo plenus vera dixit, Veritas, rogo*, I begge of thee who art Truth it selfe, as thou enabledst him to utter it, enable me to understand what he hath said. So difficult a thing seemed it to that intelligent Father, to understand this history, this mystery of the Creation. But yet though he found, that divers senses offered themselves, he did not doubt of finding the Truth: For, [c]*Deus meus lumen oculorum meorum in occulto*, sayes he, O my God, the light of mine eyes, in this

a. Aug. Con. 11.2.3.
b. c.3.
c. lib.12.c.18.

dark inquisition, since divers senses, arise out of these words, and all true, *Quid mihi obest, si aliud ego sensero, quam sensit alius, eum sensisse, qui scripsit?* What hurt followes, though I follow another sense, then some other man takes to be *Moses* sense? for his may be a true sense, and so may mine, and neither be *Moses* his. Hee passes from prayer, and protestation, to counsell, and direction; [d]*In diversitate sententiarum verarum, concordiam pariat ipsa veritas,* Where divers senses arise, and all true, (that is, that none of them oppose the truth) let truth agree them. But what is Truth? God; And what is God? Charity; Therefore let Charity reconcile such differences. [e]*Legitime lege utamur,* sayes he, let us use the Law lawfully; Let us use our liberty of reading Scriptures according to the Law of liberty; that is, charitably to leave others to their liberty, if they but differ from us, and not differ from Fundamentall Truths. (*1629*) 9:94–95

5. Lex Lux: *Scripture Is Light* (2 Cor. 4:6)

Lex Lux, says *David, The Law of God,* the Scripture, *is a light,* it is the light, it is all light; and therefore they who would take away this light, not suffer men to read the Scriptures; or if they will not snuff this light, not mend the Barbarisms, the Errours, the Contradictions which are in their Translation, and let it shine according to the Original Truth, this is a shutting of their eyes against this *Illuxit*: For, God hath showed enough, and said enough, and done enough, and suffered enough, for the salvation of his Church; he hath shined out upon all, and needs no supply of lesser lights.

So he hath shined upon all; and *Illuxit Nobis,* he hath shined abundantly upon this Nation. He shined upon us betimes; this day sprung, this Sun rose in the East; in the East, Christ lived and preached in person; but in his Beams, his Messengers, he shined quickly into the West too. And when he did so, he did not so shine upon the West, upon *Rome,* as that that light was cast upon us, as by reflection from a glass, from the walls of *Rome*: but we had it, as they had it, by persons ordained by God, to convey it over the world. I dispute not too earnestly, I determine not too vehemently any matter of fact in this point. I confess ingeniously, we had many Assistances from Rome; but truely, she hath been even with us since: and, *Computatis Computandis,* I think she may be content to give us an Acquittance. God shined upon this Island early; early in the plantation of the Gospel, (for we had not our seed-Corn from *Rome,* howsoever we may have had some waterings from thence) and early in the Reformation of the Church:

d. c.30. *e.* c.30.

for we had not the model of any other Forreign Church for our pattern; we stript not the Church into a nakedness, nor into rags; we divested her not of her possessions, nor of her Ceremonies, but received such a Reformation at home, by their hands whom God enlightned, as left her neither in a Dropsie, nor in a Consumption; neither in a superfluous and cumbersome fatness, nor in an uncomely and faint leanness and attenuation: Early in the Plantation, early in the Reformation, *Illuxit Nobis*, and we have light enough, without either seeing other light from *Rome*, or more of this light from other places. God continue to us the light of this Reformation, without readmitting any old Clouds, any old Clouts, and we shall not need any such re-Reformation, or super-Reformation, as swimming Brains will needs cross the Seas for. *The Word of God is not above thee*, says *Moses*, *nor beyond the Sea*. We need not clime up seven hills, nor wash our selves seven times in a Lake for it: God make the practise of our lives agreeable to the Doctrine of our Church; and all the world shall see that we have light enough. (*1622*) 4:106–7

6. God's Method: Last Resurrection Ground for All (1 Cor. 15:26)

Tertullian is vehement at first, but after, more supple. *Allegoricae Scripturae*, saies he, *resurrectionem subradiant aliae, aliae determinant*: Some figurative places of Scripture doe intimate a resurrection, and some manifest it; and of those manifest places he takes this vision of *Ezekiel* to be one. But he comes after to this, *Sit et corporum, et rerum, et mea nihil interest*; let it signifie a temporall resurrection, so it may signifie the generall resurrection of our bodies too, saies he, and I am well satisfied; and then the truth satisfies him, for it doth signifie both. It is true that *Tertullian* sayes, *De vacuo similitudo non competit*; If the vision be but a comparison, yet if there were no such thing as a resurrection, the comparison did not hold. *De nullo parabola non convenit*, saies he, and truly; If there were no resurrection to which that Parable might have relation, it were no Parable. All that is true; but there was a resurrection alwaies knowne to them, alwaies beleeved by them, and that made their present resurrection from that calamity, the more easie, the more intelligible, the more credible, the more discernable to them.

Let therefore Gods method, be thy method; fixe thy self firmly upon that beliefe of the generall resurrection, and thou wilt never doubt of either of the particular resurrections, either from sin, by Gods grace, or from worldly calamities, by Gods power. For that last resurrection is the ground of all. (*1622*) 4:61

7. Adherence to Augustine (Ps. 90:14)

They have made a Rule in the Councel of Trent, that no Scripture shall be expounded, but according to the unanime consent of the Fathers: But in this Book of the Psalms, it would trouble them to give many examples of that Rule, that is, of an unanime consent of the Fathers, in the interpretation thereof. In this Psalme, *Bellarmine* in his Exposition of the Psalms, finds himselfe perplexed; He sayes (and sayes truly) *Hieronymus constanter affirmat, Augustinus constanter negat,* S. *Hierome* doth confidently and constantly affirme, and S. *Augustine* with as much confidence, and constancy deny, that this Psalme, and all that follow to the hundredth Psalme, are *Moses* Psalms, and written by him. And this diverse constancy in these two Fathers, S. *Hierome* and S. *Augustine,* shake the constancy of that Canon, which binds to a following of an unanime consent, for that cannot be found. *Bellarmine* expedites himselfe herein, that way, which is indeed their most ordinary way amongst their Expositors, which is, where the Fathers differ, to adhere to S. *Augustine*. So he doth in this point; though most of the Ancients of the Christian Church, most of the Rabbins of the Jews, most of the Writers in the Reformation, take it to be *Moses* Psalme, and that way runs the greatest streame, and nearest to a concurrence. And thus far I have stopped upon this consideration, Whether this be *Moses* Psalme or no, That when it appears to be his Psalme, and that we see, that in the tenth verse of this Psalm, mans life is limited to seventy years, or at most to eighty, and then remember, that *Moses* himselfe, then when he said so, was above eighty, and in a good habitude long after that, we might hereby take occasion to consider, that God does not so limit, and measure himselfe in his blessings to his servants, but that for their good and his glory he enlarges those measures. God hath determined a day, from Sun to Sun, yet when God hath use of a longer day, for his glory, he commands the Sun to stand still, till *Joshua* have pursued his victory. So God hath given the life of man, into the hand of sicknesse; and yet for all that deadly sicknesse, God enlarges *Hezekiah's* years: *Moses* was more than fourescore, when he told us, that our longest terme was fourescore.

If we require exactly an unanime consent, that all agree in the Author of this Psalme, we can get no farther, then that the holy Ghost is the Author. All agree the words to be Canonicall Scripture, and so from the holy Ghost; and we seek no farther. The words are his, and they offer us these considerations; First, That the whole Psalme being in the Title thereof called a Prayer, *A Prayer of Moses the man of God*, it puts us justly, and pertinently upon the consideration of the many dignities and prerogatives of that part of our worship of God, Prayer; for there we shall see, That though the whole Psalme be not a Prayer, yet because there is a Prayer in the Psalme, that denominates the whole Psalme, the whole Psalme is a Prayer. When the Psalm grows formally to be a Prayer, our Text enters, *O satisfie us early with thy mercy, that we may rejoyce and be glad all our dayes*: And in that there will be two Parts more, The Prayer it selfe, *O satisfie us early with thy mercy*, And the effect thereof, *That we may rejoyce and be glad all our dayes*. So that our Parts are three; First Prayer, Then this Prayer, And lastly the benefit of all Prayer.

For the first, which is Prayer in generall, I will thrust no farther then the Text leads me in, that is, That Prayer is so essentiall a part of Gods worship, as that all is called Prayer. S. *Hierome* upon this Psalme sayes, *Difficillimum Psalmum aggredior*, I undertake the exposition of a very hard Psalme, and yet, sayes he, I would proceed so in the exposition thereof, *ut interpretatio nostra aliena non egeat interpretatione*, That there should not need another Comment upon my Comment, that when I pretend to interpret the Psalme, they that heare me, should not need another to interpret me: which is a frequent infirmity amongst Expositors of Scriptures, by writing, or preaching, either when men will raise doubts in places of Scripture, which are plaine enough in themselves, (for this creates a jealousie, that if the Scriptures be every where so difficult, they cannot be our evidences, and guides to salvation) Or when men will insist too vehemently, and curiously, and tediously in proving of such things as no man denies; for this also induces a suspition, that that is not so absolutely, so undeniably true, that needs so much art, and curiosity, and vehemence to prove it. I shall therefore avoid these errors; and because I presume you are full of an acknowledgment of the duties, and dignities of Prayer, onely remember you of thus much of the method, or elements of Prayer, That whereas the whole Book of Psalms is called *Sepher Tehillim*, that is, *Liber Laudationum*, The Book of Praise, yet this Psalme, and all that follow to the hundredth Psalme, and divers others besides these, (which make up a faire limme of this body, and a considerable part of the Book) are called Prayers; The Book is Praise, the parts are Prayer. The name changes not the nature; Prayer and Praise is the same thing: The name scarce changes the name; Prayer and Praise is almost the same word; As the duties agree in the heart and mouth of a man, so the names agree in our eares; and not onely in the language of our Translation, but in the language of the holy Ghost himselfe, for that which with us differs but so, Prayer, and

Praise, in the Originall differs no more then so, *Tehillim*, and *Tephilloth*. (*1621–1622?*) 5:268–70

B. Misinterpretation

1. Deducet *(Rev. 7:17)*

He shall *lead* them; and then, when he hath taken them into his government; for first it is *Reget*, he shall govern them, and then *Deducet*, that is, he shall lead them, in *his Church*; and therefore they that are led to baptisme, *any other way then by the Church*, they are misled; nay they are miscarried, misdriven, [f]*Spiritu vertiginis*, with the spirit of giddinesse. They that joyne any in commission with the Trinity, though but as an assistant, ([g]for so they say in the Church of *Rome*; *baptisme* may be administred, in the name of the *Father, Sonne, and holy Ghost, and the virgin Mary*) they follow not, as Christ led in his Church, *Non fuit sic ab initio, It was not so from the beginning*; for *quod extra hos tres est, totum Conservum est*; though much dignity belong to the memory of the *Saints* of God, yet whosoever is none of the three Persons, [h]*Conservus est*, he is our fellow-servant: though his service lie *above staires*, and ours *below*, his in the *triumphant*, ours in the *militant* Church, *Conservus est*, yet he, or she, is in that respect, but our *fellow-servant*, and not Christs *fellow-redeemer*. So also, [i]*if we be led to Marah*, to the *waters of bitternesse*, that we bring a bitter taste, of those institutions of the Church for the decency, and signification in Sacramentall things, things belonging to *Baptisme*, if we bring a misinterpretation of them, an indisposition to them, an aversnesse from them, and so nourish a bitternes, and uncharitablenesse towards one another, for these *Ceremonies*, if we had rather *crosse* one another, and *crosse* the Church, then *crosse* the *child*, as God shewed *Moses, a tree*, which made those waters in the wildernesse sweet, when it was cast in, so remember that there is the *tree of life*, the *crosse of Christ Jesus*, and his Merits, in this water of baptisme, and when we all agree in that, that all the vertue proceeds from the *crosse of Christ*, the God of unity and peace and concord, let us admit any representation of *Christs crosse*, rather then admit the true *crosse of the devill*, which is a bitter and *schismaticall* crossing of Christ in his Church: for it is there in his Church, that he leads us to these waters.

Well then, they to whom these waters belong, have Christ in his Church to lead them; and therefore they need not stay, till they can come *alone*; till they be of age and years of discretion, as the *Anabap-*

f. Esay 19:14.
g. Aquin.
h. Basil.
i. Exod. 15:[23–25].

tists say: for it is *Deducet*, and *Deducet eos*; generally, universally; *all* that are of this government, *all* that are appointed for the *Seal*, all *the one hundred and forty foure thousand*, all the *Innumerable multitudes of all Nations*, Christ leads them *all.* [j]*Be Baptized every one of you, in the name of Jesus Christ, for the remission of sinnes; for the promise is made unto you, and your children*. Now all promises of God, are sealed in the *holy Ghost*; To whom soever any promise of God belongs, he hath the holy Ghost; and therefore [k]*Nunquid aquam quis prohibere potest? Can any Man forbid water, that those should not be baptized, which have received the holy Ghost, as well as we?* says S. *Peter*. And therefore the *Children* of the Covenant which have the *promise*, have the *holy Ghost*, and all they are in this Regiment, *Deducet eos*, Christ shall lead *them all*. (*1624–1625?*) 5:108–9

2. Translation: Danger of Idolatrous Servility (Ps. 6:6, 7)

The difference is not of much importance, whether it be *Inveteravi*, or *Inveteravit*; in the first, or in the third person. Whether *Davids* eyes, or *David* himselfe be thus decayed, and waxen old, imports little. But yet that which *Bellarmine* collects, upon this difference, imports much. For, because the Vulgat Edition, and the Septuagint, (such a Septuagint as we have now) reade this in the first person of *David* himselfe, *Inveteravi*, and the Hebrew hath it in the third, *Inveteravit*, *Bellarmine* will needs think, that the Hebrew, the Originall, is falsified and corrupted; still in advancement of that dangerous Position of theirs, That their Translation is to be preferred before the Originall; and that is an unsufferable tyrannie, and an Idolatrous servility. The Translation is a reverend Translation; A Translation to which the Church of God owes much; but gold will make an Idol as well as wood, and to make any Translation equall, or better then the Originall, is an Idolatrous servility. (*1628*) 8:207

3. Modern Sadducees and Pharisees (Acts 23:6, 7)

The world is full of Sadduces, and Pharisees, and the true Church of God arraigned by both. The Sadduces were the greater men, the Pharisees were the greater number; so they are still. *The Sadduces denied the Resurrection, and Angels, and Spirits*; So they do still. For, those Sadduces, whom we consider now, in this part, are meere carnall men; men that have not onely no Spirit of God in them, but no soule, no spirit of their owne; meere Atheists. And this Carnality, this Atheisme, this Sadducisme is seene in some Countries to prevaile most upon great persons, (the Sadduces were great persons) upon

j. Act. 2:38. *k*. Act. 10:47.

persons that abound in the possessions, and offices, and honours of this world; for they that have most of this world, for the most part, think least of the next.

These are our present Sadduces; and then the Pharisee hath his name from *Pharas*, which is Division, Separation; But *Calvin* derives the name (not inconveniently) from *Pharash*, which is Exposition, Explication. We embrace both extractions, and acceptations of the word, both *Separation*, and *Exposition*; for the Pharisee whom we consider now, in this part, is he that is separated from us, (there it is *Pharas*, separation) and separated by following private Expositions, (there it is *Pharash*, Exposition) with a contempt of all Antiquity; and not only an undervaluation, but a detestation of all opinions but his owne, and his, whom he hath set up for his Idol. And as the Sadduce (our great and worldly man) is all carnall, all body, and beleeves no spirit: so our Pharisee is so super-spirituall, as that he beleeves, that is, considers no body; He imagines such a Purification, such an Angelification, such a Deification in this life, as though the heavenly Jerusalem were descended already, or that God had given man but that one commandement, *Love God above all*, and not a second too, *Love thy neighbour as thy selfe*. Our Sadduces will have all body, our Pharisees all soule, and God hath made us of both, and given us offices proper to each.

Now of both these, the present Sadduce, the carnall Atheist, and the present Pharisee, the Separatist, that overvalues himself, and bids us stand farther off, there are two kinds. For, for the Atheist, there is *Davids* Atheist, and S. *Pauls* Atheist; *Davids*, that ascribes all to nature, and *sayes in his heart*, [l]*There is no God*; That will call no sudden death, nor extraordinary punishment upon any enormous sinner, a judgement of God, nor any such deliverance of his servants, a miracle from God, but all is Nature, or all is Accident, and would have been so, though there had been no God: This is Natures Sadduce, *Davids* Atheist; And then S. *Pauls* Atheist is he, who though he doe beleeve in God, yet doth not beleeve God in Christ; for so S. *Paul* sayes to the Ephesians, [m]*Absque Christo, absque Deo*, If ye be *without Christ*, ye are *without God*. For as it is the same absurdity in nature, to say, There is no Sun, and to say, This that you call the Sun is not the Sun, this that shines out upon you, this that produces your fruits, and distinguishes your seasons is not the Sun: so is it the same Atheisme, in these dayes of light, to say, There is no God, and to say, This Christ whom you call the Son of God, is not God, That he in whom God hath

l. Psal. 14:1. *m*. Ephes. 2:12.

manifested himselfe, He whom God hath made Head of the Church, and Judge of the world, is not God. This then is our double Sadduce, *Davids* Atheist that beleeves not God, S. *Pauls* Atheist that beleeves not Christ. And as our Sadduce is, so is our Pharisee twofold also.

. . . .

End we all with this, That we have all, all these, Sadduces and Pharisees in our owne bosomes: Sadduces that deny spirits; carnall apprehensions that are apt to say, Is your God all Spirit, and hath bodily eyes to see sin? All Spirit, and hath bodily hands to strike for a sinne? Is your soule all spirit, and hath a fleshly heart to feare? All spirit, and hath sensible sinews to feele a materiall fire? Was your God, who is all Spirit, wounded when you quarrelled? or did your soule, which is all spirit, drink when you were drunk? Sins of presumption, and carnall confidence are our Sadduces; and then our Pharisees are our sins of separation, of division, of diffidence and distrust in the mercies of our God; when we are apt to say, after a sin, Cares God, who is all Spirit, for my eloquent prayers, or for my passionate teares? Is the giving of my goods to the poore, or of my body to the fire, any thing to God who is all Spirit? My spirit, and nothing but my spirit, my soule, and nothing but my soule, must satisfie the justice, the anger of God, and be separated from him for ever. My Sadduce, my Presumption suggests, that there is no spirit, no soule to suffer for sin; and my Pharisee, my Desperation suggests, That my soule must perish irremediably, irrecoverably, for every sinne that my body commits. (*1629*) 9:168–69, 171

C. Revelation as Interpretation

1. God Manifested in Christ, Scripture, Church (Ps. 55:19)

The fear required here, is to fear him as God, and as God presented in this name, *Elohim*; which, though it be a name primarily rooted in power and strength, (for *El* is *Deus fortis*, The powerful God; and as there is no love without fear, so there is no fear without power) yet properly it signifies his Judgment, and Order, and Providence, and Dispensation, and Government of his creatures. It is that name, which goes thorow all Gods whole work of the Creation, and disposition of all creatures, in the first of *Genesis*: in all that, he is called by no other name then this, the name *God*; not by *Jehovah*, to present an infinite Majestie; nor by *Adonai*, to present an absolute power; nor by *Tzebaoth*, to present a Force, or Conquest: but onely in the name of *God*, his name of Government. All ends in this; To fear God, is to adhere to him, in his way, as he hath dispensed and notified himself to us; that is, as God is manifested in Christ, in the Scriptures, and applied to us out of those Scriptures, by the Church: not to rest in Nature without God, nor in God without Christ, nor in Christ without the Scriptures, nor in our private interpretation of Scripture, without the Church. Almighty God fill us with these fears, these reverences; that we may reverence him, who shall at last bring us, where there shall be no more changes; and hath already placed us in such a Government, as being to us a Type and Representation of the Kingdom of heaven, we humbly beg, may evermore continue with us, without changes, in Government, or in Religion. (*1617*)   1:235

2. The Infirmity of Man and Visible Things (Gen. 32:10)

But that hath been Gods abundant and overflowing goodness, ever to succor the infirmity of Man, with sensible and visible things; with the pillars in the Wilderness; with the Tabarnacle after; and with the Temple and all the mysterious, and significative furniture thereof after all. So God leaves not *Jacob* to the general knowledge, that the Angels of God protect Gods Children, but he manifested those Angels unto him, *Occurrerunt ei*, the Angels of God met him. The word of God is an infalible guide to thee, But God hath provided thee also visible, and manifest assistants, the Pillar his Church, and the Angels his Ministers in the Church. The Scripture is thine onely *Ephod*, but *Applica Ephod*, apply it to thee by his Church, and by his visible Angels, and not by thine own private interpretation. (*1618*)   1:283

3. The Light That Illumines (2 Cor. 4:6)

The Holy Ghost hath shewed us both these, severally in *Moses*, and in St. *John*, and both together in St. *Paul*, in this Text: where, as the Sun stands in the midst of the Heavens, and shews us both the Creatures that are below it, upon Earth, and the Creatures that are above it, the Stars in Heaven; so St. *Paul*, as he is made an Apostle of the Gentiles, stands in the midst of this Text, (*God hath shined in our hearts:*) Ours, as we are Apostolical Ministers of the Gospel; and he shows us the greatness of God, in the Creation which was before, when *God commanded light out of darkness*; and the goodness of God which shall be hereafter, when he shall give us *the light of the knowledge of the glory of God, in the face of Christ Jesus*.

So that this Text, giving light, by which we see, light commanded by God out of darkness; and the Object which we are to see, *the knowledge of the glory of God*; and this Object being brought within a convenient distance to be seen *in the face of Jesus Christ*; And a fit and well-disposed *Medium* being illumined, through which we may see it, God having shined in our hearts, established a Ministry of the Gospel: for that purpose, if you bring but eyes, to that which this Text brings, Light, and Object, and Distance, and Means, then, as St. *Basil* said of the Book of Psalms, upon an impossible supposition, If all the other Books of Scripture could perish, there were enough in that one, for the catechising of all that did believe, and for the convincing of all that did not: so if all the other Writings of St. *Paul* could perish, this Text were enough to carry us through the body of Divinity, from the Cradle of the world, in the Creation, when God commanded light out of darkness, to the Grave; and beyond the Grave of the world, to the last Dissolution; and beyond it, when we shall have fully, *the light of the knowledge of the glory of God, in the face of Christ Jesus*. Now, whilst I am to speak of all this, this, which is *Omne scibile*, all, and more then can fall within the comprehension of a natural man; for it is the beginning of this world, and it is the way to the next, and it is the next world it self, I comfort my self at my first setting out, with that of St. *Gregory, Purgatas aures, et hominum gratiam nancisci, nonne Dei donu est?* I take it for one of Gods great blessings to me, if he have given me now an Auditory, *Purgatae auris*, of such spiritual and circumcised Ears, as come not to hear that Wisdom of Words, which may make the Cross of Christ of none effect; much less such itching Ears, as come to hear popular and seditious Calumnies and Scandals, and Reproaches, cast upon the present State and Government. For, a man may make a Sermon, a Satyr; he may make a Prayer, a Libel, if upon colour of preaching, or praying, against toleration of Religion, or persecution for Religion, he would insinuate, that any such tolerations are prepared for us, or such persecutions threatned against us. But if for speaking the mysteries of your salvation, plainly, sincerely, inelegantly, inartificially; for the Gold, and not for the Fashion; for the Matter, and not for the Form, *Nanciscor populi gratiam*, my service may be acceptable to Gods people, and available to their Edification. (*1622*) 4:90–91

4. Revelation: Christian Knowledge (John 14:20)

Now beloved, this knowledge, as it is opposed to inconsideration, is in this, that God by breeding us in the visible Church, multiplies unto us so many helps and assistances in the word preached, in the Sacraments, in other Sacramentall, and Rituall, and Ceremoniall things, which are auxiliary, subsidiary reliefes, and refreshings to our consideration, as that it is almost impossible to fall into this inconsideration. Here God shewes this inconsiderate man, his book of creatures, which he may run and reade; that is, he may go forward in his vocation, and yet see that every creature calls him to a consideration of God. Every Ant that he sees, askes him, Where had I this providence, and industry? Every flowre that he sees, asks him, Where had I this beauty, this fragrancy, this medicinall vertue in me? Every creature calls him to consider, what great things God hath done in little subjects. But God opens to him also, here in his Church, his Booke of Scriptures, and in that Book, every word cries out to him; every mercifull promise cries to him, Why am I here, to meet thee, to wait upon thee, to performe Gods purpose towards thee, if thou never consider me, never apply me to thy selfe? Every judgement of his anger cryes out, Why am I here, if thou respect me not, if thou make not thy profit, of performing those conditions, which are annexed to those judgements, and which thou mightest performe, if thou wouldest consider it? Yea, here God opens another book to him, his manuall, his bosome, his pocket book, his *Vade Mecum*, the Abridgement of all Nature, and all Law, his owne heart, and conscience: And this booke, though he shut it up, and clasp it never so hard, yet it will sometimes burst open of it selfe; though he interline it with other studies, and knowledges, yet the Text it selfe, in the booke it selfe, the testimonies of the conscience, will shine through and appeare: Though he load it, and choak it with Commentaries and questions, that is, perplexe it with Circumstances, and Disputations, yet the matter it selfe, which is imprinted there, will present it selfe: yea, though he teare some leaves out of the Book, that is, wilfully, yea studiously forget some sins that he hath done, and discontinue the reading of this book, the survay and consideration of his conscience, for some time, yet he cannot lose, he cannot cast away this book, that is so in him, as that it is himselfe, and evermore calls upon him, to deliver him from this inconsideration, by this open and plentifulll Library, which he carries about him. Consider, beloved, the great danger of this inconsideration, by remembring, That even that onely perfect man, Christ Jesus, who had that great way of making him a perfect man, as that he was perfect God too, even in that act of deepest devotion, in his prayer in the garden, by permitting himselfe, out of that humane infirmity, which he was pleased to admit in himselfe, (though farre from sin) to passe one petition in that prayer, without a debated and considered will, in his *Transeat Calix, If it be possible, let this Cup passe*, hee was put to a re-consideration, and to correct his Prayer, *Veruntamen, Yet not my will, but thine bee done*. And if then our best acts of praying, and hearing, need such an exact consideration, consider the richnesse, and benefit of this Legacy, knowledge, as this knowledge is opposed to inconsideration.

It is also opposed to concealing and smothering; It must be published to the benefit of others. *Paulum sepultae distat inertiae celata virtus*, sayes the Poet; Vertue that is never produced into action, is scarce worthy of that name. For that is it, which the Apostle, in his Epistle to that Church, which was in *Philemons* house, doth so much praise God for, [n] *That the fellowship of thy faith may be made fruitfull, and that whatsoever good thing is in you through Jesus Christ, may be knowne:* That according to the nature of goodnesse, and to the roote of goodnesse, God himselfe, this knowledge of God may be communicated, and transfused, and shed, and spred, and derived, and digested upon others. And therefore certainly, as the Philosopher said of civill actions, *Etiam simulare Philosophiam, Philosophia est,* That it was some degree of wisedome, to be able to seeme wise; so, though it be no degree of religion, to seeme religious, yet even that may be a way of reducing others, and perchance themselves: when a man makes a publique, an outward shew of being religious, by comming ordinarily to Church, and doing those outward duties, though this be hypocrisie in him, yet sometimes other men receive profit by his example, and are religious in earnest, and, sometimes, *Appropinquat et nescit,* (as S. *Augustine* confesses that it was his case, when he came out of curiosity, and not out of devotion, to heare S. *Ambrose* preach) what respect soever brought that man hither, yet when God findes him here, in his house, he takes hold of his conscience, and shewes himselfe to him, though he came not to see him. And if God doe thus produce good out of the hypocrite, and work good in him, much more will he provide a plentifull harvest, by their labours, who having received this knowledge from God, assist their weaker brethren, both by the Example of their lives, and the comfort of their Doctrine. (*1630?*) 9:236–38

5. The Ear: The Organ of Christian Man (Ps. 38:4)

The Organ that God hath given the naturall man, is the *eye*; he sees God in the creature. The Organ that God hath given the Christian, is the *ear*; he hears God in his Word. But when we are under water, both senses, both Organs are vitiated, and depraved, if not defeated. The habituall, and manifold sinner, sees nothing aright; Hee sees a *judgement*, and cals it an *accident*. He hears nothing aright; He hears the

n. Philem. 6.

Ordinance of *Preaching* for salvation in the next world, and he cals it an invention of the State, for subjection in this world. And as under water, every thing seems distorted and crooked, to man, so does man himself to God, who sees not his own Image in that man, in that form as he made it. [o]When *man hath drunk iniquity like water*, then, *The flouds of wickednesse shall make him afraid*; The water that he hath swum in, the sin that he hath delighted in, shall appear with horrour unto him. As God threatens the pride of *Tyrus*, [p]*I shall bring the deep upon thee, and great waters shall cover thee*, That, God will execute upon this sinner; And then, upon every drop of that water, upon every affliction, every tribulation, he shall come to that fearfulnesse, [q]*Waters flowed over my head*; then said I, *I am cut off*; Either he shall see nothing, or see no remedy, no deliverance from desperation. Keep low these waters, as waters signifie *sin*, and God shall keep them low, as they signifie *punishments*; [r]And his Dove shall return to the Ark with an Olive leaf, to shew thee that the waters are abated; he shall give thee a testimony of the return of his love, in his Oyle, and Wine, and Milk, and Honey, in the temporall abundances of this life. [s]And, *si impleat Hydrias aqua*, if he doe fill all your vessels with water, with water of bitternesse, that is, fill and exercise all your patience, and all your faculties with his corrections, yet he shall doe that, but to *change your water into wine*, as he did there, he shall make his very Judgements, Sacraments, conveyances and seals of his mercy to you, though those manifold sins be got over your heads, as a roof, as a noise, as an overflowing of waters: And, that, which is the heaviest of all, and our last consideration, *sicut Dominus*, as a Lord, as a Tyran, as an Usurper. (*1618*) 2:114

6. Christus Ratio: *Hearers of the Word (2 Cor. 4:6)*

To us then, who were created of nothing, in the first part, and called from the Gentiles in the second, in this third part, our preparation to glory, is knowledge. The Persons in this part of the Text, are, as in the former; *Not only we*, we the Ministers of Gods Word, but you also the hearers thereof: for there is a knowledge, an art of hearing, as well as of speaking. Students make up the University, as well as Doctors: and Hearers make up the Congregation, as well as Preachers. A good hearer is as much a Doctor, as a Preacher: A Doctor to him that sits by him, in example, whilst he is here: a Doctor to all his Family, in his repetition, when he comes home: a Doctor, to that which is more then

o. Job 15:16. Ps. 18:4.
p. Ezek. 26:19.
q. Lam. 3:54.
r. Gen. 8:8.
s. Joh. 2:7.

the whole world, to him, his own soul, all his life. Christ appeared to this Apostle, and said, [t]*I have appeared unto thee, for this purpose, to make thee a Minister and a witness, to open the Gentiles eyes, and to turn them from darkness to light, and from the power of Satan unto God.* There he received his Degree, his learning, and the use of it; but when *St. Paul* came abroad into the world, when he comes to preach, and to write, he says to the *Colossians, The Father hath made us meet to be partakers of the inheritance of the Saints in his light.* Us, says *St. Chrysostom,* and so says *Theophylact* too, and many more then they two; Us, that is, all Us, Us that preach, you that hear; you are bound to study this knowledge, as well as we. And truly, a Hearer hath in some respects advantage of the Preacher: for, a Preacher, though in some measure, well disposed, can hardly *exuere hominem,* put off the affections of man, by being a Preacher; they stick closer to him then his Hood and habit, even in the Pulpit. Some little Clouds, if not of ostentation, and vain glory, yet of complacencie and self-pleasing, will affect him; the hearer hath not that tentation, but hath herein a more perfect exercise of the most Christian vertue, *Humility,* then the preacher hath. Though therefore, when you cast your eye upon this part of this Text, you see in your Book, a difference of Character, in this word, *To give, to give light, etc.* which seems to fix all upon the person of the Apostle, and consequently of the Minister; yet that word is not in the Text, but the Text is only, *for the inlightning; God hath shined, for the inlightning, etc.* which is alike upon all; *and therefore let us, all us, cast off the works of darkness, and put on the armor of light*: light it self is faith; but, the armor of light is knowledge; an ignorant man is a disarmed man, a naked man.

Ignorance then is not our Usher into this presence, *to shew us the face of Christ Jesus*: almost in every one of the ancient Fathers, you shall find some passages, wherein they discover an inclination to that opinion, that before Christ came in the manifestation of his Gospel (for, since that coming, every man is bound to see him there) many Philosophers, men of knowledge, and learning, were saved without the knowledge of Christ. [u]*Christus Ratio,* says one of them, well, (for *Logos,* is *Ratio,* and not only *Verbum,* as it is ordinarily translated) Christ is Reason, rectified Reason; and *secundum Rationem vixerunt, Christiani semper,* says he, Whosoever lives according to rectified Reason, which is the Law of nature, he is a Christian; and therefore, when that Father, *Justin Martyr,* who had been before a Philosopher amongst the Gentiles, came to be a Preacher amongst the Christians, he never

t. Act. 26:16.

u. Justin Martyr.

left off his Philosophers habit, because that gave an impression of his learning, and an estimation by it.

. . . .

It was the Devils first advantage, knowledge, *The Serpent was wiser then any beast*: It is so still; Satan is wiser then any man in natural, and in Civil knowledge. 'Tis true, he is a Lyon too; but he was a Serpent first; and did us more harm as a Serpent, then as a Lyon. But now, as Christ Jesus hath nailed his handwriting, which he had against us, to the Cross, and thereby cancelled his evidence; so in his descent to hell, and subsequent acts of his glorification, he hath burnt his Library, annihilated his wisdom, in giving us a wisdome above his craft; he hath shined in our hearts by the knowledge of his Gospel.

Measure not thou therefore the growth and forwardness of thy Child, by how soon he could speak, or go; how soon he could contract with a man, or discourse with a woman: but how soon he became sensible of that great contract which he had made with Almighty God, in his Baptism: how soon he was able to discharge those sureties, which undertook for him, then, by receiving his confirmation, in the Church: how soon he became to discern the Lords Spirit, in the preaching of his Word, and to discern the Lords body, in the Administration of the Sacrament. A Christian Child must grow, as Christ when he was a Child, [v] *in wisdom and in stature*: first, *in wisdom*, then *in stature*. Many have been taller at sixteen, then ever Christ was; but not any so learned at sixty, as he when he disputed at twelve. *He grew in favour*, says that Text, *with God and Man*; first, with God, then with man. Bring up your children in the knowledge and love of God; and good, and great men, will know, and love them too. (*1622*) 4:118–21

D. Exegesis

1. Text, Context, Pretext (Matt. 19:17)

Christ saies to this Man, in this Text, *Why callest thou me good? there is none good but one, that is God.*

The words are part of a Dialogue, of a Conference, betweene Christ, and a man who proposed a question to him; to whom Christ makes an answer by way of another question, *Why callest thou me good, etc*. In the words, and by occasion of them, we consider the Text, the Context, and the Pretext: Not as three equall parts of the Building; but the Context, as the situation and Prospect of the house, The Pretext, as the Accesse and entrance to the house, And then the Text it selfe, as

v. Luc. 2:52.

the House it selfe, as the body of the building: In a word, In the Text, the Words; in the Context, the Occasion of the words; In the Pretext, the Pretence, the purpose, the disposition of him who gave the occasion.

We begin with the Context; the situation, the prospect; how it stands, how it is butted, how it is bounded; to what it relates, with what it is connected. (*1625*) 6:224

2. Church Explicates Scripture (Cant. 3:11)

That which the *Scripture* says, *God* sayes, (says St. *Augustine*) for the Scripture is his word; and that which the *Church* says, the *Scriptures* say, for she is their word, they speak *in her*; they authorize her, and she explicates them; The *Spirit* of God *inanimates* the Scriptures, and makes them *his* Scriptures, the *Church actuates* the Scriptures, and makes them *our Scriptures*: *Nihil salubrius*, says the same Father, There is not so wholsome a thing, no soule can live in so good an aire, and in so good a diet, *Quam ut Rationem praecedat authoritas*, Then still to submit a mans owne particular reason, to the authority of the Church expressed in the Scriptures: For, certainly it is very truly (as it is very usefully) said by *Calvin*, *Semper nimia morositas, est ambitiosa*, A frowardnesse, and an aptnesse to quarrell at the proceedings of the Church, and to be delivered from the obligations, and constitutions of the Church, is ever accompanied with an ambitious pride, that they might enjoy a licentious liberty; It is not because the Church doth truly take *too much* power, but because they would be under *none*; it is an ambition, to have all government in their own hands, and to be absolute Emperors of themselves, that makes them refractary: But, if they will pretend to *believe in God*, they must believe in God so, as God hath manifested himself to them, they must *believe in Christ*; so if they will pretend to *heare Christ*, they must heare him there, where he hath promised to speake, they must *heare him in the Church*. (*1625*) 6:282–83

3. Scripture—The Thing; Church—The Time (Matt. 19:17)

That which God commanded by his Word, to be done at some times (that we should humble our soules by fasting) the same God commands by his Church, to be done now: In the Scriptures you have *Praeceptum*, The thing it self, What; In the Church, you have the *Nunc*, The time, When. The Scriptures are Gods Voyce; The Church is his Eccho; a redoubling, a repeating of some particular syllables, and accents of the same voice. And as we harken with some earnestnesse, and some admiration at an Eccho, when perchance we doe not understand the voice that occasioned that Eccho; so doe the obedient children of God apply themselves to the Eccho of his Church, when perchance otherwise, they would lesse understand the voice of God, in his Scriptures, if that voice were not so redoubled unto them. This fasting then, thus enjoyned by God, for the generall, in his Word, and thus limited to this Time, for the particular, in his Church, is indeed but a continuation of a great Feast: Where, the first course (that which we begin to serve in now) is Manna, food of Angels, plentifull, frequent preaching; but the second course, is the very body and blood of Christ Jesus, shed for us, and given to us, in that blessed Sacrament, of which himselfe makes us worthy receivers at that time. Now, as the end of all bodily eating, is Assimilation, that after all other concoctions, that meat may be made *Idem corpus*, the same body that I am; so the end of all spirituall eating, is Assimilation too, That after all Hearing, and all Receiving, I may be made *Idem spiritus cum Domino*, the same spirit, that my God is. (*1625*) 6:223

4. Holy Ghost: Comments on the Comment (Rom. 13:11)

In a second sence we took these words, of Christs second *Advent*, or comming, his comming to our heart, in the working of his grace; And so the Apostles words are directed to all Christians, and not only to the new convertits of that nation; and so these three terms, salvation, nearness, and believing, (which we proposed to be considered in all the three acceptations of the words) will have this signification. Salvation is the inward means of salvation, the working of the spirit, that sets a seal to the eternal means: the *prope*, the nearness lies in this, that this grace which is this salvation in this sense, grows out of that which is in you already; not out of any thing which is in you naturally, but Gods first graces that are in you, grows into more and more grace.

. . . .

First then, salvation in this second sense is the internal operation of the holy Ghost, in infusing grace: for therefore doth St. *Basil* call the holy Ghost *verbum Dei*, the word of God, (which is the name properly peculiar to the Son) *quia interpres filii, sicut filius patris*; that as the Father had revealed his will in the Prophets, and then the Son comes and interprets all that actually, this prophecy is meant of my coming, this of my dying; and so makes a real comment, and an actual interpretation of all the prophecies, for he does come, and he does die accordingly; so the holy Ghost comes, and comments upon this comment, interprets this interpretation, and tels thy soul that all this that the Father had promised, and the Son had performed, was intended by them, and by the working of their spirit, is now appropriated to thy particular soul. (*1619*) 2:260–61

5. Role of the Holy Ghost in Application (1 Cor. 12:3)

So that this Spirit disposes, and dispenses, distributes, and disperses, and orders all the power of the Father, and all the wisdome of the Son, and all the graces of God. It is a Center to all; So S. *Bernard* sayes upon those words of the Apostle, *We approve our selves as the Ministers of God*; But by what? *By watching, by fasting, by suffering, by the holy Ghost, by love unfained. Vide, tanquam omnia ordinantem quomodo in medio virtutum, sicut cor in medio corporis, constituit Spiritum Sanctum*: As the heart is in the midst of the body, so between these vertues of fasting and suffering before, and love unfained after, the Apostle places the holy Ghost, who only gives life and soule to all Morall, and all Theologicall vertues. And as S. *Bernard* observes that in particular men, so doth S. *Augustine* of the whole Church; *Quod in corpore nostro anima, id in corpore Christi, Ecclesia, Spiritus Sanctus*; That office which the soule performes to our body, the holy Ghost performes in the body of Christ, which is the Church.

And therefore since the holy Ghost is thus necessary, and thus neare, as at the Creation the whole Trinity was intimated in that plurall word, *Elohim, creavit Dii,* but no person of the Trinity is distinctly named in the Creation, but the holy Ghost, *The Spirit of God moved upon the waters,* As the holy Ghost was first conveyed to our knowledge in the Creation, so in our Regeneration, by which we are new creatures, though our Creation, and our Redemption be religious subjects of our continuall meditation, yet let us be sure to hold this that is nearest us, to keep a neare, a familiar, and daily acquaintance, and conversation with the holy Ghost, and to be watchfull to cherish his light, and working in us. [w]*Homines docent quaerere, solus ipse, qui docet invenire, habere, frui*; Men can teach us wayes how to finde some things; The Pilot how to finde a Lande, The Astronomer how to finde a Star; Men can teach us wayes how to finde God, The naturall man in the book of creatures, The Morall man in an exemplar life, The Jew in the Law, The Christian in generall in the Gospell, But *Solus ipse, qui docet invenire, habere, frui,* Only the holy Ghost enables us to finde God so, as to make him ours, and to enjoy him. First you must get more light then nature gives, for, [x]*The naturall man perceiveth not the things of the Spirit*: When that light is so mended, that you have some sparkes of faith, you must also leave the works of the flesh, For, [y]*Fleshly men have not the Spirit*: When the Spirit offers it self in approaches, *Resist it not,* as *Stephen* accuses them to have done, *Act.* 7. When it hath prevailed, and sealed you to God, [z]*Grieve not the holy*

w. Bernard.
x. 1. Cor. 2:14.
y. Jud. 19.
z. Ephes. 4:30.

Spirit, by whom ye are sealed unto Redemption. For this preventing the Spirit, by trusting to nature, and morality, this infecting the Spirit, by living ill in a good profession, this grieving of the Spirit, by neglecting his operations, induces the last desperate work of [a]*Quenching the Spirit,* which is a smothering, a suffocating of that light, by a finall obduration.

[b]*Spiritus ubi vult spirat,* sayes our Saviour Christ; which S. *Augustine,* (and indeed most of the Fathers) interpret of the holy Ghost, and not of the winde, though it may also properly enough admit that interpretation too. But *The holy Ghost,* sayes he, *breathes where it pleases him*; *Et vocem ejus audis,* sayes Christ, *You heare the voice of the holy Ghost*; for, (sayes S. *Augustine* upon those words of Christ) *Sonat psalmus, vox est Spiritus sancti,* When you heare a Psalme sung, you heare the voice of the holy Ghost; *Sonat Evangelium, sonat sermo Divinus,* You heare the Gospell read, you heare a Sermon preached, still you heare the voice of the holy Ghost; And yet, as Christ sayes in that place, *Nescis unde venit, Thou knowest not from whence that voice comes,* Thou canst finde nothing in thy self, why the holy Ghost should delight to entertain thee, and hold discourse with thee, in so familiar, and so frequent, and so importunate a speaking to thee; *Nescis unde venit,* Thou knowest not from whence all this goodnesse comes, but meerly from his goodness; So also, as Christ adds there, *Nescis quo vadat, Thou knowest not whither it goes,* how long it will last and goe with thee. (*1624?*) 6:129–30

E. The Actions of Interpretation

1. Actions: Interpretations of God (2 Cor. 4:6)

First, *He made light*: There was none before; so first, *He shines in our hearts,* by his preventing Grace; there was no light before; not of Nature, by which any man could see any means of salvation; not of foreseen Merits, that God should light his light at our Candle, give us Grace therefore, because he saw that we would use that Grace well. He made light, he infused Grace.

And then, *He made light first of all Creatures*: *Ut innotescerent,* says St. *Ambrose,* that by that light all his other Creatures might be seen: which is also the use of this other light, that *shines in our hearts,* that by that light, the love of the Truth, and the glory of Christ Jesus, all our actions may be manifested to the world, and abide that tryal; that we look for no other approbation of them, then as they are justifiable

a. 1. Thes. 5:[19]. *b.* John 3:8.

by that light, as they conduce to the maintenance of his Religion, and the advancement of his glory: not to consider actions as they are wisely done, valiantly done, learnedly done, but onely as they are religiously done: and *ut abdicemus occulta dedecoris*, as the Apostle speaks; [c]*That we may renounce the hidden things of dishonesty, and not walk in craftiness*: that is, not sin therefore, because we see our sins may be hid from the world: For, says St. *Ambrose*, speaking of *Gyges* Ring,[1] a Ring by which he that wore it, became invisible; *Da sapienti*, says that Father, Give a wise man, (a man religiously wise) that Ring, and though he might sin invisibly before men, he would not, because God sees. [d]Nay, even the moral man goes further then that, in that point; Though I knew, says he, *hominem ignoraturum, et Deum ignosciturum*, that man should never know it, and that God would forgive it, I would not sin, for the very foulness that is naturally in sin. As God commanded light for the Manifestation of his creatures, so he hath shined in our hearts, that our actions might appear by that light. (*1622*) 4:115–16

2. The Preaching Imperative (1 Cor. 16:22)

Nothing will deale truely with thee but the Truth it selfe, and onely Christ Jesus is this Truth. He followes it thus much farther, *Si calicem aureum invenisses in terra*, If thou foundest a chalice of gold in the earth, so good a heart as thine would say, Surely this belongs to the Church, and surely thou wouldst give it to the Church: *Accepisti a Deo ingenium spiritualiter aureum*, God hath given thee a wit, an understanding, not of the gold of Ophir, but of the gold of the heavenly Jerusalem, *Et in illo, Satanae propinas teipsum?* In that chalice once consecrated to God, wilt thou drink a health to the devill, and drink a health to him in thine owne bloud, in making thy wit, thy learning, thy good parts advance his kingdome? He ends all thus, *Misereris jam mei, si tibi viluisti*, If thou undervalue thy selfe, if thou thinke not thy selfe worth hearing, if thou follow not thine owne counsels, yet *miserearis mei*, Have mercy upon me, me, whose charge it is to bring others to heaven, me, who shall not bee received there, if I bring no body with mee; bee content to goe with me, that way, which by the inspiration of the holy Ghost I do shew, and that way, which by the conduct of the holy Ghost I would fain goe. (*1621?*) 3:305

1. See the story of Gyges and Candaules, Herodotus 1.8–12 and Plato, *Republic*, 2.359. Gyges, a shepherd, descended into a chasm in the earth where, on the finger of a corpse hidden inside a bronze horse, he found a golden ring that made him invisible when he wore it.

c. v.2. *d.* Seneca.

3. Good Hearers Are Good Preachers (Acts 10:44)

A good hearer becomes a good Preacher, that is, able to edifie others. It is true, that these men were not to be literally Preachers, as the Apostles (upon whom the Holy Ghost fell, as upon them) were, and therefore the gift of tongues may seeme not to have beene so necessary to them. But it is not onely the Preacher, that hath use of the tongue, for the edification of Gods people, but in all our discourses, and conferences with one another, we should preach his glory, his goodnesse, his power, that every man might speake one anothers language, and preach to one anothers conscience; that when I accuse my selfe, and confesse mine infirmities to another man, that man may understand, that there is, in that confession of mine, a Sermon, and a rebuke, and a reprehension to him, if he be guilty of the same sin; Nay, if he be guilty of a sin contrary to mine. For, as in that language in which God spoke, the Hebrew, the same roote will take in words of a contrary signification, (as the word of *Jobs* wife signifies blessing and cursing too) so the covetous man that heares me confesse my prodigality, should argue to himself, If prodigality, which howsoever it hurt a particular person, yet spreads mony abroad, which is the right and naturall use of money, be so heavy a sin, how heavy is my covetousnesse, which, besides that it keepes me all the way in as much penuriousnesse, as the prodigall man brings himselfe to at last, is also a publique sin, because it emprisons that money which should be at liberty, and employed in a free course abroad? And so also when I declare to another, the spirituall and temporall blessings which God hath bestowed upon me, he may be raised to a thankfull remembrance, that he hath received all that from God also. This is not the use of having learnt divers tongues, to be able to talk of the wars with Dutch Captains, or of trade with a French Merchant, or of State with a Spanish Agent, or of pleasure with an Italian Epicure; It is not to entertaine discourse with strangers, but to bring strangers to a better knowledge of God, in that way, wherein we, by his Ordinance, do worship and serve him. (*at Lincoln's Inn, Whitsunday 1618 [or 1620 or 1621]?*) 5:50–51

4. The Grace of Lips (Prov. 22:11)

Ordinarily in Scriptures, where this word *lips* is not taken naturally, literally, narrowly, for that part of the body, but transferred to a figurative and larger sense, either it signifies *speaking* onely (as in *Solomon*, As, [e] *righteous lips are the delight of Kings, and the King loveth*

e. Prov. 16:13.

him that speaketh right things (That is, *Him*, in whose Counsels, and in whose relations he may confide and rely;) or else it is enlarged to all manner of expressing a mans ability, to do service to that State in which God hath made his station; and by *lips*, and *fruits* of *lips*, is well understood the fruit of all his good labors and endeavors. And so may those words be well interpreted, [f]*With the fruit of a mans mouth shall his belly be satisfied, and with the encrease of his lips shall he be filled*; That is, his honest labors in a lawful calling shall enrich him. As therefore those words, [g]*A mans gift maketh room for him, and bringeth him before great men*, are not always understood of *Gifts* given in nature of *Bribes* or gratifications for access to great persons, but also of Gifts given by God to men, that those *Gifts* and *good parts* make them acceptable to great persons; so is not *Grace of lips* to be restrained, either to a plausible and harmonious speaking, appliable to the humor of the hearer (for that's excluded in the first part, the root and fountain of all, *Pureness of heart*, for, *flattery* cannot consist with that) nor to be restrained to the good Offices and Abilities of the *tongue onely* (though they be many;) but this Grace of lips is to be enlarged to all declarations, and expressings, and utterings of an ability to serve the Publick; All that is Grace of lips. And in those words of *Osea*, [h]*We render the Calves of our lips*, is neither meant as the *Jews* say, Those Calves which we have promised with our lips, and will pay in *sacrifice*, then, when we are restored to our *Land of promise* again. Nor are those Calves of our lips only restrained to the [i]*Lip-service* of *Praise*, and *Prayer*, though of them also St. *Paul* understand them; but they include all the *sacrifices of the New Testament*, and all ways by which man can do service to God; so here the *Grace of lips* reaches to all the ways by which a man in civil functions may serve the Publick. And this *Grace of lips*, in some proportion, in some measure, every man is bound in conscience to procure to himself; he is bound to enable himself to be useful and profitable to the Publick, in some course, in some vocation.

Since even *the Angels*, which are all Spirit, be yet *administring Spirits*, and execute the Commissions and Ambassages of God, and communicate with men; should man, who is not made *all soul*, but a composed creature of body and soul, exempt himself from doing the offices of mutual society, and upholding that frame in which God is pleased to be glorified? Since *God* himself, who so many millions of ages contented himself with *himself* in Heaven, yet at last made this world for his glory; shall any man live so in it as to contribute

f. [Prov.] 18:20.
g. vers.16.
h. Hosea 14:2.
i. Heb. 13:15.

nothing towards it? Hath God made this World his Theatre, *ut exhibeatur ludus deorum*, that man may represent God in his conversation; and wilt thou play no part? (*1617*) 1:206–7

5. Interpretations of Men's Actions (Acts 23:6, 7)

First then, though it be a safer way, to suspect an action to be sin that is not, then to presume an action to be no sin, that is so, yet that rule holds better in our selves, then in other men; for, in judging the actions of other men, our suspition may soone stray into an uncharitable mis-interpretation, and wee may sin in condemning that in another, which was no sin in him that did it. But, in truth, *Transilire lineam*, To depart from the direct and straight line, is sin, as well on the right hand, as on the left; And the Devill makes his advantages upon the over-tender, and scrupulous conscience, as well as upon the over-confident, and obdurate; and many men have erred as much, in justifying some actions of holy men, as in calumniating, or miscondemning of others. If we had not evidence in Scripture, that *Abraham* received that Commandement from God, who could justifie *Abrahams* proceeding with his son *Isaac*? And therefore who shall be afraid to call *Noahs* Drunkennesse, and his undecent lying in his Tent, Or *Lots* Drunkennesse, and his iterated Incest with his Daughters, or his inconsiderate offer to prostitute his Daughters to the Sodomites, Or to call *Davids* complicated and multiplied sin, a sin? When the Church celebrates *Samsons* death, though he killed himself, it is upon a tender and holy supposition, that he might do this not without some instinct and inspiration from the Spirit of God. But howsoever the Church interprets such actions, it is a dangerous and a fallacious way, for any private man to argue so, The Spirit of God directed this man in many actions, therefore in all; And dangerous to conclude an action to be good, either because he that did it, had a good purpose in doing it, or because some good effects proceeded from it. *Bonum bene*, are the two horses that must carry us to heaven; To do good things, and to doe them well; To propose good ends, and to goe by good waies to those good ends. The Midwives lie, in the behalfe of the Israelites children, was a lie, and a sin, howsoever God, out of his own goodnesse, found something in their piety, to reward. I should not venture to say, as he said, nor to say that hee said well, when *Moses* said, [j] *Dele me, Forgive their sinne, or blot mee out of thy Booke*; Nor when S. *Paul* said, *Anathema pro fratribus, I could wish that my selfe were separated from Christ for my Brethren*. I would not, I could not without sin, be

j. Exod. 32:32. Rom. 9:3.

content that my name should be blotted out of the Booke of Life, or that I should bee separated from Christ, though all the world beside were to be blotted out, and separated, if I staid in.

The benefit that we are to make of the errors of holy men, is not that, That man did this, therefore I may doe it: but this, God suffered that holy man to fall, and yet loved that good soule well, God hath not therefore cast me away, though he have suffered me to fall too. Bread is mans best sustenance, yet there may be a dangerous surfet of bread: Charity is the bread that the soule lives by; yet there may be a surfet of charity; I may mis-lead my selfe shrewdly, if I say, surely my Father is a good man, my Master a good man, my Pastor a good man, men that have the testimony of Gods love, by his manifold blessings upon them; and therefore I may be bold to doe whatsoever I see them doe. [k]*Be perfect, even as your Father which is in heaven, is perfect,* is the example that Christ gives you. *Be yee followers of mee, as I am of Christ,* is the example that the Apostle gives you. Good Examples are good Assistances; but no Example of man is sufficient to constitute a certaine and constant rule; All the actions of the holiest man are not holy. (*1629*) 9:157–58

6. The Redemption of Time (Isa. 52:3)

He redeemed us then without money; And as he bought so he sells: He paid no money, he asks no money: but he proclaims freely to all, [l]*Ho every one that thirsteth come to the waters, and ye that have no silver, come, buy, and eat; come, I say, buy wine, and milk, without silver, and without money.* But you must come; and you must come to the market; to the Magazine of his graces, his Church; And you must buy, though you have no money: he paid obedience, and he asks obedience to himself, and his Church, at your hands. And then, as *Joseph* did to his brethren, he will give you your corn, and your money again; he will give you grace, and temporal blessings too: he will refresh and re-establish your natural faculties, and give you supernatural. He hath already done enough for all, even in his mercy, he was just; just to the Devil himself: for as we had done, so he did; he gave himself; both to the first death, as long as it could hold him, and to the second death, as far as it could reach him. But though all this be already done, yet, to conclude, there is a particular circumstance of Comfort, in this word, you shall be: that though the act of our redemption be past, the Application is future: and in the elect and regenerate child of God, though his conscience tells him every day, that he sels away

k. Mat. 5:48. 1. Cor. 11:1. *l.* Esa. 55:[1].

himself, yet his conscience shall tell him too, he shall be redeemed without money, he shall not perish finally: as we cannot carry our thoughts to so high a time, but that God elected us, before that, so we cannot continue our sins of infirmity so long, but that God will have mercy upon us after that: I cannot name a time, when Gods love began, it is eternal, I cannot imagine a time, when his mercy will end, it is perpetual. (*1615*) 1:167

10 Genre

Introduction

This final chapter is divided into biblical, liturgical, and pedagogical genres. Not all of these are strictly literary kinds, in the way *genre* is now commonly understood, but they are generally descriptive of a mode as well as of attitude and intention. Thus Donne naturally concentrates on prophecy, which is fundamental to all that he says, urging that "a Prophet was not onely *praefator*, but *praefactor*; He did not only presage, but preordain" (8 : 296–99), as if in the speaking or predicting of an event he holds the actual accomplishing of it. Hence the familiar scriptural phrases become meaningful: "This and this was thus and thus done, that such and such a Prophecy might be fulfilled." Prophecy *predicts* and at the same time *causes* events through the action of the Holy Spirit. In this light we need to understand Donne's role, or the role of any Renaissance writer who took his activity seriously, as that of the prophet-priest, or as Sidney described in his *Defense* (1583), a *maker* and *creator*.

While a prophet "causes" a thing to come to pass, he may speak in one of many ways: in praise, in denunciation (or commination), in the knowledge of things to come that have already passed (for prophecy is history), in parable, in songs, and in epithalamions. But of these biblical—and prophetical—genres, the one that most interested Donne, both historically and in his own time, was the epistle. The Old Testament is filled primarily with prophecy—of future things; but the New Testament is marked by its Epistles, accounts of things past with instruction for the present. The Epistles of St. Paul are, according to St. Augustine, *Ubera Ecclesiae*, "The Paps, the Breasts, the Udders of the Church" (6 : 114–15). In imagery that is striking for its exuberance, Donne says of Paul himself: "as he had drawne and sucked the blood of Christs mysticall body, the Church, so, in that proportion that God enabled him to, he recompensed that damage, by effusion of his owne blood."

Donne wrote verse epistles, like Ben Jonson and many others, during the flowering of this genre in the late Renaissance, from about the 1590s through the early part of the seventeenth century. The importance he attached to the Pauline Epistles may be related to this wider interest in the epistle. Recalling St. Ambrose, Donne describes the epistle in a way that points out its universal aim: "An Epistle is *collocutio scripta* . . . Though it be written far off, and sent, yet it is a Conference, and *seperatos copulat* . . . wee overcome distances, we deceive absences, and wee are together, even then when wee are asunder" (1:285). Donne delights, moreover, in the similarity of the words, related by sound and sense (though not really by etymology), for the Apostles, especially Paul, wrote epistles, and thus performed the office of their apostleship. And so it is that true instruction comes through such "holy love-letters," and that the bringing of knowledge to any congregation is a kind of lovemaking to the souls in it. In addition to the Epistles, the Acts of the Apostles likewise describe the practice of holy men, not so much by their *sermons* as by their *actions* in the world.

We move from biblical to liturgical "genres," and begin first with the "mystery of Confession" that leads us to the "mystery of the Kingdome of heaven." One begins "adversum se," "against himself," then is able to say "erubescam," "I shall blush with shame," but at last one is taken up into paradise with a "rapiemur," "we shall be caught up." There must naturally follow prayer and praise, such as the whole book of Psalms offers to those who are both penitent and thankful; for the Psalms are a golden kind of poetry, filled with closings that express new openings. The increase of our holy joy is but the interest earned from "mortification, fasting, and praying" (6:48). Indeed, praise in its various forms, particularly in the Psalms, is the subject of the remainder of this section, for they "are the Manna of the Church . . . [and some] command over all affections . . . [and] apply themselves to all necessities" (7:51).

Finally, there are the genres of teaching, governed always by the Holy Spirit, whose disciples all of us are. Once again the Psalms show a way, this time "Catechistical," in "fundamentall and easie teaching" [that is, clear to apprehend] (9:252). And in the text from Ps. 32, one of the seven Penitential Psalms, David lays the ground for all later teaching; for "Blessed is the man"—*blessedness* is the first object of man's (and David's) study and instruction. While catechizing makes up one teaching genre, and this psalm offers an especially happy example, Donne himself thought most frequently about the sermon, and it is fitting that we should end this chapter (and the volume) by showing how he treats the theory and the composition of the sermon and the action of the preacher.

For Donne, the Word is an essential complement to the sacrament of the altar, the Holy Communion. One does not properly go to the sermon and forget about the sacrament. In Donne's imagery, preaching is the "thunder," the sacrament is the "lightning." Even so clear a statement may be misleading to a modern reader because the role of preaching seems still so magnified in Donne's time, especially when compared with the attenuated or rambling "address" that frequently passes for a sermon today. Sermons normally lasted an hour and occupied the principal part of any service, which was generally the office of morning prayer. The Communion was not customarily celebrated, or offered to the people except on "solemn, and festival, and Anniversary times" (4:105), when the sermon was used to prepare the faithful to receive the sacrament with fit reverence. Although Donne is accurate in reflecting the large instructional role that sermons always occupied, he is typical only of a certain kind of churchman who urged also the primacy of the historical church and its sacraments, with preaching as the regular means for directing men toward eucharistic celebration in an apostolic continuity of worship.

Donne gave the last fifteen years of his life to preaching and to the cure of souls. He wrote very little poetry after his ordination in 1615, his sermons becoming his principal literary expression; but in a sense the 160 published sermons (he obviously preached many more) include his best poetry. Preaching is "calling," Donne says, echoing another passage on the mission of Christ, "*veni vocare,* I came to call" (p. 48). "He came to save by calling us," even as the preacher speaking to us and on our behalf calls on us, his auditors. This calling is "*Vocatio radicalis,* the calling that is the root and foundation of all" (4:109), shining in every kind of darkness. Such "calling" depends upon a two-way response; teaching implies listening, acting, coming: "*Come ye children, hearken unto mee, and I will teach you the feare of the Lord*" (6:95–96, from Ps. 34:11). Characteristically, Donne appreciates the dual nature inherent in preaching and in all worship, and he explores this vision with the imagery of war: "In every man, there are two sides, two armies: the flesh fights against the Spirit. This is but a *Civill warre.* . . . That warre *God* hath kindled, and that warre must bee maintained, and maintained by his way; and his way, and his *Ordinance* in this warre, is Preaching" (4:194).

Sermons have many varieties; they have been variously styled as homilies, conciones, lectures, enarrations, speeches, orations. But these all seek the same end and rely upon a common desire. The highest and most persuasive force of any sermon—whatever it may be called and however it may be constructed—derives from the "ethical proof" of the preacher himself. The preacher is a man who speaks more than words, for he also expresses the love of God. Like many other "learned" preachers of his time, Donne is indebted to classical oratory, as formulated by Aristotle, Cicero, and Quintillian, for the shape and plan of his sermons and for the importance ascribed to the moral example of the speaker. Oratory, of course, becomes christianized in Donne, where good character is real and never simulated, and where sermon structure is merely a convenient means for emphasizing and shoring up the faith of believing people. Truth lies in the Word of God, and the preacher is the messenger: "It becommeth me to make my selfe as accceptable a messenger as I can, and to infuse the Word of God into you, as powerfully as I can"; but, Donne continues, the greatest part lies in our own application, "and that must proceed from the Word of God it selfe, quickned by his Spirit" (8:272–73).

A. Biblical Genres

1. Prophecy

i. Venire Facio *("Lord, who hath beleeved our report?")*

The office and function of a Prophet, in the time of the Law, was not so evident, nor so ordinary an office, as the office of the Priest and Minister in the Gospel now is; There was not a constant, an ordinary, a visible calling in the Church, to the office of a Prophet. Neither the high-priest, nor the Ecclesiasticall Consistory, the *Synedrium*, did by any imposition of hands, or other Collation, or Declaration, give Orders to any man so, as that thereby that man was made a Prophet. I know some men, of much industry, and perspicacy too, in searching into those Scriptures, the sense whereof is not obvious to every man, have thought that the Prophets had an outward and a constant declaration of their Calling. And they think it proved, by that which is said to *Eliah*, [a] when God commands him to anoint *Hazael* King of Syria, and to anoint *Jehu* King of Israel, and to anoint *Elisha* Prophet in his own room: Therefore, say they, the Prophet had as much evidence of his Calling, as the Minister hath, for that unction was as evident a thing, as our Imposition of hands is. And it is true, it was so, where it was actually, and really executed. But then, nothing is more evident, then that this word *Meshiach*, which signifies *Anointing*, is not restrained to that very action, a real unction, but frequently transferred, and communicated in a Scripture use, to every kind of Declaration of any Election, any Institution, any Inauguration, any

a. 1. Reg. 19:15.

Investiture of any person to any place; And, lesse then that, of any appropriation, any application of any thing to any particular use. Any appointing was an anointing; As in particular (for many other places) where S. *Hierome* reades, [b]*Arripite clypeos, buckle your shields*; To you, which was an alarm to them, to arm, the originall hath it, and so hath our translation, *Anoint your shields*; to apply them to their right use, was called an Anointing. And when God cals *Cyrus*, the King of *Persia*, *Unctum suum, his Anointed*; it were weakly, and improperly argued from that word, that *Cyrus* King of Persia, was literally, actually, anointed; for that unction was peculiar to the Kings of Israel; but *Cyrus* was the anointed of the Lord, that is, declared and avowed by the Lord, to be his chosen Instrument. Neither could *Eliah*, literally execute this commandement, for anointing *Hasael* King of *Syria*; for *Hasael* the King of *Syria* could not be anointed by the Prophet of the Lord, for such unction was peculiar to the Kings of Israel. And for the Kings of Israel themselves, their owne Rabbins tell us, that they were not ordinarily anointed, but onely in those cases, where there arose some question, and difference, about the succession; as in *Solomons* case; [c]there, because *Adoniah* pretended to the succession; to make all the more sure, *David* proceeded with a solemnity, and appointed an anointing of *Solomon*, which, otherwise, say their Rabbins, had not been done. But howsoever it may have been for their Kings, there seemes to be a plaine distinction betweene them, and the Prophets in the Psalme, for this evidence of unction; [d]*Touch not mine Anointed*, sayes God there: They, they that were Anointed, constitute one rank, one classis; and then followes, *And doe my Prophets no harme*: They, they who were not Anointed, the Prophets, constitute another classis, another rank. So that then an internall, a spirituall unction the Prophets had, that is, an application, an appropriation to that office from God, but a constant, an evident calling to that function, by any externall act of the Church, they had not, but it was an extraordinary office, and imposed immediatly by God; and therfore the people might seem the more excusable, if they did not beleeve a Prophet presently, because the office of the Prophet did not carry with it, such a manifestation by any thing evidently done upon him, and visible to them, that by that, that man must be a Prophet. But, as God clothes himselfe with light, as with a garment; so God clothes, and apparells his works with light too: for, *frustra fecisset*, sayes S. *Ambrose*, God had made creatures to no purpose, if he had not made light to see them by. Therefore when God does any extraordinary worke, he ac-

b. Esay 21:5.
c. 1. Reg. 1.
d. Ps. 105:15.

companies that work with an extraordinary light, by which, he for whose instruction God does that work, may know that work to be his. So when he sent his Prophets to his people, he accompanied their mission, with an effectuall light, and evidence, by which, that people did acknowledge in their owne hearts, that that man was sent by God to them. Therefore they called that man at first, *Roeh, videntem*, a Seer, one whom they acknowledged to have beene admitted to the sight of God, in the declaration of his will to them: for so we have it in *Samuel*, [e] *He that is now called a Prophet, was before time called a Seer*. And then that addition of the name of a Prophet, gave them a farther qualification; for, *Nabi*, which is a Prophet, is from *Niba*; and *Niba*, is *venire facio*, to cause, to make a thing to come to passe. So that a Prophet was not onely *praefator*, but *praefactor*; He did not only presage, but preordain; that is, there was such an infallibility, such an inevitablenesse in that which he had said, as that his very saying of it, seemed to them some kind of cause of the accomplishing thereof.

For, hence it is, that we have that phrase so often in the new Testament, This and this was thus and thus done, that such and such a Prophecy might be fulfilled: They never went to that heighth, that such or such a secret purpose, or unrevealed Decree of God might be fulfilled; but they rested in the Declaration which God had made in his Church, and were satisfied in the execution of his Decrees, in his visible Ordinances. Therefore the increpation which the Prophet layes upon the people here, (*Lord, who hath beleeved our report*) is not, that they did not beleeve those Prophets to be Prophets, (for though that were an extraordinary office, yet it was accompanied with an extraordinary light) neither was it, that they did not beleeve that those things which were prophecyed by them, should come to passe, (for they beleeved that man to be *Roeh*, a Seer, one that had seen the Counsels of God concerning them; And they beleeved him to be *Nabi, venire facientem*, one upon whose word they might as infallibly rely, as upon a cause, for an effect;) But this was the sinne of this people, this was the sorrow of this Prophet, that they did not beleeve these predictions to belong to them, they did not beleeve that these judgements would fall out in their time. In one word, present security was their sinne. (*1629*) 8:296–99

ii. Imprecation as Prophecy (Ps. 6:8, 9, 10)

If this then were an Imprecation, a malediction, yet it was Medicinall, and had *Rationem boni*, a charitable tincture, and nature in it;

e. 1. Sam. 9:9.

he wished the men no harm, as men. But it is rather *Praedictorium*, a Propheticall vehemence, that if they will take no knowledge of Gods declaring himselfe in the protection of his servants, if they would not consider that God had heard, and would heare, had rescued, and would rescue his children, but would continue their opposition against him, heavy judgements would certainly fall upon them; Their punishment should be certaine, but the effect should be uncertaine; for God only knowes, whether his correction shall work upon his enemies, to their mollifying, or to their obduration. [f]Those bitter, and waighty imprecations which *David* hath heaped together against *Judas*, seeme to be direct imprecations; and yet S. *Peter* himselfe calls them Prophesies; *Oportet impleri Scripturam; They were done,* sayes he, *that the Scripture might be fulfilled*; Not that *David* in his owne heart did wish all that upon *Judas*; but only so, as fore-seeing in the Spirit of Prophesying, that those things should fall upon him, he concurred with the purpose of God therein, and so farre as he saw it to be the will of God, he made it his will, and his wish. And so have all those judgements, which we denounce upon sinners, the nature of Prophesies in them; when we reade in the Church, that Commination,[1] *Cursed is the Idolater,* This may fall upon some of our owne kindred; and *Cursed is he that curseth Father or Mother,* This may fall upon some of our owne children; and *Cursed is he that perverteth judgement,* This may fall upon some powerfull Persons, that we may have a dependance upon; and upon these we doe not wish that Gods vengeance should fall; yet we Prophesie, and denounce justly, that upon such, such vengeances will fall; and then, all Prophesies of that kinde are alwaies conditionall; they are conditionall, if we consider any Decree in God; they must be conditionall in all our denunciations; if you repent, they shall not fall upon you, if not, *Oportet impleri Scripturam, The Scripture must be fulfilled*; We doe not wish them, we do but Prophesie them; no, nor we doe not prophesie them; but the Scriptures have pre-prophesied them before; they will fall upon you, as upon *Judas*, in condemnation, and perchance, as upon *Judas*, in desperation too. (*1623*) 6:54–55

iii. History and Prophecy (Ps. 66:3)

We call *Noah, Janus,* because hee had two faces, in this respect, That hee looked into the former, and into the later world, he saw the

1. See the Book of Common Prayer, "A Commination against Sinners," which includes a litany based on the Commandments; Donne recalls three of them here.

f. Ps. 109. Acts 1:16.

times before, and after the flood. *David* in this Text, is a *Janus* too; He looks two wayes, he hath a Prospect, and a Retrospect, he looks backward and forward, what God had done, and what God would doe. For, as we have one great comfort in this, That Prophecies are become Histories, that whatsoever was said by the mouthes of the Prophets, concerning our salvation in Christ, is effected, (so prophecies are made histories) so have wee another comfort in this Text, That Histories are made Prophecies; That whatsoever we reade that God had formerly done, in the reliefe of his oppressed servants, wee are thereby assured that he can, that he will doe them againe; and so Histories are made Prophecies: And upon these two pillars, A thankfull acknowledgement of that which God hath done, And a faithfull assurance that God will doe so againe, shall this present Exercise of your devotions be raysed; And these are our two parts. *Dicite Deo, Say unto God, How terrible art thou in thy works!* (that part is Historicall, of things past) *In multitudine virtutis, In the greatnesse of thy power, shall thine enemies submit themselves unto thee,* (that part is Propheticall, of things to come.) (*1627*) 8:112

iv. Lamentations: Historical Parable—Parabolical History (Lam. 4:20)

The Booke is certainly the *Prophet Jeremies*, and certainly a *distinct booke*; But whether the Book be a *history*, or a *Prophecy*, whether *Jeremy* lament that which hee had *seen*, or that which he *foresees*, calamities past, or future calamities, things done, or things to be done, is a question which hath exercised, and busied divers Expositors. But, as we say of the *Parable of Dives*, and *Lazarus*, that it is a *Historicall parable*, and a *Parabolicall history*, some such persons there were, and some such things were really done, but some other things were figuratively, symbolically, parabolically added: So wee say of *Jeremies Lamentation*, It is a *Propheticall history*, and a *Historicall prophecy*; Some of the sad occasions of these Lamentations were past, when he writ, and some were to come after: for, we may not despise the testimony of the *Chalde Paraphrasts*, who were the first that illustrated the Bible, in that Nation, nor of S. *Hierome*, who was much conversant with the Bible, and with that Nation, nor of *Josephus*, who had justly so much estimation in that Nation, nor of those later *Rabbins*, who were the learnedest of that Nation; who are all of opinion, that *Jeremy* writ these Lamentations, after hee saw some declinations in that State, in the *death of Josiah*, and so the Book is *Historicall*, but when he onely foresaw their transportation into *Babylon*, before that calamity fell upon them, and so it is *Propheticall*. Or, if we take the exposition of the others, That the whole Booke was written after their transportation into *Babylon*, and to be, in all parts, Historicall, yet it is Propheticall still; for the Prophet laments a greater Desolation then that, in the utter ruine, and devastation of the City, and Nation, which was to fall upon them, after the death of *Christ Jesus*. Neither is any peece of this Booke, the lesse fit to be our Text, this day, because it is both Historicall, and Propheticall, for, they, from whom, God, in his mercy, gave us a Deliverance, this day, are our *Historicall Enemies*, and our *Propheticall Enemies*; historically wee know, they *have* attempted our ruine heretofore, and prophetically wee may bee sure, they *will doe so againe*, whensoever any new occasion provokes them, or sufficient power enables them.

The Text then is as the Booke presented to *Ezekiel*; [g] In it are written *Lamentations*, and *Mournings*, and *Woe*; and all they are written *within*, and *without*, says the Text there; *within*, as they concern the *Jews*, *without*, as they are applicable to *us*: And they concern the *Jews*, *Historically* (attempts upon that State *Jeremy* had certainly *seen*,) and they concern them *prophetically*, for farther attempts *Jeremy* did certainly *foresee*. They are appliable to us both ways too: *Historically*, because wee have seen, what they *would have done*, And *Prophetically*, because wee foresee what they *would doe*. So that there is but a difference of the Computation; here is *stilo veteri*, and *stilo novo*; here is the *Jews Calendar*, and the *Papists Calendar*; In the Jews Calendar, *one Babylon* wrought upon the people of God, and in the Papists Calendar, *another Babylon*: *Stilo veteri*, in the Jews Calendar, 700 yeare before Christ came, there were *pits made, and the breath of their nostrils, The anointed of the Lord, was taken in their pits*: *Stilo novo*, in the Papists Calendar, 1600 yeare after Christ came in all fulnesse, in all clearnesse, *There were pits made* againe, and *The breath of our nostrils, The anointed of the Lord, was almost taken in those pits*.

It is then *Jeremies*, and it is a *distinct* Book; It concernes the *Jews*, and it concerns *us* too; And it concernes us both, *both wayes, Historically*, and *Prophetically*. But whether *Jeremy* lament here the death of a good King, of *Josiah*, (for so Saint *Hierome*, and many of the *Ancients*, and many of the *Jewes* themselves take it, and thinke that those words in the *Chronicles*, have relation to these Lamentations, [h] *And Jeremy lamented for Josiah, and all the people speake of him, in their Lamentations*,) Or whether he lament the transportation and the misery of an ill King, of *Zedekiah*, (as is more ordinarily, and more probably held by the Expositours) we argue not, we dispute not now; we imbrace that which arises from both, That both good Kings, and bad

g. Ezek. 2:10.

h. 2. [Chron.] 35:25.

Kings, *Josiah*, and *Zedekiah*, are the *anointed* of the Lord, and the *breath of the nostrills*, that is, The life of the people; and therefore both to be lamented, when they fall into dangers, and consequently both to be preserved by all means, by *Prayer* from them who are private persons, by *counsell* from them, who have that great honour and that great charge, to be near them in that kinde, and by *support* and *supply*, from all, of all sorts, from falling into such dangers. (*1622*) 4:237–39

2. Epithalamion
Amorous Solomon (Prov. 8:17)

All affections which are common to all men, and those too, which in particular, particular men have been addicted unto, shall not only be justly employed upon God, but also securely employed, because we cannot exceed, nor go too far in imploying them upon him. According to this Rule, St. *Paul*, [i] who had been so vehement a persecutor, had ever his thoughts exercised upon that; and thereupon after his conversion, he fulfils the rest of the sufferings of Christ in his flesh, he suffers most, he makes most mention of his suffering of any of the Apostles.

And according to this Rule too, *Salomon*, whose disposition was amorous, and excessive in the love of women, when he turned to God, he departed not utterly from his old phrase and language, but having put a new, and a spiritual tincture, and form and habit into all his thoughts, and words, he conveyes all his loving approaches and applications to God, and all Gods gracious answers to his amorous soul, into songs, and Epithalamions, and meditations upon contracts, and marriages between God and his Church, and between God and his soul; as we see so evidently in all his other writings, and particularly in this text, *I love them, etc*.

In which words is expressed all that belongs to love, all which, is to desire, and to enjoy; for to desire without fruition, is a rage, and to enjoy without desire is a stupidity: In the first alone we think of nothing, but that which we then would have; and in the second alone, we are not for that, when we have it; in the first, we are without it; in the second, we are as good as if we were without it, for we have no pleasure in it; nothing then can give us satisfaction, but where those two concurr, *amare* and *frui*, to love and to enjoy.

In sensual love it is so; [j] *Quid erat quod me delectabat nisi amare et amari?* I tooke no joy in this world, but in loving, and in being be-

i. Col. 1[:24].

j. August. [Confessiones, II.2.]

loved; in sensual love it is so, but in sensual love, when we are come so far, there is no satisfaction in that; the same Father confesseth more of himself, then any Commission, any oath would have put him to, *Amatus sum, et perveni occulte ad fruendum*, I had all I desired, and I had it with that advantage of having it secretly; but what got I by all that, *Ut caederer virgis ardentibus ferreis, zeli suspicionis et rixarum*; nothing but to be scourged with burning iron rods, rods of jealousie, of suspition, and of quarrels; but in the love and enjoying of this text, there is no room for Jealousie, nor suspition, nor quarrelsome complaining.

In this text then you may be pleased to consider these two things, *Quid amare, quid frui*, what the affection of this love is, what is the blessedness of this enjoying; but in the first of these, we must first consider the persons, who are the lovers in this text; for there are persons that are incredible, though they say they love, because they are accustomed to falshood; and there are persons which are unrequitable, though they be believed to love, because they love not where, and as they should. When we have found the persons, in a second consideration we shall look upon the affection it self, what is the love in this text; and then after that, upon the bond, and union and condition of this love, that it is mutual, *I love them that love me*; and having passed those three branches of the first part, we shall in the second, which is enjoying, consider first, that this enjoying, is expressed in the word finding; and then that this finding requires two conditions, a seeking, and an early seeking, *And they that seek me early shall find me*. (*1617*) 1:237–38

3. *Epistle*

i. Ubera Ecclesiae *(1 Cor. 12:3)*

[k]We read that in the Tribe of *Benjamin*, which is, by interpretation *Filius dextrae, The Son of the right hand*, there were seven hundred left-handed Men, that could sling stones at a haires breadth, and not faile. S. *Paul* was of that Tribe; and though he were from the beginning, in the purpose of God, *Filius dextrae*, A man ordained to be a dextrous Instrument of his glory, yet he was for a time a left-handed man, and tooke sinister wayes, and in those wayes, a good mark-man, a laborious and exquisite persecutor of Gods Church; And therefore it is, that *Tertullian* sayes of him, *Paulum mihi etiam Genesis olim repromisit*, I had a promise of *Paul* in *Moses*; Then, when *Moses* said, [l]*Jacob blessed Benjamin thus, Benjamin shall ravin as a Wolfe, In the morning he shall*

k. Judg. 20:16. *l.* Gen. 49[:27].

devoure the prey, and at night he shall divide the spoile, that is, At the beginning *Paul* shall scatter the flocke of Christ, but at last, he shall gather, and re-unite the Nations to his service: [m]As he had *breathed threatnings, and slaughter against the Disciples of the Lord,* so he became *Os orbi sufficiens,* A mouth loud enough for all the world to heare: And as he had drawne and sucked the blood of Christs mysticall body, the Church, so, in that proportion that God enabled him to, he recompensed that damage, by effusion of his owne blood, [n]*He fulfilled the sufferings of Christ, in his flesh,* as himselfe saies, to the *Colossians;* And then he bequeathed to all posterity these Epistles, which are, as S. *Augustine* cals them, *Ubera Ecclesiae,* The Paps, the Breasts, the Udders of the Church, And which are, [o]as that cluster of Grapes of the Land of Canaan, which was borne by two; for here, every couple, every paire, may have their load, Jew and Gentile, Learned and Ignorant, Man and Wife, Master and Servant, Father and Children, Prince and People, Counsaile and Client, how distinct soever they thinke their callings to be towards the world, yet here every paire must equally submit their necks to this sweet and easie yoake, of confessing Jesus to be the Lord, and acknowledging that Confession to proceed from the working of the Holy Ghost, for *No man can say, that Jesus is the Lord, without the Holy Ghost.* (*1624?*) 6:114–15

ii. Seperatos Copulat *(1 Tim. 1:15)*

The greatest part of the body of the old-Testament is Prophecy, and that is especially of future things: The greatest part of the new-Testament, if wee number the peeces, is Epistles, Relations of things past, for instruction of the present. They erre not much, that call the whole new-Testament Epistle: For, even the Gospells are *Evangelia,* good Messages, and that's proper to an Epistle, and the booke of the Acts of the Apostles is superscribed, by Saint *Luke,* to one Person, to *Theophilus,* and that's proper to an Epistle; and so is the last booke, the booke of Revelation, to the severall Churches; and of the rest there is no question. An Epistle is *collocutio scripta,* saies Saint *Ambrose,* Though it be written far off, and sent, yet it is a Conference, and *seperatos copulat,* sayes hee; by this meanes wee overcome distances, we deceive absences, and wee are together even then when wee are asunder: And therefore, in this kinde of conveying spirituall comfort to their friends, have the ancient Fathers been more exercised then in any other form, almost all of them have written Epistles: [p]One of them, *Isidorus,* him whom wee call *Peluciotes,* Saint *Chrysostom's*

m. Acts 9:1. Chrysost.
n. Colos. 1:24.
o. Numb. 13:23.
p. Nicephor[us].

schollar is noted to have written Myriades, and in those Epistles, to have interpreted the whole Scriptures: St. *Paul* gave them the example, he writ nothing but in this kind, and in this exceeded all his fellow Apostles. (*1618*) 1:285

iii. Epistle and Apostle (Isa. 32:8)

By two wayes especially hath the Gospell beene propagated by men of letters, by Epistles, and by Sermons. The Apostles pursued both wayes; frequent in Epistles, assiduous in Sermons. And, as they had the name of *Apostles*, from Letters, from Epistles, from Missives, (for, the Certificates, and Testimonials, and safe-conducts, and letters of Credit, which issued from Princes Courts, or from Courts that held other Jurisdiction, were in the formularies and termes of Law called Apostles, before Christs Apostles were called Apostles) so they executed the office of their Apostleship so too, by Writing, and by Preaching. This succession in the Ministery of the Gospell did so too. Therefore it is said of S. *Chrysostome, Ubique praedicavit, quia ubique lectus*, He preached every where, because he was read every where. And, he that is said to have beene S. *Chrysostomes* disciple, *Isidore*, is said to have written ten thousand Epistles, and in them to have delivered a just, and full Commentary upon all the Scriptures. In the first age of all, they scarce went any other way, (for writing) but this, by Epistles. Of *Clement*, of *Ignatius*, of *Polycarpus*, of *Martial*, there is not much offered us, with any probability, but in the name of Epistles. (*1628*) 8:237

iv. Holy Love Letters: Instruction How to Praise (Ps. 32:8)

This verse, more then any other in the Psalme, answers the Title of the Psalme. The title is, *Davids Instruction*; and here in the Text it is said, *I will instruct thee, and teach thee, in the way thou shalt goe*. There are eleven Psalmes that have that Title, *Psalmes of Instruction*; The whole booke is *Sepher Tehillim, The booke of prayses*; and it is a good way of praysing God, to receive Instruction, Instruction how to praise him. Therefore doth the holy Ghost returne so often to this Catechisticall way, Instruction, Institution, as to propose so many Psalmes, expresly under that Title purposely to that use. In one of those, The manner how Instruction should be given, is expressed also; It must be in a loving manner, for the Title is [q] *Canticum Amorum*, A song of love for Instruction. For *Absque prudentia, et benevolentia, non sunt perfecta consilia*: True Instruction is a making love to the Congregation and to every soule in it; but it is but to the soule. And so when S. *Paul*

q. Psal. 45. Bernard.

said, *He was mad for their sakes, Insanivit Amatoriam insaniam,* sayes *Theophylact,* S. *Paul* was mad for love of them, to whom he writ his holy love-letters, his Epistles. And thereupon doe the Rabbins call this Psalme, *Leb David, Cor Davidis,* The opening and powring out of *Davids* heart to them, whom he instructs. Wee have no way into your hearts, but by sending our hearts. The Poets counsell is, *Ut ameris, ama,* If thou wouldst be truely loved, doe thou love truely; The holy Ghosts precept upon us is, *Ut credaris, crede,* That if we would have you beleeve, wee beleeve our selves. It is not to our Eloquence that God promises a blessing, but to our sincerity, not to our tongue, but to our heart: All our hope of bringing you to love God, is in a loving and hearty maner to propose Gods love to you. The height of the Spouses love to Christ, came but to that, [r] *I am sicke of love*: The love of Christ went farther, To die for love. *Love is as strong as death*; but nothing else is as strong as either; and both, Love and Death, met in Christ. How strong and powerfull upon you then should that Instruction be, that comes to you from both these, The Love and Death of Christ Jesus? and such an Instruction doth this text exhibite, *I will instruct thee, and teach thee in the way in which thou shalt goe, I will guide thee with mine eye.* God so loved the world, as that he sent his Sonne to die: The Sonne being dead so loved the world, as that he returned to that world againe; and being ascended, sent the holy Ghost to establish a Church, and in that Church, *Usque ad consummationem,* till the end of the world, shall that holy Spirit execute this Catechisticall Office, *He shall instruct thee, and teach thee in the way which thou shalt goe, He shall guide thee with his eye.*

Though then some later Expositors have doubted of the person, who doth this Office, *To Instruct,* who this *I* in our Text is, because the Hebrew word *Le David,* is as well *Davidis,* as *Davidi,* An Instruction from *David,* as an Instruction to *David,* and so the Catechist may seeme to be *David,* and no more; yet since this Criticisme upon the word, *Le David,* argues but a possibility that it may, and not a necessity that it must be so, wee accompany S. *Hierome,* and indeed the whole body of the Fathers, in accepting this Instruction from God himselfe, it is no other then God himselfe that sayes, *I will instruct thee, etc.* No other then God himselfe can undertake so much as is promised in this text. For here is first, a rectifying of the understanding, *I will instruct thee,* and in the Originall there is somewhat more then our Translation reaches to; It is there, *Intelligere faciam te, I will make thee understand.* (*winter 1624–1625?*) 9:350–51

r. Cant. 2:5; 8:6.

v. "Catholic" Epistles (James 2:12)

This [the Epistle of James] is one of those seven Epistles, which *Athanasius* and *Origen* called *Catholick*; that is, universal; perchance because they are not directed to any one Church, as some others are, but to all the Christian world: And S. *Hierom* called them *Canonical*; perchance because all Rules, all Canons of holy Conversation are comprized in these Epistles: And *Epiphanius*, and *Oecumenius* called them *Circular*; perchance, because as in a Circle, you cannot discern which was the first point, nor in which, the compass begun the Circle; so neither can we discern in these Epistles, whom the Holy Ghost begins withall, whom he means principally, King or Subject, Priest or People, Single or Married, Husband or Wife, Father or Children, Masters or Servants; but Universally, promiscuously, indifferently, they give All rules, for All actions, to All persons, at All times, and in All places; As in this Text, in particular, which is not, by any precedent, or subsequent relation, by any connexion or coherence, directed upon any company, or any Degree of Men: for the Apostle does not say, Ye Princes, nor ye people; but ye, ye in general, to all, *So speak ye, and so do, as they that shall be judged by the law of liberty*: So these Epistles are Catholick, so they are Canonical, and they are Circular so. But yet, though in a Circle we know not where the compass began, we know not which was the first point; yet we know, that the last point of the Circle returns to the first, and so becomes all one; and as much as we know the last, we know the first point. Since then the last point of that Circle, in which God hath created us to move, is a kingdome (for it is the kingdom of heaven) and it is a Court (for it is that glorious Court, which is the presence of God, in the communion of his Saints) it is a fair and a pious conception, for this Congregation, here present now in this place, to believe, that the first point of this Circle of our Apostle here, is a Court too; and that the Holy Ghost, in proposing these duties in his general *Ye*, does principally intend, ye that live in Court, ye whom God brings so neer to the sight of himself, and of his Court in heaven, as that you have always the picture of himself, and the pourtraiture of his Court in your eyes: for a Religious King is the Image of God, and a Religious Court is a Copy of the Communion of Saints. And therefore be you content to think, that to you especially our Apostle says here, *Ye*, ye who have a nearer propinquity to God, a more assiduous conversation with God, by having better helps then other inferior stations do afford (for though God be seen in a weed, in a worm, yet he is seen more clearly in the Sun) *So speak ye, and so Do, as they that shall be judged by the law of liberty*. (*1629*) 8:335–36

4. *Acts*

i. The Acts of the Apostles (Acts 23:6, 7)

We consider ordinarily in the old Testament, God the Father; And in the Gospels, God the Son; And in this Book, the Acts, and in the Epistles, and the rest, God the Holy Ghost, that is, God in the Government and Administration of his Church, as well in the ordinary Ministery and constant callings therein, as in the extraordinary use of generall Councells; of which, we have the Modell, and Platforme, and precedent in the fifteenth Chapter of this Booke. The Book is noted to have above twenty Sermons of the Apostles; and yet the Book is not called The Sermons, The Preaching of the Apostles, but the Practise, the Acts of the Apostles. Our actions, if they be good, speak louder then our Sermons; Our preaching is our speech, our good life is our eloquence. Preaching celebrates the Sabbath, but a good life makes the whole week a Sabbath, that is, [s]A savor of rest in the nostrils of God, as it is said of *Noahs* Sacrifice, when he came out of the Ark. (*1629*) 9:155–56

ii. The Stage and Acts (Acts 1:8)

There are reckoned in this booke, 22. *Sermons* of the *Apostles*; and yet the booke is not called the *Preaching*, but the *Practise*, not the *Words*, but the *Acts* of the *Apostles*: and the *Acts* of the *Apostles* were to convay that name of *Christ Jesus*, and to propagate his *Gospell*, over all the world: Beloved, you are *Actors* upon the same Stage too: the uttermost part of the Earth are your *Scene*: act over the *Acts* of the *Apostles*; bee you a light to the *Gentiles*, that sit in darkenesse; be you content to carry him over these *Seas*, who dryed up one *Red Sea* for his first people, and hath powred out another *red Sea*, his owne bloud, for them and us. (*1622*) 4:265

iii. Theatre (1 Cor. 13:12)

The whole frame of the world is the Theatre, and every creature the stage, the *medium*, the glasse in which we may see God. [t]*Moses made the Laver in the Tabernacle, of the looking glasses of women*: Scarce can you imagine a vainer thing (except you will except the vaine lookers on, in that action) then the looking-glasses of women; and yet *Moses* brought the looking-glasses of women to a religious use, to shew them that came in, the spots of dirt, which they had taken by the way, that they might wash themselves cleane before they passed any farther.

s. Gen. 8[:21]. *t.* Exod. 38:8.

There is not so poore a creature but may be thy glasse to see God in. The greatest flat glasse that can be made, cannot represent any thing greater then it is: If every gnat that flies were an Arch-angell, all that could but tell me, that there is a God; and the poorest worme that creeps, tells me that. If I should aske the Basilisk, how camest thou by those killing eyes, he would tell me, Thy God made me so; And if I should aske the Slow-worme, how camest thou to be without eyes, he would tell me, Thy God made me so. The Cedar is no better a glasse to see God in, then the Hyssope upon the wall; all things that are, are equally removed from being nothing; and whatsoever hath any beeing, is by that very beeing, a glasse in which we see God, who is the roote, and the fountaine of all beeing. The whole frame of nature is the Theatre, the whole Volume of creatures is the glasse, and the light of nature, reason, is our light, which is another Circumstance.

Of those words, *John* 1.9. *That was the true light, that lighteth every man that commeth into the* World, the slackest sense that they can admit, gives light enough to see God by. If we spare S. *Chrysostomes* sense, That *that light*, is the light of the Gospel, and of Grace, and that *that light*, considered in it self, and without opposition in us, *does enlighten*, that is, would enlighten, *every man*, if that man did not wink at that light; if we forbear S. *Augustines* sense, *That light enlightens every man*, that is, every man that is enlightned, is enlightned by that light; If we take but S. *Cyrils* sense, that this *light* is the light of naturall Reason, *which*, without all question, *enlightneth every man that comes into the world*, yet have we light enough to see God by that light, in the Theatre of Nature, and in the glasse of Creatures. God affords no man the comfort, the false comfort of Atheism: He will not allow a pretending Atheist the power to flatter himself, so far, as seriously to thinke there is no God. He must pull out his own eyes, and see no creature, before he can say, he sees no God; He must be no man, and quench his reasonable soule, before he can say to himselfe, there is no God. The difference betweene the Reason of man, and the Instinct of the beast is this, That the beast does but know, but the man knows that he knows. The bestiall Atheist will pretend that he knows there is no God; but he cannot say, that hee knows, that he know it; for, his knowledge will not stand the battery of an argument from another, nor of a ratiocination from himselfe. He dares not aske himselfe, who is it that I pray to, in a sudden danger, if there be no God? Nay he dares not aske, who is it that I sweare by, in a sudden passion, if there be no God? Whom do I tremble at, and sweat under, at midnight, and whom do I curse by next morning, if there be no God? It is safely said in the Schoole, *Media perfecta ad quae ordinantur*, How weak soever those meanes which are ordained by God, seeme to be, and be indeed in themselves, yet they are strong enough to those ends and purposes, for which God ordained them. (*1628*) 8:224–25

5. Revelation
In Principio *(2 Cor. 4:6)*

The first Book of the Bible, begins with *the beginning*; *In principio*, says *Moses*, in *Genesis*; *In the beginning God created heaven and earth*: and can there be any thing *prius principio*, before the beginning? Before this *beginning*, there is. The last Book of the Bible, (in the order as they were written) the Gospel of St. *John*, begins with the same word too; *In principio*, says St. *John*; *In the beginning was the Word*: and here, *Novissimum primum*, the *last* beginning is the *first*; St. *John*'s *beginning*, before *Moses*; *Moses* speaking but of the Creature, and St. *John* of the Creator; and of the Creator, before he took that name, before he came to the act of Creation; as, *the Word was with God, and was God* from all Eternity. Our present Text is an Epitome of both these beginnings: of the first beginning, the Creation, when *God commanded light to shine out of darkness*; and of the other beginning, which is indeed the first, of Him, in whose face we shall have *the knowledge of the glory of God, Christ Jesus*.

The first Book of the Bible, is a Revelation, and so is the last, in the order as they stand, a Revelation too. To declare a production of all things out of nothing, (which is *Moses* his work;) that when I do not know, and care not whether I know or no, what so contemptible a Creature as an Ant is made of, but yet would fain know what so vast, and so considerable a thing as an Elephant is made of; I care not for a mustard seed, but I would fain know what a Cedar is made of; I can leave out the consideration of the whole Earth, but would be glad to know what the Heavens, and the glorious bodies in the Heavens, Sun, Moon and Stars are made of; I shall have but one answer from *Moses* for all, that all my Elephants, and Cedars, and the Heavens that I consider, were made of nothing; that a Cloud is as nobly born, as the Sun in the Heavens; and a begger, as nobly, as the King upon Earth; if we consider the great Grand-father of them all, to be nothing: to produce light of darkness thus, is a Revelation, a Manifestation of that, which, till then, was not: this *Moses* does. St. *John*'s is a Revelation too: a Manifestation of that state, which shall be, and be for ever, after all those which were produced of nothing, shall be returned and resolved to nothing again; the glorious state of the everlasting *Jerusalem*, the Kingdom of Heaven. Now this Text is a Revelation of both these Revelations: the first state, that which *Moses* reveals, was too dark for man to see; for it was nothing: The other, that which St. *John* reveals, is too bright, too dazling for man to look upon; for it is no one limited, determined Object, but all at once, glory, and the seat and fountain of all glory, the face of Christ Jesus. (*1622*) 4:89–90

B. Liturgical Genres

1. Confession

i. Adversum Se *(Ps. 32:5)*

This is the Sacrament of Confession; So we may call it in a safe meaning; That is, The mystery of Confession: for true Confession is a mysterious Art. As there is a *Mystery of iniquity*, so there is a *Mystery of the Kingdome of heaven*. And the mystery of the Kingdome of heaven is this, That no man comes thither, but in a sort as he is a notorious sinner. One mystery of iniquity is, that in this world, though I multiply sins, yet the Judge cannot punish me, if I can hide them from other men, though he know them; but if I confesse them, he can, he will, he must. The mystery of the Kingdome of heaven, is, That onely the Declaring, the Publishing, the Notifying, and Confessing of my sins, possesses me of the Kingdome of heaven; There is a case, in which the notoriety of my sins does harme; when my open sinning, or my publishing of my sin, by way of glory in that sin, casts a scandall upon others, and leads them into tentation; for so, my sin becomes theirs, because they sin my sin by example, And their sin becomes mine, because I gave the example, and we aggravate one anothers sin, and both sin both. But there is a publication of sin, that both alleviates, nay annihilates my sin, and makes him that hates sin, Almighty God, love me the better, for knowing me to be such a sinner, then if I had not told him of it. Therefore doe we speak of the mystery of Confession; for it is not delivered in one Rule, nor practised in one Act.

In this Confession of *Davids*, (*I acknowledged my sin unto thee, etc.*) We shall see more then so; for, though our two Parts be but the two Acts, *Davids* Act, and Gods Act, Confession and Absolution, yet is there more then one single action to be considered in each of them. For first, in the first, there is a reflected Act, that *David* doth upon himselfe, before he come to his Confession to God; Something *David* had done, before he came to say, *I will confesse*, As he did *confesse*, before God *forgave the iniquity of his sin*. Now that which he did in himselfe, and which preceded his Confession to God, was the *Notum feci, I ackowledged my sin*; which was not his bringing it to the knowledge of God by way of Confession, for, (as you see by the Method of the

Holy Ghost, in the frame of the Text) it preceded his purpose of confessing, but it was the taking knowledge of his sin in himselfe, It was his first quickning, and inanimation, that grace gave his soul, as the soule gives the child in the Mothers wombe. And then in *Davids* act upon himselfe, followes the *Non operui, I have not hid mine iniquity*, none of mine iniquities from mine owne sight: I have displayed to my selfe, anatomized mine own conscience, left no corner unsearched, I am come to a perfect understanding of mine own case, *Non operui*, This is *Davids* act upon himselfe, the recalling, and recollecting of his sins, in his own memory. And then finding the number, the waight, and so, the oppression of those sins there, he considers where he may discharge himselfe of them; And *Dixi*, sayes *David*, which is a word that implies both Deliberation, and Resolution, and Execution too; I thought what was best to doe, and I resolved upon this, and I did it; *Dixi Confitebor*, That I would make a true, a full, a hearty Confession to God of all those sins; for such we see the Elements and Extent of his Confession to be; He will confesse *Peccata*, Transgressions, Sins; Neither by an overtendernesse, and diffidence, and scrupulosity, to call things sins, that are not so, nor by indulgent flattering, and sparing of himself, to forbear those things which are truly so; He will confesse *Peccata, Sins*, and *Peccata sua, His sins*; First, *Sua*, that is, *A se perpetrata*, He will acknowledge them to have proceeded, and to have been committed by himself, he will not impute them to any other cause, least of all to God; And then, *Sua, non aliena*, he will confesse sins that are his own sins, and not meddle with the sins of other men, that appertain not to him. This is the subject of his Confession, *Sins*, and *His sins*, and then, *Peccata sua Domino, His sins unto the Lord*, both in that consideration, That all sins are committed against the Lord, and in that also, That Confession of all sins is to be made unto the Lord; And lastly, all this, (as S. *Hierome* reads this text, and so also did our former Translation) *Adversum se, Against himself*, that is, without any hope of reliefe, or reparation in himself. He begins to think of his own sinfull state, and he proceeds to a particular inquisition upon his conscience, There is his preparation, Then he considers, and thereupon resolves, and thereupon proceeds to confesse things that are truly sins, And then all them as his own, without imputing them to others, If they be his own, without medling with others, And these to the Lord, against whom all sin is committed, and to whom all Confession is to be directed; And all this still against himself, without any hope from himself. All this is in *Davids* action, preparatorily in himself, and then declaratorily towards God. (*winter 1624–1625?*) 9:296–98 *ii.* Erubescam *[I blushed with shame] (Ps. 6:8, 9, 10)*

As soone as *Adam* came to be ashamed of his nakednesse, he presently thought of some remedy; if one should come and tell thee, that he looked through the doore, that he stood in a window over against thine, and saw thee doe such or such a sin, this would put thee to a shame, and thou wouldest not doe that sin, till thou wert sure he could not see thee. O, if thou wouldest not sin, till thou couldst think that God saw thee not, this shame had wrought well upon thee. There are complexions that cannot blush; there growes a blacknesse, a sootinesse upon the soule, by custome in sin, which overcomes all blushing, all tendernesse. White alone is palenesse, and God loves not a pale soule, a soule possest with a horror, affrighted with a diffidence, and distrusting his mercy. Rednesse alone is anger, and vehemency, and distemper, and God loves not such a red soule, a soule that sweats in sin, that quarrels for sin, that revenges in sin. But that whitenesse that preserves it selfe, not onely from being died all over in any foule colour, from contracting the name of any habituall sin, and so to be called such or such a sinner, but from taking any spot, from comming within distance of a tentation, or of a suspition, is that whitenesse, which God meanes, when he sayes, [u]*Thou art all faire my Love, and there is no spot in thee.* Indifferent looking, equall and easie conversation, appliablenesse to wanton discourses, and notions, and motions, are the Devils single money, and many pieces of these make up an Adultery. As light a thing as a Spangle is, a Spangle is silver; and Leafe-gold, that is blowne away, is gold; and sand that hath no strength, no coherence, yet knits the building; so doe approaches to sin, become sin, and fixe sin. To avoid these spots, is that whitenesse that God loves in the soule. But there is a rednesse that God loves too; which is this Erubescence that we speak of; an aptnesse in the soule to blush, when any of these spots doe fall upon it.

God is the universall Confessor, the generall Penitentiary of all the world, and all dye in the guilt of their sin, that goe not to Confession to him. And there are sins of such waight to the soule, and such intangling, and perplexity to the conscience, in some circumstances of the sin, as that certainly a soule may receive much ease in such cases, by confessing it selfe to man. In this holy shamefastnesse, which we intend in this outward blushing of the face, the soule goes to confession too. And it is one of the principall arguments against Confessions by Letter, (which some went about to set up in the Romane Church) that that took away one of the greatest evidences, and testimonies of their

u. Cant. 4:7.

repentance, which is this Erubescence, this blushing, this shame after sin; if they should not be put to speak it face to face, but to write it, that would remove the shame, which is a part of the repentance. But that soule that goes not to confession to it selfe, that hath not an internall blushing after a sin committed, is a pale soule, even in the palenesse of death, and senslesnesse, and a red soule, red in the defiance of God. And that whitenesse, to avoid approaches to sin, and that rednesse, to blush upon a sin, which does attempt us, is the complexion of the soule, which God loves, and which the Holy Ghost testifies, when he sayes, [v]*My Beloved is white and ruddy*. And when these men that *David* speaks of here, had lost that whitenesse, their innocency, for *David* to wish that they might come to a rednesse, a shame, a blushing, a remorse, a sense of sin, may have been no such great malediction, or imprecation in the mouth of *David*, but that a man may wish it to his best friend, which should be his own soule, and say, *Erubescam*, not let mine enemies, but let me be ashamed with such a shame. (*1623*) 6:57–58

iii. Rapiemur *(1 Thess. 4:17)*

Rapiemur, We shall be caught up. This is a true Rapture, in which we doe nothing our selves. Our last act towards Christ, is as our first; In the first act of our Conversion we do nothing; nothing in this last act, our Resurrection, but *Rapimur*, we are caught. In every thing, the more there is left to our selves, the worse it is done; that that God does intirely, is intirely good. S. *Paul* had a Rapture too; [w]*He was caught up into Paradise; but whether in the body, or out of the body, he cannot tell*. We can tell, that this Rapture of ours, shall be in body and soule, in the whole man. Man is but a vapour; but a glorious, and a blessed vapour, when he is attracted, and caught up by this Sun, the Son of Man, the Son of God. O what a blessed alleviation possesses that man! and to what a blessed levity, (if without levity we may so speake) to what a cheerefull lightnesse of spirit is he come, that comes newly from Confession, and with the seale of Absolution upon him! Then, when nothing troubles his conscience, then, when he hath disburdened his soule of all that lay heavy upon it, then, when if his Confessor should unjustly reveale it to any other, yet God will never speake of it more to his conscience, not upbraid him with it, not reproach him for it, what a blessed alleviation, what a holy cheerefulnesse of spirit is that man come to? How much more in the endowments which we shall receive in the Rapture of this text, where we do

v. Cant. 5:10. *w.* 2. Cor. 12:4.

not onely devest all sins past, (as in Confession) but all possibility of future sins; and put on, not onely incorruption, but incorruptiblenesse; not onely impeccancy, but impeccability. And, to be invested with this endowment, *Rapiemur, Wee shall be caught up*, and *Rapiemur in Nubibus, Wee shall be caught up in the Clouds*. (*1622*) 4:82–83

2. Prayer, Praise, Psalm

i. Prayer and the Prince of Darkness (Apoc. 7:2, 3)

None of us hath got the victory over flesh and blood, and yet we have greater enemies then flesh and blood are. Some disciplines, some mortifications we have against flesh and blood; we have S. *Pauls probatum est*, his medicine, (if we will use it) [x]*Castigo corpus, I keep under my body, and bring it into subjection*; for that we have some assistance; Even our enemies become our friends; poverty or sicknesse will fight for us against flesh and blood, against our carnall lusts; but for these powers and principalities, I know not where to watch them, how to encounter them. I passe my time sociably and merrily in cheerful conversation, in musique, in feasting, in Comedies, in wantonnesse; and I never heare all this while of any power or principality, my Conscience spies no such enemy in all this. And then alone, between God and me at midnight, some beam of his grace shines out upon me, and by that light I see this Prince of darknesse, and then I finde that I have been the subject, the slave of these powers and principalities, when I thought not of them. Well, I see them, and I try then to dispossesse my selfe of them, and I make my recourse to the powerfullest exorcisme that is, I turne to hearty and earnest prayer to God, and I fix my thoughts strongly (as I thinke) upon him, and before I have perfected one petition, one period of my prayer, a power and principality is got into me againe. [y]*Spiritus soporis*, The spirit of slumber closes mine eyes, and I pray drousily; Or *spiritus vertiginis*, the spirit of deviation, and vaine repetition, and I pray giddily, and circularly, and returne againe and againe to that I have said before, and perceive not that I do so; and *nescio cujus spiritus sim*, (as our Saviour said, rebuking his Disciples, who were so vehement for the burning of the Samaritans, [z]*you know not of what spirit you are*) I pray, and know not of what spirit I am, I consider not mine own purpose in prayer; And by this advantage, this doore of inconsideration, enters [a]*spiritus erroris*, The seducing spirit, the spirit of error, and I

x. 1. Cor. 9:27.
y. Esay 29:10. Esa. 19:14.
z. Luke 9:55.
a. 1. Tim. 4:1.

pray not onely negligently, but erroniously, dangerously, for such things as disconduce to the glory of God, and my true happinesse, if they were granted. Nay, even the Prophet *Hosea's spiritus fornicationum*, enters into me, [b]*The spirit of fornication*, that is, some remembrance of the wantonnesse of my youth, some mis-interpretation of a word in my prayer, that may beare an ill sense, some unclean spirit, some power or principality hath depraved my prayer, and slackned my zeale. And this is my greatest misery of all, that when that which fights for me, and fights against me too, sicknesse, hath laid me upon my last bed, then in my weakest estate, these powers and principalities shall be in their full practise against me. And therefore it is one great advancement of thy deliverance, to be brought by this Angel, that is, by the Ministery of the Gospel of Christ, to know that thou hast Angels to thine enemies; And then another is to know their number, and so the strength of their confederacy. (*1623?*) 10:56–57

ii. Prayer: Separare *(Ps. 6:8, 9, 10)*

When *David* found, that God had heard his *Supplications*, the voyce of his suffering, of his punishment, he was sure he would heare his *Prayer*, the voyce of his thankfulnesse too.

And this was *Davids* second reason, for his alacrity, and confidence, that God would never be weary of hearing, he had heard him, and he would heare him still, he had heard the *Supplication*, and he would heare his *Prayer*; for this word, which signifies *Prayer* here, is derived from *Palal*, which signifies properly *Separare* [to divide]: As his *Supplication* was acceptable, which proceeded *a Suppliciis*, from a sense of his afflictions; so this *Prayer*, which came *Post separationem*, after he had separated, and divorced himselfe from his former company, after his *Discedite*, his discharging of all the workers of iniquitie, must necessarily be better accepted at Gods hand. (*1623*) 6:50

iii. Rooted in Man and God (Ps. 6:2, 3)

This whole Psalme is prayer; And the whole prayer is either Deprecatory, as in the first verse, or Postulatory. Something *David* would have forborne, and something done. And in that Postulatory part of *Davids* prayer, which goes through six verses of this Psalme, we consider the Petitions, and the Inducements; What *David* asks, And why: of both which, there are some mingled, in these two verses, which constitute our Text. And therefore, in them, we shall necessarily take

b. Hosea 4:12; 5:4.

knowledge of some of the Petitions, and some of the Reasons. For, in the Prayer, there are five petitions; First, *Miserere, Have mercy upon me,* Thinke of me, looke graciously towards me, prevent me with thy mercy; And then *Sana me, O Lord, heale me,* Thou didst create me in health, but my parents begot me in sicknesse, and I have complicated other sicknesses with that, Actuall with Originall sin, O Lord, heale me, give me physick for them; And thirdly, *Convertere, Returne, O Lord,* Thou didst visit me in nature, returne in grace, Thou didst visit me in Baptisme, returne in the other Sacrament, Thou doest visit me now, returne at the houre of my death; And, in a fourth petition, *Eripe, O Lord, deliver my soule,* Every blessing of thine becomes a snare unto me, and thy benefits I make occasions of sinne, In all conversation, and even in my solitude, I admit such tentations from others, or I produce such tentations in my selfe, as that, whensoever thou art pleased to returne to me, thou findest me at the brinke of some sinne, and therefore *Eripe me,* O Lord, take hold of me, and deliver me; And lastly, *Salvum me fac, O Lord, save me,* Manifest thy good purpose upon me so, that I may never be shaken, or never overthrown in the faithfull hope of that salvation, which thou hast preordained for me. These are the five petitions of the Prayer, and two of the five, The *Miserere, Have mercy upon me,* and the *Sana, O Lord, heale me,* are in these two verses. And then, the Reasons of the prayer, arising partly out of himselfe, and partly out of God; and some being mixt, and growing out of both roots together. (*1623?*) 5:338–39

iv. Prayer and the Circle (Ps. 38:2)

This whole Psalm is a *Prayer,* and recommended by *David* to the Church; And a *Prayer* grounded upon *Reasons*. The *Reasons* are multiplyed, and dilated from the second to the 20. verse. But as the *Prayer* is made to him that is *Alpha,* and *Omega, first,* and *last*; so the *Prayer* is the *Alpha* and *Omega* of the Psalme; the *Prayer* possesses the first and the last verse thereof; and though the Reasons be not left out, (Christ himself settles that *Prayer,* which he recommended to our daily use, upon a Reason, *Quia tuum est Regnum, for thine is the Kingdome,*) yet *David* makes up his Circle, he begins, and ends in prayer. (*1618*) 2:50

v. St. Augustine's Holy Circle (Ps. 65:5)

Petition God at prayers, and God shall answer all your petitions at the Sermon. There we begin, (if wee will make profit of a Sermon) at Prayers; And thither wee returne againe, (if we have made profit by a Sermon) in due time, to prayers. For, that is S. *Augustines* holy Circle, in which hee walkes from Prayers to the Sermon, and from the Sermon, next day to Prayers againe. [c]*Invocat te fides mea,* sayes he to God; Here I stand or kneele in thy presence, and in the power of faith, to pray to thee. But where had I this faith, that makes my prayer acceptable? *Dedisti mihi per ministerium Praedicatoris*; I had it at the Sermon, I had it, saith he, by the ministery of the Preacher; but I had it therefore, because thy Spirit prepared me by prayer before; And I have it therefore, that is, to that end, that I might returne faithfully to prayers againe. (*1627*) 7:312–13

vi. "Also my prayer is pure" (Job 16:17, 18, 19)

As cleane hands denote all righteousnesse towards man, so doe pure prayers all devotion, and worship, and service of God. For, we are of the houshold of the faithfull, and the service which we are to doe, as his houshold servants, is *prayer*; for, [d]*his house is the house of prayer*. And therein onely is it possible to us, to fulfill that Commandement, *pray continually*, that continually, in all our familiar actions, we may serve God, glorifie God, (whether we eate or drink, we may doe it to his glory) and every glorifying, every thanksgiving, is prayer; there cannot be a more effectuall prayer for future, then a thankfull acknowledgement of former benefits. *Petite, et dabitur*: How often is that repeated in the Gospell, and in the Epistles? *Aske, and it shall be given yee*; no grant without prayer, no deniall upon prayer.

It must be *prayer*, and *my prayer*; *Also my prayer is pure*. I must not rely upon the prayers of others; not of Angels; Though they be Ministeriall spirits, and not onely to God himselfe, but between God and Man, and so, as they present our prayers, no doubt poure out their owne for us too, yet we must not rely upon the prayers of Angels. Nor of Saints; Though they have a more personall, and experimentall sense of our miseries then Angels have, we must not relie upon the prayers of Saints. No, nor upon the prayers of the Congregation, though we see, and heare them pray, except we make our selves parts of the Congregation, by true devotion, as well as by personall presence.

It must be mine own prayer, and no prayer is so truly, or so properly mine, as that that the Church hath delivered and recommended to me. In sudden and unpremeditate prayer, I am not alwayes I; and when I am not my self, my prayer is not my prayer. Passions and affections sometimes, sometimes bodily infirmities, and sometimes a vain desire of being eloquent in prayer, aliens me, withdraws me from my self, and then that prayer is not my prayer. Though that prayer which

c. Confes. l.1.c.1. *d.* Matt. 21:13.

Luther is said to have said upon his death-bed, *Oremus pro Domino Deo nostro Jesu Christo*, Let us pray for our Lord and Saviour Christ Jesus, may admit a good sense, because Christ being (as S. *Augustine* sayes often) *Caput et Corpus*, both the Head and the Body, as he is the Body, the Church, subject to so many pressures, he had need to be prayed for; yet, his state being considered at that time, almost at the last gasp, he being scarce he, that prayer can scarce be called his prayer.

. . . .

As the Law of the Land is my Law, and I have an inheritance in it, so the prayers of the Church are my prayers, and I have an interest in them, because I am a Son of that family. My Baptisme is mine, and my Absolution is mine, because the Church hath given them to me, and so are her prayers mine. You would scarce thank a man for an extemporall Elegy, or Epigram, or Panegyrique in your praise, if it cost the Poet, or the Orator no paines. God will scarce hearken to sudden, inconsidered, irreverent prayers. Men will study even for Complements; and Princes and Ambassadors will not speak to one another, without thinking what they will say. Let not us put God to speak to us so, (Preaching is Gods speaking to us) Let not us speak to God so, (Praying is our speaking to God) not extemporally, unadvisedly, inconsiderately. Prayer must be my prayer; and *Quid habeo quod non accepi?* Even in this kinde, what have I that I have not received? I have received my prayer altogether, as a bundle of Myrrhe, in that prayer which I have received from my Saviour, and then I have received it appropriated to me, and apportioned to my particular necessities, and sacrifices, by the piety and wisdome of the Church; so it is my prayer, and, as *Jobs* prayer was, pure prayer, Also my prayer is pure. (*1630?*) 9:218–20

vii. Psalm: Prayer and Praise (Ps. 6:8, 9, 10)

And . . . also, because out of his abundant manner of expressing his thankfulnesse to God, in every other place thereof, his whole booke of Psalmes is called, *Sepher tehillim*, a booke of praise and thankesgiving, he might reserve his thanks here to the last place; And lastly, because naturall and morall men are better acquainted with the duty of gratitude, of thankesgiving, before they come to the Scriptures, then they are with the other duty of repentance, which belongs to Prayer; for in all *Solomons* bookes, you shall not finde halfe so much of the duty of thankfulnesse, as you shall in *Seneca* and in *Plutarch*. No book of Ethicks, of morall doctrine, is come to us, wherein there is not, almost in every leafe, some detestation, some Anathema against ingratitude; but of repentance, not a word amongst them all. And therefore in that dutie of prayer, which presumes repentance, (for he must stand *Rectus in curia* that will pray) *David* hath insisted longest; and because he would enter, and establish a man, upon a confidence in God, he begins with a deprecation of his anger; for but upon that ground, no man can stand; and because he would dismisse him with that which concerns him most, he chooseth to end in a Thanksgiving.

Therefore at last he comes to his thanks. Now this is so poore a duty, if we proportion it to the infinitenesse of Gods love unto us, our thanks, as we may justly call it nothing at all. But [e]*Amor Dei affectus, non contractus*, The love of God is not a contract, a bargaine, he looks for nothing againe, and yet he looks for thanks, for that is nothing, because there is nothing done in it, it is but speaking; [f]*Gratias dicere, est gratias agere*, To utter our thanks to God, is all our performance of thankfulnesse. It is not so amongst us; [g]*Vix, aut nunquam apud nos purum, et merum beneficium*; Every man that gives, gives out of designe, and as it conduces to his ends: [h]*Donat in hamo*, There is a hook in every benefit, that sticks in his jawes that takes that benefit, and drawes him whither the Benefactor will. God looks for nothing, nothing to be done in the way of exact recompence, but yet, as he that makes a Clock, bestowes all that labour upon the several wheeles, that thereby the Bell might give a sound, and that thereby the hand might give knowledge to others how the time passes; so this is the principall part of that thankfulnesse, which God requires from us, that we make open declarations of his mercies, to the winning and confirming of others.

. . . .

Here is an admirable readinesse in God, that heares a voyce in that, which hath none. They have described God by saying he is all eye, an universall eye, that pierceth into every darke corner; but in darke corners, there is something for him to see; but he is all eare too, and heares even the silent, and speechlesse man, and heares that in that man, that makes no sound, his teares. [i]When *Hezekias* wept, he was turned to the wall, (perchance, because he would not be seene) and yet God bad the Prophet *Esay* tell him, *Vidi lacrymam*; though the text say, *Hezekias wept sore*, yet *Vidit lacrymam*, God saw every single teare, his first teare, and was affected with that. But yet this is more strange; God heard his teares. And therefore the weeping of a penitent sinner, is not improperly called, [j]*Legatio lacrymarum*, An embas-

e. Bernar.
f. August.
g. Philo Judae.
h. Martial.
i. Esay 38.
j. Gregor.

sage of teares; To Embassadours belongs an audience, and to these Embassages God gives a gracious audience; [k]*Abyssus abyssum invocat, One depth cals upon another*; And so doth one kinde of teares call upon one another. Teares of sorrow call upon teares of joy, and all call upon God, and bring him to that ready hearing which is implied in the words of this text, *Shamang*; a word of that largenesse in the Scriptures, that sometimes in the Translation of the Septuagint, it signifies hearing, *Shamang*, is *audit*, God gives eare to our teares; sometimes it is beleeving, *Shamang*, is *Credit*, God gives faith, and credit to our teares; sometimes it is Affecting, *Shamang*, is *Respondet*, God answers the petition of our teares; and sometimes it is Publication, *Shamang*, is *Divulgat*, God declares and manifests to others, by his blessings upon us, the pleasure that he takes in our holy and repentant teares. And therefore *Lacrymae foenus*, sayes S. *Basil*, Teares are that usury, by which the joyes of Heaven are multiplied unto us; the preventing Grace, and the free mercy of God, is our stock, and principall; but the Acts of obedience, and mortification, fasting, and praying, and weeping, are *Foenus*, (sayes that blessed Father) the interest, and the increase of our holy joy. (*1623*) 6:41–42, 47–48

viii. Petition and Evidence (Ps. 90:14)

If we compare these two incomparable duties, Prayer, and Praise, it will stand thus. Our Prayers besiege God, (as *Tertullian* speakes, especially of publique Prayer in the Congregation, *Agmine facto obsidemus Deum*) but our praises prescribe in God, we urge him, and presse him with his ancient mercies, his mercies of old; By Prayer we incline him, we bend him, but by praise we bind him; our thanks for former benefits, is a producing of a specialty, by which he hath contracted with us for more. In Prayer we sue to him, but in our Praise we sue him himselfe; Prayer is as our petition, but Praise is as our Evidence; In that we beg, in this we plead. God hath no law upon himselfe, but yet God himselfe proceeds by precedent: And whensoever we present to him with thanksgiving, what he hath done, he does the same, and more againe. Neither certainly can the Church institute any prayers, more effectuall for the preservation of Religion, or of the State, then the Collects for our deliverances, in the like cases before: And when he heares them, though they have the nature of Praise onely, yet he translates them into Prayers, and when we our selves know not, how much we stand in need of new deliverances, he delivers us from dangers which we never suspected, from Armies and Navies which we

k. Psal. 42:7.

never knew were prepared, and from plots and machinations which we never knew were brought into Consultation, and diverts their forces, and dissipates their counsels with an untimely abortion. And farther I extend not this first part of Prayer in generall, in which, to that which you may have heard often, and usefully of the duty and dignity of Prayer, I have only added this, of the method and elements thereof, that prayer consists as much of praise for the past, as of supplication for the future. (*1622?*) 5:272

ix. Religion Is Praise (Rom. 13:7)

Now Glory is, *Clara cum laude notitia*, sayes S. *Ambrose*: It is an evident knowledge, and acknowledgement of God, by which, others come to know him too; which acknowledgement is well called a recognition, for it is a second, a ruminated, a reflected knowledge: Beasts doe remember, but they doe not remember that they remember; they doe not reflect upon it, which is that that constitutes memory: Every carnall and naturall man knowes God, but the acknowledgement, the recognition, the manifestation of the greatnesse and goodnesse of God, accompanied with praise of him for that, this appertaines to the godly man, and this constitutes glory. If God have delivered me from a sicknesse, and I doe not glorifie him for that, that is, make others know his goodnesse to me, my sicknesse is but changed to a spirituall apoplexy, to a lethargy, to a stupefaction. If God have delivered us from destruction in the bowels of the Sea, in an Invasion, and from destruction in the bowels of the earth, in the Powder-treason,[2] and we grow faint in the publication of our thanks for this deliverance, our punishment is but aggravated, for we shall be destroyed both for those old sins which induced those attempts of those destructions, and for this later and greater sin, of forgetting those deliverances; God requires nothing else; but he requires that, Glory and Praise. And that booke of the Scriptures, of which, S. *Basil* sayes, That if all the other parts of Scripture could perish, yet out of that booke alone, we might have enough for all uses, for Catechizing, for Preaching, for Disputing; That whole Booke, which containes all subjects that appertaine to Religion, is called altogether *Sepher Tehillim, The Booke of praises*, for all our Religion is Praise. And of that Book every particular Psalme is appointed by the Church, and continued at least for a thousand and two hundred yeares, to be shut up with that humble and glorious acclamation, Glory be to the Father, and to the Son, and to the Holy Ghost; *O that men would therefore praise the Lord, and de-*

2. Allusions to the defeat of the Spanish Armada (1588) and to the Gunpowder Plot (1605).

clare the wonderfull works that he doth for the sons of men! *Nil quisquam debet nisi quod turpe est, non reddere,* sayes the Law: It is *Turpe,* an infamous and ignominious thing, not to pay debt; And, infamous and ignominious, are heavy and reproachfull words in the Law; and the Gospell would adde to that *Turpe, Impium*: It is not onely an infamous but an impious, an irreligious thing, not to pay debts. As in debts, the State, and the Judge is my security, they undertake I shall be paid, or they execute Judgement; so, consider our selves as Christians, God is my security, and he will punish where I am defrauded. Either thou owest God nothing, (And then, if thou owe him nothing, from whom, or from what hath she stollen that face, that is faire; or he that estate, that is rich; or that office, that commands others; or that learning, and those orders and commission, that preaches to others; or they their soules, that understand me now? If you owe nothing, from whom had you all these, all this?) Or if thou dost owe, *Turpe est, Impium est,* It is an unworthy, it is an unhonest, it is an irreligious thing, not to pay him, in that money, which his owne Spirit mints, and coynes in thee, and of his owne bullion too, praise and thanksgiving. Not to pay him then, when he himselfe gives thee the money that must pay him, the Spirit of Thankfulnesse, falls under all the reproaches, that Law or Gospell can inflict in any names. How many men have we seen molder and crumble away great estates, and yet pay no debts? It is all our cases: What Poems, and what Orations we make, how industrious, and witty we are, to over-praise men, and never give God his due praise? Nay how often is the Pulpit it selfe, made the shop, and the Theatre of praise upon present men,[3] and God left out? How often is that called a Sermon, that speakes more of Great men, then of our great God? (*1623?*) 4:306–7

x. In villula Christi *(Ps. 90:14)*

And though S. *Hierome* tell us this, with some admiration, and note of singularity, That *Paula* could say the whole book of Psalmes without booke, in Hebrew; yet he presents it as a thing well known to be their ordinary practise; *In villula Christi Bethlem, extra psalmos silentium est,* In the village where I dwell, sayes he, where Christ was borne, in Bethlem, if you cannot sing Psalmes, you must be silent, here you shall heare nothing but Psalmes; for, (as he pursues it) *Arator stivam tenens,* The husbandman that follows the plough, he that sowes, that reapes, that carries home, all begin and proceed in all their labours with singing of Psalmes. Therefore he calls them there, *Can-*

3. Those who are present or in attendance, with a likely pun signifying "attentive."

tiones amatorias, Those that make or entertaine love, that seeke in the holy and honorable way of marriage, to make themselves acceptable and agreeable to one another, by no other good parts, nor conversation, but by singing of Psalmes. So he calls them, *Pastorum sibilum,* and *Arma culturae,* Our shepheards, sayes S. *Hierome,* here, have no other Eclogues, no other Pastoralls; Our labourers, our children, our servants no other songs, nor Ballads, to recreate themselves withall, then the Psalmes. (*1622?*) 5:288

xi. Manna of the Church (Ps. 63:7)

The Psalmes are the Manna of the Church. [l]As Manna tasted to every man like that that he liked best, so doe the Psalmes minister Instruction, and satisfaction, to every man, in every emergency and occasion. *David* was not onely a cleare Prophet of Christ himselfe, but a Prophet of every particular Christian; He foretels what I, what any shall doe, and suffer, and say. And as the whole booke of Psalmes is [m]*Oleum effusum,* (as the Spouse speaks of the name of Christ) an Oyntment powred out upon all sorts of sores, A Searcloth that souples all bruises, A Balme that searches all wounds; so are there some certaine Psalmes, that are Imperiall Psalmes, that command over all affections, and spread themselves over all occasions, Catholique, universall Psalmes, that apply themselves to all necessities. (*1626*) 7:51

C. The Genres of Teaching

1. The Holy Ghost

Docebimur *(John 14:26)*

Wee passe from the Person to his working; we come from his comming, to his operation, from his Mission, and Commission, to his Executing thereof, from the Consideration, who he is, to what he does. His Specification, his Character, his Title, *Paracletus, The Comforter,* passes through all. Therefore our first comfort is, *Docebimur,* we shall be Taught, *He shall teach you;* As we consider our selves, The Disciples of the Holy Ghost, so it is a meere teaching, for, we, in our selves are meerly ignorant; But when we consider the things we are to be taught, so it is but a remembring, a refreshing of those things, which Christ in the time of his conversation in this world, had taught before; *He shall bring all things to your remembrance, whatsoever I*

l. Wisd. 16:20. *m.* Cant. 1:3.

have said unto you. These two then, The comfort in the Action, (we shall be Taught) and the comfort in the Way and Manner, (we shall not be subject to new Doctrines, but taught by remembring, by establishing us in things formerly Fundamentally laid) will be our two parts at this time. (*1628*) 8:253

2. Catechism

David's "Blessed is the man" (Ps. 32:1, 2)

That then which constitutes our first part, is this, That *David*, then whom this world never had a greater Master for the next, amongst the sonnes of men, delivers himselfe, by way of Catechising, of fundamentall and easie teaching. As we say justly, and confidently, That of all Rhetoricall and Poeticall figures, that fall into any Art, we are able to produce higher straines, and livelier examples, out of the Scriptures, then out of all the Orators, and Poets in the world, yet we reade not, we preach not the Scriptures for that use, to magnifie their Eloquence; So in *Davids* Psalmes we finde abundant impressions, and testimonies of his knowledge in all arts, and all kinds of learning, but that is not it which he proposes to us. *Davids* last words are, and in that *Davids* holy glory was placed, [n]That he was not onely *the sweet Psalmist*, That he had an harmonious, a melodious, a charming, a powerfull way of entring into the soule, and working upon the affections of men, but he was *the sweet Psalmist of Israel*, He employed his faculties for the conveying of the God of Israel, into the Israel of God; [o]*The spirit of the Lord spake by me, and his word was in my tongue*; Not the spirit of Rhetorique, nor the spirit of Poetry, nor the spirit of Mathematiques, and Demonstration, But, [p]*The spirit of the Lord, the Rock of Israel spake by me*, sayes he; He boasts not that he had delivered himselfc in strong, or deepe, or mysterious Arts, that was not his Rock; but his Rock was the Rock of Israel, His way was to establish the Church of God upon fundamentall Doctrines. [q]*Moses was learned in all the wisedome of the Egyptians*, sayes *Stephen*. Likely to be so, because being adopted by the Kings daughter, he had an extraordinary education; And likely also, because he brought so good naturall faculties, for his Masters to worke upon, [r]*Ut Reminisci potius videretur, quam discere*, That whatsoever any Master proposed unto him, he rather seemed to remember it then, then to learne it but then; And yet in *Moses* books, we meet no great testimonies, or deepe impressions

n. 2. Sam. 23:1.
o. ver.2.
p. ver.3.
q. Act. 7:22. Exod. 2:10.
r. Philo.

of these learnings in *Moses*: He had (as S. *Ambrose* notes well) more occasions to speak of Naturall philosophy, in the Creation of the world, and of the more secret, and reserved, and remote corners of Nature, in those counterfeitings of Miracles in *Pharaohs* Court, then he hath laid hold of. [s]So *Nebuchadnezzar* appointed his Officers, that they should furnish his Court, with some young Gentlemen, of good bloud and families of the Jews; And (as it is added there) *well favoured youths, in whom there was no blemish, skilfull in all wisedome, and cunning in knowledge, and understanding science*; And then farther, *To be taught the tongue, and the learning of the Chaldeans*. And *Daniel* was one of these, and, no doubt, a great Proficient in all these; and yet *Daniel* seemes not to make any great shew of these learnings in his writings. S. *Paul* was in a higher Pedagogy, and another manner of University then all this; [t]*Caught up into the third heavens, into Paradise,* as he sayes; and there he learnt much; but (as he sayes too) *such things as it was not lawfull to utter*; That is, It fell not within the lawes of preaching to publish them. So that not onely some learning in humanity, (as in *Moses* and *Daniels* case) but some points of Divinity, (as in S. *Pauls* case) may be unfit to be preached. Not that a Divine should be ignorant of either; either ornaments of humane, or mysteries of divine knowledge. For, sayes S. *Augustine,* Every man that comes from Egypt, must bring some of the Egyptians goods with him. *Quanto auro exivit suffarcinatus Cyprianus,* sayes he, How much of the Egyptian gold and goods brought *Cyprian,* and *Lactantius,* and *Optatus,* and *Hilary* out of Egypt? That is, what a treasure of learning, gathered when they were of the Gentils, brought they from thence, to the advancing of Christianity, when they applied themselves to it? S. *Augustine* confesses, [u]that the reading of *Cicero's Hortensius, Mutavit affectum meum,* began in him a Conversion from the world, *Et ad teipsum, Domine, mutavit preces meas,* That booke, sayes he, converted me to more fervent prayers to thee, my God; *Et surgere jam coeperam ut ad te redirem,* By that help I rose, and came towards thee. And so *Justin Martyr* had his Initiation, and beginning of his Conversion, from reading some passages in *Plato*. S. *Basil* expresses it well; They that will dye a perfect colour, dip it in some lesse perfect colour before. To be a good Divine, requires humane knowledge; and so does it of all the Mysteries of Divinity too; because, as there are Devils that will not be cast out but by Fasting and Prayer, so there are humours that undervalue men, that lacke these helps. But our Congregations are not made of such persons; not of meere naturall men, that must be con-

s. Dan. 1:[3,] 4.
t. 2. Cor. 12:2.
u. L.3.c.4.

verted out of *Aristotle*, and by *Cicero's* words, nor of Arians that require new proofes for the Trinity, nor Pelagians that must be pressed with new discoveries of Gods Predestination;[4] but persons imbracing, with a thankfull acquiescence therein, Doctrines necessary for the salvation of their soules in the world to come, and the exaltation of their Devotion in this. This way *David* calls his, a Catechisme. And let not the greatest Doctor think it unworthy of him to Catechize thus, nor the learnedest hearer to be thus catechized; Christ enwraps the greatest Doctors in his Person, and in his practise, when he sayes *Sinite parvulos, Suffer little children to come unto me;* and we do not suffer them to come unto us, if when they come, we doe not speak to their understanding, and to their edification, for that is but an absent presence, when they heare, and profit not; And Christ enwraps the learnedest hearers, in the persons of his owne Disciples, when he sayes, *Except yee become as these little children, yee cannot enter into the Kingdome of heaven;* Except you nourish your selves with Catechisticall, and Fundamentall Doctrines, you are not in a wholesome diet. Now in this Catechisme, the first stone that *David* layes, (and that that supports all) the first object that *David* presents, (and that that directs to all) is Blessednesse; *Davids* Catechisme; *Blessed is the man.* (*winter 1624–1625?*) 9:252–54

3. Sermon

i. Word and Sacrament (2 Cor. 4:6)

[v]*The Gospel is preached to every Creature under heaven:* The properties, the qualities of every Creature, are in man; the Essence, the Existence of every Creature is for man; so man is every Creature. And therefore the Philosopher draws man into too narrow a table, when he says he is *Microcosmos*, an Abridgement of the world in little: *Nazianzen* gives him but his due, when he calls him *Mundum Magnum*, a world to which all the rest of the world is but subordinate: For all the world besides, is but Gods Foot-stool; Man sits down upon his right hand: and howsoever God be in all the world, yet how did God dwell in man, in the assumption of that nature? and what care did GOD take of that dwelling, that when that house was demolished, would yet dwell in the ruines thereof? for the Godhead did not depart from the dead body of Christ Jesus in the Grave. And then how much

4. Arianism denies the Trinity by rejecting the divinity of Christ, and Pelagianism teaches that man himself must take the steps toward salvation independently of God's grace or intervention.

v. Colos. 1:23.

more gloriously then before, did he re-edifie that house, in raising it again to Glory? Man therefore is [w]*Cura Divini ingenii*, a creature upon whom, not onely the greatness, and the goodness, but even the study and diligence of God is employed. And being thus a greater world then the other, he must be greater in all his parts, and so in his lights; and so he is: for, instead of this light, which the world had at first, Man hath a nobler light, an immortal, a discerning soul, the light of reason. Instead of the many stars, which this world hath, man hath had the light of the Law, and the succession of the Prophets: And instead of that Sun, which this world had, a Sun from God; man hath had the Son of God; God hath spoken to us by his Son; God hath shined upon us in his Son. The whole work of Almighty God, in the Conversion of man, is many times expressed by this act of shining; an effectual, a powerful shining. [x]The infusion of the Holy Ghost into the Apostles at Pentecost, was with fire: [y]The light which shined upon St. *Paul*, going to *Damascus*, struck him to the ground. And in both those cases, there were tongues too. The Apostles fire, was fiery tongues, and St. *Pauls* light, was accompanied with a voice; for then does God truely shine to us, when he appears to our eyes and to our ears, when by visible and audible means, by Sacraments which we see, and by the Word which we heare, he conveys himself unto us. In *Pauls* case, there were some that saw the light, but heard not the voice: God hath joyned them, separate them not: Upon him that will come to hear, and will not come to see; will come to the *Sermon*, but not to the *Sacrament*; or that will come to see, but will not come to hear; will keep his solemn, and festival, and Anniversary times of receiving the *Sacrament*, but never care for being instructed in the duties appertaining to that high Mystery, God hath not shined. They are a powerful thunder, and lightning, that go together: Preaching is the thunder, that clears the air, disperses all clouds of ignorance; and then the *Sacrament* is the lightning, the glorious light, and presence of Christ Jesus himself. And in the having and loving of these, the *Word* and *Sacraments*, the outward means of salvation, ordained by God in his Church, consists this Irradiation, this Coruscation, this shining. (*1622*) 4:104–5

ii. Preaching and Calling (Ps. 34:11)

What name soever we took in our *baptisme*, and contract between God and us, that name, in which we come to you, is *that, The Ministers of Christ, The Stewards of the Mysteries of God, And so let men ac-*

w. Tertul.
x. Act. 2:3.
y. Act. 9:3.

count of us, says the Apostle. *Invention*, and *Disposition*, and *Art*, and *Eloquence*, and *Expression*, and *Elocution*, and *reading*, and *writing*, and *printing*, are secondary things, accessory things, auxiliary, subsidiary things; men may account us, and make account of us, as of *Orators* in the pulpit, and of *Authors*, in the shop; but if they account of us as *of Ministers and Stewards*, they give us our due; that's our name to you. All the Evangelists mention *John Baptist* and his *preaching*; but two of the foure say never a word of his *austerity of life*, his *Locusts*, nor his *Camels haire*; and those two that do, *Matthew* and *Marke*, they insist, *first*, upon his *calling*, *then* upon his *actuall preaching*, how he pursued that Calling, And *then* upon the *Doctrine* that he preached, *Repentance*, and *Sanctification*, and *after that*, they come to these secondary and subsidiary things, which added to his estimation, and assisted the passage of his Doctrine, His good life. Learning, and other good parts, and an exemplar life fall into second places; They have a first place, in *their* consideration who are to call them, but in *you*, to whom they are sent, but a second; fixe you, in the first place, upon the *Calling*. [z]Calling circumcised *Moses* uncircumcised lips; This made *Jeremy* able to speak, though he called himself a childe; This is *Esays coale from the Altar, which takes away even his sinne, and his iniquity*. Be therefore content to passe over some infirmities, and rest your selves upon the *Calling*. And when you have thus taken the simplicity of *Children*, (they are the *persons*, which was our first step) and are *come* to the *Congregation*, (that is your *Action*, and was our second) and have conformed your selves to *hearken*, (that also is the *Disposition* here, which was our third) And all this with a reverence to the *Calling* before an affection to the *man*, (that is your submission to Gods Ordinance, and was our fourth and last step) you have then built up our first part in your selves, and laid together all those peeces which constitute *your Duty, Come ye Children, and hearken unto me*. (*1624*) 6:103–4

iii. Vocatio Radicalis *(2 Cor. 4:6)*

If we take Gods Word into our mouths, and pretend a Commission, a Calling, for the calling of others, we must be sure that God hath shined in our hearts. There is *vocatio intentionalis*, an intentional Calling, when Parents, in their intention and purpose, dedicate their children to this service of God, the Ministry, even in their Cradle. And this is a good and holy intention, because though it bind not in the nature of a Vow, yet it makes them all the way more careful, to give them such an Education, as may fit them for that profession. And

z. Exod. 6:12. Jer. 1:6. Esa. 6:6.

then there is *Vocatio Virtualis*, when having assented to that purpose of my Parents, I receive that publick Seal, the Imposition of hands, in the Church of God: But it is *Vocatio radicalis*, the calling that is the root and foundation of all, that we have this light shining in our hearts, the testimony of Gods Spirit to our spirit, that we have this calling from above. First then, it must be a light; not a calling taken out of the darkness of melancholy, or darkness of discontent, or darkness of want and poverty, or darkness of a retired life, to avoid the mutual duties and offices of society: it must be a light, and a light that shines; it is not enough to have knowledge and learning; it must shine out, and appear in preaching; and it must shine in our hearts, in the private testimony of the Spirit there: but when it hath so shined there, it must not go out there, but shine still as a Candle in a Candlestick, or the Sun in his sphere; shine so, as it give light to others: so that this light doth not shine in our hearts, except it appear in the tongue, and in the hand too. (*1622*) 4:109

iv. The Dynamics of Preaching (Ps. 34:11)

To every Minister and Dispenser of the word of God, and to every Congregation belong these words; And therefore we will divide the Text between us; To you one, to us appertains the other part. You must *come*, and you must *hearken*; we must *teach*, and teach to *edification*; There is the *Meum et Tuum*, your part, and our part. From each Part, these branches flow out naturally; In yours, first, the *capacity, as children*; Then the *action*, you *Come*; Then your *Disposition* here, you *hearken*; And lastly, your *submission* to Gods Ordinance, you *hearken* even *unto me*, unto *any* Minister of *his* sending. In our Part, there is first a *Teaching*; for, else, why should you *come* or *hearken unto me*, or *any*? It is a *Teaching*, it is not onely a *Praying*; And then, there is a *Catholique* doctrine, a *circular* doctrine, that walks the round,[5] and goes the *compasse* of our whole lives, from our first, to our *last childhood*, when *age* hath made us children again, and it is the *Art of Arts*, the root, and fruit of all true wisdome, *The true feare of the Lord. Come ye children, hearken unto mee, and I will teach you the feare of the Lord*. (*1624*) 6:95–96

v. Preaching and the Civil War of Self (Judges 5:20)

Every man is a little world, sayes the *Philosopher*; Every man is a little *Church* too; and in every man, there are two sides, two armies: the flesh fights against the Spirit. This is but a *Civill warre*, nay it is

5. A round is a watch under the command of an officer, who circles or goes around a camp, a fortress, etc., to see that the sentinels are vigilant.

but a *Rebellion* indeed; and yet it can never be absolutely quenched. So every Man is also a Souldier in that great and generall warre, between *Christ*, and *Beliall*, the Word of *God*, and the will of man. Every man is bound to hearken to a peace, in such things as may admit peace, in differences, where men differ from men; but bound also to shut himselfe up against all overtures of peace, in such things, as are in their Nature irreconcileable, in differences where men differ from *God*. That warre *God* hath kindled, and that warre must bee maintained, and maintained by his way; and his way, and his *Ordinance* in this warre, is Preaching.

If *God* had not said to *Noah*, *Fac tibi Arcam*; and when he had said so, if he had not given him a *Deseigne*, a *Modell*, a *Platforme* of that *Arke*, we may doubt credibly, whether ever man would have thought of a *Ship*, or of any such way of trade and Commerce. Shipping was Gods owne Invention, and therein *Laetentur Insulae*, as *David* sayes, *Let the Ilands rejoyce*. So also, if *Christ* had not said to his *Apostles*, *Ite praedicate, Goe and preach*: And when hee had said so, said thus much more, *Qui non crediderit damnabitur, Hee that beleeves not your Preaching shall bee damned*: certainly man would never have thought of such a way of establishing a kingdome, as by Preaching. No other Nation had any such Institution, as Preaching. In the *Romane* State, there was a publique Officer, *Conditor Precum*, who upon great emergent occasions, deprecations of imminent dangers, or Gratulations for evident benefites, did make particular *Collects* answerable to those occasions: And as some such occasionall *Panegyriques*, and gratulatory Orations for temporall benefites, they had in that state. But a fixt and constant course of conteyning Subjects in the Religious and Civill duties, by preaching, onely *God* ordained, onely his Children enjoyed. Christ when he sent his *Apostles*, did not give them a particular command, *Ite orate*, goe and pray in the publique Congregation; All Nations were accustomed to that; Christ made no doubt of any mans opposing, or questioning Publique Prayer; and therefore for that, he onely said, *Sic orabitis*, Not go, and pray, but, *when you pray, pray thus*, he instructed them in the forme; the dutie was well knowne to all before. But, for Preaching, He himselfe was anointed for that, [a]*The Spirit of the Lord is upon me, because the Lord hath anointed mee to preach:* His unction was his function. Hee was anointed with that power, and hee hath anointed us with part of his owne unction: [b]*All power is given unto me*, sayes he, *in Heaven and in Earth*; and therefore (as he adds there) *Go ye, and preach*: Because I have all power, for preaching, take yee part of my power, and preach too. For, Preaching

a. Esa. 61:1.   *b*. Math. 28:[18,] 19.

is *the power of God unto Salvation, and savour of life unto life.* When therefore the *Apostle* saies, [c]*Quench not the Spirit, Nec in te, nec in alio,* sayes *Aquinas;* Quench it not in your selfe, by forbearing to heare the Word preached, quench it not in others, by discouraging them that doe preach. For so Saint *Chrysostome,* (and not he alone) understood that place, *That they quench the spirit, who discountenance preaching, and dishearten Preachers.* St. *Chrysostome* tooke his example from the *Lampe* that burnt by him, when hee was preaching; (It seemes therefore hee did preach in the afternoone) and he sayes, *you may quench this Lampe, by putting in water, and you may quench it by taking out the oyle.* So a Man may quench the spirit in himselfe, if hee smother it, suffocate it, with worldly pleasures, or profits, and he may quench it in others, if he withdraw that favour, or that helpe, which keepes that Man, who hath the spirit of Prophesie, the unction of Preaching,[6] in a cheerefull discharge of his duty. Preaching then being *Gods Ordinance,*[7] to beget Faith, to take away preaching, were to disarme *God,* and to quench the spirit; for by that *Ordinance, he fights from heaven.* (*1622*) 4:194–95

vi. Show vs. Sermon (Ps. 90:14)

And therefore, beloved, as they, whom lighter affections carry to Shewes, and Masks, and Comedies; As you your selves, whom better dispositions bring to these Exercises, conceive some contentment, and some kinde of Joy, in that you are well and commodiously placed, they to see the Shew, you to heare the Sermon, when the time comes, though your greater Joy bee reserved to the comming of that time; So though the fulnesse of Joy be reserved to the last times in heaven, yet rejoyce and be glad that you are well and commodiously placed in the meane time, and that you sit but in expectation of the fulnesse of those future Joyes: Returne to God, with a joyfuyll thankfulnesse that he hath placed you in a Church, which withholds nothing from you, that is necessary to salvation, whereas in another Church they lack a great part of the Words, and halfe the Sacrament; And which obtrudes nothing to you, that is not necessary to salvation, whereas in another Church, the Additionall things exceed the Fundamentall; the Occa-

6. The "unction of Preaching" refers to spiritual feeling manifested in speech. See 1 John 2:20 and the medieval hymn "Veni Creator Spiritus" ("Come Holy Ghost, our soules inspire . . . Thy blessed unction from above / Is comfort, life, and fire of love").

7. Donne uses a metaphor of war, with ordinance indicating the arrangement of forces into ranks, as for a battle, as well as the orderly disposition of things, as the parts of a sermon.

c. 1. Thess. 5:19.

sionall, the Originall; the Collaterall, the Direct; And the Traditions of men, the Commandements of God. Maintaine and hold up this holy alacrity, this religious cheerfulnesse; For inordinate sadnesse is a great degree and evidence of unthankfulnese, and the departing from Joy in this world, is a departing with one piece of our Evidence, for the Joyes of the world to come. (*1621–1622?*) 5:294–95

vii. Variety of the Sermon (Isa. 32:8)

When Christians gathered themselves with more freedome, and Churches were established with more liberty, Preaching prevailed; And there is no exercise, that is denoted by so many names, as Preaching. *Origen* began; for, (I thinke) we have no Sermons, till *Origens*. And though hee began early, (early, if wee consider the age of the Church, (a thousand foure hundred yeares since) and early, if wee consider his owne age, for, *Origen* preached by the commandement, and in the presence of Bishops, before he was a Churchman) yet he suffered no Sermons of his to be copied, till he was sixty yeares old. Now, *Origen* called his Homilies; and the first *Gregory*, of the same time with *Origen*, that was Bishop of Neocesaria, hath his called Sermons. And so names multiplied; Homilies, Sermons, Conciones, Lectures, S. *Augustins* Enarrations, *Dictiones*, that is, Speeches, *Damascens* and *Cyrils* Orations (nay, one exercise of *Caesareus*, conveied in the forme of a Dialogue) were all Sermons. (*1628*) 8:237–38

viii. In City and in Country (Acts 1:8)

Preachers that binde themselves alwaies to *Cities* and *Courts*, and *great Auditories*, may learne new Notes; they may become *occasionall* Preachers, and make the emergent affaires of the time, their *Text*, and the humours of the hearers their *Bible*; but they may loose their Naturall Notes, both the *simplicitie*, and the *boldnesse* that belongs to the Preaching of the *Gospell*: both their power upon lowe understandings to raise them, and upon high affections to humble them. They may thinke that their errand is but to knocke at the doore, to delight the eare, and not to search the House, to ransacke the conscience. *Christ* left the *Ninetie and nine* for one Sheepe; populous *Cities* are for the most part best provided; remoter parts need our labour more, and should not make such differences. *Yeoman*, and *Labourer*, and *Spinster*, are distinctions upon Earth; in the Earth, in the grave there is no distinction. The *Angell* that shall call us out of that dust, will not stand to survay, who lyes naked, who in a Coffin, who in Wood, who in Lead, who in a fine, who in a courser Sheet; In that one day of the Resurrection, there is not a forenoone for Lords to rise first, and an afternoone for meaner persons to rise after. *Christ* was not whipped to save Beggars, and crowned with Thornes to save Kings: he dyed, he suffered all, for all; and we whose bearing witnesse of him, is to doe, as hee did, must conferre our labours upon all, upon *Jerusalem*, and upon *Judaea* too, upon the *Citie*, and upon the *Country* too. You, who are his witnesses too, must doe so too; preach in your just actions, as to the *Citie*, to the *Countrey* too. (*1622*) 4:276–77

ix. Sermons and Lectures (Matt. 22:30)

Of all Commmentaries upon the Scriptures, *Good Examples* are the best and the livelyest; and of all Examples those that are nearest, and most present, and most familiar unto us; and our most familiar Examples, are those of our owne families; and in families, the Masters of families, the fathers of families, are most conspicuous, most appliable, most considerable. Now, in exercises upon such occasions as this, ordinarily, the instruction is to bee directed especially upon those persons, who especially give the occasion of the exercise; that is, upon the persons to bee united in holy wedlock: or, as that's a difference between *Sermons* and *Lectures*, that a Sermon intends *Exhortation* principally and *Edification*, and a holy stirring of religious affections, and then *matters of Doctrine*, and points of *Divinity*, occasionally, secondarily, as the words of the text may invite them; But *Lectures* intend principally *Doctrinall points*, and matter of *Divinity*, and matter of *Exhortation* but *occasionally*, and as in a *second* place: so that's a difference between *Christening sermons*, and *Mariage sermons*, that the first, at Christnings, are especially directed upon the *Congregation*, and not upon the persons who are to be christened; and these, at mariages, especially upon the *parties* that are to be united; and upon the congregation, but by reflexion. (*1627*) 8:95

4. Preacher

i. Life as a Sermon (2 Cor. 4:6)

Vehementer destruit Ecclesiam Dei, laicos esse meliores Clericis: Nothing shakes the Church more, then when Church-men are no better then other men are. Where we read in *Genesis*, [d]*Vox sanguinis, The voice of* Abel's *blood calls*; it is in the Original, *Vox sanguinum*, of bloods, in the plurall; many bloods, much blood: the blood of a whole Parish, of a whole Province, cries out against the life of such a man: for his Sermons are but his Texts; his life is his Sermon that preaches; *Aaron* and *Moses* were joyned in Commission; *Aaron* had the tongue,

d. 4:10.

the power of speaking; *Moses* had the Rod, the power of doing great works. [e]When the *Lystrians* called *Paul, Mercury,* for his Eloquence, they called his Companion *Barnabas, Jupiter*; their eye was upon their great work as well as their sweet words. Clearly and ingenuously, we, we the Ministers of the Gospel, acknowledge our selves to be principally intended by the Apostle in this Text; this light, that is the knowledge, and the love of Gods truth, must shine in our hearts, sincerely there; and in our tongues, assiduously there; and in our hands, evidently there; and so we are the persons; but yet not we alone, though the Apostle express it in that phrase, *in Cordibus nostris.*
(*1622*) 4:112

ii. Wings of the Eagle (Rev. 4:8)

Now besides these generall qualifications, laid downe as the foundation of the text, in the verse before it, in the text it selfe these foure Creatures, being first the foure Evangelists, and consequently, or by a just and faire accommodation, all the Preachers of the Gospell, which limit themselves in the doctrine laid downe in the foure Evangelists, have also *wings* added unto them; Wings, first for their owne behoofe and benefit, and then, wings for the benefit and behoofe of others. They have wings to raise themselves from the earth; that they doe not entangle themselves in the businesses of this World; but still to keepe themselves upon the wing, in a Heavenly conversation, ever remembring that they have another Element, then Sea or Land, as men whom Christ Jesus hath set apart, and in some measure made mediatours betweene him, and other men, as his instruments of their salvation. And then as for themselves, so have they wings for others too, that they may be alwaies ready to succour all, in all their spirituall necessities. For as those words are well understood by many of the Ancients, [f]*To the Woman were given two wings of an Eagle,* that is, to the Church were given able and sufficient Ministers, to carry and convey her over the Nations: So are those words which are spoken of God himself, appliable to his Ministers, that first, [g]*The Eagle stirreth up her nest,* The Preacher stirres and moves, and agitates the holy affections of the Congregation, that they slumber not in a senselesnesse of that which is said, *The Eagle stirreth up her nest,* and then as it is added there, *She fluttereth over her young*; The Preacher makes a holy noise in the conscience of the Congregation, and when hee hath awakened them, by stirring the nest, hee casts some claps of thunder, some intimidations, in denouncing the judgements of God, and he flings open

e. Act. 14:12.
f. Revel. 12:14.
g. Deut. 32:11.

the gates of Heaven, that they may heare, and look up, and see a man sent by God, with power to infuse his feare upon them; *So she fluttereth over her young*; but then, as it followes there, *She spreadeth abroad her wings*; she over-shadowes them, she enwraps them, she armes them with her wings, so as that no other terror, no other fluttering but that which comes from her, can come upon them; The Preacher doth so infuse the feare of God into his Auditory, that first, they shall feare nothing but God, and then they shall feare God, but so, as he is God; and God is Mercy; God is Love; and his Minister shall so spread his wings over his people, as to defend them from all inordinate feare, from all suspition and jealousie, from all diffidence and distrust in the mercie of God; which is farther exprest in that clause, which followes in the same place, *She taketh them and beareth them upon her wings*; when the Minister hath awakened his flocke by the stirring of the nest, and put them in this holy feare, by this which the Holy Ghost cals a Fluttering; and then provided, by spreading his wings, that upon this feare there follow not a desperation; then he sets them upon the top of his best wings, and shewes them the best treasure that is committed to his Stewardship, hee shewes them Heaven, and God in Heaven, sanctifying all their crosses in this World, inanimating all their worldly blessings, rayning downe his blood into their emptinesse, and his balme into their wounds, making their bed in all their sicknesse, and preparing their seate, where he stands soliciting their cause, at the right hand of his Father. And so the Minister hath the wings of an Eagle, that every soule in the Congregation may see as much as hee sees, that is, a particular interest in all the mercies of God, and the merits of Christ.

So then, these Ministers of God have that double use of their Eagles wings; first, [h]*Ut volent ad escam*, (as it is in *Job*) that they may flie up to receive their own food, their instructions at the mouth and word of God; And then, [i]*Ut ubi cadaver sit, ibi statim adsit*, (as it is in *Job* also) where the dead are, they also may be; That where any lie, [j]*Pro mortuis*, (as S. *Paul* speaks) *for dead*, as good as dead, ready to die, upon their death-bed, they may be ready to assist them, and to minister spirituall Physick, opportunely, seasonably, proportionably to their spirituall necessities. (*1627*) 8:43–45

iii. No Plaudite *(2 Cor. 5:20)*

When we consider the manner of hearing Sermons, in the Primitive Church, though we doe not wish that manner to be renewed, yet we

h. Job 9:26.
i. Job 39:30.
j. 1. Cor. 15:29.

cannot deny, but that though it were accompanied with many inconveniences, it testified a vehement devotion, and sense of that that was said, by the preacher, in the hearer; for, all that had been formerly used in Theatres, *Acclamations* and *Plaudites*, was brought into the *Church*, and not onely the vulgar people, but learned hearers were as loud, and as profuse in those declarations, those vocall acclamations, and those plaudites in the passages, and transitions, in Sermons, as ever they had been at the Stage, or other recitations *of their Poets, or Orators*. S. *Hierom* charges *Vigilantius*, that howsoever he differed from him in opinion after, yet when he had heard him preach of the Resurrection before, he had received that Doctrine with Acclamation and *Plaudites*. And as Saint *Hierome* saith of himselfe, that he was thus applauded in his Preaching; he saith it also of him whom he called his Master, *Gregory Nazianzen*, a grave and yet a facetious man, of him he telleth us this Story; That he having intreated *Nazianzen*, to tell him the meaning of that place, [k] *What that second Sabbath after the first was?* he played with me, he jested at me, saith he, *Eleganter lusit*, and he bad me be at Church next time he preached, and he would preach upon that Text, *Et toto acclamante populo, cogeris invitus scire quod nescis*, and when you see all the Congregation applaud me, and cry out that they are satisfied, you will make your self beleeve you understand the place, as they doe, though you doe not; *Et si solus tacueris, solus ab omnibus stultitiae condemnaberis*, And if you doe not joyne with the Congregation in those *Plaudites*, the whole Congregation will thinke you the onely ignorant person in the Congregation; for, as we may see in Saint *Augustin*, the manner was, that when the people were satisfied in any point which the Preacher handled, they would almost tell him so, by an acclamation, and give him leave to passe to another point; for, so saith that Father, *Vidi in voce intelligentes, plures video in silentio requirentes*, I heare many, to whom, by this acclamation, I see, enough hath been said, but I see more that are silent, and therefore, for their sakes, I will say more of it. Saint *Augustine* accepted these acclamations more willingly, at least more patiently, then some of the Fathers before had done; *Audistis, laudastis; Deo gratias;* you have heard that that hath been said, and you have approved it with your praise; God be thanked for both; *Et laudes vestrae folia sunt arborum, sed fructus quaero;* Though I looke for fruit from you, yet even these acclamations are Leafes, and Leafes are Evidences that the tree is alive. Saint *Chrysostome* was more impatient of them, yet could never overcome them. To him, they came a little

k. Luc. 6:1.

closer; for it was ordinary, that when he began to speake, the people would cry out, *Audiamus tertiumdecimum Apostolum*; Let us hearken to the thirteenth Apostle. And he saith, [l] *Si placet, hanc nunc legem firmabimus*, I pray let us now establish this for a Law, between you and mee, *Ne quis auditor plaudat, quamdiu nos loquimur*; That whilest I am speaking, I may heare no *Plaudite*; yet he saith in a Sermon preached after this, *Animo cogitavi Legem ponere*, I have often purposed to establish such a Law, [m] *Ut decore, et cum silentio audiatis*, that you would be pleased to heare with silence, but he could never prevail. (*after 1625?*) 10:132–33

iv. The Honey and the Honeycomb (Prov. 14:31)

[n] *Eloquia Domini, eloquia casta*, saith *David, The words of the Lord are chaste words, sincere, pure words*, no drosse, no profanenesse, no such allay mingled with them; for, as it followeth there, *They are as silver tried and purified seaven times in the fire*. They are as *that silver*, that is so tried, and they are as *that fire* that trieth it. It is *Castum*, a *Pure* Word in it self, and then it is *powerfull* upon the Hearer too; *Ignitum Eloquium tuum vehementer*, saith he, Thy word hath the vehement operation of fire; and [o] *therefore, thy servant loveth it well*, as it followeth there; Therefore, because it *pierces*; But therefore especially, because it carrieth a *sweetnesse* with it. For, the *sting of the Serpent* pierces, and the *toothe of the Viper* pierces, but they carry *venenosam salivam*, a venimous and mischievous liquor with them. But [p] *Dulcia faucibus super Mel, Thy words are sweeter to my mouth, then Hony*; then Hony it selfe. For, [q] *verba composita*, saith *Solomon*, chosen words, *studied*, premeditated words, *pleasing* words, (so we translate it) are *as a Hony-combe*. Now, in the Hony-combe, the Hony is collected and gathered, and dispensed, and distributed from the Hony-combe, And of this Hony-combe is wax, wax apt for *sealing*, derived too. The distribution of this Hony to the Congregation, The sealing of this Hony to the Conscience, is in the *outward Ordinance of God*, and in the labour of the *Minister*, and his conscionable fitting of himselfe for so great a service. But the *Hony-Combe* is not the *Hony*, The gifts of the man, is not the Holy Ghost.

. . . .

It becommeth me to make my selfe as acceptable a messenger as I can, and to infuse the Word of God into you, as powerfully as I can, but all that I can doe, is but a small matter, the greatnesse of the worke lieth in your Application, and that must proceed from the

l. Hom. 30 in Act.
m. Hom. 31.
n. Psal. 12:6.
o. Psal. 119:140.
p. 103.
q. Prov. 16:24.

Word of God it selfe, quickned by his Spirit, and therefore *Ascribe all Greatnesse unto our God*, for that is the Hony, whatsoever, or whosoever be the Hony-combe. Truely, when I reade a Sermon of *Chrysostome*, or of *Chrysologus*, or of *Ambrose*, Men, who carry in the very signfication of their *Names*, and in their *Histories*, the attributes of *Hony-mouthed* and *Golden-mouthed Men*, I finde my selfe oftentimes, more affected, with the very Citation, and Application of *some sentence of Scripture*, in the middest or end of one of their Sermons, then with any witty, or forcible passage of their owne. (*1628*) 8:271–73

v. The Garment of Style (Ezek. 34:19)

Tertullian in his Book *De habitu muliebri*, notes two excesses in womens dressing; One he cals *Ornatum*, the other *cultum*; One *mundum muliebrem*, the other, (according to the liberty that he takes in making words) *Immundum muliebrem*; the first is a *superfluous diligence* in their dressing, but the other an *unnaturall addition* to their complexion; the first he pronounces to be always *ad ambitionem*, for *pride*, but the other, *ad prostitutionem*, for a worse, for the worst purpose. These two sorts of Excesses doe note these two kindes of treading down the grasse, which we intend; of which one is, the mingling of too much *humane ornament*, and secular *learning* in *preaching*, in presenting the word of God, which word is our grasse; The other is of mingling *humane Traditions*, as of things of equall value, and obligation, with the Commandements of God. For the first, *humane ornament*, if in those pastures, which are ordained for sheep, you either plant rare and curious flowers, delightfull onely to the eye, or fragrant and odoriferous hearbs delightfull onely to the smell, nay, be they medicinall hearbs, usefull, and behovefull for the preservation, and restitution of the health of man, yet if these specious and glorious flowers, and fragrant, and medicinall hearbs, be not proper nourishment for sheep, this is a *treading down* of the grasse, a pestering and a suppressing of that which appertained to them. So if in your spirituall food, our preaching of the Word, you exact of us more secular ornament, then may serve, as *Saint Augustine* says, *Ad ancillationem*, to convey, and usher the true word of life into your *understandings*, and *affections*, (for both those must necessarily be wrought upon) more then may serve *ad vehiculum*, for a chariot for the word of God to enter, and triumph in you, this is *a treading down of the grasse*, a filling of that ground which was ordained for sheep, with things improper, and impertinent to them. If you furnish a *Gallery* with stuffe proper for a Gallery, with *Hangings* and *Chairs*, and *Couches*, and *Pictures*, it gives you all the conveniences of a Gallery, walks and prospect, and ease; but if you pester it with improper and impertinent furniture, with *Beds*, and *Tables*, you lose the use, and name of a *Gallery*, and you have made it a *Wardrobe*; so if your curiosity extort more then convenient ornament, in delivery of the word of God, you may have a good *Oration*, a good *Panegyrique*, a good *Encomiastique*, but not so good a *Sermon*. It is true that Saint *Paul* applies sentences of secular Authors, even in matters of greatest importance; but then it is to persons that were accustomed to those authors, and affected with them, and not conversant, not acquainted at all, with the phrase and language of Scripture: amongst us now, almost every man (God be blessed for it) is so accustomed to the text of Scripture, as that he is more affected with the name of *David*, or Saint *Paul*, then with any *Seneca* or *Plutarch*. I am far from forbidding secular ornament in divine *exercises*, especially in some *Auditories*, acquainted with such learnings. I have heard men preach against witty preaching; and doe it with as much wit, as they have; and against learned preaching, with as much learning, as they could compasse. If you should place that *beast*, which makes the *Bezoar stone*,[8] in a pasture of pure, but onely grasse, it is likely, that out of his naturall faculty, he would petrifie the juyce of that grasse, and make it a stone, but not such a medicinall stone, as he makes out of those herbes which he feeds upon. Let all things concur in the name of God, to the advancing of his purpose, in his ordinance, which is, to make his will *acceptable* to you, by his word; onely avoid excesse in the manner of doing it. Saint *Augustines* is an excellent rule, when after in his book *De Doctrina Christiana*, he had taught a use of all Arts in Divinity, he allows them onely thus far, *ut cum ingenia his reddantur exercitatiora, cavendum ne reddantur maligniora*, that when a man by these helps is the more ful, and the more ready and the more able for Church-service, he be not also thereby made the more bold and the more confident; *Nec ament decipere verisimili sermone*, lest because he is able to make any thing seem probable and likely to the people, by his eloquence, he come to infuse paradoxicall opinions, or schismaticall, or (which may be beleeved either way) problematicall opinions, for certain and constant truths, and so be the lesse conversant, and the lesse diligent in advancing plaine, and simple, and fundamentall doctrines and catechisticall, which are truely necessary to salvation, as though such plaine, and ordinary, and catechisticall doctrines were not worthy of his gifts and his great parts. (*1625?*) 10:146–48

8. A calculus or concretion found in the stomach or intestines of some animals, chiefly ruminants, formed of layers of animal matter deposited round some foreign substance. (OED)

Glossary

Words appear in alphabetical order, in lower case except for proper nouns. They are given in the first or most common form in which they occur, definitions being those of the *Oxford English Dictionary*.

abastardise. To render bastard, that is, to debase.
abortion. A coming to nothing.
acceptation. Acceptance.
accessary. Accessory, additional to.
affections. Feelings, emotions.
aggravating. Increasing the burden or load; aggravated, that is, made worse or more burdensome.
aliens (verb). Alienates.
anatomist. One who anatomizes, dissects, as a physician; used figuratively of anyone who is skilled in dissection.
anhelation. Difficulty with breathing; panting.
appertaines. Belonging, appropriate or proper to.
appliable(ness). Well-disposed(ness).
apprehends and reprehends. Understands and reproves.
apt. Appropriate.
artificial. Scholarly, that is, having reasonableness and intellectual merit.
asseveration. A solemn affirmation.
avow. To own or acknowledge (a person) as one's own.

bendes. To direct oneself towards an end.
bestiall. Brutish, barbarous.
bravery. Daring.
bullion. Raw metal, especially gold or silver in the lump.
bundle. A gathering, an amount (of something).
byasse. "To clap on a byass," or suddenly force an inclination toward something.

callings. Summons, as in a divine calling or vocation.
casuist. One who studies cases of moral conscience.
catechistical. Referring to the catechism, or a question and answer form for Christian instruction, denoted by versicle (V/) and response (R/); denoting also a person who teaches by means of the catechism.
character. "To give a character," that is, to describe a person's qualities.
Chimera. A mere wild fancy; from the Greek monster, slain by Bellerophon, with a lion's head, a goat's body, and a serpent's tail.
citation. Citing, calling up, summonsing.
clamber(-ing). Climb(-ing) with difficulty; to struggle to rise.
classis. A division according to rank.
cleane. Completely.

clout(s). Clot of earth, clod; cf. "clouds," with which the word is associated, in the general sense of "darkening with trouble."
coaction. A coercive action or force.
collaterall. Parallel.
collation. Comparison with other parts (of the text).
collection. Coming together, gathering.
colluctation. A wrestling or struggling together; a conflict.
commonefaction. An admonition, warning.
compasse. To close round, encircle, circumscribe.
compellation. Style of address, an appellation or name.
complacency. Pleasure, contentment.
complements. That is, compliments.
complexion. Mental temperament, as opposed to bodily constitution.
comprehend(ed). Embraced or described inclusively; understood, opposed to incomprehensibleness.
computatis computandis. A reckoning of what is owed.
concurrence. A running together.
concentred. Directed towards a common center.
concinnity. A harmony; a skilful fitting together of parts.
concision. In Phil. 3:2, from Greek κατατομή "cutting up," applied to the Judaizing Christians (OED). See Chap. 1, selection A.8.
concoction. A mixture of ingredients, as (figuratively) of ideas.
concupiscences. Desire(s) for the things of the world.
condition (verb). To place (something) as a stipulation.
conferences. Conversations, especially of a serious and formally organized kind.
consanguinity. Blood-relationship.
conscionable. Conscientious.
contemn(ed). To view with contempt or consider of small value; to despise, scorn.
continency. Self-restraint, especially in sexual matters.
contumelies. Reproaches, despite.
contumelious. Despiteful, superciliously insolent.
conversation. a. Sexual intimacy; b. social familiarity.
convertits. Professed converts to religion.
coveraling. Donne's coinage, based evidently on "overall," to cover every part.
cordials. Medicines which invigorate the heart and stimulate the circulation.
corrasives. Variant of corrosives, a substance that eats away or consumes, as an acid or a drug.
coruscation. A sparkling or quivering flash of light.
criticall. Fault finding, probably with the sense of fastidious or over discriminating.
crooken. To make, be, or become crooked.
Crucifiges. Latin, "Crucify Him!," the cry of the Jews to Pilate (Matt. 27:22), a term (now archaic) used to call for the death of a victim. Donne opposes it to *Hosannaes*, or shouts of praise (see Matt. 21:9).
crying (sins). See note 2, p. 71.
cure. Care, especially spiritual and pastoral.

curious frame. A skilful form (of words).
customary. Habitual.

damnification. The action of damnifying, injuring, or destroying.
dampe. As "a dampe," a depression or despondent state.
dangerously. Injuriously, with harmful effect.
debatement. Action of debating, strife.
declination. Declining, falling off.
deflectings. Things slightly turned from their natural course.
delating. Obsolete form of dilating, that is, enlarging, expanding.
demonstration. Referring to logical or deductive proofs.
deprecations. Prayers for the averting or removal of evil, etc.
deprehend. Capture, seize.
derogate. To take away (from) so as to lessen or impair.
design. Mark out, designate.
determinate. Determined, clearly defined.
determine (in). As intransitive verb, to have resolution of or conclusion in (something).
deviation. Divergence from (a righteous course).
diametrally. In the way of a diameter, diametrically; directly.
diffidence. Doubt.
diffusive. Dispersive.
dilatation. Expansion, dilation.
dilated. Explained at length.
dimensions. Measurable parts.
disconduce. To be non-conducive to (OED quotes Donne's usage).
discretive. Discriminating, ability to distinguish one thing from another.
dis-estimation. To hold in low esteem, despise.
distasted. Disgusted, offended.
distemper. Generally, ill health, disease, derangement, disorder.
distinct. Separated from others of its class by especially characteristic features.
distributive(ly). To deal out or bestow in individual portions.
downright. Thorough, absolute.
dress. To adorn, take care of.
drousiness. Dullness, lethargy.
ductile. Malleable, flexible.

ebullition. Sudden outburst, agitation.
effused. Poured out freely.
entendred. Made tender.
εὐλογία. A eulogy, implying a blessing.
evacuation. Depletion, emptying out (of spirit, energy, or life).
Evangelicall. Referring to the Gospels, "directed upon Christ."
erogations. Money expended.
erubescence. Erubescent state, that is, reddened or blushing.
exaltation . . . exultation. Ascension, lifting up . . . joyousness.
Exchange. A place or building where merchants gather for transacting business.
excremental. Of nails and hair, outgrowths of the body.

execrations. Curses.
exinanition. The action of emptying or exhausting; humiliation.
expansion. Space to which anything is extended; circumference.
exprobation. Reproach; the action of upbraiding.
expunction. Removal.
extasies . . . stupidities. Rapturous delight . . . dullness; that is, contrasting and equally invalid emotions.
extemporall. Unpremeditated, arising out of the immediate occasion.
extended. Of voice, continued or prolonged, as in the sustaining of a musical tone.

facetious. Witty, humorous.
facile. That which can be managed with little effort, easily moved.
false fires. A blank discharge of firearms, "without shot."
fashionall. Fashionable.
file(s). A rough metal instrument used for abrading, or smoothing out.
filiation. Descent from, the becoming, or the being, a son; implying sonship.
fold. Sheepfold; a place of warmth and comfort.
foment(s). To rouse, stir up, excite.
fomentations. Encouragements; specifically, cloths soaked in some medicinal substance which are then applied to the body.
free-hold, freehold. A tenure by which an estate or office is held for life.
froward. Refractory; inclined to go counter to what is expected.
furniture. That with which a place or person is provided; equipment, necessaries.
funerals. Funeral.
fusil. Fusile, capable of being melted.

gammut. Musical scale.
gratulatory. Congratulatory, or expressing praise.
graving. Engraving.
gremial. Of the bosom, intimate.
gripe. Grip, to grasp or seize firmly, in a fierce or rapacious way.

habit. Custom, use, or deportment.
habitude. Habit, that is, condition.
heaped. Piled up, accumulated.
heart. Figuratively, to signify love and affection.
herding (noun). The coming together as a herd of animals.
homely. Unpolished, rough.
Homoousion, Homoiousion. See note 6, p. 77.
honest. Of persons, honorable.

idiot. One whose reasoning is defective and permanently impaired, but not used here reproachfully.
idiotisme. The peculiar character of language, or (by transference) a peculiarity of action or manner.
illation. The action of drawing a conclusion from premises; a deduction or conclusion.
immarcessible. Unfading; imperishable.
impeccability. The quality of being impeccable, that is, not liable to sin.
impeccancy. Sinlessness.

imprecation. A curse, the invoking of evil on one. Cf. malediction.
impression. Used in the general sense of influence, but also with the technical significance of printing, that is, the publication of a book in any one edition, press run, or issue.
impropriation. The action of impropriating, that is, of annexing property, as an ecclesiastical benefice, or figuratively of making something one's own.
imputative. Characterized by being imputed; existing or arising by imputation, that is, by vicarious substitution.
inanimate (verb), inanimation (noun). To put life into; infusion of life or vitality.
inartificial. Natural, lacking in constructive or added skills.
inchoation, inchoative. Beginning, starting; incipient.
incomprehensible. That which cannot be contained or kept within limits; unintelligible, inconceivable.
inconsideration. Indiscretion; want of consideration.
inconstancy. Fickleness, changeableness.
increpation. Rebuke.
incurvation. The action of bending.
indevotions. Indevout feeling or action.
indifferent. Of an observance that may be equally well observed or neglected; non-essential; of appearance, neither good nor bad.
infectious, infection. Contagious, contaminating; referring specifically to the pestilence or plague.
ingeminate(s), ingemination. To emphasize by repetition.
integrity. Innocence, sinlessness; original perfect condition, wholeness.
intendment. That which is intended.
intepidate(s). To make tepid or lukewarm.
intermitted. Suspended, deprived of feeling. Cf. stupified.
invention(s). Devices or contrivings; discovery(-ies).
irradiations. Figuratively, a beaming forth of spiritual light.
irrefragable. Incontrovertible, inviolable.
irremediably. Irreparably.
irremissible. For or of which there can be no remission.
iterated. Repeated frequently.

Jod. Jot, referring to Greek *ἰῶτα*, "i," the smallest letter.

lead (noun). Lead-line, used for plumbing or sounding sea depth.
left-handed. Ill omened, of happiness that is false.
legitime. The portion of his movable estate to which children are entitled on the death of their father.
levity. a. Lightness; b. lack of seriousness.
liberality. Munificence.
lineament(s). Distinctive features, applied particularly to a human outline or form.
luted. Cemented or closed and sealed over with lute (that is, clay).

macerate. Of the mind, to be distressed; of the body, to be enervated, to waste or wear away, especially by fasting.
magazine. A storehouse.

malediction. The utterance of a curse.
matrice. Matrix or womb; a place in which something is bred.
melancholy. Personified, as "a melancholy," denoting a gloomy or depressed state.
meridionall. That is, southern, southerly, but also pertaining to the noontide position of the sun, when at its brightest and warmest.
mortifications. The practice of austere living; the regulated controlling of bodily desire.
motions. Inclinations.
myriades. Countless numbers.
mysterious. "Mysterious arts," that is, speech which is wrapt in mystery.
mystery. An obscurity of faith beyond human reason, but known by divine revelation, applied to the sacraments.

naturall (man). Without spiritual enlightenment; also, unaffected, unspoiled, as "naturall Idiot"; innate, as "Naturall Reason."

obduration. Obduracy, to be hardened and insensible of heart; obstinacy.
obscure. Literally, in darkness.
obtruded. Thrust forward forcibly or unduly.
ordinance. Practice, rule, or custom (of the Church); "ordnance," that is, artillery, as "his Ordinance in this warre."
ordinary. Customary.

parabolical. Pertaining to parable, having a figurative or non-literal sense.
parle. Parley, a conference called for by sounding a drum or trumpet.
particular. Individual, private.
parts. Capacities, abilities.
passible, passibility. Sufficient, sufficiency; *not* passable, that which is unable to be passed.
patefaction. The action of making open, visible, or known.
patheticall. Stirring of the emotions; moving, affecting.
penurious. In want, needy; meagre, parsimonious.
peregrination. Traveling, used also (as here) to denote the "journey" of life.
perspicacy. Alternative form of perspicacity; keenness of sight or understanding.
phantasie. Fantasy, the imagination.
physick. Medicine, or a course of medicine.
positive. Absolute, unconditional, not subject to alteration.
pregnant. Convincing, cogent.
preparatives. Medicines used to prepare the system for a course of treatment.
presentiall. Implying actual presence with a person.
pretended. Counterfeit, feigned.
preteritions. Omissions, the action of passing over.
pretermit(s). Omit mention of, as in a narrative.
prevaricate. To deviate, go astray.
prevent, preventing, prevention. To act in anticipation of or in preparation for a future event; to come before the time; said of God, or of His Grace, anticipating human action or need; preventing Grace predisposes the heart to seek God, thus anticipating other graces.
privative. Depriving, tending to take away, applied to loss or variation; expresses a negative quality.

progresse. A journey or expedition, especially by a royal personage; "progresse house," a temporary stopping place.
promoved. Promoted, advanced; provoked, incited.
proprietary. Proprietor.
protestation. A solemn affirmation or public assertion.

quarrell (intransitive verb). To find fault with, dispute.
quickning. An enlivening, a begetting; a becoming alive.

radicall. Root or basis.
rapture. Transport of mind, ecstasy.
ratiocination. A conclusion arrived at by reasoning.
recidivation. Relapse into sin or error.
recompact. To rejoin together.
rectified. Amended, set right (of one's conscience).
redintegration. Renewal, restoration.
religation. The action of tying or binding up.
reluctation. Opposition, reluctance (from the verb, reluct).
removes (noun). The act of removing a thing from one place to another.
reprehension. Reproof.
respiration. The act of breathing out.
roote. Basis of connection or union.
ruffle. To turn over the leaves (of a book) hurriedly.

sanation. Curative or healing force.
satyricall. Satirical; ridiculing a vice.
scantling. Measure or amount of a prescribed or appropriate size.
scattered. Disordered.
scedulously. Sedulously, diligently, assiduously.
screwed up (unto thee). Closed up and secured.
scruple, scruples. An uncertainty of the conscience; doubts, especially of an over-refined kind.
scurrile, scurril. Scurrilous (archaic).
servility. Mean submissiveness.
settles. To come to rest, to reside.
shrewd. Mischievous; "sportfull shrewd turne," a playful trick.
shutting up. Conclusion.
signification. Significance.
significative. Serving as a sign or indication of something.
silliness. Foolishness.
single. Only.
singular, singularity. Singleness, oneness; distinctiveness, individuality.
sodain. Hasty, impetuous.
solecism. A violation of the rules of grammar or syntax.
sophistry. The use of specious reasoning as a deliberate art.
sordid . . . barbarous . . . negligent. Mean or common . . . uncultured or rude . . . inattentive.
specious. Fair and pleasing, or fair-seeming.
stamp. The die by which a coin is made or "impressed," and so made "currant."
stationary hours. Fixed hours, applied to prayer.
statuaries. Those who make statues.
stewes. A brothel.

story. One level or floor of a building; Donne puns on the other sense, that is, a narrative.
stuff. a. Material for making garments; b. equipment, furnishings.
stupidities. See 'extasies.'
stupidity. A state of numbness, stupor; incapacity for understanding.
stupified, stupefied. To become stupid or torpid, insensible.
sub-obscurely. Donne's coinage: used to intensify "dimly," with which the word is coordinate.
substraction. Subtraction.
suffered. Endured, put up with.
sullen. Gloomy.
superedifications. Instruction of the highest kind.
supererogation. Doing more than one is expected, or that is needed.
supple. Pliant, flexible; as a verb, to soften or mollify.
suppled . . . matured . . . entendred. Softened . . . fully developed . . . made tender.
surfeit. An excessive indulgence in food or drink.
swimming. A state of giddiness.
syntaxis. The arrangement of words in a statement.

tentation. Temptation.
text hand. Referring to the fair handwriting of a professional copiest.
through. Variant of *thorough*.
title (to). A claim or right (to).
tractable. Easily managed.
transitory. Transient, but with the sense also of trifling, of little moment.
translated. Transformed.
transmigration. Passage from this life, by death, into another state.
tried. Tested and proved.
tumultuary. Disorderly, confused, tumultuous.
turne. Mischievous trick.
turned. Changed.
Tzebaoth. [The Lord God] of hosts.

unanime. Variant of unanimous.
undertakes. To receive or accept.

vae('s). Latin, alas! or woe!
viscerall. Of the bowels or viscera, the seat of emotion; touching deeply inward feelings.
vulgar. That is, the Vulgate Bible.
vulgarly. Commonly, regularly, that is, in ordinary usage.

washy. Weak, feeble.
whispering sin(s). See note 2, p. 71.
winding sheet. A sheet in which a corpse is wrapped for burial.
witty waggish thing. A clever practical joke.
worky-day. Workaday, workday, opposed to Sunday and holidays (=holydays).
wrangle. An empty dispute.

Biblical Texts

Chapter 1: The Speech of the Trinity

A. God's Creative Speaking

1. 2 Cor. 4:6. "For, God who commanded light to shine out of darkness, hath shined in our hearts, to give the light of the knowledge of the glory of God, in the face of Jesus Christ."

2. Isa. 50:1. "Thus sayeth the Lord: where is the bill of your mothers Divorcement whom I have put away? Or which of my creditors is it, to whom I have sold you? Behold, for your iniquities have you sold your selves, and for your transgressions, is your mother put away."

3. 2 Pet. 3:13. "Neverthelesse, we, according to his promises, looke for new heavens, and new earth, wherein dwelleth righteousnesse."

4. Judges 5:20. "They fought from heaven; the stars in their courses fought against Sisera."

5. Job 36:25. "Every man may see it, man may behold it afar off."

6. Job 36:25. See above.

7. Acts 9:4. "And he fell to the earth, and heard a voyce, saying, Saul, Saul, why persecutest thou me?"

8. Phil. 3:2. "Beware of the concision."

9. "Lord, who hath beleeved our report?" (Donne: "These words are written, in more then one, in more then two places of the Bible.")

B. God's Word: His Son

1. 1 Cor. 16:22. "If any man love not the Lord Jesus Christ, let him be Anathema, Maranatha."

2. Acts 7:60. "And when he said this, he fell asleep."

3. 1 John 5:7, 8. "For there are three which beare record in heaven; the Father, the Word, and the Holy Ghost; and these three are one: / And there are three which beare record in the earth; the spirit, and the water, and the bloud; and these three agree in one."

4. Mark 4:24. "Take heed what you heare."

5. 2 Cor. 1:3. "Blessed be God, even the Father of our Lord Jesus Christ, the Father of mercies, and the God of all comfort."

6. 1 Cor. 16:22. See B.1 above.

7. Lam. 4:20. "The breath of our nostrils, the anointed of the Lord, was taken in their pits."

8. James 2:12. "So speak ye, and so do, as they that shall be judged by the law of liberty."

9. Ps. 6:6, 7. "I am weary with my groaning; all the night make I my bed to swim, I water my couch with my teares. Mine eye is consumed because of griefe; it waxeth old, because of all mine enemies."

C. The Eloquence of the Holy Ghost

1. John 14:26. "But the Comforter, which is the Holy Ghost, whom the Father will send in my name, hee shall teach you all things, and bring all things to your remembrance, whatsoever I have said unto you."
2. Phil. 3:2. See A.8 above.
3. Prov. 14:31. "He that oppresseth the poore, reproacheth his maker, but he that honoureth him, hath mercy on the poore."
4. 1 Tim. 1:15. "This is a faithful saying, and worthy of all acceptation, that Christ Jesus came into the world to save sinners; of which I am the chiefest."
5. Ps. 90:14. "O satisfie us early with thy mercy, that we may rejoyce and be glad all our dayes."
6. Ps. 6:6, 7. See B.9 above.
7. 1 John 5:7, 8. See B.3 above.

D. The Showing Forth of the Word

1. Rev. 4:8. "And the foure beasts had each of them sixe wings about him, and they were full of eyes within; and they rest not day and night, saying, Holy, Holy, Holy, Lord God Almighty, which was, and is, and is to come."
2. Ps. 66:3. "Say unto God, how terrible art thou in thy works! Through the greatnesse of thy power shall thine enemies submit themselves unto thee."
3. Ps. 90:14. See C.5 above.
4. Ps. 65:5. "By terrible things in righteousnesse wilt thou answer us, O God of our salvation; who art the confidence of all the ends of the earth, and of them that are a far off, upon the sea."
5. Ps. 90:14. See C.5 above.
6. Ps. 66:3. See D.2 above.

Chapter 2: The Word Transcribed into Art

A. The Premises of Poetry

1. Gen. 1:26. "And God said, let us make man, in our image, after our likenesse."
2. 1 Tim. 1:15. "This is a faithful saying, and worthy of all acceptation, that Christ Jesus came into the world to save sinners; of which I am the chiefest."
3. James 2:12. "So speak ye, and so do, as they that shall be judged by the law of liberty."
4. Lam. 3:1. "I am the man, that hath seen affliction, by the rod of his wrath."
5. Ps. 32:5. "I acknowledged my sin unto thee, and mine iniquity have I not hid. I said, I will confesse my transgressions unto the Lord, and thou forgavest the iniquity of my sin."
6. 1 Pet. 1:17. "And if ye call on the Father, who without respect of persons judgeth according to every mans works, passe the time of your sojourning here in feare."
7. Job 13:15. "Loe, though he slay me, yet will I trust in him."

8. Ps. 68:20. "And unto God the Lord belong the issues of death."
9. 1 Cor. 12:3. "Also no man can say, that Jesus is the Lord, but by the Holy Ghost."

B. The Caveat: The Limitations and Dangers of Art

1. Matt. 12:31. "Wherefore I say unto you, all manner of sin and blasphemy shall be forgiven unto men; but the blasphemy against the Holy Ghost shall not be forgiven unto men."
2. Rom. 8:16. "The Spirit it selfe beareth witnesse with our spirit, that we are the children of God."
3. John 16:8, 9, 10, 11. "And when he is come, he will reprove the world of sin, and of righteousnesse, and of judgement. / Of sin, because ye beleeve not on me. / Of righteousnesse, because I goe to my father, and ye see me no more. / Of judgement, because the Prince of this world is judged."
4. Deut. 12:30. "Take heed to thy self, that thou be not snared by following them after they be destroyed from before thee; and that thou inquire not after their gods, saying, how did those nations serve their gods? Even so will I do likewise."

C. Possibilities, Style, and Form

1. Ezek. 33:32. "And lo, thou art unto them a very lovely song, of one that hath a very pleasant voyce, and can play well on an instrument; for they hear thy words, but they doe them not."
2. Micah 2:10. "Arise and depart, for this is not your rest."
3. Job 36:25. "Every man may see it, man may behold it afar off."
4. Gen. 32:10. "I am not worthy of the least of all thy mercies, and of all the truth which thou hast shewed unto thy servant; for with my staff I passed over this *Jordan* and now I am become two bands."
5. Ps. 32:6. "For this shall every one that is godly pray unto thee, in a time when thou mayest be found; surely in the floods of great waters they shall not come nigh unto him."
6. Luke 2:29, 30. "Lord now lettest thou thy servant depart in peace, according to thy word: for mine eyes have seen thy salvation."
7. Matt. 6:21. "For, where your treasure is, there will your heart be also."
8. Ps. 32:3, 4. "When I kept silence, my bones waxed old, through my roaring all the day long. / For day and night thy hand was heavy upon me; my moysture is turned into the drought of summer. Selah."
9. Ps. 6:2, 3. "Have mercy upon me, O Lord, for I am weake; O Lord, heale me, for my bones are vexed: my soule is also sore vexed; but thou, O Lord, how long?"
10. Ps. 6:8, 9, 10. "Depart from me, all ye workers of iniquitie; for the Lord hath heard the voyce of my weeping. / The Lord hath heard my supplication; the Lord will receive my prayer. / Let all mine enemies be ashamed and sore vexed: / Let them returne and be ashamed suddenly."

Chapter 3: Grammar and Theology

A. The Grammar of Devotion

1. 2 Cor. 1:3. "Blessed be God, even the Father of our Lord Jesus Christ, the Father of mercies, and the God of all comfort."
2. Ps. 55:19. "Because they have no charges, therefore they fear not God."
3. Ps. 32:8. "I will instruct thee, and teach thee in the way which thou shalt goe, I will guide thee with mine eye."
4. James 2:12. "So speak ye, and so do, as they that shall be judged by the law of liberty."

B. Salvation: Verb, Tense, Mood, Voice

1. Matt. 18:7. "Wo unto the world, because of offences."
2. Ps. 32:8. See A.3 above.
3. 1 Thess. 4:17. "Then we which are alive, and remain, shall be caught up together with them in the clouds, to meet the Lord in the ayre; and so shall we be ever with the Lord."
4. Job 19:26. "And though, after my skin, wormes destroy this body, yet in my flesh shall I see God."
5. Mark 16:16. "He that beleeveth not, shall be damned."
6. Matt. 12:31. "Wherefore I say unto you, all manner of sin and blasphemy shall be forgiven unto men; but the blasphemy against the Holy Ghost shall not be forgiven unto men."

C. Great Things of Small: Prepositions, Adverbs, Pronouns

1. Gen. 1:26. "And God said, let us make man, in our image, after our likenesse."
2. Ps. 11:3. "If the foundations be destroyed, what can the righteous doe?"
3. Ps. 32:8. See A.3 above.
4. 1 Cor. 13:12. "For now we see through a glasse darkly, but then face to face; now I know in part, but then I shall know, even as also I am knowne."
5. John 10:22. "And it was at Jerusalem, the feast of the dedication; and it was winter; and Jesus walked in the Temple in Salomons porch."
6. Gen. 17:24. "Abraham himselfe was ninety nine yeares old, when the foreskin of his flesh was circumcised."
7. Ps. 38:2. "For thine arrowes stick fast in me, and thy hand presseth me sore."
8. Ps. 144:15. "Blessed are the people that be so; yea blessed are the people, whose God is the Lord."
9. Ps. 6:6, 7. "I am weary with my groaning; all the night make I my bed to swim, I water my couch with my teares. Mine eye is consumed because of griefe; it waxeth old, because of all mine enemies."
10. Matt. 5:16. "Let your light so shine before men, that they may see your good works, and glorifie your Father which is in heaven."

D. Singular and Plural in God and His Church

1. Deut. 25:5. "If brethren dwell together, and one of them die, and have no childe, the wife of the dead shall not mary without, unto a stranger; her hus-

bands brother shall goe in unto her, and take her to him to wife, and performe the duty of an husbands brother unto her."

2. Gen. 1:26. "And God said, let us make man, in our image, after our likenesse."

3. Apoc. 7:9. "After this, I beheld, and loe, a great multitude, which no man could number, of all nations, and kindreds, and people, and tongues, stood before the throne, and before the lambe, clothed with white robes, and palmes in their hands."

4. Cant. 3:11. "Goe forth ye daughters of Sion, and behold King Solomon, with the crown, wherewith his mother crowned him, in the day of his espousals, and in the day of the gladnesse of his heart."

5. Gen. 1:26. See 2 above.

6. Rom. 8:16. "The Spirit it selfe beareth witnesse with our spirit, that we are the children of God."

7. John 10:10. "I am come that they might have life, and that they might have it more abundantly."

8. 1 Thess. 5:16. "Rejoyce evermore."

E. Hebrew: The Language in Which God Spake

1. Ps. 63:7 "Because thou hast been my helpe, therefore in the shadow of thy wings will I rejoyce."

2. Ps. 64:10. "And all the upright in heart shall glory."

3. Ps. 32:7. "Thou art my hiding place; thou shalt preserve mee from trouble; thou shalt compasse me about with songs of deliverance."

4. 1 Tim. 1:15. "This is a faithful saying, and worthy of all acceptation, that Christ Jesus came into the world to save sinners; of which I am the chiefest."

5. Ps. 90:14. "O satisfie us early with thy mercy, that we may rejoyce and be glad all our dayes."

6. Isa. 7:14. "Therefore the Lord shall give you a signe; behold, a virgin shall conceive, and beare a son, and shall call his name Immanuel."

7. Prov. 22:11. "He that loveth pureness of heart, for the grace of his lips, the King shall be his friend."

8. Lam. 3:1. "I am the man, that hath seen affliction, by the rod of his wrath."

Chapter 4: Logic and the Son

A. The Premises of Poetry

1. Rev. 7:17. "For the lamb which is in the midst of the throne, shall govern them, and shall leade them unto the lively fountains of waters, and God shall wipe away all teares from their eyes."

2. 2 Cor. 4:6. "For, God who commanded light to shine out of darkness, hath shined in our hearts, to give the light of the knowledge of the glory of God, in the face of Jesus Christ."

3. Micah 2:10. "Arise and depart, for this is not your rest."

4. Apoc. 7:2, 3. "And I saw another angel ascending from the east, which had the seale of the living God, and he cryed with a loud voyce to the foure

angels, to whom power was given to hurt the earth, and the sea, saying, hurt yee not the earth, neither the sea, neither the trees, till we have sealed the servants of our God in their foreheads."

5. Eccles. 8:11. "Because sentence against an evil work, is not executed speedily, therefore the heart of the children of men, is fully set in them, to do evil."

6. John 14:26. "But the Comforter, which is the Holy Ghost, whom the Father will send in my name, hee shall teach you all things, and bring all things to your remembrance, whatsoever I have said unto you."

7. Luke 23:24. "Father forgive them, for they know not what they do."

8. Ps. 6:2, 3. "Have mercy upon me, O Lord, for I am weake; O Lord, heale me, for my bones are vexed: my soule is also sore vexed; but thou, O Lord, how long?"

B. The Dangers of Reason

1. Ps. 55:19. "Because they have no charges, therefore they fear not God."

2. Acts 28:6. "They changed their minds, and said, that he was a God."

C. Logical Conjunctions: How, Why, For, Therefore

1. Micah 2:10. "Arise and depart, for this is not your rest."

2. Micah 2:10. See above.

3. Col. 1:19, 20. "For, it pleased the Father, that in him should all fulnesse dwell; and, having made peace through the bloud of his Crosse, by him, to reconcile all things to himselfe, by him, whether they be things in earth, or things in heaven."

4. Matt. 28:6. "He is not here, for he is risen, as he said; come, see the place where the Lord lay."

5. Acts 2:36. "Therefore let all the house of Israel know assuredly, that God hath made that same Jesus, whom ye have crucified, both Lord, and Christ."

D. Common Sense and Grammatical Logic

1. John 14:20. "At that day shall ye know, that I am in my Father, and you in me, and I in you."

2. 2 Cor. 4:6. "For, God who commanded light to shine out of darkness, hath shined in our hearts, to give the light of the knowledge of the glory of God, in the face of Jesus Christ."

3. Matt. 19:17. "And he said unto him, why callest thou me good? There is none good but one; that is, God."

4. John 16:8, 9, 10, 11. "And when he is come, he will reprove the world of sin, and of righteousnesse, and of judgement. / Of sin, because ye beleeve not on me. / Of righteousnesse, because I goe to my father, and ye see me no more. / Of judgement, because the Prince of this world is judged."

5. Acts 9:4. "And he fell to the earth, and heard a voyce, saying, Saul, Saul, why persecutest thou me?"

6. Job 4:18. "Behold, he put no trust in his servants, and his angels he charged with folly."

7. Exod. 4:13. "O my Lord, send I pray thee, by the hand of him whom thou wilt send."

8. Ps. 62:9. "Surely men of low degree are vanity, and men of high degree are a lie; to bee laid in the balance, they are altogether lighter then vanity."

9. Ps. 32:5. "I acknowledged my sin unto thee, and mine iniquity have I not hid. I said, I will confesse my transgressions unto the Lord, and thou forgavest the iniquity of my sin."

E. Formal Logic: Relation and Privation

1. Prov. 22:11. "He that loveth pureness of heart, for the grace of his lips, the King shall be his friend."

2. Gen. 1:26. "And God said, let us make man, in our image, after our likenesse."

3. Ephes. 5:25, 26, 27. "Husbands love your wives, even as Christ loved the Church, and gave himselfe for it. / That he might sanctifie it, and cleanse it, by the washing of water, through the Word: / That he might make it unto himselfe a glorious Church, not having spot, or wrinkle, or any such thing; but that it should be holy, and without blame."

4. Matt. 19:17. See D.3 above.

5. Acts 7:60. "And when he had said this, he fell a sleep."

6. Rev. 4:8. "And the foure beasts had each of them sixe wings about him, and they were full of eyes within; and they rest not day and night, saying, Holy, Holy, Holy, Lord God Almighty, which was, and is, and is to come."

Chapter 5: Voice and Character—The Revelation of Self

A. To Put on the Person of Christ: Redefining Self

1. Gal. 3:27. "For, all yee that are baptized into Christ, have put on Christ."

2. Deut. 12:30. "Take heed to thy self, that thou be not snared by following them after they be destroyed from before thee; and that thou inquire not after their gods, saying, how did those nations serve their gods? Even so will I do likewise."

3. Lam. 3:1. "I am the man, that hath seen affliction, by the rod of his wrath."

4. Ps. 38:4. "For mine iniquities are gone over my head, as a heavy burden, they are too heavy for me."

B. Redemption: The Role of Voice

1. Matt. 9:13. "I am not come to call the righteous, but sinners to repentance."

2. Matt. 3:17. "And lo, a voyce came from heaven, saying, this is my beloved Sonne, in whom I am well pleased."

3. Acts 9:4. "And he fell to the earth, and heard a voyce saying, Saul, Saul, why persecutest thou me?"

4. James 2:12. "So speak ye, and so do, as they that shall be judged by the law of liberty."

5. Matt. 9:13. See 1 above.

C. The Uniqueness of Human Voice

1. Ps. 38:3. "There is no soundnesse in my flesh, because of thine anger, neither is there any rest in my bones, because of my sinne."
2. Matt. 3:17. See B.2 above.
3. Ezek. 33:32. "And lo, thou art unto them a very lovely song, of one that hath a very pleasant voyce, and can play well on an instrument; for they hear thy words, but they doe them not."

D. Resurrection: The Role of Voice

1. John 5:28, 29. "Marvell not at this; for the houre is comming, in which, all that are in the graves, shall heare his voice; and shall come forth, they that have done good, unto the resurrection of life; and they that have done evill, unto the resurrection of damnation."
2. 1 Thess. 4:17. "Then we which are alive, and remain, shall be caught up together with them in the clouds, to meet the Lord in the ayre; and so shall we be ever with the Lord."

Chapter 6: Human Personality and the Faculties of the Soul

A. Trinitarian Theory

1. 1 John 5:7, 8. "For there are three which beare record in heaven; the Father, the Word, and the Holy Ghost; and these three are one: / And there are three which beare record in the earth; the spirit, and the water, and the bloud; and these three agree in one."
2. Ps. 2:12. "Kisse the Son, lest he be angry."
3. Rom. 8:16. "The Spirit it selfe beareth witnesse with our spirit, that we are the children of God."
4. Prov. 22:11. "He that loveth pureness of heart, for the grace of his lips, the King shall be his friend."
5. Matt. 12:31. "Wherefore I say unto you, all manner of sin and blasphemy shall be forgiven unto men; but the blasphemy against the Holy Ghost shall not be forgiven unto men."
6. John 16:8, 9, 10, 11. "And when he is come, he will reprove the world of sin, and of righteousnesse, and of judgement. / Of sin, because ye beleeve not on me. / Of righteousnesse, because I goe to my father, and ye see me no more. / Of judgement, because the Prince of this world is judged."

B. The Mirror of the Trinity in Personality

1. Gen. 1:26. "And God said, let us make man, in our image, after our likenesse."
2. 1 Cor. 13:12. "For now we see through a glasse darkly, but then face to face; now I know in part, but then I shall know, even as also I am knowne."
3. John 14:26. "But the Comforter, which is the Holy Ghost, whom the Father will send in my name, hee shall teach you all things, and bring all things to your remembrance, what soever I have said unto you."

4. Ps. 38:3. "There is no soundnesse in my flesh, because of thine anger, neither is there any rest in my bones, because of my sinne."
5. Eccles. 12:1. "Remember now thy Creator in the dayes of thy youth."

C. Body, Soul, and Spirit

1. Gen. 17:24. "Abraham himselfe was ninety nine yeares old, when the foreskin of his flesh was circumcised."
2. Ps. 38:4. "For mine iniquities are gone over my head, as a heavy burden, they are too heavy for mee."
3. Ps. 38:3. See B.4 above.
4. Ps. 38:2. "For thine arrowes stick fast in me, and thy hand presseth me sore."
5. Gen. 28:16, 17. "Then Jacob awoke out of his sleep, and said, surely the Lord is in this place, and I was not aware. And he was afraid, and said, how fearfull is this place! This is none other but the house of God, and this is the gate of heaven."
6. Rom. 13:11. "For now is our salvation nearer then when we believed."
7. Ps. 6:2, 3. "Have mercy upon me, O Lord, for I am weake; O Lord, heale me, for my bones are vexed: my soule is also sore vexed; but thou, O Lord, how long?"

D. Salvation and the Natural Faculties

1. Isa. 52:3. "Ye have sold your selves for nought, and ye shall be redeemed without money."
2. Col. 1:19, 20. "For, it pleased the Father, that in him should all fulnesse dwell; and, having made peace through the bloud of his Crosse, by him, to reconcile all things to himselfe, by him, whether they be things in earth, or things in heaven."
3. Job 36:25. "Every man may see it, man may behold it afar off."
4. Ps. 32:9. "Be not as the horse, or the mule, who have no understanding; whose mouth must be held in with bit and bridle, lest they come neare unto thee."
5. Matt. 28:6. "He is not here, for he is risen, as he said; come, see the place where the Lord lay."
   John 10:10. "I am come that they might have life, and that they might have it more abundantly."
6. Gen. 3:14. "And dust shalt thou eat all the dayes of thy life."
7. 2 Cor. 4:6. "For, God who commanded light to shine out of darkness, hath shined in our hearts, to give the light of the knowledge of the glory of God, in the face of Jesus Christ."
8. Ps. 32:8. "I will instruct thee, and teach thee in the way which thou shalt goe, I will guide thee with mine eye."
9. Ps. 32:9. See 4 above.
10. Job 19:26. "And though, after my skin, wormes destroy this body, yet in my flesh shall I see God."

Chapter 7: Names and Typology

A. The Name of God

1. Ps. 6:1. "O Lord, rebuke me not in thine anger, neither chasten me in thy hot displeasure."
2. Exod. 4:13. "O my Lord, send I pray thee, by the hand of him whom thou wilt send."
3. 1 Thess. 4:17. "Then we which are alive, and remain, shall be caught up together with them in the clouds, to meet the Lord in the ayre; and so shall we be ever with the Lord."
4. Ps. 63:7. "Because thou hast been my helpe, therefore in the shadow of thy wings will I rejoyce."
5. Ps. 6:1. See 1 above.
6. 2 Pet. 3:13. "Nevertheless, we, according to his promises, looke for new heavens, and new earth, wherein dwelleth righteousnesse."
7. 1 Cor. 12:3. "Also no man can say, that Jesus is the Lord, but by the Holy Ghost."
8. Ps. 55:19. "Because they have no charges, therefore they fear not God."
9. Ps. 34:11. "Come ye children, hearken unto me, I will teach you the fear of the Lord."
10. Ps. 38:9. "Lord all my desire is before thee, and my groninge is not hid from thee."

B. Typology

1. Lam. 4:20. "The breath of our nostrils, the anointed of the Lord, was taken in their pits."
2. Gal. 3:27. "For, all yee that are baptized into Christ, have put on Christ."

C. The Postdated Bible

1. Acts 9:4. "And he fell to the earth, and heard a voyce, saying, Saul, Saul, why persecutest thou me?"
2. Ps. 38:3. "There is no soundnesse in my flesh, because of thine anger, neither is there any rest in my bones, because of my sinne."
3. Gen. 32:10. "I am not worthy of the least of all thy mercies, and of all the truth which thou hast shewed unto thy servant; for with my staff I passed over this *Jordan* and now I am become two bands."
4. Gen. 17:24. "Abraham himselfe was ninety nine yeares old, when the foreskin of his flesh was circumcised."
5. Ps. 38:4. "For mine iniquities are gone over my head, as a heavy burden, they are too heavy for mee."
6. Ps. 38:2. "For thine arrowes stick fast in me, and thy hand presseth me sore."
7. Isa. 32:8. "But the liberall deviseth liberall things, and by liberall things he shall stand."
8. 1 Cor. 15:26. "The last enemie that shall be destroyed, is death."
9. Ps. 38:2. See 6 above.
10. 1 Cor. 15:26. See 8 above.

11. Matt. 28:6. "He is not here, for he is risen, as he said; come, see the place where the Lord lay."

12. Luke 2:29, 30. "Lord now lettest thou thy servant depart in peace, according to thy word: for mine eyes have seen thy salvation."

13. John 1:8. "He was not that light, but was sent to beare witnesse of that light."

14. John 1:8. See above.

15. John 1:8. See above.

16. Acts 7:60. "And when he had said this, he fell a sleep."

17. Acts 9:4. See 1 above.

Chapter 8: Image, Idol, Example, and Imitation

A. Image: The Sight of God in Man

1. Image in Self

i. 1 Cor. 13:12. "For now we see through a glasse darkly, but then face to face; now I know in part, but then I shall know, even as also I am knowne."

ii. Apoc. 7:9. "After this, I beheld, and loe, a great multitude, which no man could number, of all nations, and kindreds, and people, and tongues, stood before the throne, and before the lambe, clothed with white robes, and palmes in their hands."

iii. Ps. 6:4, 5. "Returne, O Lord; deliver my soule; O Lord save me, for thy mercies sake. / For in death there is no remembrance of thee; and in the grave, who shall give thee thanks?"

iv. Col. 1:19, 20. "For, it pleased the Father, that in him should all fulnesse dwell; and, having made peace through the bloud of his Crosse, by him, to reconcile all things to himselfe, by him, whether they be things in earth, or things in heaven."

v. 2 Cor. 4:6. "For, God who commanded light to shine out of darkness, hath shined in our hearts, to give the light of the knowledge of the glory of God, in the face of Jesus Christ."

vi. Gal. 3:27. "For, all yee that are baptized into Christ, have put on Christ."

vii. Ps. 38:2. "For thine arrowes stick fast in me, and thy hand presseth me sore."

viii. Acts 7:60. "And when he had said this, he fell a sleep."

ix. Eccles. 12:1. "Remember now thy Creator in the dayes of thy youth."

x. Gen. 1:26. "And God said, let us make man, in our image, after our likenesse."

xi. Prov. 14:31. "He that oppresseth the poore, reproacheth his maker, but he that honoureth him, hath mercy on the poore."

2. Image in the Church

i. Cant. 3:11. "Goe forth ye daughters of Sion, and behold King Solomon, with the crown, wherewith his mother crowned him, in the day of his espousals, and in the day of the gladnesse of his heart."

ii. Ps. 32:8. "I will instruct thee, and teach thee in the way which thou shalt goe, I will guide thee with mine eye."

iii. Rom. 13:7. "Render therefore to all men their dues."

B. The Danger of Images and Their Idolatrous Worship

1. Idolatrous Love

i. Prov. 22:11. "He that loveth pureness of heart, for the grace of his lips, the King shall be his friend."

ii. Judges 5:20. "They fought from heaven; the stars in their courses fought against Sisera."

2. Use and Abuse

i. Acts 28:6. "They changed their minds, and said, that he was a God."

ii. Matt. 5:8. "Blessed are the pure in heart, for they shall see God."

iii. Ps. 32:6. "For this shall every one that is godly pray unto thee, in a time when thou mayest be found; surely in the floods of great waters they shall not come nigh unto him."

iv. Micah 2:10. "Arise and depart, for this is not your rest."

C. Pattern and Example

1. Ps. 63:7. "Because thou hast been my helpe, therefore in the shadow of thy wings will I rejoyce."

2. 2 Cor. 4:6. "For, God who commanded light to shine out of darknesse, hath shined in our hearts, to give the light of the knowledge of the glory of God, in the face of Jesus Christ."

3. Matt. 5:16. "Let your light so shine before men, that they may see your good works, and glorifie your father which is in heaven."

4. Ps. 32:3, 4. "When I kept silence, my bones waxed old, through my roaring all the day long. / For day and night thy hand was heavy upon me; my moysture is turned into the drought of summer. Selah."

5. Gen. 1:26. "And God said, let us make man, in our image, after our likenesse."

6. Cant. 5:3. "I have washed my feet, how shall I defile them?"

D. Emblems, Characters, and Signs

1. Lam. 3:1. "I am the man, that hath seen affliction, by the rod of his wrath."

2. Matt. 5:16. See C.3 above.

3. Ps. 6:6, 7. "I am weary with my groaning; all the night make I my bed to swim, I water my couch with my teares. Mine eye is consumed because of griefe; it waxeth old, because of all mine enemies."

4. Isa. 7:14. "Therefore the Lord shall give you a signe; behold, a virgin shall conceive, and beare a son, and shall call his name Immanuel."

5. Isa. 7:14. See above.

E. Some Specific Images

1. The Circle

i. Ps. 63:7. "Because thou hast been my helpe, therefore in the shadow of thy wings will I rejoyce."

ii. Ps. 32:10, 11. "Many sorrows shall be to the wicked; but he that trusteth in the Lord, mercy shall compasse him about. / Be glad in the Lord, and rejoyce yee righteous; and shout for joy all yee that are upright in heart."

iii. 1 Tim. 3:16. "And without controversie, great is the mystery of godliness: God was manifest in the flesh, justified in the spirit, seen of angels, preached unto the Gentiles, believed on in the world, received up into glory."

iv. Ps. 89:48. "What man is he that liveth, and shall not see death?"

v. Isa. 32:8. "But the liberall deviseth liberall things, and by liberall things he shall stand."

vi. Hosea 2:19. "And I will mary thee unto me for ever."

vii. Rev. 4:8. "And the foure beasts had each of them sixe wings about him, and they were full of eyes within; and they rest not day and night, saying, Holy, Holy, Holy, Lord God Almighty, which was, and is, and is to come."

2. On the Work and Expression of the Holy Ghost

i. Gen. 1:26. "And God said, let us make man, in our image, after our likenesse."

ii. Ps. 32:6. See B.2.iii above.

iii. Ps. 63:7. See E.1.i above.

iv. Ezek. 34:19. "And as for my flock, they eate that, which yee have troden with your feet, and they drink that which yee have fouled with your feet."

v. Ps. 63:7. See iii above.

vi. Cant. 3:11. "Go forth ye daughters of Sion, and behold King Solomon, with the crown, wherewith his mother crowned him, in the day of his espousals, and in the day of the gladnesse of his heart."

3. Sacred Place

i. Gen. 28:16, 17. "Then Jacob awoke out of his sleep, and said, surely the Lord is in this place, and I was not aware. And he was afraid, and said, how fearfull is this place! This is none other but the house of God, and this is the gate of heaven."

ii. Gen. 1:26. See E.2.i above.

iii. Ps. 6:4, 5. See A.1.iii above.

iv. Matt. 28:6. "He is not here, for he is risen, as he said; come, see the place where the Lord lay."

Chapter 9: Hermeneutics—Interpretation and Revelation

A. Methods of Interpretation

1. Apoc. 20:6. "Blessed and holy is he that hath part in the first Resurrection."

2. Ps. 38:4. "For mine iniquities are gone over my head, as a heavy burden, they are too heavy for mee."

3. John 1:8. "He was not that light, but was sent to beare witnesse of that light."

4. Gen. 1:2. "And the Spirit of God moved upon the face of the waters."

5. 2 Cor. 4:6. "For, God who commanded light to shine out of darkness, hath shined in our hearts, to give the light of the knowledge of the glory of God, in the face of Jesus Christ."

6. 1 Cor. 15:26. "The last enemie that shall be destroyed, is death."

7. Ps. 90:14. "O satisfie us early with thy mercy, that we may rejoyce and be glad all our dayes."

B. Misinterpretation

1. Rev. 7:17. "For the lamb which is in the midst of the throne, shall govern them, and shall leade them unto the lively fountains of waters, and God shall wipe away all teares from their eyes."
2. Ps. 6:6, 7. "I am weary with my groaning; all the night make I my bed to swim, I water my couch with my teares. Mine eye is consumed because of griefe; it waxeth old, because of all mine enemies."
3. Acts 23:6, 7. "But when Paul perceived that one part were Sadduces, and the other Pharisees, he cryed out in the Councel, men and brethren, I am a Pharisee, and the son of a Pharisee; of the hope and Resurrection of the dead I am called in question. / And when he had so said, there arose a dissention between the Pharisees and the Sadduces, and the multitude was divided."

C. Revelation as Interpretation

1. Ps. 55:19. "Because they have no charges, therefore they fear not God."
2. Gen. 32:10. "I am not worthy of the least of all thy mercies, and of all the truth which thou hast shewed unto thy servant; for with my staff I passed over this *Jordan* and now I am become two bands."
3. 2 Cor. 4:6. For, God who commanded light to shine out of darkness, hath shined in our hearts, to give the light of the knowledge of the glory of God, in the face of Jesus Christ."
4. John 14:20. "At that day shall ye know, that I am in my Father, and you in me, and I in you."
5. Ps. 38:4. See A.2 above.
6. 2 Cor. 4:6. See 3 above.

D. Exegesis

1. Matt. 19:17. "And he said unto him, why callest thou me good? There is none good but one; that is, God."
2. Cant. 3:11. "Goe forth ye daughters of Sion, and behold King Solomon, with the crown, wherewith his mother crowned him, in the day of his espousals, and in the day of the gladnesse of his heart."
3. Matt. 19:17. See 1 above.
4. Rom. 13:11. "For now is our salvation nearer then when we believed."
5. 1 Cor. 12:3. "Also no man can say, that Jesus is the Lord, but by the Holy Ghost."

E. The Actions of Interpretation

1. 2 Cor. 4:6. See C.3 above.
2. 1 Cor. 16:22. "If any man love not the Lord Jesus Christ, let him be Anathema, Maranatha."
3. Acts 10:44. "While Peter yet spake these words, the Holy Ghost fell on all them, which heard the word."
4. Prov. 22:11. "He that loveth pureness of heart, for the grace of his lips, the King shall be his friend."
5. Acts 23:6, 7. See B.3 above.
6. Isa. 52:3. "Ye have sold your selves for nought, and ye shall be redeemed without money."

Chapter 10: Genre

A. Biblical Genres

1. Prophecy

i. "Lord, who hath beleeved our report?" (Donne: "These words are written, in more then one, in more then two places of the Bible.") See Chapter 1, A.9, above.

ii. Ps. 6:8, 9, 10. "Depart from me, all ye workers of iniquitie; for the Lord hath heard the voyce of my weeping. / The Lord hath heard my supplication; the Lord will receive my prayer. / Let all mine enemies be ashamed and sore vexed: let them returne and be ashamed suddenly."

iii. Ps. 66:3. "Say unto God, how terrible art thou in thy works! Through the greatnesse of thy power shall thine enemies submit themselves unto thee."

iv. Lam. 4:20. "The breath of our nostrils, the anointed of the Lord, was taken in their pits."

2. Epithalamion

Prov. 8:17. "I love them that love me, and they that seek me early shall find me."

3. Epistle

i. 1 Cor. 12:3. "Also no man can say, that Jesus is the Lord, but by the Holy Ghost."

ii. 1 Tim. 1:15. "This is a faithful saying, and worthy of all acceptation, that Christ Jesus came into the world to save sinners; of which I am the chiefest."

iii. Isa. 32:8. "But the liberall deviseth liberall things, and by liberall things he shall stand."

iv. Ps. 32:8. "I will instruct thee, and teach thee in the way which thou shalt goe, I will guide thee with mine eye."

v. James 2:12. "So speak ye, and so do, as they that shall be judged by the law of liberty."

4. Acts

i. Acts 23:6, 7. "But when Paul perceived that one part were Sadduces, and the other Pharisees, he cryed out in the Councel, men and brethren, I am a Pharisee, and the son of a Pharisee; of the hope and Resurrection of the dead I am called in question. / And when he had so said, there arose a dissention between the Pharisees and the Sadduces, and the multitude was divided."

ii. Acts 1:8. "But yee shall receive power, after that the Holy Ghost is come upon you, and yee shall be witnesses unto me both in Jerusalem, and in all Judea, and in Samaria, and unto the uttermost part of the earth."

iii. 1 Cor. 13:12. "For now we see through a glasse darkly, but then face to face; now I know in part, but then I shall know, even as also I am knowne."

5. Revelation

2 Cor. 4:6. "For, God who commanded light to shine out of darkness, hath shined in our hearts, to give the light of the knowledge of the glory of God, in the face of Jesus Christ."

B. Liturgical Genres

1. Confession

i. Ps. 32:5. "I acknowledged my sin unto thee, and mine iniquity have I not hid. I said, I will confesse my transgressions unto the Lord, and thou forgavest the iniquity of my sin."

ii. Ps. 6:8, 9, 10. See A.1.ii above.

iii. 1 Thess. 4:17. "Then we which are alive, and remain, shall be caught up together with them in the clouds, to meet the Lord in the ayre; and so shall we be ever with the Lord."

2. Prayer, Praise, Psalm

i. Apoc. 7:2, 3. "And I saw another angel ascending from the east, which had the seale of the living God, and he cryed with a loud voyce to the foure angels, to whom power was given to hurt the earth, and the sea, saying, hurt yee not the earth, neither the sea, neither the trees, till we have sealed the servants of our God in their foreheads."

ii. Ps. 6:8, 9, 10. See A.1.ii above.

iii. Ps. 6:2, 3. "Have mercy upon me, O Lord, for I am weake; O Lord, heale me, for my bones are vexed: my soule is also sore vexed; but thou, O Lord, how long?"

iv. Ps. 38:2. "For thine arrowes stick fast in me, and thy hand presseth me sore."

v. Ps. 65:5. "By terrible things in righteousnesse wilt thou answer us, O God of our salvation; who art the confidence of all the ends of the earth, and of them that are a far off, upon the sea."

vi. Job 16:17, 18, 19. "Not for any injustice in my hands: also my prayer is pure. / O Earth cover not thou my blood; and let my cry have no place. / Also now behold, my witnesse is in heaven, and my record is on high."

vii. Ps. 6:8, 9, 10. See A.1.ii above.

viii. Ps. 90:14. "O satisfie us early with thy mercy, that we may rejoyce and be glad all our dayes."

ix. Rom. 13:7. "Render therefore to all men their dues."

x. Ps. 90:14. See viii above.

xi. Ps. 63:7. "Because thou hast been my helpe, therefore in the shadow of thy wings will I rejoyce."

C. The Genres of Teaching

1. The Holy Ghost

John 14:26. "But the Comforter, which is the Holy Ghost, whom the Father will send in my name, hee shall teach you all things, and bring all things to your remembrance, whatsoever I have said unto you."

2. Catechism

Ps. 32:1, 2. "Blessed is he whose transgression is forgiven, whose sinne is covered; / Blessed is the man, unto whom the Lord imputeth not iniquitie, and in whose spirit there is no guile."

3. Sermon

i. 2 Cor. 4:6. See A.5 above.

ii. Ps. 34:11. "Come ye children, hearken unto me, I will teach you the fear of the Lord."

iii. 2 Cor. 4:6. See i above.

iv. Ps. 34:11. See ii above.

v. Judges 5:20. "They fought from heaven; the stars in their courses fought against Sisera."

vi. Ps. 90:14. See B.2.viii above.

vii. Isa. 32:8. "But the liberall deviseth liberall things, and by liberall things he shall stand."

viii. Acts 1:8. "But yee shall receive power, after that the Holy Ghost is come upon you, and yee shall be witnesses unto me both in Jerusalem, and in all Judea, and in Samaria, and unto the uttermost part of the earth."

ix. Matt. 22:30. "For, in the Resurrection, they neither mary nor are given in marriage, but are as the angels of God in heaven."

4. Preacher

i. 2 Cor. 4:6. See A.5 above.

ii. Rev. 4:8. "And the foure beasts had each of them sixe wings about him, and they were full of eyes within; and they rest not day and night, saying, Holy, Holy, Holy, Lord God Almighty, which was, and is, and is to come."

iii. 2 Cor. 5:20. "We pray yee in Christs stead, be ye reconciled to God."

iv. Prov. 14:31. "He that oppresseth the poore, reproacheth his maker, but he that honoureth him, hath mercy on the poore."

v. Ezek. 34:19. "And as for my flock, they eate that, which yee have troden with your feet, and they drink that which yee have fouled with your feet."

Bibliography

This selected bibliography aims to give only works directly connected with Donne's sermons, but it includes a few supporting works of background interest. Further books about Donne are cited in a number of the references given below, but especially in the two volumes edited by John R. Roberts: *John Donne: An Annotated Bibliography of Modern Criticism, 1912–1967* (Columbia, Mo.: University of Missouri Press, 1973) and *John Donne: An Annotated Bibliography of Modern Criticism, 1968–1978* (Columbia, Mo.: University of Missouri Press, 1982). The standard bibliography of Donne's works is by Geoffrey Keynes, *A Bibliography of Dr. John Donne*, 4th ed. (Oxford: Clarendon Press, 1973).

Allen, Don Cameron. "Dean Donne Sets His Text." *ELH* 10 (1943): 208–29.

———. "Donne and the Bezoar." *MLN* 56 (1941): 609–11.

Asals, Heather. "David's Successors: Forms of Joy and Art." *Proceedings of the PMR Conference: Annual Publications of the International Patristic, Mediaeval, and Renaissance Conference* 2 (1977): 31–37.

Baker-Smith, Dominic. "John Donne's *Critique of True Religion*," in *John Donne: Essays in Celebration*, ed. A. J. Smith, pp. 404–32. London: Methuen, 1972.

Bald, R. C. *John Donne: A Life*. Oxford: Clarendon Press, 1970.

Baldwin, C. S. *Medieval Rhetoric and Poetic*. New York: Macmillan, 1928.

Blench, J. W. *Preaching in England in the Late Fifteenth and Sixteenth Centuries*. Oxford: Basil Blackwell, 1964.

Bollier, E. P. "T. S. Eliot and John Donne: A Problem in Criticism." *Tulane Studies in English* 9 (1959): 103–18.

Boston, Rosemary. "The Variable Heart in Donne's Sermons." *Christian Scholar's Review* 2 (1971): 36–41.

Bozanich, Robert. "Donne and Ecclesiastes." *PMLA* 90 (1975): 270–76.

Carey, John. *John Donne: Life, Mind and Art*. London: Faber and Faber, 1981.

Carrithers, Gale H., Jr. *Donne at Sermons: A Christian Existential World*. Albany: State University of New York Press, 1972.

Chamberlin, John S. *Increase and Multiply: Arts-of-Discourse Procedure in the Preaching of Donne*. Chapel Hill: University of North Carolina Press, 1976.

Colie, Rosalie. *Paradoxia Epidemica: The Renaissance Tradition of Paradox*. Princeton: Princeton University Press, 1966.

Croll, Morris W. *Style, Rhetoric, and Rhythm*. Ed. J. Max Patrick et al. Princeton: Princeton University Press, 1966.

Danielou, Jean, S.J. *The Bible and the Liturgy*. London: Darton, Longman, and Todd, 1960.

Doebler, Bettie Anne. *The Quickening Seed: Death in the Sermons of John Donne*. Salzburg: Institut für englische Sprache und Literatur, University of Salzburg, 1974.

Donne, John. *Devotions upon Emergent Occasions*. Ed. Anthony Raspa. Montreal: McGill-Queen's University Press, 1975.

———. *The Divine Poems*. Ed. Helen Gardner. 2d ed. Oxford: Clarendon Press, 1978.

———. *The Poems of John Donne*. Ed. Herbert J. C. Grierson. 2 vols. Oxford: Clarendon Press, 1912.

———. *Donne's Prebend Sermons*. Ed. Janel M. Mueller. Cambridge, Mass.: Harvard University Press, 1971.

———. *Essays in Divinity*. Ed. Evelyn M. Simpson. Oxford: Clarendon Press, 1952.

———. *The Sermons of John Donne*. Ed. Evelyn M. Simpson and George R. Potter. 10 vols. Berkeley: University of California Press, 1953–1962.

Eliot, T. S. *For Lancelot Andrewes: Essays on Style and Order*. London: Faber and Faber, 1928.

Farrer, Austin. *Reflective Faith: Essays in Philosophical Theology*. Ed. Charles C. Conti. London: SPCK, 1972.

Galdon, Joseph A., S.J. *Typology and Seventeenth-Century Literature*. The Hague: Mouton, 1975.

Gifford, William. "John Donne's Sermons on the 'Grand Days.'" *Huntington Library Quarterly* 29 (1966): 235–44.

———. "Time and Place in Donne's Sermons." *PMLA* 82 (1967): 388–98.

Halewood, William H. *The Poetry of Grace: Reformation Themes and Structures in English Seventeenth-Century Poetry*. New Haven: Yale University Press, 1970.

Hall, Michael L. "Searching the Scriptures: Meditation and Discovery in Donne's Sermons," in *New Essays on Donne*, ed. Gary A. Stringer. Salzburg: Institut für englische Sprache und Literatur, University of Salzburg, 1977.

Hathaway, Baxter. *Marvels and Commonplaces: Renaissance Literary Criticism*. New York: Random House, 1968.

Hattori, Akio. "Donne's Sacred Eloquence." *Doshisha Literature* (Doshisha Daigaku) 27 (November 1973): 13–27.

Hayward, John. "A Note on Donne the Preacher," in *A Garland for John Donne*, ed. Theodore Spencer, pp. 75–97. Cambridge, Mass.: Harvard University Press, 1931.

Henricksen, Bruce. "Donne's Orthodoxy." *Texas Studies in Literature and Language* 14 (1972): 5–16.

———. "The Unity of Reason and Faith in Donne's Sermons." *Papers on Language and Literature* 11 (1975): 18–30.

Hickey, Robert L. "Donne's Art of Memory." *Tennessee Studies in Literature* 3 (1958): 29–36.

———. "Donne's Art of Preaching." *Tennessee Studies in Literature* 1 (1956): 65–74.

———. "Donne's Delivery." *Tennessee Studies in Literature* 19 (1964): 39–47.

Howell, Wilbur S. *Logic and Rhetoric in England, 1500–1700*. Princeton: Princeton University Press, 1956.

Husain, Itrat. *The Dogmatic and Mystical Theology of John Donne*. London: SPCK, 1938.

Jones, Richard Foster. *The Triumph of the English Language*. Stanford: Stanford University Press, 1953.

Krueger, Robert. "The Publication of John Donne's Sermons." *Review of English Studies* 15 (1964): 151–60.
Lanham, Richard A. *The Motives of Eloquence*. New Haven: Yale University Press, 1976.
Lewalski, Barbara Kiefer. "Donne's Epideictic *Personae*." *Southern Quarterly* 14 (1976): 195–202.
———. *Protestant Poetics and the Seventeenth-Century Religious Lyric*. Princeton: Princeton University Press, 1979.
———. "Typological Symbolism and the 'Progress of the Soul' in Seventeenth-Century Literature," in *Literary Uses of Typology from the Late Middle Ages to the Present*, ed. Earl Miner, pp. 79–114. Princeton: Princeton University Press, 1977.
Lonergan, Bernard, S.J. *Method in Theology*. London: Darton, Longman, and Todd, 1972.
Lowe, Irving. "John Donne: The Middle Way. The Reason-Faith Equation in Donne's Sermons." *Journal of the History of Ideas* 22 (1961): 389–97.
McAdoo, H. R. *The Spirit of Anglicanism: A Survey of Anglican Theological Method in the Seventeenth Century*. London: A. and C. Black, 1965.
McGee, Michael C. "The Thematic Reduplication in Christian Rhetoric." *Quarterly Journal of Speech* 56 (1970): 196–204.
MacLure, Millar. *The Paul's Cross Sermons, 1534–1632*. Toronto: University of Toronto Press, 1958.
Mazzeo, Joseph A. "St. Augustine's Rhetoric of Silence: Truth vs. Eloquence and Things vs. Signs," in *Renaissance and Seventeenth-Century Studies*, pp. 1–28. New York: Columbia University Press, 1964.
Merchant, W. Moelwyn. "Donne's Sermon to the Virginia Company, 13 November 1622," in *John Donne: Essays in Celebration*, ed. A. J. Smith, pp. 433–52. London: Methuen, 1972.
Merrill, Thomas F. "John Donne and the Word of God." *Neuphilologische Mitteilungen* 69 (1968): 597–616. Reprinted as "The Sermon as Sacrament" in his *Christian Criticism* (Amsterdam: Rodopi, 1976), chap. 9.
Mitchell, W. Fraser. *English Pulpit Oratory from Andrewes to Tillotson*. London: SPCK, 1932.
Mueller, William R. *John Donne: Preacher*. Princeton: Princeton University Press, 1962.
Nelly, Una. *The Poet Donne: A Study in His Dialectic Method*. Cork: Cork University Press, 1969.
Novarr, David. *The Disinterred Muse: Donne's Texts and Contexts*. Ithaca, N.Y.: Cornell University Press, 1980.
Ong, Walter J., S.J. *The Presence of the Word*. New Haven: Yale University Press, 1967.
———. *Ramus: Method, and the Decay of Dialogue*. Cambridge, Mass.: Harvard University Press, 1958.
Owst, G. R. *Literature and Pulpit in Medieval England*. Cambridge: Cambridge University Press, 1933.
———. *Preaching in Medieval England*. Cambridge: Cambridge University Press, 1926.
Palmer, Richard E. *Hermeneutics*. Evanston: Northwestern University Press, 1969.

Partridge, A. C. *John Donne: Language and Style*. London: Andre Deutsch, 1978.
———. *Tudor to Augustan English: A Study in Syntax and Style from Caxton to Johnson*. London: Andre Deutsch, 1969.
Quinn, Dennis B. "Donne's Christian Eloquence." *ELH* 27 (1960): 276–97.
———. "John Donne's Principles of Biblical Exegesis." *JEGP* 41 (1962): 313–29.
Rooney, William J. J. "John Donne's 'Second Prebend Sermon'—a Stylistic Analysis." *Texas Studies in Literature and Language* 4 (1962): 24–34.
Roston, Murray. *The Soul of Wit: A Study of John Donne*. Oxford: Clarendon Press, 1974.
Rugoff, Milton A. *Donne's Imagery: A Study in Creative Sources*. New York: Corporate Press, 1939.
Schleiner, Winfried. *The Imagery of John Donne's Sermons*. Providence: Brown University Press, 1970.
———. "The Hand of the Tongue: Emblematic Technique in One of Donne's Sermons." *English Miscellany* 25 (1976): 183–90.
Sennbenn, Carl Braun. "John Donne, Poet in the Pulpit," in *New Essays on Donne*, ed. Gary A. Stringer. Salzburg: Institut für englische Sprache und Literatur, University of Salzburg, 1977.
Sherwood, Terry G. *Fulfilling the Circle: A Study of John Donne's Thought*. Toronto: University of Toronto Press, 1984.
———. "Reason in Donne's Sermons." *ELH* 39 (1972): 353–74.
Simpson, Evelyn M. *A Study of the Prose Works of John Donne*. Oxford: Clarendon Press, 1924. 2d ed., 1948.
Slights, Camille Wells. *The Casuistical Tradition in Shakespeare, Donne, Herbert, and Milton*. Princeton: Princeton University Press, 1981.
Smalling, Michael. "Donne's Medieval Aesthetics and His Use of Morally Distant *Personae*: Two Questions, One Answer," in *New Essays on Donne*, ed. Gary A. Stringer. Salzburg: Institut für englische Sprache und Literatur, University of Salzburg, 1977.
Smyth, Charles. *The Art of Preaching*. London: SPCK, 1940.
Sparrow, John. "John Donne and Contemporary Preachers: Their Preparation of Sermons for Delivery and for Publication." *Essays and Studies by Members of the English Association* [of 1930] 16 (1931): 144–78.
———. "Donne's Religious Development." *Theology* (London), March 1931, pp. 144–54.
Stanwood, P. G. "Contemporary and Patristic Borrowing in the Caroline Divines." *Renaissance Quarterly* 23 (1970): 421–29.
———. "John Donne's Sermon Notes." *Review of English Studies* 29 (1978): 313–20. See I. A. Shapiro's responses in *Review of English Studies* 30 (1979): 194 and 31 (1980): 54–56.
———. "Time and Liturgy in Donne, Crashaw, and T. S. Eliot." *Mosaic*, 12, no. 2 (1979), 91–105.
Stapleton, Laurence. "John Donne: The Moment of the Sermon," in his *The Elected Circle: Studies in the Art of Prose*, pp. 17–44. Princeton: Princeton University Press, 1973.
Thompson, M. Geraldine, Sister. "John Donne and the Mindes Indeavours." *Studies in English Literature* 5 (1965): 115–31.

———. "'Writs Canonicall': The High Word and the Humble in the Sermons of John Donne," in *Familiar Colloquy: Essays Presented to Arthur Edward Barker*, ed. Patricia Bruckmann, pp. 55–67. Ottawa: Oberon Press, 1978.

Tuve, Rosemond. *Elizabethan and Metaphysical Imagery*. Chicago: University of Chicago Press, 1947.

Umbach, H. H. "The Merit of Metaphysical Style in Donne's Easter Sermons." *ELH* 12 (1945): 108–29.

———. "The Rhetoric of Donne's Sermons." *PMLA* 52 (1937): 354–58.

Wallerstein, Ruth. *Studies in Seventeenth-Century Poetic*. Madison: University of Wisconsin Press, 1950.

Warren, Austin. "The Very Reverend Dr. Donne." *Kenyon Review* 16 (1954): 268–77.

Webber, Joan. "Celebration of Word and World in Lancelot Andrewes's Style." *JEGP* 64 (1965): 255–69.

———. *Contrary Music: The Prose Style of John Donne*. Madison: University of Wisconsin Press, 1963.

Wellek, René. "The Criticism of T. S. Eliot." *Sewanee Review* 64 (1956): 398–443.

White, Helen C. "John Donne and the Psychology of Spiritual Effort," in *The Seventeenth Century: Studies in the History of English Thought and Literature from Bacon to Pope by Richard Foster Jones and Others Writing in His Honor*, pp. 355–68. Stanford: Stanford University Press, 1951.

INDEX